D1520741

The Spiritual Turn

The Spiritual Turn

The Religion of the Heart and the Making
of Romantic Liberal Modernity

GALEN WATTS

OXFORD
UNIVERSITY PRESS

OXFORD
UNIVERSITY PRESS

Great Clarendon Street, Oxford, OX2 6DP,
United Kingdom

Oxford University Press is a department of the University of Oxford.
It furthers the University's objective of excellence in research, scholarship,
and education by publishing worldwide. Oxford is a registered trade mark of
Oxford University Press in the UK and in certain other countries

First Edition published in 2022

Impression: 1

Published in the United States of America by Oxford University Press
198 Madison Avenue, New York, NY 10016, United States of America

British Library Cataloguing in Publication Data

Data available

Library of Congress Control Number: 2021951810

ISBN 978-0-19-285983-9

DOI: 10.1093/oso/9780192859839.001.0001

Printed and bound in the UK by
TJ Books Limited

For my parents

This deeply thoughtful and important work draws on classical sociological theory and a range of empirical data to offer a unique insight into the nature and significance of 'the spiritual turn' in modern Western democracies. It should be of great interest, not just to sociologists of religion, but to all sociologists of culture.

Colin Campbell
Professor Emeritus of Sociology, University of York, UK

Galen Watts covers an immense amount of intellectual and ethnographic ground with great clarity, intelligence, and passion. In doing so, he challenges received ideas about liberalism, spirituality, and the individual; but he also presents a positive ethical vision in critical yet constructive dialogue with such figures as Émile Durkheim, Robert Bellah and Charles Taylor. *The Spiritual Turn* is an indispensable read for anybody interested in the moral underpinnings of contemporary liberal democracies.

Simon Coleman
Chancellor Jackman Professor, University of Toronto

Efforts to salvage religion as a form of personal spirituality have been recurrent since the nineteenth century, and Watts brings keen cultural, sociological, and ethnographic analysis to those sundry projects of self-realization and experiential insight, especially as they have found expression since the 1960s. He artfully balances empathy and critique in his pursuit of those spiritual inquirers who tune themselves—both creatively and predictably—to the discursive norms of romantic, liberal modernity.

Leigh Eric Schmidt
Edward C. Mallinckrodt Distinguished University Professor
in the Humanities at Washington University in St. Louis and author
of *Restless Souls: The Making of American Spirituality*

A nuanced look at the modern "turn" to individual-centered spiritualities. Watts draws on new empirical research to challenge conventional wisdom about modern spirituality fostering self-absorption and eroding communal bonds. This even-handed sociological analysis reveals that although these unchurched spiritualities are sometimes guilty as charged, they can also be as morally demanding and as much a source of social solidarity as their institution-centered counterparts.

Robert C. Fuller
Distinguished Professor of Religious Studies at Bradley University and
author of *Spiritual, But Not Religious* and *Spirituality in the Flesh*

Written by one of the rising stars in the field of cultural sociology, Galen Watts brings readers on a fascinating theoretical and empirical journey to tease out the social realities and roots of current-day spiritualities. The author takes a bold leap in expanding our definition of religion and to light the way for the next 20 years of work in the field that will be sure to generate much discussion and debate. Combining political and philosophical thought with grounded social scientific research, the author convincingly demonstrates how today's spiritualities, focused on personal experience and authenticity, are in fact grounded in the social conditions and cultural framework of modern romantic liberal Western societies. The author undertakes a deep analysis into how spiritualities and the religion of the heart are both a product of expressive individuality as well as milieus to curb its excesses in our society today.

Sarah Wilkins-Laflamme
Associate professor, Sociology and Legal Studies, University of Waterloo

Acknowledgements

The debts I owe for the completion of this book are many—too many, unfortunately, for me to recount in full. Alas, such is the nature of scholarship; we stand on the backs of so many giants that it becomes near impossible to name them all. I will therefore give thanks to those who most readily come to mind, and hope the rest will not be offended by my lapses in memory.

I must begin by thanking my informants. I am deeply grateful to all those who sat down with me for an interview, allowing me into your life worlds. I gained far more from our conversations than I could have known.

I've had the extreme fortune of working and conversing with an array of brilliant scholars that, in both direct and indirect ways, have made me a much better academic than I otherwise would be. Thanks must especially go to my doctoral supervisor, Will Kymlicka, whose breadth of learning and intellectual depth continue to astound and inspire me. Special thanks also to the rest of my doctoral committee: Simon Coleman and Sharday Mosurinjohn. Simon was gracious enough to give up his time to oversee my fieldwork and teach me about the nature of ethnographic research, not to mention tolerate my philosophical musings during our weekly meetings. Sharday, for her part, has been a friend and stimulating conversation partner for some time. I would also like to highlight the contributions of my examiners, Lori Beaman and Richard Ascough, whose searching questions shone necessary light on key issues that I'd overlooked. Next, thanks are owed to Dick Houtman, who has been immensely helpful since we first met at a conference in Las Vegas (of all places!). Dick kindly invited me to present my work to him and his colleagues at the Centre for Sociological Research at KU Leuven while I was living in Cambridge. Moreover, he read significant portions of early drafts of this book, always offering incisive commentary in turn. Others who read and offered their comments on early drafts of specific chapters include (in alphabetical order): Nancy Ammerman, Polina Batanova, Peter Beyer, Mark Cladis, Liza Cortois, Robert Fuller, James Laidlaw, Alasdair Lockhart, Anna Halafoff, Craig Martin, Gillian McCann, Matthew McManus, Hugh McLeod, Deborah Orr, Bill Parsons, Sam Reimer, Leigh Eric Schmidt, Tim Stacey, Riyaz Timol, Steven Tipton, Paul Tromp, C. Travis Webb, and Linda Woodhead. This book is immeasurably improved as a result of their contributions. Still, I have no doubt that they, along with many others, will find it lacking in important respects. For these errors or omissions, I take full responsibility.

I am especially beholden to the inimitable James Miller, who, as my MA supervisor, gave me the freedom to pursue my intellectual interests widely, without concern for disciplinary boundaries. And I would also like to single out two people who have been instrumental to my academic career: Jacqueline Davies and Christine Sypnowich. I've learned much from Jackie, both by attending her lectures as an undergraduate philosophy student, and chatting with her over coffee. And Christine has long inspired me with her ability to combine erudition, analytical acumen, humility, and kindness in a single character.

During 2017–18 I had the privilege of studying in the Department for the Study of Religion at the University of Toronto, where I was privy to a number of rousing conversations and graduate seminars, which were instrumental to my research. And during the Lent term of 2019 I had the great fortune of studying in the Faculty of Divinity at Cambridge University. For the latter I am ever grateful to Tim Jenkins, who sponsored my trip and supervised my stay. It was a wonderful privilege (not to mention incredibly daunting) to sit with Tim every week and discuss my work-in-progress. And with Cambridge in mind, I must also give thanks to Fraser Watts (no relation), who for years has served as an intellectual mentor of sorts, not to mention been a close friend.

Material presented in this book has previously appeared in various journal publications. Ideas discussed in Chapter 1 can be found in "Religious Studies and the Spiritual Turn," *Theory and Method in the Study of Religion* 33/5 (2021): 482–504 (co-authored with Sharday Mosurinjohn). Parts of Chapter 2 have been published in "Religion, Science, and Disenchantment in Late Modernity," *Zygon: Journal of Science and Religion* 54/4 (2019): 1022–35. An earlier version of Chapter 3 was published as "The Religion of the Heart: 'Spirituality' in Late Modernity," *American Journal of Cultural Sociology* 10/1 (2022): 1–33. And Chapter 7 draws on ideas presented in "Making Sense of the Study of Spirituality: Late Modernity on Trial," *Religion* 50/4 (2020): 591–614. I want to thank these journals for granting me permission to reprint this material here. And thanks also to University of California Press, University of Chicago Press, Penguin Random House, and Harvard University Press for their permission to include the epigraphs in this book.

Naturally, I have significantly benefitted from presenting my work at various conferences. These include: in 2017, the annual meeting of the Canadian Society for the Study of Religion, the annual meeting of the International Society for the Sociology of Religion, the annual meeting of Socrel, the BSA's Sociology of Religion Study Group, the American Academy for the Study of Religion, and the annual Universitair Centrum Sint-Ignatius Antwerpen Summer School on Religion, Culture and Society in Antwerp; in 2018, the International Conference on Religion & Film, the Nonreligion and Secularity Research Network annual conference, the World Congress of Sociology, and the annual meeting of the Society for the Scientific Study of Religion; in 2019, the annual meeting of the Epiphany Philosophers at Cambridge University, the Religion, Faith, and Society Research Group Workshop hosted by the Center for the Study of Islam in the UK (thank you Riyaz Timol for the invite), a research seminar hosted by the Woolf Institute in Cambridge, and the annual meeting of the Society for the Anthropology of Religion. And, of course, none of this would have been possible were it not for financial support from the following institutions: the Social Sciences and Humanities Research Council of Canada, the Ontario Confederation of University Faculty Associations, and the Cultural Studies Graduate Program at Queen's University. Finally, I would like to thank Tom Perridge, the two discerning anonymous readers he found, and the rest of the team at OUP, all of whose feedback and guidance did much to improve the original manuscript.

*　*　*

Once I extend my vision beyond the academic world, the debts begin to rack up very rapidly. Indeed, it is striking to reflect on the degree to which the completion of a work of scholarship like this depends upon a whole array of relationships, support systems, and social networks. The end product—which obscures these background forces and factors—belies the truth: that we are little without the people around us.

First and foremost, I need to thank my parents, Kingsley and Pearl—whose unwavering support has been the cornerstone of any success I can justifiably claim. Thank you for being the people you are, and for setting the examples you have. This book is dedicated to you.

I would also like to give a shout out to my sister, Kelsey—whose love and friendship I cherish.

Scholarship, in my experience, demands long periods of solitary work, and many episodes of agony and frustration. As a result, it has been a necessity for me to have means of escape. I have many friends and extended family to thank for grounding me in these moments, and for just being good company over the years. To all of you (you know who you are): thank you for being a part of my life.

Last, I must give thanks to my best friend, my partner, my wife—Chantel. To you, I owe more than words can express, and more than any metric can measure. Life without you, our daughter, Audrey, and our two dogs, Mick and Lily, would be incalculably worse—so much so that I dare not contemplate it. Thank you for being a light in my life. Thank you for being you. You have my love.

G. W.
Toronto

Contents

... religion seems destined to transform itself rather than disappear.
(Émile Durkheim, *The Elementary Forms of Religious Life*)

Introduction

> We have argued that any living tradition is a conversation, an argu-
> ment in the best sense, about the meaning and value of our
> common life.
>
> (Robert Bellah et al. 1985, 303)

What ideals and visions of the good underpin and animate the social order of
twenty-first-century liberal democracies? From what traditions, moral and religious, do we—their citizens—draw to divine guidance and inspiration? In what
ways do we depend upon our institutions to make sense of the world both within
and around us? And what is the nature and substance of our common life?

Many of us who live in post-1960s liberal democracies struggle with these
questions. While we might have a faint notion of what it is we share, we have
trouble articulating it. In fact, we are much better at defining who and what we are
not, than who and what it is we *are*—so much so that mere talk of "we" tends to
immediately rouse our suspicions. One reason for this has to do with the complexity of our societies—Euro-American liberal democracies are diverse, multidi-
mensional, and conflictual by nature. The by-product of centuries of vast social
change, the basic structures and constitutive dynamics of our societies are not
easily perceived or comprehended. In some ways, then, we can be forgiven for
failing to provide answers to these probing queries—or even dismissing them
outright. Yet this explanation alone is insufficient. For, as I see it, the greatest
impediment to achieving clarity on these questions is the self-understanding post-
1960s liberalism tacitly encourages.

It is commonly remarked that what makes liberal citizens distinctive is their
individualism. A hardened cliché, this descriptor is regularly taken as self-evident.
As a result, few think to interrogate its substance. There are, in actual fact, many
different kinds of individualism—*individualisms*, if you will. But what our
most common individualisms share is a specific self-conception; one which
encourages their adherents to see themselves as *independent* of, and even perennially *in conflict* with, their society's traditions, institutions, and norms. It is
this self-understanding—widespread in post-1960s liberal democracies (and
beyond)—that makes it so difficult for us to respond confidently to the queries
listed above, and which leads us to raise our hackles whenever the infamous "we"
is invoked. For as a result of our individualism, many of us do not see ourselves as
inheritors of shared traditions, or as dependent upon institutions for our sense of

The Spiritual Turn: The Religion of the Heart and the Making of Romantic Liberal Modernity. Galen Watts,
Oxford University Press. © Galen Watts 2022. DOI: 10.1093/oso/9780192859839.003.0001

self. Rather, we tend to perceive our ideals as emerging from deep within us, as opposed to the society in which we live. In other words, we see ourselves as *individuals*—those whose true selves *pre-exist* society, and whose realization is the hard-won achievement of having railed *against* its dictates and discourses.

Of course, there is some truth to this self-understanding. Immense social and political progress has been achieved as a result of liberals challenging engrained and enduring laws and customs which oppressively stifled individual freedoms while protecting social hierarchies. Nevertheless, it remains a peculiar feature of post-1960s liberal democracies that they tend to produce subjects who, by virtue of their self-conception, fail to acknowledge their cultural, social, and institutional debts. That is, we regularly overlook the fact that, in our quest for greater freedom and moral equality, we have not so much done away with tradition, as rejected one in favour of another.

This is perhaps no more evident than in the way we tend to tell the history of religion in the West. It has become a truism that the overarching trend since the Enlightenment has been one of religious decline—and that, roundabout the 1960s, this trend took off, reaching ever new heights. For instance, in a *New York Times* article provocatively titled "The Crisis for Liberalism," one reads that pre-1960s liberalism relied on the "substructure" of family life, religion, and patriotism, whereas "Much of post-1960s liberal politics, by contrast, has been an experiment in cutting Western societies loose from those foundations...No heaven or religion, no countries or borders or parochial loyalties of any kind" (Douthat 2016). On this view—widespread in twenty-first-century liberal democracies—religion is antithetical to the basic thrust of late modern liberal life, destined to end up in the dustbin of history.

While plausible, this is not merely a just-so story. For in conceiving of religion as a kind of hangover from the archaic past, it plays an active role in defining the post-1960s liberal identity. Recall: we may not know exactly what we are, but we certainly know what we are *not*—that being, "religious." Thus, many of us commonly assume that while our pre-modern ancestors may have depended on institutions, relied on tradition, participated in collective rituals, and indeed been "religious," we have outgrown such primitive things. In short, the story of liberal modernity, as habitually recounted by both proponents and detractors alike, is intimately bound up with a grand narrative of religious decline.

In his perspicacious *A Secular Age* philosopher Charles Taylor (2007) critically refers to this type of narrative as a "subtraction story" because it occludes "the way in which each stage of this process has involved new constructions of identity, social imaginary, institutions and practices" (530). Taylor does not deny that secularization has occurred; he recognizes that organized religion is not faring well in the West and that this trend is inextricably linked to modern social conditions. Rather, his point is that conceptualizing the birth and ascent of liberal modernity as a mere decline of pre-modern characteristics is profoundly myopic, for it conceals what has positively emerged in their place. In other words, the problem with this type of narrative is that it reinforces the self-understanding accompanying much post-1960s liberalism—fostering a self-induced blindness to what we have in common, along with our social and institutional debts.

This book aims to demystify, and ultimately challenge, this self-understanding. It does so by adopting a cultural sociological approach to the study of religion, which, rather than focusing on what has been lost over the past fifty years, foregrounds what has positively arisen in its stead—giving concerted attention to the new constructions of identity, social imaginary, and institutional trans-formations that have crystallized in the West. More broadly, this book seeks to analyse and assess the character and constitution of post-1960s liberal democra-cies by, counterintuitively, surveying the specific kind of religion they tend to foster.

It is a striking fact that roundabout the time when secularization is said to have kicked into high gear—the 1960s—North Americans and Western Europeans began increasingly identifying as "spiritual" rather than "religious." Indeed, the semantic shift from "religion" to "spirituality"—what scholars have taken to calling the *spiritual turn*—has become a staple of the contemporary religious landscape, yet it is rarely interpreted as contradicting the subtraction narrative commonly told. The reason for this is that, for a large majority, to be "spiritual" is to have shed or rejected the shackles of "religion"—that is, those aspects of religion which are institutional, or bind one to tradition—in lieu of a unique quest of one's own. It is to have taken the road less travelled as a means of realizing one's true self, unencumbered by societal norms, cultural expectations, or religious conven-tions. In this way, the self-understanding implicit in talk of "spirituality" is strikingly similar to that espoused by post-1960s liberals. In fact, they are not merely similar, they are, in crucial respects, identical. This explains why, as we shall explore at length later, the many criticisms targeting what goes by "spiritu-ality" today mirror, in remarkable respects, broader criticisms of post-1960s liberalism. Picking up on this, religious studies scholar Gordon Lynch (2007) has called studying the spiritual turn "a kind of religious and cultural Rorschach test, where what the researcher sees is often a projection of their own values, hopes and concerns" (7). In actual fact, it reveals much more than this—what one thinks of the shift from "religion" to "spirituality," in large measure, tracks what one thinks of post-1960s liberal democracies (and vice versa). Thus, examining the character of the spiritual turn and the debates it has engendered illuminates much about twenty-first-century liberal democracies and their discontents.

* * *

In the pages that follow, I synthesize a wide array of disparate scholarship on "spirituality," draw from a number of disciplines—cultural sociology, sociology of religion, religious and cultural studies, intellectual history, and political philosophy—as well as my own empirical research in order to excavate historical trends, chart cultural connections, and map socio-political developments that have heretofore remained largely invisible. In so doing, I make the case that far from signalling an escape from traditions, institutions, and norms, the self-understanding typical of both post-1960s liberals and those who self-identify as "spiritual"—as we shall, quite often one and the same—in fact, *derives* from their social condition. In other words, the self-evident or taken-for-granted character of this self-understanding is *itself* the by-product of key societal transformations—specifically, the crystallization and consolidation of a distinct social imaginary and social order, whose roots can be roughly traced back to the 1960s.

This will undoubtedly seem counterintuitive to many. But this should not surprise us, given how prevalent this self-understanding has become. We are so accustomed to viewing ourselves as having broken free of the chains of the past that we fail to see the myriad ways we remain dependent upon it. Of course, as mentioned above, this self-conception is often inspired by good intentions—a means of challenging and transcending oppressive historical legacies and cultural forms. But the tragic irony is that in failing to acknowledge our social and institutional debts we may, in the end, stifle our ability to realize our own ideals.

In sum, contemporary liberals—and those among us who self-identify as "spiritual"—require a new self-understanding. This calls for a new story with which to understand our past and present—one that enables us to answer, with moral clarity and confidence, the questions I posed at the outset of this chapter. The aim of this book is to supply this story.

Retracing My Steps: *Habits* and the Spiritual Turn

But before I begin, it will prove useful to retrace my steps and make clear why I ended up undertaking this project in the first place.

Admittedly, these issues have not always been top of mind for me. Born and raised in Toronto, Canada, for much of my life I had little sense of the traditions to which I belonged, and could not have fathomed the notion that my conception of the world, nor my convictions, depended upon cultural structures and social institutions that preceded my existence. While I might have been able to articulate my values, I was quite convinced that these sprung from my true inner self—something categorically independent of my society. And having grown up in a nonreligious household, it was self-evident to me that religion was a relic of the past—wholly alien to the secular society I called my own.

All of this changed after reading *Habits of the Heart: Individualism and Commitment in American Life*—a book that woke me from what I now refer to as a dogmatic slumber. Written collaboratively by four sociologists and one philosopher, *Habits* is a profound meditation on the nature of individualism in

America. That is, its authors—Robert Bellah, Richard Madsen, William Sullivan, Ann Swidler, and Steven Tipton—are concerned with the problems thrown up by liberal modernity, or how to create a decent, just, and cohesive society in a world of multiple and conflicting moral traditions and social institutions. What makes *Habits* distinctive, then, is its cultural sociological character. Rooted in a classical sociological paradigm, which sees the fact of institutional differentiation—the process whereby modern society's primary institutional spheres (e.g., the economy, politics, religion, etc.) become differentiated, or governed by distinct moral logics, ethical styles, and organizational structures—as the defining characteristic of modern societies, Bellah and his co-authors do not view the birth of modernity as entailing the erosion of tradition per se. On the contrary, they argue that liberal modernity is characterized by the existence of multiple moral traditions, each of which finds a rightful place in a distinct institutional sphere. Thus, rather than speak of individualism in the singular, they describe various vocabularies of individualism—expressive, utilitarian, biblical, and republican—which they conceive as "living cultural traditions" or "distinctive patterns of meaning" that "make different kinds of common-sense out of our experience of different institutional spheres of social life" (Tipton 1986, 166).

No doubt, for those who are not sociologists this is likely an extremely unintuitive way of thinking about society. But Bellah and his co-authors make clear that this has long been the reality in America—regardless of whether or not individuals have recognized it. At the same time, *Habits*'s main thesis is that, since the 1960s, the moral traditions of expressive and utilitarian individualism have become "overgeneralized"—that is, they have lamentably overtaken and diminished the authority of the biblical and republican traditions in American life, producing what the authors perceive as worrying consequences. Indeed, expressive individualism, which, according to Bellah et al. (1985, 334), "holds that each person has a unique core of feeling and intuition that should unfold or be expressed if individuality is to be realized," receives particularly harsh treatment.

I say *Habits* woke me from a dogmatic slumber because, for one, it opened my eyes to the way in which the past lives on in the present. It helped me to see what I earlier did not: the particularity of my own liberal identity. For another, the first time I read it, despite over twenty-five years having passed since its original publication, the picture it painted of post-1960s liberal democratic life seriously disturbed me. I saw myself in its pages and I did not like it. I was especially struck by their treatment of expressive individualism, which Bellah and his co-authors contend lies at the root of many of our most acute social ills. This moral tradition is intimately familiar to me; it permeates my life world, and rolls easily off my tongue. Indeed, it is—I have come to see—central to my sense of self. Thus, while I found reading *Habits* incredibly illuminating, I also found it deeply distressing.

*   *   *

It is no accident that religion receives sustained attention in *Habits*. Following Alexis de Tocqueville in *Democracy in America*, Bellah and his co-authors observe that, historically, religion has been central to social and political life in America, what with puritanism and sect religion playing a key role in giving life to the republican virtues and values that were pivotal to the birth of American democracy. Moreover, well attuned to contemporary religious change, they were some of the first to draw attention to the shift from "religion" to "spirituality." In taking a cultural sociological approach, Bellah and his co-authors contend that the spiritual turn signals not the demise of religion, so much as the triumph of a distinct kind—which they call "religious individualism" (a term borrowed from Ernst Troeltsch). They observe, "Contemporary religious individualists often speak of themselves as 'spiritual' rather than 'religious,' as in 'I'm not religious but I'm very spiritual'" (Bellah et al. 1985, 246). They even offer an exemplary case, a woman they call Sheila Larson. When asked to define her religiosity, Larson answered, "My faith has carried me a long way. It's Sheilaism. Just my own little voice." According to Bellah and his co-authors Sheilaism reflects a kind of *religious expressive individualism*, which posits "personal religious experience as the basis of belief" and holds "'self-realization' as the highest aspiration" (235, 234). Accordingly, for these social critics, the spiritual turn is emblematic of the worrying moral-cum-institutional trends they seek to bring to light—specifically, the overgeneralization of expressive individualism in American life.

The analysis in *Habits* is notable for two reasons. First, Bellah and his co-authors flat out reject the simplistic subtraction version of secularization, which holds that, with the birth of modernity, religion inevitably declines. Instead, they contend that post-1960s liberal democracies are characterized as much by *religious transformation* as by religious decline, and that studying this transformation—symbolized by the shift from "religion" to "spirituality"—can teach us much about the nature of these societies. Second, *Habits* makes evident the striking degree to which debates about "spirituality" reflect larger debates about the nature of twenty-first-century liberal democracies. Indeed, for Bellah and his co-authors, the shift from "religion" to "spirituality" epitomized all that had gone awry in liberal democracies in the wake of the 1960s. And many have followed in their footsteps. As we shall see, concerns abound regarding the decline of civic consciousness, community, and moral commitment as a result of the spiritual turn. And in recent years, critics have argued that "spirituality" serves to conceal and perpetuate social and economic injustices. Thus, not only did *Habits* put the shift from "religion" to "spirituality" on the sociological map, but in making evident the elective affinities shared between the spiritual turn and the social order of post-1960s liberal democracies, its authors made a persuasive case for studying the former in order to make sense of the latter.

Toward a Cultural Sociology of Twenty-First-Century Liberal Democracies

Habits
Say you are
the sequel
to Habits

This book extends as well as challenges the legacies of *Habits*. It extends them as follows. First, though principally a work of cultural sociology it draws freely from a host of disciplines and theoretical traditions, thereby operating "in the border areas between philosophy, the humanities, and the social sciences" (Bellah 1990, 1063). In other words, it seeks to embody what Bellah et al. (1985, 298) felicitously call "social science as public philosophy." I therefore reject the positivist assumption that the competent social scientist must cease to be a general citizen of society, as well as the postmodern supposition that the social critic must take a position of detachment from their own society and its ideals.

Second, like the authors of *Habits*, I use classic sociological methods—the interview and participant observation—and interlace my sociological analysis with philosophical reflection as a means of illuminating the issues at stake. Between 2014 and 2018, I conducted semi-structured in-depth interviews with fifty Canadian millennials (born between 1980 and 2000) who self-identify as "spiritual but not religious" (SBNR). And in addition to this, over the course of 2018, I conducted participant observation at three sites in downtown Toronto—a Twelve Step group, a neo-Pentecostal church, and a Toastmasters public speaking club—in order to better understand the nature of "spirituality" in its myriad forms.[1] Of course, given my limited empirical sample, some might reasonably question my pretensions to speak of post-1960s liberal democracies in general. In response, while my sample may be limited, I've made sure to avail myself of extensive secondary literatures—both on "spirituality" and contemporary liberalism—in order to bolster my empirical claims. In other words, the arguments presented in this book rely considerably upon scholarship and empirical research that is not just my own. At the same time, others may be troubled by my lack of attention to regional particularities—for while I occasionally highlight national developments, my "big picture" analysis in Parts I and II gives primacy to international trends. While I do not deny that twenty-first-century Euro-American democracies vary in significant and wide-ranging respects, I also think there is value in pinpointing and reflecting upon their equally profound similarities. Indeed, it seems to me quite instructive that since its original publication *Habits* has found a receptive audience far outside of the US. Clearly, it is not just Canadians like myself who have seen themselves in its pages.

Lastly, this book concerns itself fundamentally with the consequences—social, political, economic, and existential—of the shift from "religion" to "spirituality" and seeks to contribute to the public discussion about the moral traditions, ideals,

---

[1] For more on research methods see the Appendix.

and political aspirations that animate twenty-first-century liberal democracies. So, while I recognize that parts of this book can make for tough going, given the somewhat technical and specialized nature of the theories and debates with which I engage, I have tried to write in a lucid and accessible manner, defining concepts and terms where necessary, so that it might find an audience beyond the ivory tower. In my view, one of the great virtues of *Habits* is its democratic use of language—which I suspect explains at least some of its broad and enduring appeal. Moreover, it is this public stance that underlies my repeated use of that perennially fraught pronoun—"we." Of course, my invocation of this term naturally raises the question: who is this "we" of which I speak? While at times I use it to refer exclusively to those who are citizens of one or other Euro-American liberal democracy, I generally use it in a more inclusive manner: as an invitation to the reader to *mutual recognition* and *identification*. What I mean by this is that while I hope this book may be of interest to (and potentially even persuade) those who are hostile to the spirit of post-1960s liberal democracies, I envisage it chiefly as contributing to a conversation among those who willingly identify with these societies and their animating ideals—regardless of whether or not they are citizens of the West. And so, when I invoke "we," it is to this imagined community that I appeal. Undoubtedly, there will be some citizens of liberal democracies who do not see themselves in the picture I paint. That is fine. I do not purport to speak for everyone—an ambition that would be as foolish as it is incoherent. Rather, my principal aims are humbler: to offer a descriptive account of twenty-first-century liberal societies and the social imaginary that animates them, which I hope at least a significant number will be able to see themselves in. And, then, to spur amongst this self-selected group a critical awareness of our social and institutional debts.

At the same time, this study diverges from *Habits* in a number of ways. In the intervening years, I have been able to make sense of, and grapple with, my initial response to that book. I see now, in a way that eluded me before, just how American *Habits* is. By this I am not suggesting that the issues it throws into light are only of relevance to Americans. By no means. Again, the spread of expressive individualism is far from exclusive to America, so the challenges this poses (as well as the opportunities it brings) are endemic to all post-1960s liberal democracies. But what is undeniably American about *Habits*, I have come to believe, are the specific challenges its authors diagnose *as* problems, as well as the remedies they prescribe in turn.

This is no more evident than in their discussion of religion. Following Tocqueville, *Habits* assumes a "tight linkage of religion and public life" (Bellah et al. 1985, 221)—that is, Bellah and his co-authors view religion as "indispensable to the maintenance of republican institutions" (Tocqueville [1835] 1998, 120). This is why they are far from enthused about the rise of "spirituality," and why they instead champion the revival of a "public church" (Bellah et al. 1985, 237). Moreover, their call to revitalize the biblical and republican moral traditions reflects a distinctly American genealogy. Of course, few can fault them for this, given their intended audience. But one cannot help but wonder whether such a prescription makes sense even for America in the twenty-first century—let alone other liberal democracies.

Second, this study diverges from *Habits* insofar as it makes the issue of meaning in modernity just as central as those of community and justice. Indeed, I believe studying the spiritual turn is important because it reflects a shift in meaning-structures—the way individuals make sense of their selves, especially in relation to a greater order. Accordingly, while I am concerned with the state of social and political life in post-1960s liberal democracies my focus on the religious sphere is chiefly motivated by a recognition of the need for ultimate or transcendent meaning, or what we might call *enchantment*—and an acute awareness of the forces that stifle its fulfilment.

Finally, I seek to offer a, though parallel and at times overlapping, nevertheless distinct narrative of our past and present. With a richer understanding of the nature of social theory, as well as what is at stake in debates about "spirituality" and liberalism today, I have come to see that *Habits* was powerful and persuasive because from within the interpretive lens through which it filtered the world its conclusions were inescapable. As a result, I have chosen a different lens through which to gaze upon liberal modernity.

Émile Durkheim as Guide and Interlocutor

Instead of Tocqueville, I place a different Frenchman, Émile Durkheim, front and centre, treating him as both guide and interlocutor. Of course, *Habits* was undeniably Durkheimian in character. The stress Bellah and his co-authors place on institutional differentiation, and their overall cultural sociological approach, owe much to this founding father of sociology. But I nevertheless think they fail to fully heed the wisdom of the Durkheimian tradition—a tradition whose insights have, in my view, never been more relevant.

Though it is all too often forgotten, Durkheim came of age during a period not unlike today. The Industrial Revolution was a time of immense cultural and social change, creating massive rifts in society, and spurring great social unrest. Indeed, sociology, as a discipline, emerged in response to these changes. Durkheim hoped that the social sciences would help to shed light on what was happening around him. But this was not merely an academic exercise. During his lifetime, liberalism in France received sustained assaults from both the conservative Catholic right and the socialist left. A committed left-liberal, Durkheim sought to fend off these attacks, arguing that the picture of modern liberal societies afforded by a sociological perspective makes evident the oversights and omissions in these critics' accounts. For instance, advancing what has come to be an axiom of contemporary cultural sociology, Durkheim contended that shared cultural structures and sacred forms are constitutive of *all* societies—including liberal democracies. In other words, *contra* critics who charge liberal societies with moral and cultural incoherence, Durkheim maintained that liberalism reflects a moral tradition like any other—which he referred to as *moral individualism*. Moral individualism, from a Durkheimian perspective, represents a distinctive collective representation, rooted in social life and shared institutions, which admirably sacralizes the ideals of individual liberty and moral equality.

And yet, while committed to the liberal settlement, Durkheim was also sensitive to the risks associated with individualism and unfettered capitalism, spending much of his career studying what he saw as the central pathologies of liberal modernity—*anomie* (a lack of social integration) and *egoism* (a lack of moral regulation). In other words, Durkheim was not solely interested in proving critics wrong. He was equally interested in warning his fellow liberals of the challenges intrinsic to the liberal democratic project, as well as identifying the social conditions necessary for the realization of its animating ideals. In turn, he championed the existence of voluntary associations in civil society, which he argued must serve as sources of social integration and moral regulation for liberal citizens by means of collective rituals and shared moral norms. At the same time, he also endorsed institutional differentiation and moral pluralism, which he saw as crucial to preserving individual freedom and individuality, along with a healthy balance between private and public life. In sum, Durkheim impressively managed to combine both sociological and political theoretical insights in order to advance a unique sociological defence of liberal societies, as well as an inspiring vision of the good society—both of which we would be wise to recover.

Of course, Durkheim did not live to see post-1960s liberal democracies, and as a product of the nineteenth century it is likely that he would have struggled to comprehend their character and constitution. Thus, in treating Durkheim as a guide and interlocutor in the pages that follow, I do not do so dogmatically. I recognize that, in many instances, supplementary theoretical and normative frameworks have much to contribute—and I make sure to adopt these where appropriate. For instance, in order to produce a workable definition of religion with which to chart the spiritual turn, I borrow from and combine the theoretical insights of both Durkheim and Max Weber. In spelling out the appropriate relationship between private and public life, and the reasons for this division, I look to Jean-Jacques Rousseau for guidance. And in assessing the various philosophical positions informing the popular criticisms of both "spirituality" and post-1960s liberal democracies, I rely significantly on the political philosophical scholarship of recent liberal theorists.

Still, despite these qualifications, I am convinced that the Durkheimian tradition remains immensely fruitful to think with. Indeed, what is most valuable about a Durkheimian perspective is that it helps us to see the stunning degree to

which the self-understanding of so many today is deeply at odds with their social
condition.

The Story in Brief

For the sake of clarity, let me state plainly the argument that underlies this book.
Following in the footsteps of contemporary cultural sociologists, I contend the
spiritual turn signals the ascent of an enduring cultural structure in liberal
modernity. Bellah and his co-authors called this "religious individualism,"
whereas I call it *the religion of the heart.* By cultural structure, I mean a symbolic
framework that orders and animates distinct discourses—both "secular" and
"religious." The religion of the heart has longstanding roots in the Western
tradition. We can see it at work in the Romantic, Transcendentalist,
Theosophist, and New Thought movements of the eighteenth and nineteenth
centuries, as well as the New Age, Charismatic Christian, and Human Potential
movements of the 1960s. Indeed, the 1960s play a central role in the story I tell.
Sociologists of religion tend to speak of this period as "unusually irreligious" (Voas
and Chaves 2016, 1543). I disagree. If we expand our definition of religion to
include unchurched forms of religion, we see that the 1960s were a period of
tremendous religious ferment—that is, they mark the era when the religion of the
heart moved from the cultural margins into the mainstream.

Yet it would be wrong to view this shift in isolation from wider societal
developments. In my view, the spiritual turn is best thought of as *the religious
wing of a more general moral-cum-political revolution.* This revolution was characterized by a widespread embrace of expressive individualism, a reformulation of
liberal values, and the concomitant reform of key primary institutions—along
with the creation of a whole collection of secondary institutions—in order to reflect
these new romantic expressivist dispensations. This explains the close elective
affinities shared between the religion of the heart (which goes by "spirituality"
today) and the social order of post-1960s liberal democracies.

As a result of the upheavals of the 1960s, we in the West inhabit a social order
that remains animated, and indeed legitimated, by what I call a *romantic liberal*
social imaginary. *Romantic liberalism* seeks to reconcile romantic disenchantment
with liberal institutions by means of enchanting the private sphere. Accordingly,
romantic liberals interpret the value of individual freedom in a particular way, one
that resonates strongly with a romantic expressivist conception of the human
condition. This distinctive—if widespread—interpretation of the liberal tradition
can be traced back, in different ways, to the writings of Wilhelm von Humboldt
and John Stuart Mill, but it came of age in the 1960s, and has since become the
dominant conception of liberalism. I therefore refer to the social order of twenty-
first-century liberal democracies as *romantic liberal modernity.* As we shall see, the

religion of the heart bears deep elective affinities with this social order; so deep that it can be justifiably thought of as *the spirit of romantic liberal modernity*.

To many, this story will seem farfetched. I aim to show that it is not.

Overview of the Chapters

This book comprises three parts. In Part I (Chapters 1–3), I introduce the reader to the academic study of spirituality and the problems therein, make the case for a cultural sociological approach to the study of religion, offer a brief history of the religion of the heart, and then outline its basic character.

In Chapter 1, I argue that, while the secularization paradigm remains tremendously insightful, secularization theorists' preoccupation with charting the decline of church religion has nevertheless stifled our ability to grasp the substantive character of what goes by "spirituality." At the same time, alternative cultural approaches within the sociology of religion have tended to obscure the underlying unity of the spiritual turn. As a result, the study of spirituality has taken place across a host of subfields and disciplines, each of which has contributed much to our understanding of the spiritual turn, but whose theoretical and empirical insights have yet to be comprehensively compared or synthesized. In turn, I lay out the foundations of the distinctly cultural sociological approach to the study of religion that I use to synthesize and clarify the existing scholarship on "spirituality."

In Chapter 2, I draw from a wide array of historical, philosophical, and sociological studies—primarily Anglo-American though not exclusively—in order to provide a brief history of the religion of the heart, by examining some of its key carrier movements and representative voices, while offering supportive examples from my empirical research. The reason for this historical foray is to provide compelling evidence that identifying as "spiritual" does not signal an escape from religious tradition, so much as place one squarely within a longstanding "third way" tradition in the West that, paradoxically, denies its status as a tradition.

In Chapter 3, I draw from the existing scholarship on "spirituality," my interviews with SBNRs, the informal and formal interviews conducted at my three field sites, and discourse analysis of several popular "spiritual" and self-help books in order to systematically outline the ten tenets that comprise today's religion of the heart. No doubt, in offering such a synthesis, I retrace steps and cover tracks that have been trodden before. However, I argue such a synthesis, given the insights it affords, is enormously productive. For instance, not only does it enable us to place into conversation disparate academic literatures—connecting scholarship on the New Age, Charismatic Christian, and Human Potential movements—but it also helps us to see just how intimately the spiritual turn is related to the consolidation of romantic liberal modernity—the story I tell in Part II (Chapters 4–6).

In Chapter 4, I trace the ascent of the religion of the heart to the 1960s. Inspired by an eclectic mix of innovative historical and political theoretical scholarship, especially the work of Nancy Rosenblum, I argue that it was during this era that an unprecedented alliance between romanticism and liberalism took root and blossomed. I link key cultural and political developments of this period, demonstrating that they were equally motivated by a romantic liberal social imaginary. I conclude that the rise of the religion of the heart reflects the religious wing of a wider romantic liberal revolt, to which the rights revolutions and liberation movements of the period also belong.

In Chapter 5, guided by the Durkheimian tradition, I advance an institutionalist analysis of the 1960s. I make clear how the counter-culturalists of the 1960s relied upon a whole series of secondary institutions in order to launch a moral crusade against the competing economic, legal-political, and private spheres. Next, I demonstrate how they successfully transformed both the private sphere, while reforming the legal-political sphere, thereby giving life to romantic liberal modernity. I conclude with a discussion of the moral, political, epistemic, and economic developments that have precipitated not only the decline of Christendom but also the flourishing of the religion of the heart.

In Chapter 6, I map the array of secondary and primary institutions that comprise the religious sphere in romantic liberal modernity—which I call the *romantic liberal institutional order*. These include: (1) the holistic milieu, (2) the Charismatic wing of the congregational domain, (3) popular culture and entertainment media institutions, (4) arts institutions, (5) healthcare institutions, (6) educational institutions, and (7) certain sectors of the economic sphere. These various institutional fields, I argue, offer social support and plausibility to the religion of the heart. I then draw from my interviews and fieldwork in order to make the case that attraction to "spirituality" in romantic liberal modernity follows one of a number of distinct social pathways.

Upon narrating the rise of the religion of the heart and the making of romantic liberal modernity, in Chapter 7, I turn to the popular and academic debates their emergence has provoked. Though it has rarely been acknowledged explicitly, the spiritual turn is, for many, a paradigmatic test case for the ills of romantic liberal modernity; critics view in "spirituality" all of the sins of the contemporary social order. These range from the erosion of the authority of reason and science, the corrosion of community and the weakening of moral commitment, the devaluation of civic membership and political solidarity, the legitimation of neoliberal capitalism, and the mystification of insidious forms of social control. Of course, while the target of these censures may be quite new, they reflect longstanding concerns and anxieties about the nature of liberal democracy.

Admittedly, it is not easy to get a handle on these sweeping criticisms. Even in their most sophisticated versions, they remain informed by a host of controversial and contestable theoretical and normative assumptions. And yet, to dismiss them outright would be both disingenuous and short-sighted. They indisputably contain important truths, and flag noteworthy issues. How, then, to tease these out?

Here, the Durkheimian tradition is especially helpful. Inspired by the interpretive work of Mark Cladis and W. Watts Miller, in Chapter 7, I set out the building blocks of a Durkheimian reformulation of the romantic liberal tradition that enables us to disentangle those aspects of critics' concerns that are antithetical to the animating ideals of romantic liberalism from those that are not. In other words, I draw from the Durkheimian tradition in order to defend romantic liberal modernity against its detractors, while at the same time flagging the concerns that romantic liberals cannot afford to ignore. These are as follows: (1) To what extent does the religion of the heart ("spirituality") mitigate or exacerbate the pathologies of romantic liberal modernity—anomie and egoism? (2) Does the religion of the heart lead to a colonization of competing social spheres, thereby impeding shifting involvements and the adoption of rival social perspectives and moral traditions?

These unresolved concerns call out for careful empirical investigation. However, not just any methodological approach will do. One of the problems with critics' sweeping criticisms is their abstract nature. Armchair theorizing is easy, but often misleading—divorced, as it is, from everyday life. Durkheim understood this better than most. He argued that examining discourse alone reveals little about how it gets encoded and enfleshed (internalized in bodily habits and dispositions) amongst particular groups of people, and therefore what its real-world effects are. Heeding this lesson, in Part III (Chapters 8–10), I offer three cultural sociological case studies of distinct moral communities where the religion of the heart is institutionalized.

The purpose of the case studies is threefold. First, to build on the argument that I introduce in Part I, and which is integral to the book as a whole—that we find a specific iteration of the religion of the heart at each of these otherwise quite dissimilar field sites. Second, to make clear why paying attention to the role of ritual is essential for grasping the social and political implications of the spiritual turn. And third, to enable us to glean the partial truths contained in critics' accounts of the spiritual turn and romantic liberal modernity, more generally— while at the same time illuminating their deficiencies and limitations.

In Chapter 8, I examine the way the religion of the heart is institutionalized at New Life Fellowship (NLF), a meeting of Alcoholics Anonymous. In Chapter 9, I turn my gaze to C3 Toronto (C3T), a neo-Pentecostal church that belongs to the wider C3 Church movement. And in Chapter 10, I look at Tomorrow's Leaders (TL), a Toastmasters International public speaking club. In light of the evidence presented in the case studies, I argue, first, that critics of "spirituality" lack an appreciation of the distinctive features of romantic liberal modernity and its animating ideals—specifically, the ramifications of institutional differentiation, the romantic liberal attempt to balance public discipline with private enchantment, and romantic liberal modernity's privileging of distinctly liberal virtues.

Second, critics tend to equate "spirituality" with atomistic individualism, when in fact, as I demonstrate in Parts I and II, it signals a cultural structure—the religion of the heart—which is both culturally coherent and institutionally rooted. Consequently, these scholars have failed to see that, in some cases, the religion of the heart is both morally demanding and serves as a source of solidarity.

* * *

The story I tell in this book is less one of corrosion or corruption than one of complexity and contradiction. While I firmly believe romantic liberal modernity has brought with it great achievements which deserve the term progress, I can also empathize with those who look longingly at the past with a sense of nostalgia, as well as those who condemn its gratuitous and vain excesses. What this means is that while I may endorse the core ideals of romantic liberal modernity, I am not oblivious to its failings. Indeed, one of my chief aims in writing this book is to alert those of us who find ourselves defending the romantic liberal project—especially in its egalitarian forms—to our blind spots.

PART I
THE SPIRITUAL TURN

1

From "Religion" to "Spirituality"

Leslie Parker

"Being spiritual just means being who you really are." Leslie Parker, 28, is adamant that there's a world of difference between "religion" and "spirituality." The former, she says, involves "a specific set of beliefs, or dogma" and "an organized, institutional, and hierarchical community that forces you to be something you're not." Whereas the latter is "more free, and feeling-based," simply encouraging individuals to "be themselves." Although neither of her parents ever took their Roman Catholicism very seriously, they still thought it best for the family to join the local church "as a way to become part of the community." So, Leslie has vivid memories of reluctantly attending Catholic mass as a child. "I got my baptism, my communion, my confirmation. I hated it." Just after her confirmation, Leslie's parents got divorced. While she sees this as "the best decision they ever made," the church felt differently. In the wake of the divorce, Leslie and her family were ostracized and shamed. Faced with the church's hostility, her parents gave Leslie and her brothers a choice. "They sat us down and told us, 'OK, guys. We're not going back to church anymore. You are free to form whatever opinion and beliefs that you want to in terms of spirituality or religion.'" Leslie says she "can never thank them enough" for this. She describes her family life, post-church, as "very hippy and earth-based." "My family's ground rules were simple: do no harm." Her father, a teacher by profession, became interested in "native medicine practices," while her mother, a librarian, explored various New Age practices—astrology, tarot cards, and crystals.

While she views her parents' divorce as ultimately for the good, Leslie admits that, as a child, it significantly affected her. "In high school I was very angry and troubled, and I had a lot of emotional problems." It would be years before Leslie was diagnosed with bipolar disorder. Until then, she used drugs and alcohol to self-medicate. The first time Leslie overdosed she was sixteen. By that point, she was regularly taking painkillers to quell feelings of anxiety and depression. She describes her late teens and early twenties as "seriously dark." In university, hangovers and blackouts became commonplace, as did feelings of shame and guilt. Drinking became part of Leslie's daily routine. The turning point came when she decided to get sober. "I remember waking up in the morning and I was doing drugs and drinking, and something just quietly tipped over. I was just like, 'I can't

The Spiritual Turn: The Religion of the Heart and the Making of Romantic Liberal Modernity. Galen Watts, Oxford University Press. © Galen Watts 2022. DOI: 10.1093/oso/9780192859839.003.0002

do this anymore.' I was just done." Leslie eventually found her way to New Life Fellowship (NLF), a group of Alcoholics Anonymous (AA) popular with young people in downtown Toronto. At first, she was confused. But she warmed up to the group quickly. "I saw that it was friends and community, and taking a life back, having fun, and being happy." The first few months in AA were emotionally turbulent, but Leslie sensed she was in the right place: "They spoke in the language of the heart. I loved it." Today, she proudly refers to herself as "spiritual but not religious," as talk of "religion" conjures up memories of the small-town Catholic church which excluded her family, whereas her involvement in AA has been nothing short of liberating—the catalyst for self-discovery and "spiritual exploration." Moreover, Leslie looks back on her life with amazement and gratitude. Although she acknowledges she's had her fair share of ups and downs, she remains convinced that "everything happens for a reason."

Amy Lee

It wouldn't be an exaggeration to say that Leslie Parker and Amy Lee, 30, have lived worlds apart. While Leslie was being raised by lapsed Catholics with New Age curiosities in small-town Ontario, Amy was learning to recite Bible verses at a conservative evangelical church in a sprawling urban metropolis, just outside of Toronto. "Religion was the cornerstone of our household. And my parents are very conservative." Amy's father is a pastor and missionary, who believes that biblical principles should govern all aspects of both public and private life. So, the portrait she paints of her childhood differs markedly from that of Leslie. Not only did her family drive two hours every Sunday in order to attend the Korean evangelical church where her father preached, but Amy's life was governed by what she calls "very strict rules." In high school she was prohibited from sleeping over at friends' houses, dating, or questioning her parents' authority. She was expected to dress modestly, and wasn't allowed to get piercings or tattoos, or wear nail polish or makeup. Naturally, Amy learned to see her Christian identity and beliefs as all-encompassing. Ironically, it was because of the taken-for-granted quality of her religious upbringing that, in Amy's view, she struggled with her faith when she left home in order to study fashion. "I realized that my church life was very routine-based. Deep down I knew that I didn't have that intimacy with God." This feeling only intensified when, after graduating, she found employment in Toronto's hospitality industry—where many workers burn the candle at both ends. This set off a period of moral disorientation and self-doubt. "I had no focus and no idea what I was doing. I was standing on nothing." After working in the industry for five years and getting burnt out, Amy yearned for change. So, she did what her parents had always taught her to: pray about it. As she tells it, this is what led her to C3 Toronto (C3T), a neo-Pentecostal church in the downtown core. Amy still remembers her first service vividly: "The presence of God was undeniable." "In worship, I was just consumed by what I felt was a deepening intimacy with God that I'd never felt before. I was inviting Jesus into my heart." It didn't take long for her to go "all in"—going through the church's Next Steps program, signing up for a volunteer team, and taking part in "connect groups." Over a year later, Amy thinks of herself as a part of the "C3 Toronto family." When asked what distinguishes C3T from the church she was raised in, she's decisive: "the Holy Spirit encounter. My old church was very theology-driven, which is great, but it didn't really have any emphasis on the Holy Spirit—or it being relational, you know? And that's a huge thing for me." Although Amy prefers to call herself "religious and spiritual," as opposed to "spiritual but not religious," what she finds appealing about C3T is that they "are trying to show people that Christianity is not a religion. It's a faith. It's a relationship." She admits this is not exactly what she was raised to believe. But this doesn't bother her. "At C3, I've come to see that it has to be relational—your relationship with God is personal." Today, Amy is committed to C3's mission of "connecting people to God." She holds a number of leadership roles and invests considerable time, energy, and finances into the church. But most importantly for her, she feels a newfound confidence with respect to her faith: "I feel like I hear God in a different way now. I can hear His voice, and hear His direction for me in ways that I never would have expected."

Michael Wallace

Michael Wallace, 24, was born and raised in the suburbs outside of Toronto. He attended an Anglican church at his parents' behest up until his mid-teens, when he persuaded them to let him leave. "I'm not a big fan of institutionalized religion because it seems sort of like a money grab. And it seems very traditional and old-fashioned." Michael associates "religion" less with experiences of exclusion than apathy and incomprehension; as he sees it, being "religious" is basically a holdover of a bygone era. And yet, he happily identifies as "spiritual"—which he sees as "more open, less rigid, and conservative." Still, Michael admits that for much of his childhood, and into his teens, talk of "spirituality" didn't interest him. In fact, it wasn't until university that things changed. "In first year, I had a bit of a crisis. There were so many new people, cliques, and social hierarchies. I couldn't place myself. And I knew I was missing something, but I had no idea what it was." A friend of Michael's lent him Tony Robbins's *Awaken the Giant Within*. And soon after, he read Eckhart Tolle's *The Power of Now*. He says these books were "life changing." They helped him see that he'd "just accepted certain things" about himself that he "should have been questioning." They also stimulated his interest in self-help—a concept Michael believes is closely related to "spirituality." He began reading more widely in the genre, delving into business and life-coaching literatures, but also practising meditation, yoga, and other "spiritual practices"—all of which he sees as components of his "self-development project." In his twenties, Michael joined Tomorrow's Leaders (TL), a Toastmasters International public speaking group in the downtown core. He insists that it's been pivotal to his "personal transformation." "In a strangely weird way, Toastmasters changed my life." Today, Michael harbours dreams of being a professional public speaker and life coach. He spends much of his time reading self-help and positive psychology books. And he continues to hone his public speaking skills at TL. Having conquered his insecurities, he aspires to help others "follow their hearts"—which, he argues, lies at the core of "spirituality without religion." Indeed, for Michael, "being spiritual" has nothing to do with accepting a tradition, being loyal to an institution, or following prescribed rules. Rather, it's far simpler: "I'm spiritual because I believe being the best me I can be is being spiritual."

Institutional Religion vs. Subjective Spirituality

In many respects, Leslie, Amy, and Michael are vastly different people. Their life histories reflect distinct life paths and social influences. Moreover, the social institutions that have formatively influenced their self-understandings are considerably dissimilar, leading them to use contrasting languages to describe themselves and their outlooks on life. And yet, despite these differences, they share something crucial in common. In their own idiosyncratic ways, they champion a conceptual distinction that has become a staple of the post-1960s religious landscape—that between "religion" and "spirituality."

Although Leslie, Amy, and Michael are probably unaware of this, "spirituality" has not always been considered categorically distinct from "religion." In fact, in its earliest formulation, "spirituality"—derived from the Greek noun, *pneuma*—signified the spirit of God (Sheldrake 2013, 2). Of course, as is customary with language, its meaning over the centuries has morphed, changing with its surrounding social context. Yet, it wasn't until the twentieth century that "spirituality" seems to have divorced "religion" in the popular imagination (Huss 2014).

Nevertheless, the novelty of this conceptual distinction has done little to slow its spread. As sociologist Reginald Bibby (2017, 143) observes, "While religion has been scorned and stigmatized and rejected by many, spirituality has known something of celebrity status." Indeed, a recent survey conducted by the Public Religion Research Institute reports that about one in five Americans identifies as "Spiritual but not Religious" (or, as has become the fashion in academic circles, SBNR) (Lipka and Gecewicz 2017). And while the number of SBNRs in Western Europe may be smaller, it is still substantial (see Pew Center 2018) (see also

Wilkins-Laflamme 2021). Moreover, walk into any bookstore today and you're likely to find the "mind-body-spirit" or "spirituality" section stocked, with new titles being added monthly. Yoga studios, meditation workshops, and personal development seminars are popping up left and right, enthusiastically offering people help along their "spiritual paths." It is thus little surprise that leading media outlets from *The New York Times*, to *The Atlantic*, to the BBC have taken notice (Castella 2013; Oppenheimer 2014; Kitchener 2018). As religious studies scholars Heinz Streib and Constantin Klein (2016, 79) remark, "it is an empirical fact that talking about spirituality and self-identifying as spiritual (and not religious) is growing in prominence." It would seem, then, whether Leslie, Amy, or Michael realize it or not, they are representative of a great many people today.

But what should we make of this distinction? This is a more complex question than you might think. As the accounts of Leslie, Amy, and Michael illustrate, when invoked, the distinction between "religion" and "spirituality" is often believed to reflect the personal histories of the speaker, used to indicate their seemingly sundry views and commitments. And yet, scholars agree that it almost always signals an implicit *normative opposition*, which can be summed up: "religion" the "institutional bad-guy" versus "spirituality" the "individual good-guy" (Zinnbauer and Pargament 2005). We see this opposition invoked starkly in both Leslie's and Michael's accounts. However, it also shows up, in a distinct way, in Amy's self-understanding. Recall that, for Amy, "Christianity is not a religion. It's a faith." Indeed, while Amy might be willing to acknowledge the *institutional* nature of C3T, she nevertheless downplays its significance—for what matters first and foremost, as for many Charismatic Christians, is her *personal* relationship with God.

This polarization of what we might call *institutional religion* versus *subjective spirituality* (or *faith*) is widespread today—so widespread, in fact, that it has become something of a truism. The problem with this, as Durkheim would be quick to point out, is that it is sociologically vacuous. Subjective beliefs (especially those that are widely shared) and institutions are co-constitutive—we rarely have one without the other. Moreover, no matter how unique our experiences may *feel* to us, we cannot escape the influence of the social world. Thus, from a cultural sociological perspective, reproducing this binary *presupposes what needs to be explained*—the origins and nature of the *opposition itself*. Put otherwise, the key question posed by the accounts of Leslie, Amy, and Michael is as follows: how did the distinction between "religion"—understood as *institutional* and *public* in nature—and "spirituality"—understood as *individual* and *private*—become cultural common sense?

Parts I and II of this book provide an answer to this question. But it will prove useful to first consider what others have said on the matter. For, as we shall see, those who identify as "spiritual" are not the only ones guilty of reproducing this cultural binary.

The Secularization Paradigm

The secularization paradigm holds that modernization spells trouble for religion (see Tschannen 1991). Central to the theory is a thesis of *institutional differentiation*: in modern Euro-American societies the religious sphere is said to have separated from other institutional spheres—the economy, politics, education, the family, etc.—and therefore no longer functions as a comprehensive "sacred canopy" for society as a whole (Berger 1967). Instead, each sphere is said to be governed by its own specialized institutions, which entail their own symbolic orders and moral logics. As a result, the religious sphere becomes merely one institutional sphere among many others, and its scope and authority are drastically reduced (Fenn 1972; Chaves 1994). Notably, the process of institutional differentiation is said to have occurred in the shift to liberal modernity—indeed, it is constitutive of it—especially with the advent of the separation of church and state.

Following from the thesis of differentiation are two sub-theses: a *thesis of privatization* and a *thesis of religious decline* (Casanova 1994). The thesis of privatization holds that with institutional differentiation, and the evacuation of religion from the public sphere, individuals *privatize* their religiosity, that is, "people limit religion to the private realm so as to avoid public controversy over competing world views" (Thiessen 2015, 18). In turn, religion in modernity becomes a "private affair," intrinsically related to the emergence of a private sphere free from government intrusion as well as ecclesiastical control.

In the 1970s the privatization thesis was offered support by work emerging from the sociology of knowledge, especially that of Peter Berger. Berger (1979) famously argued that institutional differentiation creates a context of religious pluralism, which encourages not only privatization but also religious decline, as it undermines the plausibility of any single religious worldview. What he called "the heretical imperative"—constitutive of the modern condition—refers to the *necessity to choose* one's beliefs, as opposed to being able to take them for granted ("heresy" derives from the Greek word *hairein*, meaning "to choose"). Thus, in modernity, Berger proposed, religion becomes merely a matter of choice bereft of strong "plausibility structures," referring to the social institutions that make a specific religious belief-system plausible to its adherents. In turn, secularization theorists argue that religious decline is an irreversible by-product of modernization. According to Steve Bruce (2017, 6), the paradigm's most tireless advocate, "Modernization changes the status and nature of religion in ways that weaken it and make it difficult to pass successfully from generation to generation."

Not surprisingly, proponents of the paradigm have tended to conceive of the shift from "religion" to "spirituality" as evidence of religious decline.[1] No doubt,

---

[1] See, for example, Bruce 2002, 2011, 2013, 2017; Voas and Crockett 2005; Crockett and Voas 2006; Glendinning and Bruce 2006; Voas 2009, Turner 2014; Thiessen 2015; Voas and Chaves 2016.

this is, in part, because the spiritual turn has coincided with the growth of "religious nones" (see Drescher 2016; Thiessen and Wilkins-Laflamme 2020). These scholars have largely drawn on the theoretical insights outlined above, tailoring them to suit their purposes when necessary, but leaving them basically intact. Thus, a preference for "spirituality" over "religion" has been interpreted by secularization theorists in the following way: institutional differentiation has produced a privatized religiosity (what goes by "spirituality"), which is individualistic and ineffectual—that is, it lacks the institutional support and plausibility structures necessary to sustain itself over time.

It follows that secularization theorists would tend to interpret the accounts of Leslie and Michael through a framework of religious decline. For, on this view, to be "spiritual" without the institutional support of an organized religion is, in effect, to stand on a travellator whose final destination is wholesale secularity. Bruce (2011, 119) captures this aptly: "Far from refuting the secularization paradigm, both the nature and the extent of alternative spirituality offer strong support for a key element of the paradigm: individualism undermines religion." Even more interestingly, Bruce would also interpret the account of Amy as evidence of religious decline, despite her embrace of a "religious and spiritual" identity. The reason for this is that her neo-Pentecostalism, which stresses subjective "faith" over and above all else, reflects an individualistic approach to Christianity (see Bruce 1998).

To be clear, I do not think the theoretical premises of the secularization paradigm are mistaken. In fact, I think they are extremely illuminating. And yet, there are good reasons to resist the paradigm in its entirety. The most important centres on its conception of "religion." Linda Woodhead (2010, 31–2) has persuasively argued that underlying the secularization paradigm is "a submerged norm of 'real religion'" which represents "an unacknowledged 'commitment to historically influential forms of church Christianity'." Of course, there are historical reasons for privileging this form of religion. As Bruce (2011, 99) notes, church religion has been dominant for centuries in the West, and it is important to be able to capture its decline. Yet as a result of casting it as the protagonist in their narrative of religious decline, all rival forms of religiosity are necessarily placed in supporting (that is, subordinate) roles—if not left out entirely. The following remark by David Voas and Mark Chaves (2016, 1524) is illustrative: "There may be more diffuse spirituality now than previously, but it should not be mistaken for an increase in traditional religiosity. On the contrary, it is probably a consequence of the waning of traditional religiosity." Here we see the spiritual turn presented as a mere chapter in a larger story of religious decline—an interest in "spirituality" marks one last step on the road to religion's demise. While this may well be true, it nevertheless rests on a number of contestable assumptions.

First, the existence of a lost golden age of faith. Indeed, comparative claims about the impotent and socially insignificant nature of "spirituality" rely heavily on assumptions about the past which, while possibly correct, are by no means uncontested (see Stark 1998). Second, this position assumes that we have the appropriate data and survey metrics to accurately map such trends. But what justifies this? As Voas (2009) himself notes, studies tend to rely on self-reports about how "religious" a person is. Given the associations carried by the terms "religious" and "religion" in the West—a sample of which are plainly provided by the accounts of Leslie, Amy, and Michael—it is hard to accept this as reliable. Thus, many studies rooted in the secularization paradigm fail to account for the myriad ways the meaning of questions and terms has changed over time (Smith et al. 2013, 925). Indeed, this is why Dick Houtman and Paul Tromp (2021) have recently argued that quantitative sociologists need new survey metrics with which to map what today goes by "spirituality." Third, due to their privileging of church Christianity, many secularization theorists, wittingly or not, are guilty of reifying the sociologically vacuous claim—implicit in the SBNR moniker—that "religion" is institutionally rooted while "spirituality" floats free of institutions. Indeed, whether or not "spirituality" is "filling the gap left by the decline of the churches" (Bruce 2011, 106), it is simply mistaken to suppose that it lacks plausibility structures and institutional support. As I will demonstrate in Part II, discourses of "spirituality," like those invoked by Leslie, Amy, and Michael, are not without precedent, and in fact find social support across a broad array of institutions in twenty-first-century liberal democracies—both "secular" and "religious."

Part of the problem, then, is that owing to their definition of religion secularization theorists have been reluctant to look *beyond* the churches and other explicitly "religious" institutions for religion. And as a result, they have missed much. For instance, I met Leslie while conducting fieldwork at NLF, a place where self-identifying as SBNR is the norm. I came across Amy while conducting participant observation at C3T, an organization which, by contrast, most would deem "religious." And finally, I encountered Michael at TL, a public speaking group that presents itself as "nonreligious." And yet, as I demonstrate in Part III, despite being located at vastly different points along what might be called the religious-secular spectrum, these respective organizations play a key role in providing plausibility to the discourses of "spirituality" that each of these individuals invoke.

Finally, even if we lay these concerns aside and accept their larger story of decline, secularization theorists' myopic preoccupation with the decline of church religion has arguably distracted from, and marginalized, other equally important questions. Of course, this observation was made much earlier by the Durkheimian sociologist Thomas Luckmann. In *The Invisible Religion* Luckmann (1967, 26) condemned the sociology of religion of his day for conducting what he described as a "sociography of the churches." He argued that the "shrinking of church religion" is "only one—and the sociologically less interesting—dimension of the problem of secularization" (40). For Luckmann, what should interest sociologists of religion is not merely whether a nineteenth-century conception of religion is in decline, but also answering the question: "What are the values overarching contemporary culture? What is the social-structural basis of these values and what is their function in the life of contemporary man?" (40). Answering these questions is important, I would argue, not merely in order to advance scholarly knowledge, but also to provide those who inhabit romantic liberal modernity with a more accurate self-understanding. Though Bruce is correct that one can both endorse the secularization paradigm as a descriptive account of social change, without normatively endorsing it, he is strikingly silent about the degree to which "theories of secularization double as empirically descriptive theories of modern social processes and as normatively prescriptive theories of modern societies" (Casanova 1992, 20). Indeed, while Bruce may be capable of distinguishing between these two modes, he remains very much in the minority. For as sociologist José Casanova (2006, 15) observes, the secularization paradigm, as a folk theory, tends to accompany a secularist self-understanding, which interprets the decline of religion as a "quasi-normative consequence of being a 'modern' and 'enlightened'" person—a point that is illustrated sharply in the account of Michael Wallace.

Such a conception legitimates what I called in the Introduction, following Charles Taylor (2007, 530), a "subtraction story" of modernity, which frames secularization as a mere shedding of traditional vestiges, thereby occluding what is newly emerging. Fascinating, then, is that while the secularization paradigm, beginning in the 1980s, progressively lost its hegemonic status in the sociology of religion, it simultaneously rose to become the de facto folk theory among the publics of liberal democracies. Ask anyone unfamiliar with the discipline of religious studies whether the West has experienced secularization and the chances that they will answer affirmatively are extraordinarily high. What this reveals is that, despite their sincere and thoughtful attempts to bring nuance to their accounts, secularization theorists have conspired with the populaces of liberal democracies to legitimate a crude subtraction story of religious decline.

And yet the thesis of religious decline is not, understood on its own terms, incorrect. I am perfectly happy to concede that post-1960s liberal democracies are not traditionally Christian, and that we have experienced the erosion of Christendom (see Clarke and Macdonald 2017). Moreover, I recognize, with sociologists Joel Thiessen and Sarah Wilkins-Laflamme (2020, 172) that "secularization" and "spiritualization" may well be "occurring simultaneously." But I also agree with Taylor (2007, 437) when he writes that "the interesting story is not simply one of decline, but also of a new placement of the sacred or spiritual in relation to individual and social life." And this remains the case, irrespective of whether liberal democracies are *as* religious as they once were. Thus, the thesis of decline is less wrong than uninteresting. I see no reason why the study of spirituality must narrowly focus on establishing whether "spirituality" is "filling the gap left by the decline of the churches." In fact, why must we assume anything about the degree of religiousness expressed in the past?

In line with Luckmann (1999), I argue that the secularization paradigm remains immensely fruitful for theorizing the character of the contemporary religious landscape, but secularization theorists' preoccupation with religious decline—born of their conception of religion—has stifled our ability to take full advantage of its theoretical insights.

Cultural Approaches in the Sociology of Religion

Alongside the secularization paradigm, cultural approaches to the study of "spirituality" have grown in prominence in recent years. We can divide these into two types, each of which can be distinguished according to the research question they prioritize. The first type focuses on the question "What does it mean to be 'spiritual but not religious'?" whereas the second type foregrounds the question "Why has this moniker become so ubiquitous in post-1960s liberal democracies?" Both approaches have strengths and weaknesses, and both have inadvertently served to naturalize the self-understanding implicit in the spirituality/religion binary.

Focused Approaches

These approaches seek to establish what "spirituality" as distinct from "religion" signifies by means of focusing narrowly on either forms of self-identification or classifying particular *emic* (insider) understandings (e.g., Marler and Hadaway 2002; Ammerman 2014; Bibby 2017, 2019; Marshall and Olson 2018; Steensland et al. 2018). For instance, Brian Steensland et al. (2018) identify a range of emic meanings associated with the term "spirituality," concluding there exists little consensus on the ground regarding what it means to be "spiritual." Similarly, Reginald Bibby (2017, 72) observes that "a majority of individuals who say they are 'spiritual and religious' are inclined to embrace religion and seldom reject it." And Nancy Ammerman (2014) argues that, at least among a large percentage of Americans, "spirituality" and "religion" are not viewed as wholly at odds, but rather as complementary. According to these scholars, then, the distinction between "religion" and "spirituality" is not so clear-cut, for many continue to identify as "religious and spiritual"—especially in America. This would suggest the preference for "religion" over "spirituality" is less substance than mere semantics.

What should we make of this? Unfortunately, these studies tend to confound more than they illuminate for two reasons. First, they fail to make a crucial distinction—that between the label "spirituality" and the cultural structure it imperfectly signals. Consider: it is undeniably the case that Leslie, Amy, and Michael differ in the way they talk about "spirituality." They each grab for different key terms, and narrate its content within contrasting discursive registers. If they were to fill out a survey which asked them how they define "spirituality," it is quite likely that their responses would differ markedly. But would this be foolproof evidence that they lack a shared conception? It goes without saying that it's a rare individual who can articulate, in systematic terms, their theological or philosophical commitments and how they fit together. Moreover, it remains possible that the superficial differences that distinguish the accounts of Leslie, Amy, and Michael belie their more fundamental cultural structural similarities. Indeed, as I show in Chapters 2 and 3, this is precisely the case.

Second, Ammerman notes that the "spiritual but not religious" label "reflects moral and political categories more than analytic ones" (Ammerman 2014, 52). This leads her to conclude that when individuals make distinctions between "spirituality" and "religion" they are merely drawing symbolic boundaries around those whom they disagree with morally or politically. Indeed, we see this clearly in the accounts of Leslie, Amy, and Michael. Ammerman is therefore correct that the categories of "spirituality" and "religion" are used to shore up specific moral or political identities. Yet there is more to the story. For those who identify as "spiritual but not religious" (Leslie and Michael) and those who identify as "spiritual and religious" (Amy) may *share a religious orientation* while nevertheless *diverging in their moral and political views*. Indeed, sociologists Michael Hout and Claude Fischer (2014, 430) have suggested identification with "religion" in America is, in large measure, explained by political polarization (see also Braunstein 2021). This suggests that social scientists studying "spirituality" need to concern ourselves with two distinct levels of analysis: first, the way individuals and groups construct boundaries in order to shore up a moral or political identity; second, the degree to which these groups may be caught up in similar socio-cultural processes. As we shall see, studying the latter reveals that while the "spiritual but not religious" cohorts and the "religious and spiritual" cohorts may, in general, differ in some ways (for instance, politically), in others they may be quite similar.

Broad Approaches

In foregrounding the question "Why has the 'spiritual but not religious' moniker become so ubiquitous in post-1960s liberal democracies?" the second type of approach takes a broader, more historical, perspective of "spirituality." In other words, these scholars are more sensitive to the way changes in the religious landscape are related to those occurring in other spheres of society, as well as the degree to which the late modern religious landscape is distinctive.

An example is sociologist Robert Wuthnow's *After Heaven: Spirituality in America since the 1950s*, which describes a shift from a "spirituality of dwelling" to a "spirituality of seeking" taking place in post-1960s liberal democracies. According to Wuthnow (1998a, 11), Americans are "reshaping deep religious traditions in ways that help make sense of the new realities of their lives." And in *After the Baby Boomers: How Twenty- and Thirty-Somethings Are Shaping the Future of American Religion*, Wuthnow relates these transformations to the "high value our culture places on individual freedom" (2007, 133). Similarly, Grace Davie (1994) advances her well-known "believing without belonging" thesis, whereby religion at the end of the twentieth century is said to be unmoored from institutional constraints, redirected toward individual religious feelings and experiences. And in *Spiritual Marketplace* Wade Clark Roof (1999, 8, 7) describes an "expanding consumer-oriented culture targeting the self as an arena for marketing," further remarking that religious life today is characterized by a preoccupation with "inwardness, subjectivity, the experiential, the expressive."

There is much to commend these approaches for. They handily aid us to make sense of the accounts of Leslie, Amy, and Michael—picking up on, and teasing out, key themes and motifs. However, despite their very real insights, they share with secularization theorists a crucial flaw—the tendency to theorize the shift from "religion" to "spirituality" as one from an institutionalized form of religiosity to one that is free-floating, relatively bereft of institutional support, and lacking internal consistency. This is summed up in Wuthnow's claim that the religious landscape at the end of the twentieth century is characterized by a fundamental "messiness" (1998a, 198). Unfortunately, these approaches fail to theorize, at any depth, the degree to which "spirituality" is shaped and supported by entrenched cultural norms and social structures (Altglas 2018, 83). Not only does this reproduce the self-understanding typical of those who champion "spirituality" over "religion," but it also fails as sociological analysis—that is, it fails to capture both the cultural structural coherence of what goes by "spirituality" as well as the degree to which it is bound to a vast institutional order.

Beyond the Sociology of Religion

Since the 1960s, manifold studies have sprouted up across a host of subfields and disciplines beyond the sociology of religion, yielding tremendously fertile insights into the spiritual turn. The problem, however, is that these studies have rarely been placed into conversation with one another—thereby leading to a vicious siloing effect.[2] For instance, New Age Studies began as a branch growing off of the

---

[2] For a detailed account of the sources of fragmentation within the study of spirituality see Watts 2022.

tree of the study of New Religious Movements. Other branches included the study of self-help, humanistic psychology, or what is sometimes called therapeutic culture (associated with the Human Potential movement), and the study of Pentecostalism and the wider Charismatic movement. These three subfields have for decades existed independently of one another, with strikingly little engagement between them. No doubt, this has made good sense to many, given the glaring differences between their respective objects of study. However, a number of recent socio-historical studies make evident that, while distinct, the cultural logics undergirding these various cultural-cum-religious forms share much by way of origins. Moreover, studies produced within these respective fields demonstrate that their historical debts continue to exert a sizeable influence on contemporary expressions. One problem, then, is that the insights garnered in each of these independent fields have yet to be synthesized. Another is that there now exist in the academic literature innumerable terms used to describe what today goes by "spirituality."[3] As a result, the study of spirituality remains scattered across the many corners of academia.

I therefore argue a more cultural sociological approach to the study of religion is called for. As noted in the Introduction, the rubric for such an approach was offered some time ago in *Habits of the Heart*. Bellah and his co-authors' (1985, 235) analysis of what they called "Sheilaism" is most promising, if negatively charged. Although they agreed with secularization theorists that Sheilaism is a form of "religious individualism," they also saw it as the heir of a well-worn American religious tradition, one exemplified by the likes of Ralph Waldo Emerson, Henry David Thoreau, and Walt Whitman. In turn, what makes the analysis offered in *Habits* instructive is the degree to which Bellah and his co-authors frame the shift from "religion" to "spirituality" as the eclipse of one kind of religion by another. A cultural sociological approach seeks to heed and refine this theoretical insight. Scholars that have contributed to this paradigm acknowledge that romantic liberal modernity is not only characterized by real religious change, but have sought to provide an empirically grounded account of what this change consists of.[4] This theoretical framework holds great potential for illuminating the religious form that gives coherence and meaning to the disparate accounts of Leslie, Amy, and Michael, while also capturing its *social* and *institutional* nature.[5]

---

[3] In earlier publications I used the terms "self-spirituality" and "holistic spirituality." However, one finds many others in the academic literature: "self-religion," "subjective-life spirituality," "alternative spirituality," "post-Christian spirituality," "contemporary spirituality," "spiritualities of life," and "popular spirituality," to name a few.

[4] For a good example of this kind of approach see Houtman and Aupers 2010.

[5] In working within a sociological paradigm, I maintain that any study of "spirituality" must treat its object as a social phenomenon. At the same time, I remain wholly agnostic regarding the question of religious truth. For, as I see it, whether the cultural structures and discourses we study correspond to anything not socially constructed is simply not a question the sociologist *qua* sociologist can answer.

A Cultural Sociological Approach to the Study of Religion

A cultural sociological approach to the study of religion, as I understand it, returns to, rereads, and synthesizes the thought of Max Weber and Émile Durkheim. Indeed, I believe that a pragmatic synthesis of Weber's and Durkheim's social thought provides us with a more expansive and therefore useful conception of religion, which enables us to delimit, and make sense of, the cultural structure undergirding talk of "spirituality."[6]

Max Weber's Contribution: The Human Need for Meaning in Disenchanted Modernity

"Max Weber's vision of modernity," Chris Shilling and Philip Mellor (2001, 73) write, "is perhaps best known for its analysis of self-determining human subjects struggling to invest their actions with meaning in an increasingly rationalised world." Indeed, central to Weber's sociology of religion and modernity are problems of *meaning*—those features of human life such as suffering and death, which are, as Bellah (1970, 7) puts it, "inescapable in human life but insoluble in purely scientific terms." Thus, cultural sociologists often speak of *theodicies*, those cultural frameworks which enable an individual to situate herself in a horizon of ultimate meaning that both transcends her and gives meaning to what Weber ([1922] 1991, 139) felicitously called the "the world's imperfections."

According to Weber, modernity is distinctive as an epoch insofar as it dissolves the solid grounds upon which a plausible theodicy might emerge. Indeed, in a famous lecture entitled "Science as a Vocation," he diagnosed the disenchantment of the world, by which he meant that the world was no longer mysterious, or that it could, in principle, be understood by means of calculation or reason (Weber [1922] 1946). This occurs, fundamentally, due to increasing rationalization; he argued that with the systematic application of modern science and instrumental rationality to technological and governance systems comes the disenchantment of the world. Weber's is therefore a tragic and pessimistic account of modernity: humans require ultimate meaning, but rationalization makes this increasingly difficult to ascertain.

---

[6] I have chosen to describe what informs talk of "spirituality" today as a *religion* because I think the recent trend of using "spirituality" as an *etic* (scholarly) category obscures fundamental similarities between what goes by "spirituality" and what goes by "religion" in romantic liberal modernity. In other words, I use this category in a particular way because it allows me to capture a dimension of cultural life that I wish to understand (not because I believe it to be universal). I do not consider myself advancing a cross-cultural definition, to be applied any and everywhere. On the contrary, mine is a conception of religion which emerges from, and is quite specific to, the liberal democratic contexts that I study. Moreover, it has been formulated with the aim of synthesizing the existing academic literature on "spirituality" and shedding light on what I take to be substantive and pressing public issues.

It is not hard to see just how indebted the secularization paradigm is to Weber's thought. However, contemporary cultural sociologists have employed his theoretical framework to come to a quite different conclusion about religion in modernity. While Weber may have diagnosed the modern world as disenchanted, he nevertheless contended that humans exhibit a basic drive toward transcendent meaning, and that such a drive cannot be extinguished (Parsons [1964] 1991, lvii). A revised version of Weber's theory therefore seeks to identify how this drive toward meaning manifests in late modern conditions.

Émile Durkheim's Contribution: The Sacred and Symbolic in Modern Life

Rather than conceiving of religion as bound to the individual need for ultimate meaning in an imperfect world, Émile Durkheim took a wholly sociological approach, insisting on viewing religion as an "eminently social thing" (Durkheim [1912] 1995, 9). In turn, he produced the following definition: "A religion is a unified system of beliefs and practices relative to sacred things, that is to say, things set apart and forbidden—beliefs and practices which unite into one single moral community called a Church, all those who adhere to them" (44). A number of things follow from this. First, according to Durkheim, *every society has a religion*, whether "secular" or not. Second, religion for Durkheim consists of "two basic categories: beliefs and rites" (34). Indeed, a religion only has moral force insofar as both of these elements are present and active. I will wait until Chapter 7 to discuss Durkheim's conception of ritual—the second elementary form of religious life—for here I wish to focus exclusively on the first: collective representations, symbols, and ideals. Durkheimian scholar W. S. F. Pickering (1984, 73) observes, "Durkheim's theoretical argument rests on the proposition that at the heart of every society there are collective representations which are necessary for its existence." Indeed, for Durkheim, *collective representations are what make social life possible*. However, it is not merely that symbols enable individuals in society to communicate; they also underwrite social cohesion by being classified as either sacred or profane. And those that are deemed *sacred* are "set apart and forbidden"—that is, they are viewed and experienced by the community as having *a special aura and being authoritative*. It is therefore not surprising that Durkheim's discussion of religion is often indistinguishable from the way he speaks about morality. In fact, we can say that religion and morality, for Durkheim, express two aspects of the same phenomenon: Religion refers to the cultural system of beliefs and rites that circumscribe a society's sacred forms, while morality refers to the norms and sanctions that compel action because they are deemed sacred.

Durkheim has played a pivotal role in shaping what is known as the strong program in cultural sociology (see Alexander and Smith 2010). Outlining the basic tenets of the strong program Jeffrey Alexander (2013, 3) writes, "At the foundation of cultural sociology is the anti-historicist claim that structures of meaning—cultural codes, symbols, and narratives—are a permanent, not transitory element of consciousness and society." The strong program in cultural sociology therefore assumes the *centrality of meaning* in social life. While it acknowledges the role of "hard" factors such as the economy and politics, it nevertheless rejects the claim that these are wholly determinant of social life. For this reason, strong program cultural sociologists grant analytic autonomy to culture, as they argue that we must first identify and articulate the meaning systems alive in society before we can establish their causal effects. In agreement, I believe it is only by granting analytic autonomy to the cultural structure underlying the shift from "religion" to "spirituality" that we can bring clarity to the contemporary religious landscape.

Toward a Cultural Sociology of "Spirituality"

We can now sum up the theoretical basis of the cultural sociological paradigm to which this study belongs. The paradigm begins by drawing on Weber's insights regarding the disenchantment of modernity and the human need for ultimate meaning. According to Weber, what makes religion distinctive is that it offers a theodicy, or a framework of meaning, by which individuals can come to terms with fundamental existential questions. Next, the paradigm combines these insights with a Durkheimian cultural sociology that conceives of religion as constituted by symbols of classification, or shared cultural structures, which bind individuals to one another by virtue of delineating that which they hold sacred.

Still, before I move on, it is important to make clear how, and why, I distinguish between *cultural structures* and *discourses*. By the former I refer to deep ideational structures which *order and organize distinct discourses*, whereas the latter I think of as *concrete meanings which instantiate implicit codes in discursive form*. In this sense, we can think of cultural structures as ideal types, or analytic abstractions, which are only made manifest through specific discourses (Simko and Olick 2021). Moreover, cultural structures, while deeply constraining and enabling of social life, are often invisible to their adherents (Rambo and Chan 1990). This is why Alexander (2003, 3) analogizes the strong program in cultural sociology to a "social psychoanalysis," the goal of which is "to bring the social unconscious up for view." It also explains why a cultural sociological approach is needed in the study of spirituality: even the most innovative studies have failed to identify the deeper *cultural structure* that informs specific *discourses* associated with "spirituality"—such as those invoked by Leslie, Amy, and Michael. So, scholars studying New Age, Charismatic Christianity, and humanistic psychology and the movements they have spawned, while perhaps noting shared affinities between them, have generally highlighted their theological or philosophical—that is, discursive—differences. While this is an important task, it has unfortunately led scholars to overlook the *more basic symbolic framework* upon which these discourses collectively rest—which I call the *religion of the heart*.

a direct plaganication of Bellah?

2

A Brief History of the Religion of the Heart

Out of the abundance of the heart the mouth speaketh.

(Matthew 12:34)

For it is an immutable truth, that what comes from the heart, that alone goes to the heart; what proceeds from a divine impulse, that the godlike alone can awaken.

(Coleridge [1912] 1951, 527)

Trust thyself: every heart vibrates to that iron string.

(Emerson [1841] 2000, 133)

In this chapter, I chart, in broad terms, the history of the religion of the heart in the West, highlighting some of its key carrier movements and representative figures. And in the following chapter I use my cultural sociological approach to systematically reconstruct its ten logically interrelated tenets. In so doing, I synthesize the disparate scholarship that comprises the study of spirituality. Yet I also supplement these studies, where applicable, with findings from my own empirical research, regularly invoking the voices of my SBNR interviewees, along with data collected while conducting participant observation at my three field sites—NLF, C3T, and TL. And to further strengthen my case, I make repeated reference to popular "spiritual" and self-help literatures. However, before I begin, let me explain why I chose this specific designation.

Why the Religion of the Heart?

The *heart* is a central concept and metaphor for much of what goes by "spirituality" today. Recall: In explaining her attraction to NLF, Leslie extolls what she calls the "language of the heart," characteristic of AA discourse. Amy, for her part, speaks of "inviting Jesus into my heart"—a common trope among Charismatic Christians. And finally, Michael is adamant that the essence of living "spiritually" can be boiled down to a simple maxim: "follow your heart." These are not coincidences. I regularly heard allusions to the *heart* over the course of my research. Moreover, they are a staple of popular "spiritual" literature. In *The Monk Who Sold His Ferrari*, Robin Sharma counsels, "Be guided by your heart. The rest will take care of itself" (1997, 134). And in *Conversations with God* Neale

The Spiritual Turn: The Religion of the Heart and the Making of Romantic Liberal Modernity. Galen Watts, Oxford University Press. © Galen Watts 2022. DOI: 10.1093/oso/9780192859839.003.0003

Donald Walsch writes, "Every heart which earnestly asks, 'Which is the path to God?' is shown. Each is given a heartfelt Truth" (1995, 94).

The heart beckons themes of sincerity and authenticity, central to "spirituality." It also portends a preoccupation with one's inner life—especially intuitions and feelings. In *The Seven Spiritual Laws of Success*, Deepak Chopra instructs, "Consciously put your attention in the heart and ask the heart what to do... Only the heart knows the correct answer" (1994, 43). And during our interview an SBNR interviewee lamented, "I'm a very cerebral person, so I feel like I've neglected my heart." Indeed, the notion that "spirituality" gives primacy to the heart and not the mind is a common theme. Chopra writes, "the heart is intuitive; it's holistic, it's contextual, it's relational... At times it may not even seem rational, but the heart has a computing ability that is far more accurate and far more precise than anything within the limits of rational thought" (44). While Joseph Murphy, well-known preacher of New Thought, writes in *Within You Is the Power*, "The great truth is that as a man thinketh in his heart... so does he act, experience, and function in life" (1977, 160).

In *Heart Religion*, historian John Coffey notes that the *Oxford English Dictionary* defines the "heart" as "the seat or repository of a person's inmost thoughts, feelings, inclinations, etc.; a person's inmost being; the depths of the soul; the soul, the spirit" (2001, 6). To know oneself, for those I spoke to, requires getting in touch with one's heart, not one's head. In this sense, the rational is not contrasted with the irrational, but with the emotional or affective. Moreover, the heart is where you find the divine or superempirical. As evangelical pastor Joyce Meyer (1995, 106) asserts, "God has placed faith in our heart."

An SBNR interviewee, in describing how she thinks about "spirituality," shared, "love has a lot to do with it." Of course, love—however we might understand it—is often symbolized by the heart. As an emblem we associate it with that which we are most attached to, that which fills us with joy, serenity, and peace. "When I talk about spirituality and being spiritual," writes New Age author Wayne Dyer (1995, 5), "I am speaking of expanding the godlike qualities of love, forgiveness, kindness and bliss within ourselves." And in *Your Best Life Now,* evangelical pastor Joel Osteen (2004, 249) counsels, "Keep your heart of compassion open. Learn to be quick to follow that flow of love God puts in your heart." The religion of the heart models religious commitment on romantic love; we don't come to know God through rational reflection, or by accepting a creed on someone else's authority, but rather through submission to an overwhelming experience, of being overcome by a spontaneous sense of union with a force greater than ourselves. As a metaphor for a religious form the heart suggests the primacy of experience— ecstatic, effervescent, transcendent in nature.

Of course, the heart in Western culture is also used to symbolize health or wellness. We exercise in order to develop a strong heart, and perhaps to feel good. In this, we see how the heart, given its polyvalence as symbol and concept, gestures toward a mind-body-spirit connection. Very rarely do we associate the heart with negativity or depression, unless of course we are referring to a broken or heavy heart. But in this register, we would commonly see the need for healing; hearts may break, but their natural state is one of wholeness.

And finally, the heart is something that can be more or less pure. Osteen cautions, "Don't let your heart get polluted," and then instructs, "Examine your own heart and see if there are attitudes and motives you need to change" (2004, 157, 208). So, despite the seemingly innocuous and innocent self-presentation of heart rhetoric it can, and often does, come bearing a moral system, replete with its own disciplines, virtues, and taboos.

For these reasons, and many more which we will soon examine, I have come to think it fitting to call the cultural structure that shapes and gives meaning to much of the post-1960s religious landscape the *religion of the heart*. However, this is not a wholly novel term. Jean-Jacques Rousseau used "the religion of the heart" to capture his preferred form of religion. Theologian Ted Campbell (1991) uses the "religion of the heart" to categorize a number of religious movements which emerged in the seventeenth and eighteenth centuries. Historian Richard Hofstader (1963) uses it to capture the spirit of American evangelicalism in the eighteenth century. Elisabeth Jay (1979) uses it to describe Anglican evangelicalism as it is expressed in the nineteenth-century novel. Harvey Cox calls Charismatic Christianity not merely an "experiential religion" but also a "religion of the heart" (1995, 11, 12). And sociologist Linda Woodhead has used this term to describe the religiosity of Princess Diana, for whom "it was not institutions which were important, but individual human beings and their feelings" (1999, 127). Woodhead argued, presciently, "it is possible to discern the outlines of this religion, a religion more widespread in contemporary society than is often recognised, and a religion superbly adapted to life in late modernity" (120).

While my own conception of the religion of the heart isn't identical to these others, it comes quite close and overlaps considerably. The religion of the heart, as I understand it, can be understood as a cultural structure that has deep roots in the West, constituting a tradition of sorts. By this I mean that, while it takes distinct discursive forms at different times in history, one can find its symbolic structures recur over time. That said, I'm not suggesting the current expressions of the religion of the heart are universal. Having been shaped by contemporary social conditions they are clearly not. Yet while acknowledging this fact, we must beware of perpetuating an ahistoricism that refuses to understand the cultural present in relation to its past. The religion of the heart both belongs to a long-standing tradition and simultaneously reflects a novel constellation of beliefs, tropes, and ideals which have been significantly influenced by recent societal developments.

The Religion of the Heart in Historical Context

[handwritten margin notes: "why before Moravians etc. (Gnostics?) pre-Refor."]

According to historian Ted Campbell (1991, 2), what he calls the "religion of the heart movements," emerged in the seventeenth and eighteenth centuries. He includes in this tradition Jansenism, Quietism, English puritanism, Quaker spirituality, Pietism (especially the Moravian Church), and early Methodism. Despite their theological differences Campbell argues what unites these movements is that, for each of them, "Affective experience became the center of the religious life" (3). They all maintained that "sacraments are ineffective without appropriate inward affections" and posited "experience as the basis of knowledge" (3, 17). Among the puritans, the "heart" was contrasted with the "head," with the religious life ultimately being concerned with the former, not the latter. In a similar vein, Pietism stressed an "epistemology of religious experience" (62) which was taken up, notably, by Friedrich Schleiermacher, as well as, in a more extra-theistic mode, the German and English Romantics. Campbell concludes, "The power that held this unique cluster of men and women, of ideas and movements, together was a fresh way of approach to the religious ultimate, an insistence that 'the heart,' the human will and the affections, was the crucial link between divinity and humanity, that the way to God was the way of heartfelt devotion" (177).

Ernst Troeltsch's "Spiritual" or "Mystic" Religion

In *The Social Teaching of the Christian Churches*, Ernst Troeltsch ([1912] 1992, 731, vol. 2) refers to this tradition as "spiritual and mystic religion," which, he contends, expresses itself "in subjective religious experience and 'inwardness', in concentration upon the purely interior and emotional side of religious experience." Though spiritual or mystic religion has been much "maligned" by scholars of religion in the twentieth century (see Garrett 1975), Troeltsch was adamant that it warrants our attention. Within this tradition, direct experience of God or the divine becomes an "independent religious principle"—that is, spiritual and mystic religion "sees itself as the real universal heart of all religion, of which the various myth-forms are merely the outer garment." Furthermore, while Troeltsch argues it emerged from within the Christian tradition he also notes that its adherents have often believed "non-Christian religious souls" can also be in touch with the divine, for they assume "the universal unity of the Spirit" (Troeltsch [1912] 1992, 745, 747). Accordingly, the mystic's tendency is "to identify Christianity with an entirely personally differentiated and entirely inward spiritual religion" (795).

A Third Way

A useful means of understanding the religion of the heart is as a kind of "third way" tradition. According to historian Wouter Hanegraaff, the West has been constituted by three traditions, each of which stresses a distinct approach to truth: *reason* (represented by the Ancient Greeks and Enlightenment rationalists), *faith* (represented by traditional Christianity), and *gnosis* (represented by occultist and esoteric movements) (1996, 517–19). Whether or not the religion of the heart is fundamentally a gnostic tradition, as Hanegraaff, among others (e.g., Herrick 2003; Versluis 2014) suggest, I remain undecided. In any case, Hanegraaff's analysis enables us to make a useful analytic distinction—that between epistemologies that stress reason, doctrine, and feeling/intuition. The movements that carry the religion of the heart are united insofar as they give primacy to the last of these: *feeling* and *intuition*. Resultantly, the religion of the heart has historically found itself in conflict with movements that champion either of the other two epistemic stances (Campbell 1991, 169). For its adherents, "God is experienced rather than believed in, and on that basis His existence is usually regarded as fairly self-evident and non-problematic" (Hanegraaff 1996, 183). One SBNR interviewee asserted, "I think, when it comes to spirituality, you can't really ignore it. You have to acknowledge that there are other things going on in the universe." Another shared, "For the past year, and even more now, my goal has been to really strengthen my intuitive voice." The religion of the heart rejects rationalistic and scientific reductionism while at the same time criticizing dogmatic traditionalism. That is, it "rejects neither religion and spirituality nor science and rationality, but combines them in a higher synthesis" (Hanegraaff 1996, 517).

The Romantic Movement

Since the Enlightenment the most important carrier of the religion of the heart has been the Romantic movement. The primary actors were poets and writers, who sought to relocate the sacred to the aesthetic, exalting unconstrained self-expression. In his study of the Romantics, *Natural Supernaturalism*, M. H. Abrams (1973, 13) argues that far from rejecting Christian thought, the Romantics, in fact, translated biblical themes and ideas into a language of immanence. Indeed, Romantics were far more hostile to the structure of Enlightenment rationalist philosophy than to biblical prophecy. In fact, they borrowed much from the latter in order to critique the former (32). Yet it would be wrong to view Romanticism as a mere extension of biblical morality. As Isaiah Berlin (1999, 135) notes, Romanticism, far from endorsing traditionalism, railed against tradition as such; what the Romantics shared, over and above all else, was the desire to "break up the nature of the given." Bertrand Russell (1946, 658) concurs: "The romantic movement, in its essence, aimed at liberating human personality from the fetters of social convention and social morality." Thus, the primary targets of Wordsworth's censure were "custom" and "habit"—what he perceived as sources of despotism. Indeed, Berlin (2006, 247) contends that for the Romantics "self-expression, self-realization, is the goal of man, as of everything in the universe." This we find in both the counter-enlightenment thought of Herder, as well as the poetry and prose of Coleridge. Crucially, the command to self-expression is rooted in a particular conception of the universe: "to live is to do something, to do is to express your nature. To express your nature is to express your relation to the universe" (Berlin 1999, 106). Moreover, it emerges from a view of society as corrupting, or as the source of vice—summed up powerfully in proto-Romantic Jean-Jacques Rousseau's dictum, "Man is born free, and everywhere he is in chains."

The irony, of course, is that in railing against tradition as such, the early Romantics paved the way for a *new* cultural tradition—that of Romanticism—which has, over the past two centuries or so, played a critical role in shaping the modern identity (Taylor 1989). Furthermore, in their quest to re-enchant the modern world, the Romantics left us a host of religious ideals and themes, which today inform "spirituality."

Metaphysical or Harmonial Religion

It should come as no surprise, then, that historian Leigh Eric Schmidt (2012) finds the Romantic impulse at the core of the religious and metaphysical movements that swept across America in the eighteenth and nineteenth centuries. Most notably, Unitarians, Universalists, followers of Emmanuel Swedenborg, and Transcendentalists—spinoffs of early American Protestantism—propagated what Catherine Albanese (2007, 161) calls "self-culture," as they followed "a spiritual logic...from outer to inner." The religion of the heart was championed in particularly potent terms by Ralph Waldo Emerson—whom historian Sydney Ahlstrom (1977, 152) calls America's "national poet."

A Unitarian-turned-Transcendentalist, Emerson ([1841] 2000, 69, 134, 109) iconoclastically preached, "That is always best which gives me to myself," and "It is my desire...to do nothing which I cannot do with my whole heart." And in a famous essay, "The Over-Soul," he clearly presages the "spiritual but not religious" disposition: "When we have broken our god of tradition and ceased from our god of rhetoric, then may God fire the heart with his presence. It is the doubling of the heart itself, nay, the infinite enlargement of the heart with a power of growth to a new infinity on every side" (248–9). For Emerson, the authentic spiritual life is one of unrelenting self-expression and self-discovery, and an untiring quest for the ineffable—a view we find equally championed in the work of Walt Whitman and Henry David Thoreau (both close confidantes of Emerson). For these American spokesmen of the religion of the heart, rituals, liturgies, and norms must always come second to that which matters most: "spontaneous, direct, unmediated spiritual insight into reality" (Versluis 2014, 2).

Transcendentalists—and Theosophists after them—channelled the Romantic fascination with non-Western cultures and looked to the East for religious inspiration. Emerson held an abiding fascination with the *Upanishads*, while Thoreau became enamoured with the *Bhagavad Gita*. And yet, as historian Amanda Porterfield (2001, 130–1) notes, these New Englanders tended to interpret Hindu and Buddhist scriptures "within an idealistic intellectual framework that involved a distinctively American combination of German philosophy and English Romanticism."

These new religious movements gave birth to a number of offshoots such as Spiritualism, Mesmerism, Theosophy, Christian Science, and New Thought, among other nineteenth-century metaphysical religions that have been carriers of the religion of the heart. Historian Robert Fuller observes in *Spiritual but not Religious: Understanding Unchurched America* that these movements stressed direct personal experience above all else, preaching that "Genuine spirituality . . . has to do with personal efforts to achieve greater harmony with the sacred" (2001, 4). Similarly, anthropologist Peter van der Veer (2009, 1115) describes a yearning for a "core spirituality" that seeks to transcend tradition, and which has crossed oceans, shaping both Western and Eastern cultural contexts. This was especially true of Theosophy, which sought, in esoteric fashion, to synthesize Eastern and Western religions, and even prophesied the coming of a "new age" of spiritual consciousness (Fuller 2001, 54).

Nevertheless, following what Schmidt (2012, xv) calls "the Emersonian turn"— that is, "the sense that religion was fundamentally about the sacredness of the individual"—the religion of the heart took on a quintessentially American hue. Schmidt writes in *Restless Souls: The Making of American Spirituality*, "Much of what has come to be labeled 'spirituality' in contemporary culture and in contemporary scholarship is better seen as a complex artifact of nineteenth century religious liberalism" (2012, 90). For instance, New Thought, which emerged in the 1880s, emphasized the holistic connection between right thought and human health, happiness, and prosperity, and preached that "men were actually individualizations of God" (Meyer [1965] 1980, 268, 77). Ralph Waldo Trine, one of the best-known American New Thought leaders, forged the popular notions that "worrying minds and disordered emotions—fear, anger, jealousy, sorrow, or malice—wreaked havoc on people's bodies" and that seekers must therefore learn to calm their minds in order to allow the "harmony" of the divine flow in and through them. Schmidt (2012, 12) thus concludes, "Religious liberalism, with its motley bedfellows of romantics and reformers, led the way in redefining spirituality and setting out its essentials."

The Triumph of the Therapeutic

In the late nineteenth century, there was no spokesperson of the religion of the heart more noteworthy than Harvard psychologist and philosopher William James. Significantly influenced by religious innovators like Swedenborg and Emerson, in his *Varieties of Religious Experience* James both carries forward and extends what Taylor (1991) calls the "massive subjective turn" of modern culture. "Of all his penetrating insights into religious psychology" Wade Clark Roof (1999, 16) writes, "James's comment on the power of a religious experience to redeem and vivify—to fill an empty interior world—is especially fitting to our time." Indeed, James's pragmatic, experience-based, approach to religion is a staple of much literature on "spirituality," new and old. For instance, in *The Power of Positive Thinking* Norman Vincent Peale informs us that positive thinking is "a system of creative living based on spiritual techniques" (1952, x). While New Age authors Esther and Jerry Hicks (2004, 4) write in *Ask and It Is Given: Learning to Manifest Your Desires*: "Your true knowledge comes from your own life experiences." And James's pragmatic and experiential approach to self-development lies at the core of much secular self-help as well. In *Awaken the Giant Within* life coach Tony Robbins (1991, 29) assures his readers, "you don't have to believe or use everything within [this book]. Grab hold of things you think are useful; put them into action immediately."

Another noteworthy figure is Carl Jung, a disciple of Freud until they had a falling out. The crux of their conflict lay in Jung's turning away from Freud's scientific materialism towards a more Jamesian approach to nature and the psyche. Sociologist Philip Rieff (1966, 116, 114) suggests that in supplying a "fresh statement of opposition between reason and spontaneity, thought and feeling, restriction and freedom, distortion and honesty," Jung developed a "fresh rhetoric of spirituality." Indeed, Jung argues in *Modern Man in Search of a Soul* that moderns have outgrown their willingness to accept the purported truths of religion, yet they still retain a deep hunger for spiritual meaning—interpreting the emergence of modern psychology as "symptomatic of a profound convulsion of spiritual life" (1933, 202).

Since James and Jung, psychology has become a key carrier of the religion of the heart. As Fuller (2001, 124) remarks, "Some mistakenly assume that the rise of modern psychology has gone hand-in-hand with a loss of interest in spiritual issues," when the reality is rather that "on the whole, psychology has had a special affinity with America's unchurched spiritual traditions" (see also Parsons 2010). Indeed, it was a synthesis of metaphysical religion and early psychological discourses that paved the way for what Rieff calls the "triumph of the thera-peutic"—denoting the eclipse of the language of biblical religion by that of psychology.

The 1960s Counter-Culture and Its Religious Wings

A crucial period in the flowering of the religion of the heart, however, was the counter-culture of the 1960s. It was at this time that this cultural structure was embraced by a large swath of the population in the West—predominantly youth—and consequently found its way into the primary institutional spheres of liberal democratic societies. Its success was most apparent in the popularity of three movements, which, while overlapping, it is useful to separate analytically: the New Age movement, the Human Potential movement, and the Charismatic movement.

The New Age Movement

"New Age ideas about God reflected a marked aversion to rigid, doctrinal defin-itions," writes Hanegraaff (1996, 183) in *New Age Religion and Western Culture*. Similarly, Colin Campbell (2007, 130) contends that within the New Age move-ment there was a "strong emphasis . . . on the importance attached to each person finding his own spiritual path." Much of what goes by New Age can be traced back to Transcendentalism, Theosophy, and Spiritualism. New Agers channelled the romantic aversion to all forms of reductionism, and celebrated feelings and intuition above all else. For them, "personal experience [was] the sole and exclusive yardstick for reality testing" (Campbell 2007, 227). However, as a result of the Emersonian turn, in tandem with the triumph of the therapeutic, the religion of the heart in its New Age form became something different from that of Romantics like Wordsworth and Coleridge. Elline Kay Eskenazi describes the religion of the heart as it crystallized in the New Age:

> For this style of Romantic, the most urgent task is self-actualization: to realize all one potentially is by discovering personal values, living authentically, cultivating artistic and intellectual gifts, and using them to express the personal vision. From the Romantic's perspective, it is society that hinders his progress by insisting that he subordinate personal to traditional values, self-expression to social harmony, and self-actualization to social functionality. Subject to such coercion, he becomes alienated from himself, and enters adulthood unaware of his true values, and estranged from his true self. From this perspective, self-discovery is the precondition to authentic living. Despite the fact that social authorities discour-age the journey toward self-actualization, the Romantic feels it is his highest priority.   (Eskenazi 2010, 4)

Here we see how the religion of the heart takes different forms at different times, adapting to its surrounding socio-cultural conditions. Nevertheless, within New Age literature one finds motifs that resonate powerfully with the self-culture once trumpeted by the likes of Emerson, Whitman, and Thoreau. For instance, in James Redfield's bestselling New Age novel *The Celestine Prophecy*, the protagonist describes his encounter with the divine as such: "I felt this euphoric connection with everything, and this total kind of security and confidence...a mystical experience" (1993, 105). While New Age author Deepak Chopra writes, "If you embrace the present and become one with it, merge with it, you will experience a fire, a glow, a spark of ecstasy throbbing in every living sentient being" (1994, 61). Though never cohesive and utterly contested, there is little doubt that the New Age movement was one of the most important carriers of the religion of the heart in the twentieth century.

The Human Potential Movement

As with the New Age, the Human Potential movement is difficult to pin down, for its core groups and membership fluctuated over time. Still, Jessica Grogan (2013) is certainly right that by the 1970s the movement was strongly associated with humanistic psychology and other post-psychoanalytic schools of thought. Moreover, tracing its intellectual origins, Taylor (1989, 497) writes, "many of the ideas of the 'human potential' movements in the United States...go back to the original expressivism, partly through the indigenous American line of descent, including Emerson and Whitman."

Abraham Maslow is arguably the best-known of all humanistic psychologists, responsible for bringing the legacies of James and Jung to a wider audience. In fact, the debt owed by Maslow to Jung is far from small for, as we've seen, it was Jung who first saw psychology as the future language of "spirituality." But it was Maslow who made this notion palatable for the public. As sociologist Véronique Altglas (2014, 205) remarks, "Maslow celebrated religious experience as a source of self-realization—therapy then becomes a means to attain spiritual fulfillment." Indeed, Maslow defined "religion" in precisely the same terms as SBNRs do today (see Maslow 1970).

He was not alone. Inspired by the writings of Emerson, Carl Rogers received his doctorate in psychology in 1931 and went on to develop what became known as client-centred therapy. Rogers's clinical approach presumes that within each and every individual lies an "innate valuing process" that will guide him or her morally. He proposed that when an individual connects with their true self via therapy well-being naturally follows. In *On Becoming a Person*, Rogers describes his philosophy of client-centred therapy in especially illustrative terms: "Experience is, for me, the highest authority....Neither the Bible nor the prophets—neither Freud nor research—neither the revelations of God nor man—can take precedence over my own direct experience" (1961, 23, 24).

The works of Maslow and Rogers have together played a formative role in shaping what we might call "secular" variants of the religion of the heart (Browning and Cooper 2004; Fuller 2006). Their stature as renowned public intellectuals facilitated the mass adoption of expressive individualism, and its absorption into various spheres of late modern social life. Owing to their legacies it became both acceptable and commonplace to hear the term "spirituality" used without reference to traditional religion, and to equate it with the task of self-realization. Thus, religious studies scholars Jeremy Carrette and Richard King (2005, 72) contend that it was "the development of humanistic psychology in the USA that had the greatest impact in forging the modern, privatized sense of spirituality."

The Charismatic Christian Movement

Too few have noticed the striking degree to which the Charismatic movement, associated with the global spread of Pentecostal style worship, largely exhibits the cultural structure of the religion of the heart. Yet, there are exceptions. For instance, anthropologist Tanya Luhrmann (2004, 518) observes, "Mainstream churches have seen their congregations dwindle; evangelical, New Age, and other more demanding faiths have seen their memberships explode. And what US citizens seem to want from these new religiosities—and from evangelical Christianity in particular—is intense spiritual experience." And in *Pentecostalism: The World and Their Parish* David Martin (2002, 3) argues, "Insofar as Pentecostalism spreads it does so principally through a charismatic movement partly inside the older churches and partly 'breaking bounds' in every sense, even displaying faint affinities with New Age 'spirituality'." Similarly, writing about the North American Charismatic movement Margaret Poloma (2003, 22) observes, "What can be said about the movement ever since its inception . . . is that it is more about a distinct 'spirituality' rather than about 'religion'."

How do we explain this? A historical perspective illuminates much. Scholars have shown that the Charismatic revivals find their origins in German Pietism, puritanism, and Methodism (Walker 1997; Coleman 2006; Neuhouser 2017). Other precursors include the liberal Protestantism of Schleiermacher, and the Holiness movement of the nineteenth century, whose grandfather was John Wesley (Hollenweger 1986, 4). Clearly, then, Charismatic Christianity owes much to what Ted Campbell calls the "religion of the heart movements," whose theological outlooks gave primacy to heartfelt religious experience. Indeed, according to Stephen Hunt (1995, 269) Pentecostals were "the earliest articulators of 'emotionalism'," which "marked a revolt against the spiritual 'deadness' and 'worldiness' of the mainstream churches." Yet in addition to these explicitly Christian currents, we also find substantive linkages to the American metaphysical religious traditions discussed above. In her history of the American prosperity gospel—a close cousin to neo-Pentecostalism—Kate Bowler (2013, 12) reminds

us, "Victorian America was a hotbed of mind-power, bursting with transcendentalism, spiritualism, Free Masonry, Christian Science, and...an offshoot of
Christian Science called New Thought. Out of this miasma came the thinkers
who nurtured a particular species of mind-power, planting the seeds of the
present-day prosperity gospel." These alternative metaphysical movements—
especially Theosophy and New Thought—have played a significant role in shaping the New Age, Human Potential, *and* Charismatic movements. Hence why "the
form of Christianity that flourishes in the West today...bears considerable
resemblance to the New Age movement" (Campbell 2007, 345).

Conclusion

While the New Age, Human Potential, and Charismatic Christian movements
may have employed quite different vocabularies, what has often gone unnoticed is
the degree to which they subscribed to the same underlying cultural structure. We
might say, then, while those like Leslie and Michael who self-identify as "spiritual
but not religious" (heirs to the New Age and Human Potential movements) are
generally more committed to mystical illumination, understood in extra-theistic
terms, Charismatic Christians like Amy celebrate direct communion with a
theistic God through the Holy Spirit.[1] Needless to say, the rhetoric belies the
similarities.

---

[1] I borrow the terms "theistic" and "extra-theistic" from Ammerman 2014.

3

"Spirituality" Today

In the last chapter I charted the development of the religion of the heart over time, identifying some of its historical precursors. But I wouldn't wish to give the impression that today's religion of the heart is identical to its earlier renditions. What goes by "spirituality" among my informants is undeniably shaped by contemporary social conditions. In other words, the voices that I invoke to represent the religion of the heart are voices that inhabit a particular socio-cultural context—broadly, North America in the twenty-first century. Still, as I explicate the various dimensions of what goes by "spirituality" today, I shall regularly make connections to past iterations of the religion of the heart, thereby establishing my historical claim that these disparate voices do, in fact, belong to a tradition, if variegated in nature.

The religion of the heart consists of ten logically interrelated tenets, which together form a coherent *cultural structure* upon which distinct *discourses* are erected, organized, and made meaningful. They are the following:

1) Experiential Epistemology
2) Immanence of God or the Superempirical
3) Benevolent God or Universe
4) Redemptive Self as Theodicy
5) Self-Realization as Teleology
6) Self-Ethic (Voice from Within)
7) Virtue is Natural
8) Sacralization of Individual Liberty
9) Mind-Body-Spirit Connection
10) Methodological Individualism

[handwritten marginal note: the sacred + profane don't make an appearance...]

Experiential Epistemology

The religion of the heart is fundamentally characterized by an *experiential epistemology*. To quote Neale Donald Walsch (1995, 3): "Feeling is the language of the soul." While my informants might vary in the weight they give to reason, or abstract principles and doctrines in other spheres of social life, nothing trumps direct *personal experience* when it comes to their "spirituality." For instance, an

The Spiritual Turn: The Religion of the Heart and the Making of Romantic Liberal Modernity. Galen Watts,
Oxford University Press. © Galen Watts 2022. DOI: 10.1093/oso/9780192859839.003.0004

SBNR interviewee asserted, "For me it's your own truth." While another stated, "I found it was more encouraging to find the truth within myself."

Margaret Poloma (2003, 23) observes that Pentecostal and Charismatic Christians "tend to be anticreedal, believing that 'knowing' comes from a right relationship with God rather than through reason or even through the five senses." She concludes, "the P/C worldview is experientially centered." Giving credence to this claim, in a sermon at C3 Toronto, one of the pastors declared, "God's love cannot be taught. It cannot be understood. It cannot be theologically grasped. It can only be *experienced*." When it comes to the religion of the heart, the more intense, ecstatic, and effervescent the experience, the more authoritative.

For SBNRs, "spirituality" is signalled in moments of quiet contemplation or unexpected bliss—be it while in meditation, climbing a mountain, or dancing at a rave. While for Charismatics, God's presence is most often felt in moments of praise and joy (Lee et al. 2013). Their form of worship, which excites the emotions and encourages a letting go of inhibitions, becomes a primary gateway into God's presence. Furthermore, among both SBNRs and Charismatics "spiritual" or "God" moments stand for those times when everything in life seems to align, as if unfolding according to a divine or cosmic plan. These experiences are interpreted as evidence for the existence of "something more," and it is these moments which, as one Charismatic put it, "cannot be ignored," that encourage the adherent to pursue their "spiritual" interests—to read more, to talk to others about these experiences, to delve deeper into their "spiritual journey." In other words, for my informants, these experiences—of absolute joy, of self-transcendence, of synchronicity—contain within them, if not proof, then at least the possibility of a greater force in the world, or a superempirical order.

Immanence of God or the Superempirical

In light of the intimate relationship between ecstatic and effervescent experiences and the religion of the heart, it should come as no surprise that, from within this cultural structure, the superempirical—however it is described or labelled—is something that can be *experienced*.[1] In other words, God or the superempirical is conceived as not categorically separate from humans, but rather as accessible *through* the self. In this, the religion of the heart not only encourages a thirst for a "direct communion with God," as Troeltsch ([1912] 1931, 731) would say, but also assumes its potentiality.

In *The Easternization of the West* Colin Campbell (2007, 66) argues that "belief in a transcendental, personal god is giving way to belief in an immanent and

---

[1] I use the term "superempirical" as opposed to "supernatural" on the grounds that supernatural implies that the "spiritual" cannot be a part of nature, and that nature solely consists of physical matter (see Smith 2003, 98).

impersonal one." While I agree that the religion of the heart generally entails an ontology that is more monistic than dualistic, what one finds among Charismatic Christians is not so much a rejection of a transcendental, personal God in favour of an immanent and impersonal one, but rather one that is simultaneously transcendent, immanent, and personal (Poloma and Pendleton 1989; Richter 1997). As anthropologist Simon Coleman (2000, 235) observes, "These Christians worship a God who is both within the self and a permanently moving force on the earth as a whole." This harkens back to John Wesley's Methodism, whose "primary and original sphere of action was finding the supernatural in the fabric of everyday life" (Martin 2002, 7). But it also echoes the poetic spirit of Walt Whitman ([1855] 2005), who avers in *Leaves of Grass*, "Divine am I inside and out" (55). Moreover, it remains a central theme in much New Age literature as well. For instance, Wayne Dyer (1995, 139) asserts, "Everything in life is energy." Of course, Charismatic Christians do not use the terms "impersonal spirit," "energy," or "life force," but this doesn't mean they do not subscribe to this cultural structure. For much like SBNRs, these Christians assume a "continuity of the self with [an] ever-present divine reality" (Fuller 2001, 85)—albeit preferring to speak in terms of the "Holy Spirit." In sum, we can say that "spirituality" today postulates a *God within* insofar as one can access God or the divine *through the self*, but also a *God without* insofar as the superempirical permeates the universe.

[handwritten note: Whitman has already done this work.]

Benevolent God or Universe

For adherents of the religion of the heart, whatever it is that informs the "something more," it is *good*. That is, the religion of the heart breeds what William James ([1901] 1992, 79) once called the "optimistic type," for whom, the superempirical, "if you will only trust her sufficiently, is absolutely good." And it also entails what James called the "religion of healthy-mindedness," committed to exploring and mapping the "wonderful inner paths to a supernatural kind of happiness" (77). Indeed, the religion of healthy-mindedness is a staple of much contemporary "spiritual" literature. Joel Osteen—known colloquially as the "smiling preacher"— assures his readers, "God wants you to have a good life, a life filled with love, joy, peace, and fulfillment" (2004, 76), adding, "individuals who view themselves as God sees them are usually happy about who they are" (57). And echoing these ideas in New Age parlance, Neale Donald Walsch (1995, 296) writes, "The Highest Thought is always that thought which contains joy." While Wayne Dyer (1995, 296) asserts, "Your higher self wants you to be at peace." Thus, the religion of the heart today affirms the goodness of "God," "Nature," or "the Universe" (however it is labelled), assuring its adherents that subjective well-being and inner peace are the natural state of things.

Redemptive Self as Theodicy

Colin Campbell (2007) contends theodicies are comprised of three components, which serve to meet distinct needs for meaning: cognitive, emotional, and moral. The religion of the heart's conception of an immanent superempirical force supplies *cognitive meaning* to its adherents by offering a descriptive account of the reality they experience. It assures them that they are in contact with an immanent reality that transcends them, and which they can access through their bodily senses, feelings, and intuitions. It offers *emotional meaning* by means of a teleology of self-realization which encompasses an ethical framework that orients daily interactions and long-term goals.[2] And finally, the religion of the heart meets the human need for *moral meaning* by providing an account of why suffering exists. Simply put, the religion of the heart postulates that *all suffering is redemptive*. In this, it shares much with what narrative psychologist Dan McAdams (2006) calls the "redemptive self." Now, this is not an otherworldly redemption—it doesn't presume redemption will only (or, in some cases, ever) come in an afterlife. Rather, the religion of the heart presupposes redemption in *this* life. As a result, adherents learn to find meaning in their darkest moments, to extract lessons from their pain, and to discover how their suffering fits into a larger divine or cosmic plan.

For example, Tony Robbins (1991, 285) writes, "our disappointments may truly be opportunities in disguise." Joel Osteen (2004, 170, 204) urges: "God has a divine purpose for every challenge that comes into our lives." And Wayne Dyer (1995, 7) writes, "If it is true that we are part of an intelligent system, we can assume that we go from no-where to now-here for some purpose. With this realization you can stop doubting that you are a divine creation with purpose and just accept that you are. You are part of this intelligent system *and* you are here for some divine reason" (10). While these authors may have quite different theological or discursive understandings, they nevertheless share the conviction that our lives and the events we experience are not meaningless. By postulating that all experiences and events unfold according to a larger plan, they enable their readers to both make sense of, and cope with, the existence of suffering. Accordingly, the religion of the heart provides an interpretive lens, or symbolic filter, through which to experience one's life. No longer do mundane or ordinary moments pass by without significance; instead, they are understood as imbued with great personal (even cosmic) meaning.

---

[2] I examine this in the following section.

Class + hierarchy or touched so far.

Self-Realization as Teleology

What ultimate end, or telos, does suffering serve? Simply put: *self-realization*—
that is, suffering is necessary to actualize one's potential and realize one's true self.
Accordingly, the religion of the heart is underwritten by the moral tradition of
expressive individualism, which holds that we all have within us a *pre-social* self
that reflects *who we truly are*, and which it is *our life's goal to realize*.

Charles Taylor (1989) refers to this as a *romantic expressivist* conception of the
human condition, and we see it endorsed time and again in the literature on
"spirituality." For instance, Deepak Chopra (1994, 97) writes, "Each of us is here
to discover our higher self or our spiritual self." Wayne Dyer (1995, 5) directs
people to locate their "sacred self." Esther and Jerry Hicks (2004, 5) tell us, "Your
life is about the continuing expression of who you truly are." And Joel Osteen
counsels, "Be an original, not a copycat" (2004, 91, 92). Furthermore, we also find
expressive individualism in secular psychological and self-help discourse. For
instance, in *Awaken the Giant Within* Tony Robbins writes, "I believe our *true*
identity is something that's indefinable and greater than anything that's describ-
able. We are soul; we are spirit" (1991, 431). And in *On Becoming a Person* Carl
Rogers contends that the ultimate goal of client-centred therapy is, "to be that self
which one truly is" (1969, 166).

Accordingly, from within the religion of the heart, "'personal growth' can be
understood as the shape 'religious salvation' takes" (Hanegraaff 1996, 46)—and
this is as true of Charismatic Christians as it is of those who are heirs to the New
Age and Human Potential movements (Nadesan 1999; Coleman 2000). What's
more, it is generally believed by both Charismatics and SBNRs that we ought to
engage in a constant process of work upon ourselves in order to actualize our
potential. It would seem, then, the "spiritual" life demands work—self-work.[3]

Self-Ethic (Voice from Within)

Implicit in this teleological conception of human life is a *self-ethic*. The basic idea
is that individuals must look *within*—specifically, to their intuitions and feelings—
in order to discern what is true and good. In short, "The 'individual' serves as his
or her own source of guidance" (Heelas 1996, 23). Moreover, following in the

---

[3] Importantly, while humanistic psychological and self-help discourses are certainly coherent
without the background metaphysical picture provided by the religion of the heart, taking on little in
the way of religious meaning for a great many persons, they nevertheless naturalize expressive
individualism, and also often presuppose the theodicy and teleology this cultural structure propagates.
Thus, they are easily combined with this picture—and when this occurs, they become *existentially
meaningful*. That is, it is in such instances when these secular discourses become carriers of the religion
of the heart. This process is discussed in Chapter 10.

footsteps of the Romantics, adherents of the religion of the heart conceive of the *true self* as *a conduit of God or the superempirical.* For instance, Deepak Chopra (1994, 3) celebrates, "the divinity within us." Wayne Dyer (1995, 5) writes, "there dwells within all human beings a divine energy." While Joseph Murphy (1977, 3) directs his readers toward "the Presence of God within you." In assuming a mystical access to divine power, adherents of the religion of the heart believe that they need not suffer hesitation, self-doubt, or ambivalence about how to lead their lives, nor need they seek inspiration outside of themselves, since they already have everything they need within themselves.

Recall that for the Romantics, the good life is a matter of discerning the voice within, thought to be the voice of God or Nature, and then heeding it without compromise. Similarly, among adherents of the religion of the heart, the true self is conceived as *pre-social*, and therefore *not constituted by society.* Accordingly, one must pave one's own way and be who one truly is, *in spite of* established social norms and conventions. And to the extent that one is taking on external roles, or trying to live up to expectations derived from society, one is not being authentic to oneself.

Furthermore, "spirituality" encourages the development *self-awareness*, for if the ultimate end of life is to achieve the self that one truly is, then one must first become aware of *who that is.* This can be achieved through a variety of practices of self-cultivation, but fundamentally it requires reflexively *going within* in order to delineate those parts of the self that are seen to be by-products of society from those that are authentic to oneself. Of course, how the "social self" is conceptualized varies—SBNRs are more likely to speak in terms of the "ego," whereas Charismatics might instead speak of the "enemy." The problem for both of these groups, however, remains the same: *societal norms and institutions are believed to stifle the true self by hemming it in, manipulating it, or repressing it.* Crucially, then, today's religion of the heart *naturalizes the romantic self-understanding.*

Virtue Is Natural

How do adherents of the religion of the heart conceive of the source of virtue or moral action? If not society, then what encourages individuals to be good? From within this cultural structure, a person who lives as their true self *will naturally act virtuously*. As Wayne Dyer (1995, 17) explains, "Every problem—be it with relationships, finances, health or self-image—has a solution in the sacred self. When you are peaceful, experience silence, meditate and listen, really listen to God, you will be directed away from the worldly and toward the divinity that is within you. You will know what you need to do." *Becoming virtuous is ultimately a by-product of realizing one's true self.*

This is why my informants are far more comfortable speaking in terms of "healthy and ill" than "good and evil."[4] What leads individuals to cause harm either to themselves or to others is, in their view, some combination of oppressive social structures and psychological trauma—hence the focus on "healing" among those who identify as "spiritual." As Wayne Dyer (1995, 359) puts it, "transcend the false self that we call the ego. That is when healing will occur." Similarly, Norman Vincent Peale (1959, 149) writes, "You have to give God a chance to reach into your soul with His healing power." Becoming whole, healing, realizing one's true self—these are all synonyms as regards the religion of the heart (see Bowman 1999, 181; McGuire 2008, 130). In short, *all healing entails moral reform*.

Lastly, not only is virtue the natural result of achieving one's true self, but one is also promised happiness, understood as subjective well-being or inner peace. An SBNR interviewee shared, "When I feel a state of permeating calm, that to me feels spiritual and it feels like the true self." And Eckhart Tolle (1995, 5) writes, "the unhappy and deeply fearful self . . . is ultimately a fiction of the mind." The idea is that in realizing one's true self, one simultaneously becomes moral and achieves subjective well-being—the religion of the heart promises *a perfect harmony between personal authenticity, virtue, and inner peace*.

Sacralization of Individual Liberty

There is no value more sacred to the religion of the heart than *individual liberty*. What this amounts to in practice is, first and foremost, a commitment to allowing individuals to "listen to the voice within" and "follow their heart"—that is, *negative freedom*. Adherents of the religion of the heart demand that individuals be granted a sphere within which they cannot be interfered with, where they have *freedom from* external obstructions and constraints.

This derives from the expressive individualism at its core. Moreover, today's religion of the heart is essentially egalitarian. As Eeva Sointu and Linda Woodhead (2008, 273) suggest, "spirituality" recognizes "the uniqueness—and unique worth—of each and every individual." Indeed, evincing the Protestant principle, and sharing in the Emersonian celebration of "individuality," its adherents reject all attempts to order, tame, or control the true self. Because they hold self-realization in such high esteem, they give great weight to *self-expression*—the ability to express, and be recognized as, one's true self. Leslie Parker explains, "When I think of religion, it's very obviously . . . tainted and very limiting; placing limitations on life and life experiences, whereas spirituality to me is more about exploration and freedom." One hears strikingly similar claims among Charismatic Christians.

---

[4] Admittedly, this is less true of Charismatic Christians than SBNRs.

Nevertheless, this commitment to negative freedom derives from a more fundamental commitment to *positive freedom*. By this I mean a *freedom to* realize one's true self. Here again, we see the romantic self-understanding tacitly naturalized: realizing one's true self requires shedding *all* external attachments—only the individual who lives *as* their true self is truly free. Thus, Wayne Dyer (1995, 48) encourages his readers, "Begin by making your decision to be free by letting go of your personal history." While Robin Sharma (1997, 170) warns, "Never be a prisoner of your past." Of course, much psychotherapy is premised upon a similar ideal. For example, Phil McGraw (1999, 48) encourages his readers to "adopt the attitude of questioning and challenging everything in your life that you can identify as having been accepted on blind faith or as having been adopted out of tradition or history."

In sum, the religion of the heart sacralizes individual liberty in the following senses: because cultural traditions and social institutions are believed to stifle individual authenticity, adherents challenge and contest external constraints that are seen to regulate or deform their true selves. However, because cultural traditions and social institutions are considered *aspects of the self*—the "ego" or the "enemy"—adherents endorse a conception of positive freedom that requires them to shed these aspects in order to become truly free (Houtman and Aupers 2010, 15).

Mind-Body-Spirit Connection

Colin Campbell (2007, 66) writes of the spiritual turn, "all dualisms are being rejected, whether that of god and mankind, mankind and nature, mind and body, or body and soul, in favor of generally holistic assumptions." Indeed, at its most basic, the religion of the heart inspires *a general hostility to dualisms*. However, as far as I can tell, there exists no consensus as to which dualisms are necessarily opposed, and which are not. For instance, among my informants the specific dualisms Campbell identifies are sometimes challenged, sometimes validated. Yet what is abundantly clear is that the religion of the heart presupposes some version of the idea that *thought shapes reality*. Deepak Chopra (1994, 31) writes, "Thought has the power to transform." Tony Robbins (1991, 75) assures us, "Beliefs have the power to create and the power to destroy." Joel Osteen (2004, 121) preaches, "Our words are self-fulfilling prophecies." Robin Sharma (1997, 63) asserts, "the quality of your thinking determines the quality of your life." And Esther and Jerry Hicks (2004, 18) assure us, "You *do* create your own reality." And should one think only best-selling authors make these claims, I heard variations on this theme from nearly all of my informants. For instance, Michael Wallace asserted, "I believe in the power of the mind." While an SBNR interviewee admitted, "I've always believed some element of 'perception is reality'." And one regularly hears from the pulpit at C3 Toronto, "You will reproduce what you repeat." All the same, what remains puzzling is how best to interpret all of these statements. I don't believe there exists a consensus on this. So, it would seem the meaning of the mind-body-spirit connection—its generally holistic direction—remains amenable to many interpretations.

Methodological Individualism

One way or another, the "spiritual" life involves taking responsibility for oneself. Whether it is one's happiness, success, past trauma, or simply one's attitudes, adherents of the religion of the heart locate responsibility in the individual. As anthropologist Susannah Crockford (2017, 41) observes, "the individual self, not society, is the locus of change and power." That is, the religion of the heart endorses a strict *methodological individualism*. Or put another way, this cultural structure prescribes mass self-transformation, or mass self-realization, to combat the ills of the world. For instance, the idea that "God helps those who help themselves" is a staple at C3 Toronto. And this anti-structuralist lens was also endorsed by SBNRs when discussing "spirituality," as the following interviewee's account vividly illustrates: "I think moving people close to their potential definitely is their spirituality, and if more people approach that as their spirituality, as finding their passion and working through that passion, then I think the world is definitely going to improve. Not by one person's action, but by everybody's smaller actions." Finally, we see this vision outlined in popular "spiritual" literature as well. Wayne Dyer (1995, 347) writes, "The world is encountering a spiritual deficit that reflects our need to consciously get on the path of our sacred quest. The solution to individual global problems is to overcome the spiritual deficit. When you make the shift in consciousness allowing yourself to be an agent of heightened awareness, you are contributing to the transformation of our world."

Bringing Clarity to the Contemporary Religious Landscape

As should be clear by now, from within the cultural schema naturalized by the religion of the heart any activity, event, or experience can potentially be interpreted as "spiritual" in nature. In fact, what makes an event or experience "spiritual," fundamentally, is not whether it conforms to traditional "religious" or "secular" boundaries and conventions, but rather *its quality* (ecstatic/effervescent) and the *purpose it serves* (self-awareness, self-expression, self-realization). This explains why scholars have observed the tendency towards religious bricolage—that is, "the joining together of seemingly inconsistent, disparate contents" (Wuthnow 2007, 15)—among many today. Indeed, the contemporary religious landscape has been described variably as replete with "do-it-yourself-religion" (Baerveldt 1996), "religious consumption à la carte" (Possamai 2003), and characteristic of the "postmodern condition" (Lyon 1993). There is some truth in this. For those I spoke to, exercising, listening to music, or hiking can be considered "spiritual," as what matters foremost is whether they *experience* a connection to a force greater than themselves—be it God or the Universe—and whether or not it helps them to grow personally, heal, or realize their true self. Adherents of the religion of the heart do not respect traditional semantic boundaries, believing with Emerson ([1841] 2000) that "Words are finite organs of the mind" (23). Because the superempirical pervades everything, it can be connected with anywhere, and at any time, provided one is open to it. Similarly, among Charismatics, bricolage is also commonplace—if always interpreted *within* a theistic frame.

We can see, then, why studies that have focused narrowly on the semantics associated with the term "spirituality" have tended to produce a more disjointed picture of the religious landscape than is warranted. The fact that adherents engage in an eclectic "pick and mix" form of bricolage is not evidence of cultural incoherence, but rather derives from a consistent and underlying cultural logic. And although the religion of the heart may encourage a postmodern incredulity towards metanarratives, this is not the case with respect to its own. Furthermore, the fact that individuals who self-identify as "spiritual" don't all agree about what this term means is not evidence that they don't collectively subscribe to a shared cultural structure, but rather evinces the fact that they do—one that prizes subjective experience and self-realization over and above labels of self-identification. As Troeltsch knew well, "mystic" or "spiritual" religion tends to induce a suspicion of labels because labels are human constructions, which are believed to constrain the individual spirit from flowing where it wishes. Indeed, what has made the religion of the heart so difficult for social scientists to study is that, *as a result of their self-understanding, its adherents deny adhering to it.* In romantic fashion, they prefer instead to view themselves as nomadic traditionless seekers in touch with a universal spiritual core that cannot be captured by language. Yet I've tried to show that a closer look at their accounts illustrates something quite different. The truth is that much, if not most, of what goes by "spirituality" today is animated by an underlying and shared cultural structure—the religion of the heart.[5]

---

[5] From hereon I assume a basic commensurability between what scholars refer to as "spirituality" and the religion of the heart, as I have defined it. In other words, I use these terms interchangeably. As argued in Chapter 1, the study of spirituality has suffered due to a lack of shared nomenclature. So, I think it justified to impose my own analytic framework, to the extent that it serves the pragmatic purpose of delineating that which scholars agree upon and that which we do not. While doing so undoubtedly risks reifying my etic term, "the religion of the heart," I ultimately think it's worth it.

PART II
ROMANTIC LIBERAL MODERNITY

4

The 1960s and the Rise of Romantic Liberalism

In Part I of this book I delineated the cultural structure underlying much of what goes by "spirituality" today. In Part II, I locate the religion of the heart in space and time, as it relates to the past half-century. It is no mere accident that the religion of the heart rolls off the tongues of so many in twenty-first-century Euro-American liberal democracies (and beyond). Though it might be as old as the Christian tradition from which it arose, the religion of the heart's recent popularity is incomprehensible without accounting for the transformations that took place during and in the wake of the 1960s. So, while I recognize that speaking of epochal change always risks sacrificing nuance and reducing social complexity, I am convinced that such language is warranted. As historian Callum Brown (2009, 8) observes, "The 1960s revolution was about how people constructed their lives—their families, their sex lives, their cultural pursuits, and their moral identities of what makes a 'good' or 'bad' person." Without question, the seeds of this cultural revolution were centuries in the making, but the events of the 1960s precipitated their flowering to an unprecedented degree. Moreover, this occurred on an international scale, affecting nearly all liberal democracies, at least to some extent. As a result, we in the West continue to live out the legacies of this tumultuous period—whether we realize it or not.

In this chapter I tell the story of the 1960s. I relate the rise of the religion of the heart to the wider moral, social, and political developments which swept across liberal democracies during this period. My argument is that it was during the 1960s that an unprecedented alliance between romanticism and liberalism took root and blossomed. Although unstable and lacking self-consciousness in its early days, this alliance eventually crystallized into a stable social imaginary, which today offers legitimation to both the religion of the heart and the institutions that support it.[1] In order to understand how this came about we need to examine the nature of these two schools of thought and feeling. I therefore begin with a philosophical examination of the roots of romanticism. Crucial, in this regard, is

Benedict Arnold

[1] In speaking of a "social imaginary" I follow Taylor (2004, 23), for whom it refers to "the ways people imagine their social existence, how they fit together with others, how things go on between them and their fellows, the expectations that are normally met, and the deeper normative notions and images that underlie these expectations."

The Spiritual Turn: The Religion of the Heart and the Making of Romantic Liberal Modernity. Galen Watts, Oxford University Press. © Galen Watts 2022. DOI: 10.1093/oso/9780192859839.003.0005

what spurred the Romantic movement—its dissatisfaction and disenchantment with modernity. Second, I explain what I mean by liberalism. I understand liberalism as a broad tradition of political thought constituted by a commitment to securing "the political conditions that are necessary for the exercise of personal freedom" (Shlkar 1989, 21). While liberals might disagree over how best to interpret this fundamental value, they are nevertheless liberals by virtue of this shared commitment.[2] As we shall see, romantic liberalism, in contrast to rational liberalism, seeks in modernity a compromise: it accepts the legalistic, bureaucratic, and fragmenting aspects of liberal regimes, in exchange for a space of privacy, or personal retreat, where "romantic impulses and expressions of personality remerge" (Rosenblum 1989, 210). Accordingly, romantic liberals endorse a vision of the good society whereby citizens are treated with equal concern and respect in the public sphere, and have equal opportunities to lead their lives from the inside and realize their true selves in the private sphere. It follows that romantic liberals interpret liberty through a romantic expressivist lens, while also espousing the liberal separation of private and public spheres. For this reason, the religion of the heart is usefully thought of as the religious expression typical of romantic liberals. Lastly, I examine the 1960s counter-culture and the various social and political developments it spawned—which I argue reflected the rise of romantic liberalism. I outline the key religious developments that took place during this era, and then relate these to the social and political transformations that accompanied them. My aim in this chapter is to link the religious, moral, social, and political developments of this period, offering a comprehensive picture of how, despite their differences, they collectively served to animate, propagate, and embed the romantic liberal imaginary that legitimates the social order of twenty-first-century liberal democracies.

The Romantic Response to Modernity

In the popular imagination, the Romantic movement was chiefly aesthetic in nature, yet it has proved incredibly politically consequential. It represented a rebellion against the classical stress on rationalism, tradition, and formal harmony, in lieu of the individual, the imagination, and raw feeling. The Romantics came of age during a period of tremendous upheaval—industrialization, urbanization, and economic turbulence were dramatically transforming the nature of social life. They looked out at their budding industrial societies and shuddered, experiencing nothing short of world-weariness, the sense that everything they

---

[2] Accordingly, the political Left and Right in North America largely share a commitment to the liberal tradition, but simply hold dramatically different interpretations of what liberal principles entail in practice. I return to this point in Chapter 10.

valued—authenticity, individuality, sensuality, self-expression, eroticism, and the imagination—was being stunted and degraded as a result of modern industrialism. In a word, "They sought to liberate the human spirit from the mechanistic prison" of modernity (Ahlstrom 1977, 156).

Historian Michael Saler (2006, 694) remarks, "There is one characteristic of modernity...that has been emphasized fairly consistently by intellectuals since the eighteenth century: that modernity is 'disenchanted'." It was this sense of disenchantment that spurred the Romantic movement. Thus, while Weber may have articulated the thesis of disenchantment in social scientific terms, it began as a form of romantic cultural criticism (Josephson-Storm 2017). The Romantics, when looking out at modernity and contemplating the view of humanity proffered by modern science, asked, "What is the place of the Good, or the True, or the Beautiful, in a world entirely determined mechanistically?" (Taylor 1989, 459).

As we saw in Chapter 2, the Romantic movement was deeply religious in nature. Its iconoclastic proponents sought to identify and articulate a "subtler language" which could "make manifest the higher or the divine." In the wake of the Romantics, "Deeply felt personal insight" became the "most precious spiritual resource" (Taylor 2007, 489). Although they bore the imprints of Enlightenment thought, the Romantics simultaneously railed against the culture of rationalism and the materialist outlooks championed by the *philosophes*. They detested the "ugliness" and the "spiritual emptiness" of the budding modern world, and the utilitarian individualism of the marketplace (Campbell 1987, 218). And they especially railed against what they saw as the repressive, routinizing, and instrumentalizing aspects of modern public life—which Taylor (2007, 633) calls the "disciplines of civilized life." But rather than propose political revolution, the Romantics instead sought to re-enchant the world by means of *turning inward*. They offered as an antidote "the ideal of self-expression," that is, "the aim of realizing individuality through creativity" (218). In short, *in the self the Romantics found the source of re-enchantment* (Gay 1995, 37).

We can see, then, the great extent to which today's religion of the heart carries forward the Romantic legacy. We see this, first, in its championing of the ideals of self-expression and authenticity (Trilling 1971). But we also see it in the self-understanding it naturalizes. Recall, the "spiritual" journey inward requires identifying and expressing one's true self—a self which is considered entirely *pre-social*, and thus fundamentally antithetical to society's norms and traditions. Moreover, the romanticism of today's religion of the heart is evident when its adherents reject all reductionist explanations for human life and its beauty (Berlin 1999). Just as for Wordsworth "to dissect is to murder," so, too, is it "unspiritual" to study human life analytically.

Furthermore, romanticism's hatred of the disciplines of civilized life continue to exert much force in the contemporary era. When popular commentators point out the deadening or soul-crushing effect of modern rationalism, bureaucratization, and mechanization, they are drawing from the Romantic tradition. Romantic expressivism, given its commitment to an ideal of personal authenticity, generally distrusts all forms of impersonality, calculation, and unspontaneous collective action. All of this was evident in the counter-culture of the 1960s. However, what made the era's romanticism distinct was its alliance with liberal political ideals—that is, a commitment to the moral equality of individuals and the value of individual liberty.

What Is Liberalism?

Philosopher John Gray (1995, 78) argues liberalism is the political theory of modernity and the Enlightenment. Similarly, Robert Bellah (1970, 70) contends liberalism is "the primary ideology of modernization." Why is this? Larry Siedentop (2014, 349) supplies an answer: "the only birthright recognized by the liberal tradition is individual freedom." Indeed, the Universal Declaration of Human Rights, ratified in 1948, is a fundamentally liberal document, as are the United States Constitution and the Canadian Charter of Rights and Freedoms. Thus, it is quite common for critics of liberalism to equate it with individualism. This is correct if by "individualism" we mean that the individual is conceived as the basic unit of society. For the primary preoccupation of liberals is "securing the conditions of personal liberty" (Rosenblum 1994, 541). To this extent, liberals are concerned with individual autonomy and the conditions that make it possible.

It was for this reason that early liberals introduced the distinction between public and private spheres. Interested in securing conditions of peace among warring Protestants and Catholics, these liberals proposed this conceptual distinction to demarcate state affairs from those they claimed were the business of private citizens (e.g., religious belief). They were primarily concerned about the potential despotism of the state, and the need to identify political principles upon which to co-exist peacefully (Laborde 2017). Thus, in response to the wars of religion, early liberals sought peace and security, and formed their principles on this basis. Accordingly, religious belief (basically Protestant in nature) was relegated to the private sphere, the role of the state was severely restricted, and commerce and science were given an enlarged status in public life (Owen 2015).

Bertrand Russell (1946, 578) adds, "Implicitly, the tendency of early liberalism was towards democracy tempered by the rights of property. There was a belief—not at first wholly explicit—that all men are born equal." Indeed, in principle, liberalism conceives of every individual as having an equal moral status, which requires that they be treated "with equal concern and respect" (Kymlicka 1989a, 140).[3] It was on

---

[3] This is not to say liberals have always lived up to their principles, as the moral stains of slavery and colonial genocide (among other historic injustices) on the liberal conscience make evident.

this basis that early liberals rejected the doctrine of the divine right of kings. For liberals, moral equality between persons favours democracy on the grounds that citizens ought to have an equal say in who governs. Accordingly, the notion of consent is a key liberal value, as it follows from the liberal commitment to individual autonomy, that is, self-rule. Citizens must consent to those public decisions that will infringe on their liberty (Rawls [1971] 1999).[4]

Lastly, liberalism is fundamentally concerned with pluralism. Liberals assume that a free society will necessarily produce social and moral diversity, and on this basis make central specifying "the terms of peaceful coexistence in a pluralist society, whereby the form of pluralism is characterized by incommensurable worldviews" (Gray 1995, 85). Whether or not this makes liberalism neutral towards all worldviews is a matter I will return to in later chapters.

Rational vs. Romantic Liberalism

We can distinguish between two broad versions of liberalism that I call *rational* and *romantic*—and which Russell (1946, 618) refers to as the "hard-headed" and "soft-hearted" schools of liberalism.[5] In describing the former, Russell stresses its "[e]mphasis on prudence" (593). In other words, the disciplines of civilized life— regularity, disinterestedness, impartiality—which the early Romantics believed stifle human flourishing and expressive freedom, rational liberals deem both essential and praiseworthy. For rational liberals, modern life necessarily requires discipline of various kinds; a peaceful and prosperous polity requires citizens to cultivate the habits of self-restraint, detachment, and temperance. This emphasis on prudence and self-discipline, rational liberals argue, is necessary in order to secure the conditions of personal liberty (Shklar 1989, 21).

Yet, in her remarkable book *Another Liberalism: Romanticism and the Reconstruction of Liberal Thought*, Nancy Rosenblum (1987, 4) notes that liberalism in its rational, conventional, mode wards "off everything affective, personal, and expressive." Indeed, the vision of liberalism espoused by rational liberals is "cold, contractual, and unlovely—without emotional or aesthetical appeal" (2). In other words, rational liberalism is a by-product of Enlightenment thought, mistrustful of the emotions, afraid of arbitrariness, and wary of anything that smacks of irrationalism. It celebrates commitment to impersonal government, impartial rule of law, public reason, and rational calculation. Rational liberalism, in short, "distrusts the law of the heart" (34). Moreover, as Nomi Maya Stolzenger (2009)

---

[4] That said, there is no necessary connection between liberalism and democracy, as the recent emergence of "illiberal democracies" around the globe is demonstrating (see Mounk 2018).

[5] Judith Shklar (1989, 28) makes a similar distinction between the "liberalism of natural rights" and the "liberalism of personal development."

argues, rational liberalism endorses a conception of freedom as self-mastery, whereby autonomy is conceived as the willingness and ability to submit to a higher authority—be it secular or religious in nature. Since Durkheim, scholars have spoken of this moral tradition as *moral individualism*. Perhaps the clearest example is Immanuel Kant, who saw moral action as characterized by rational obedience to the categorical imperative.

But, as Rosenblum notes, due to its arid legalism, rational liberalism has often provoked a romantic counter-response, describing the relationship between romanticism and liberalism as "one of mutual tension, reconciliation, and reconstruction" (Rosenblum 1987, 3). She writes, "When liberalism imposes its severe discipline of legalism, it excites a romantic reaction" (Rosenblum 1989, 207). This is because romantic expressivism resists homogenization and routinization, that is, "its nemesis is generality and regularity, security of expectation" (207). History bears this out.

For instance, John Stuart Mill, a quintessential liberal if there ever was one, sought solace in the poetry of Wordsworth in the midst of a prolonged depression, and after having been rescued by romantic pieties, allowed romantic convictions to inform his liberal theory. One of the primary motivators for Mill's famous harm principle was the expressivism of Wilhelm von Humboldt—for whom privatism was necessary to cultivate one's individuality (Humboldt 1969). In *On Liberty* Mill rails against what he calls "social tyranny"—meaning the "tyranny of the prevailing opinion and feeling"—which he argues is "more formidable than many kinds of political oppression" as it "leaves fewer means of escape, penetrating much more deeply into the details of life, and enslaving the soul itself" (Mill [1859] 2016, 8). For Mill,

> The only freedom which deserves the name, is that of pursuing our own good in our own way, so long as we do not attempt to deprive others of theirs, or impede their efforts to obtain it. Each is the proper guardian of his own health, whether bodily, or mental and spiritual. Mankind are greater gainers by suffering each other to live as seems good to themselves, than by compelling each to live as seems good to the rest.   (16)

In turn, Rosenblum (1987, 24) contends that Mill came to believe "liberalism might be open to a romantic justification of private liberty as the condition for imaginative expression." In agreement, Robert Devigne argues that Mill endorsed liberal legal structures and institutions on the basis that they provided the conditions for self-development. "Mill is a romantic-expressive liberal. The focus of Mill's attention is upon the relation of reason to self-realization, and the idea, underlined by such terms as 'self-development' and 'inner consciousness,' is that the best life is distinctive and authentic, something every individual can discover for himself" (2006, 76).

Translating Mill's view into contemporary philosophical parlance, philosopher Will Kymlicka (1989a, 12) argues the romantic liberal is morally committed to the belief that "my life goes better if I'm leading it from the inside, according to my beliefs about value." It is for this reason, as Kymlicka (1995, 80) acknowledges, that romantic liberalism "grants a very wide freedom of choice in terms of how [people] lead their lives." That is, "It allows people to choose a conception of the good life, and then allows them to reconsider that decision, and adopt a new and hopefully better plan of life." Indeed, it was romantic-influenced liberals who reformulated the private/public distinction to mean the distinction between the *personal* and *social*; that is, they were "concerned not only to protect the private sphere of social life, but also to carve out a realm *within the private sphere* where individuals can have *privacy*" (Kymlicka 2007, 395). Thus, within a romantic liberal social imaginary the private sphere is conceived as a protected space of personal retreat from public life, necessary in order to cultivate one's individuality and realize one's true self.

While romantic liberalism owes much to Humboldt and Mill, one of its best-known advocates in recent years is philosopher Richard Rorty. According to Rorty (1989, 84), "The social glue holding together the ideal liberal society . . . consists in little more than a consensus that the point of social organization is to let every-body have a chance at self-creation to the best of his or her abilities, and that that goal requires, besides peace and wealth, the standard 'bourgeois freedoms'." Crucially, for Rorty, the private sphere is a place of self-realization, whereas the public sphere is a place of civic duties and public reason. And it is the former where he consigns religion: "the only role left for religious belief will be to help individuals find meaning in their lives, and to serve as a help to individuals in their times of trouble" (Rorty 2003, 142). Religion, Rorty submits, can and should serve the important and felt need for private enchantment, but it must not stray into the public sphere—the site of rational deliberation and civic virtue.[6]

Although the seeds of romantic liberalism long presaged the 1960s, it was not until this boisterous era that it reached maturation. Indeed, Stolzenberg (2009, 196) argues that in the wake of the sixties it became common for liberals to recast *autonomy* as *self-expression*, which she argues "exalts the irrational side of human nature, disparages psychological repression, and elevates 'the heart' over 'the head'." Similarly, legal theorist Lawrence M. Friedman (1990, 3) describes a shift

---

[6] Importantly, my conception of romantic liberalism should be read as operating at a level once removed from political philosophy proper. And the reason for this is that while I believe thinkers as diverse as Humboldt, Mill, Kymlicka, and Rorty can be justifiably called "romantic liberal," I do not claim they are equally so. Moreover, I recognize that there exist important differences between these philosophers' theories that my purposefully broad conception cannot account for. Ultimately, then, my conception of romantic liberalism is more cultural sociological than political theoretical insofar as it seeks to capture, less the fine-grained theoretical systems of particular professional philosophers, than what I consider the broad political tradition that animates both the social order of contemporary liberal democracies as well as the personal philosophies of many of their citizens.

during these years whereby "*expression* [became] favored over *self-control.*" While Thomas Franck (1999, 39) argues the 1960s gave birth to a "new individualism," which "challenge[d] the limits on personal self-determination so long imposed by the traditional objects of allegiance."

We can see then how sixties' romanticism gave life to a distinctive kind of liberalism, which finds fresh justifications for supporting liberal institutions, principles, and policies (Rosenblum 1987, 208). Of course, pure romanticism rejects the very terms of political theory. But romantics need not be (indeed have not been) so consistent. In truth, in the late twentieth century many romantics made peace with liberalism. This is not only because romantic discontents arise in response to the disciplines of civilized life but also because they arise "in response to romantics' own compensatory visions" (Rosenblum 1987, 4). In other words, chastened romantics are likely to find in liberal society a reasonable compromise—as occurred en masse in the sixties.

The 1960s and the Rise of Our Romantic Liberal Imaginary

The 1960s marked the beginning of epochal moral, social, and political change that continues to shape life in twenty-first-century liberal democracies.[7] Indeed, this era is associated with no less than second-wave feminism, gay liberation, the environmental movement, mass religious disaffiliation, and the spread of multiculturalism. And while these certainly had national contours, they were in many respects global developments. Below, I am primarily concerned with what came to be known as the counter-culture in the West, which I argue reflected a distinctly romantic liberal development. Framing it as such serves to illuminate the degree to which the spread of the religion of the heart is bound up with the historical movements listed above.

In *The Religious Crisis of the 1960s* historian Hugh McLeod (2007, 1) writes, "The 1960s were a period of decisive change in the religious history of the Western world." So decisive, that "these years may come to be seen as marking a rupture as profound as that brought about by the Reformation." What made them so? The sixties marked the widespread acceptance of romanticism. Indeed, as Colin Campbell (2007, 188) observes, the counter-culture was the "social expression of romanticism." Romantic attitudes and ideals were, of course, a much earlier innovation, but it was only in the sixties that they became a mass phenomenon (16). Hence why Talcott Parsons ([1974] 1984) famously called the 1960s the "Expressive Revolution." This revolution was spawned by a host of both social and economic factors—the post-Second World War affluence boom, the rise of

---

[7] By the "1960s" I am referring to the years roughly between 1958 and 1975.

consumer culture, and increased urbanization, among others. But from a cultural sociological perspective, the counter-culture of the sixties reflected a romantic revival in order to re-enchant what was perceived as a culturally disenchanted world (cf. Roszak 1969).

This attempt at re-enchantment manifested itself as a wholesale critique against "the system." During the 1960s, institutions—both private and public—were perceived by youth as repressive and alienating, stifling individuals from being truly creative and autonomous (Houtman et al. 2011, 13). "There was considerable disaffection with various facets of the industrial civilization, including science, technology, and the institutions of capitalist political economy," writes Peter Clecak (1983, 18). In short, romantic attitudes became pervasive among the youthful baby boomers.

David Bouchier (1983, 48) observes, "With hindsight it is possible to see the various protests of the 1960s as one protean social movement for greater human freedom." But this was freedom in a *romantic liberal*, or *expressivist*, register. Hence why "the biggest revolution in Western societies during the 1960s involved a redrawing of the boundaries between public and private" (McLeod 2007, 67). Within the counter-culture and associated movements, the traditionalist expectation to submit and obey familial and social customs, the rationalist focus on disinterest-edness, legalism, and scientific calculation, and the utilitarian focus on the narrow pursuit of one's economic self-interest were all rejected in favour of finding and expressing one's individuality. Roof (1993, 63) sums things up: "there was more to the sixties than politics or drugs, there was also freedom. Freedom from the old conformity. Freedom to break out of social structures that impoverish or exploit. Freedom to be yourself." Indeed, the 1960s gave life to what Taylor (1991) calls the "culture of authenticity" that we in the liberal democratic West inhabit today.

Sociologist Robert Wuthnow (1976) once referred to this era as the "Consciousness Reformation," as he interpreted the counter-culture as an attempt to upend the traditional categories of Western thought. But I would argue counter-cultural youth were simply reinterpreting Western ideals. As Campbell (2007, 224) notes, youth activists shared a "deep respect for individual human dignity, autonomy, and self-determination." The counter-culture combined this liberal reverence for individual freedom with a romantic critique of modernity.

Furthermore, while secularization theorists tend to conceive of the 1960s as unusually irreligious, there is an alternative interpretation available. Sydney Ahlstrom (1980, 511) argues that the 1960s ushered in "another Great Awakening." And Doug Rossinow (1998, 12) similarly argues, "the search for authenticity that infused American radicalism generally in the 1960s had a notable spiritual aspect." Indeed, while the rising authority of a romantic liberal social imaginary may have spelt trouble for traditional church Christianity, it simultan-eously privileged other religious forms. This becomes evident when we examine the quintessential religious expression of the counter-culture—the New Age Movement.

The New Age Attack on Traditional Biblical Religion

Although New Agers may have given the impression that they had no predecessors, it is indisputable that they were reviving the romantic thesis of disenchantment. As Taylor (2007, 510) writes, "much of the spirituality we call 'New Age' is informed by a humanism which is inspired by the Romantic critique of the modern disciplined, instrumental agent." Indeed, New Age thought harmonized fluently with the romantic liberal imaginary animating wider developments in society (Heelas 2008, 30).

The New Age, and the counter-culture more generally, took aim at Christianity principally, or what Bellah et al. (1985) call the tradition of biblical religion, for they perceived it as the chief bulwark of moral traditionalism. One axis upon which New Agers targeted biblical religion was its conception of "original sin." They rejected the Christian doctrine of human depravity, in favour of a romantic conception of human benevolence (Woodhead 1993). Additionally, New Agers challenged the Calvinist notion of a distant and wholly transcendent God, instead championing an immanent conception of the divine, often equated with "Nature."

Increasing the New Age movement's appeal were the responses to the counter-culture by the Christian churches. These took one of two forms. The first was reactionary. In his 1968 encyclical *Humanae Vitae*, Pope Paul VI denounced the use of birth control, while the bulk of Protestant churches fought to "drive back the forces of sexual liberalization" (Brown 2007, 412). Responses like these solidified the counter-cultural association between "being religious" and being "part of the [conservative] establishment" in the minds of baby boomers (Brown 2010, 475). The other response was reformist. In light of counter-cultural critiques liberal theologians, like those associated with the Death of God movement, began to rail against their own tradition (see Hollinger 2011). In turn, criticism of the church and institutions more generally, a rejection of legalism, and suspicion of any kind of claim to respectability became features of mainstream theology in the 1960s (Putnam and Campbell 2010, 95). The theological radicalism preached from the pulpit tended to alienate the more conservative laity while failing to attract the younger generation. As a result, the 1960s gave rise to "the eclipse of the Protestant establishment" (Ahlstrom 1970, 10). Hence why Brown (2009) and McLeod (2007) both trace the decline of Christendom to this period.

The Charismatic Movements and the Spirit of Romanticism

Yet some forms of Christianity not only survived but flourished. They did so by adapting to the new cultural climate, by acknowledging and catering to the sweeping "demand for immediate, powerful, and deep religious experience" (Bellah 1976, 340). Steve Bruce (2011, 14) highlights the striking degree of affinity between the counter-culture and the neo-Pentecostal and Charismatic movements of the time (see also Walker 1997; Coleman 2000). Likewise, Roof (1993, 75) observes, "The evangelical and charismatic revivals of the 1970s and 1980s served to infuse new experiential meanings into old images." As we've seen, despite its theistic commitments (and Charismatics' claims to the contrary) Charismatic Christianity is significantly romantic—concerned, as it is, with "[e]xperiencing the love of God" above all else (Lee et al. 2013, 27). It is therefore no exaggeration to call what occurred in the wake of the 1960s a religious revolution, one that impacted both those outside and within the churches. As romantic expressivist ideals and attitudes spread throughout both the cultural and religious spheres, infiltrating mass media, fashion, publicity and advertising, the entertainment industry, and even the household, Western liberal democracies were changed "in immeasurable ways" (Campbell 2007, 238).

Of course, this isn't to suggest that the New Age and Charismatic movements, as respective carriers of the religion of the heart, were, or are, identical. On the contrary, while they might have both been infused with expressive individualism, they were often opposed politically. This is because the sixties also witnessed the emergence of the infamous "culture wars" (Hunter 1991). Thus, while Charismatics in the 1980s may have adopted much of the expressivist language of the counter-culture, they nevertheless remained theologically conservative (McLeod 2007, 137). Andrew Walker (1997, 30) clarifies: "The 1960s was a revolution of experience—sexual and chemical—and in some quarters this revolution was seen as counter-cultural. The Charismatic movement in the churches reflected the idealism, the heightened experience, and the hedonism of this counter-culture even though ideologically they were opposed to each other." Indeed, in the wake of the sixties, Charismatics were able to reconfigure the religion of the heart towards theological and political conservatism, thereby hiding the degree to which they had accommodated to the counter-cultural ethos (Shibley 1998).

The Environmental Movement and the Church of Nature

The religion of the heart has long served to animate environmentalist aspirations and ideals. For instance, in romantic fashion, Emerson preached to his fellows that they were alienated from the natural world, and should therefore "seek mystical union with the Divine in the woods" (Stoll 2015, 41). Moreover, his Transcendentalism inspired a panoply of early American environmentalists: notably, architect Frank Lloyd Wright who "worshipped in the church of Nature," along with conservationist John Muir, "the patron saint of the Era of Ecology" (126, 175). In fact, by the mid-twentieth century, historian Mark Stoll informs us, Transcendentalism had become "environmentalism's effective spiritual reed" (115).

As Rossinow (1998, 279) remarks in his history of the New Left, many in the counter-culture revived the Emersonian ideal of "a harmony between humans and the rest of nature and a belief in a spirit-life that connected all living things." This was even true, to an extent, of Rachel Carson, whose *Silent Spring* catalysed the modern environmental movement. Though Carson was a committed natural scientist, she did not shy away from praising "the spiritual value of nature" (Stoll 2015, 197). Of course, the environmental movement was far from homogeneous; there were no doubt deeply anti-humanist strands to it. But as Campbell (2007, 86) notes, many environmentalists saw their cause in romantic terms—as premised upon the need for humans to reconnect with nature in order to realize their true selves. For example, Norwegian philosopher Arne Næss (1989, 8), the pioneer of the Deep Ecology movement, rooted his ecological movement in the quest for "self-realization."

Stoll's religious history of the American environmental movement identifies a striking trend: many environmentalists followed in the footsteps of Wright, who travelled "a religious journey away from orthodoxy toward a spiritual (and not merely scientific) relationship to nature" (Stoll 2015, 158). This trend hit full stride in the 1960s. Sociologist Courtney Bender (2007) writes, "some parts of the environmental movement and alternative health movement claimed a 'spirituality' that was counter to organized religion's non-organic, non-holistic, materialist foundations, and urged an alternative, countercultural spirituality." Indeed, as we saw above, many progressives in the sixties rejected wholesale the Christianity of their youth in lieu of a more extra-theistic conception of the religion of the heart. It's fair to say, then, that the expressivism of the counter-culture developed in such a way that it generally supported progressive causes—environmentalism becoming something of a signature issue (Höllinger 2004, 2017).

But its reach extended much further than this. The crystallization and spread of a romantic liberal social imaginary played no small part in inspiring the second-wave feminist, gay liberation, and multiculturalism movements—all of which pitted themselves discursively against the establishment (of which the Christian church was deemed a primary representative). In this way, the romanticism of the 1960s gave life to a romantic liberal imaginary that both inspired and shaped the rights revolution of the late twentieth century.

The Romantic Liberal Legal Revolution

A vast array of legal developments accompanied these cultural-cum-religious changes, amounting to no less than a "revolution in legal culture" (Friedman 1990, 178). As Robert Putnam and David Campbell (2010) remark, the 1950s were characterized by an, although tenuous, considerable moral traditionalism (82). Indeed, the "1950s was a deeply old-fashioned era," writes historian Callum

Brown (2009, 6), "so old that it has often been described as the last Victorian decade." The Second World War left Westerners craving security and stability, and this was reflected in legal-political institutions. For instance, in the 1950s it *not u* *prod.* was commonly accepted that nation-states could legally enforce moral behaviour. *of ty,* Most countries had obscenity laws, which severely restricted representations of sex *1950?* in public media of any kind, and some even had blasphemy laws. Homosexuality was illegal in many states, and contraception wasn't widely available.

Although no doubt a generalization, I think it fair to suggest that prior to the sixties, Western nation-states interpreted the distinction between private and public according to an *authoritative ethic*, rooted in a conservative interpretation of biblical religion. According to sociologist Steven Tipton (2002, 21), an authoritative ethic "presupposes a set of social roles and relations that feature superordinate and subordinate members, whether parent and child, officer and soldier, foreman and laborer, or rulers and subject." From within this ethical style, moral action demands submission to tradition, irrespective of the individual's inner desires, as an authoritative ethic "places a much higher value on self-control and discipline, on traditional values, and on the norms of the group" (Friedman 1990, 2). As a result, in the 1950s an intense moral scrutiny pervaded in private life at the same time as states felt it appropriate to enforce moral behaviour. McLeod writes,

Race

> In the 1950s, concepts of decency and discretion ensured that much that was normal in private was excluded from the public sphere, and some forms of behaviour which were regarded as abnormal, but were nonetheless known to be widespread, were surrounded with secrecy and taboo. At the same time, the state penetrated the private sphere in order to punish these widespread, yet morally unacceptable and seldom openly discussed practices, including most notably homosexuality and abortion. Attacks on religion and open expressions of religious doubt lay on a borderline. On the one hand the Western world had a long and widely known history of religious scepticism going back to the seventeenth century; on the other hand the idea continued to be widely accepted that in a Christian country it was bad manners to air one's religious doubts publicly, and that at the very least the convictions of what were assumed to be the believing majority should be treated with respect. There was also a suspicion that those who openly attacked religion were likely to be political subversives or crazed fanatics.   (McLeod 2007, 67)

But, as McLeod notes, in the 1960s all of this began to change. As a result of the counter-culture and the great swelling up of romantic liberalism across the West, taboos were broken, laws revised, norms upended, and longstanding traditions done away with. This was fundamentally a *moral* shift; what occurred was no less than a generation-wide rejection of moral traditionalism—informed by nineteenth-century Christianity—which pervaded in the 1950s, in lieu of a full-throated romantic expressivism (Franck 1999; Fukuyama 2018). And as a result of this cultural shift, the years between 1959 and 1969 marked what McLeod (2007, 218) calls a "legislative revolution." He outlines the range of legal changes instituted within the UK during this period:

> The beginning was the Obscene Publications Act of 1959, which protected works of literary or scientific merit from prosecution for obscenity. Restrictions on gambling were relaxed in 1960 and on drinking in 1961. Attempted suicide was decriminalized in 1961. The death penalty for murder was suspended in 1965 and abolished in 1969. The year 1967 saw the decriminalization of male homosexuality and a major extension of the legally permitted grounds for abortion, and also for the first time contraceptives were made available to unmarried couples through the National Health Service. In 1968 theatre censorship was abolished. And in 1969 the divorce law was liberalized... (McLeod 2007, 218)

Similar changes occurred across nearly all liberal democracies (Fawcett 2014, 366–7). What took place during this period was no less than a radical process of liberalization. That is, these legal reforms were justified in virtue of extending the sphere of individual freedom. But as I have stressed, this was freedom understood in a romantic expressivist sense, which challenged the presumption that the state could dictate how individuals ought to lead their private (personal) lives.

Obscenity, censorship, and blasphemy laws, from a romantic liberal perspective, infringe on the space of private life. The criminalization of attempted suicide and homosexuality is a violation of an individual's right to act on their desires, however much others may disapprove—as is the criminalization of divorce. Recall, for romantic liberals, one's private life is a sphere where the state has no right to intrude, a view powerfully captured by Canadian prime minister Pierre Elliot Trudeau's 1967 pronouncement: "There's no place for the state in the bedrooms of the nation." But perhaps more than any other legal change, it was the legalization of abortion that most reflected this new romantic understanding of freedom. *Roe v. Wade* struck down the anti-abortion statutes in the US on the basis that they violated the *right to privacy*; it was now accepted that the state had no right to interfere with a woman's right to choose what to do with her own body. This relied on a reinterpretation of the fundamental dividing line between the private and public. In other words, these reforms were only possible because, as Brown (2009, 196) reminds us, "the 'personal' changed so much in the 1960s."

Feminism and the Religion of the Heart

This is also true of the women's liberation movement, which political theorist Martha Nussbaum (1997, 89) argues was fundamentally *liberal* in character.

Although this movement was of course not politically homogeneous, as many members championed various forms of neo-Marxism and political radicalism, with hindsight it is clear the liberal wing won out. As Rossinow (1998, 332) puts it, "the feminist left of the early 1970s made its most lasting political contribution to political liberalism."[8] It did this by challenging, in romantic liberal fashion, the traditional drawing of the boundaries between public and private (McLeod 2007, 67).

Again, this relied on the very same conception of freedom that lies at the core of the religion of the heart: the notion that freedom means *freedom to be oneself as one feels oneself to be*. By claiming, "the personal is political" second-wave feminists challenged the traditionalist assumption that women's place is in the home, and shone a light on the various injustices manifested in the private sphere. And in their quests for personal authenticity, they also sought to topple the systemic barriers that prevented women from achieving equal concern and respect in the public sphere.

This is apparent in the writing of Betty Friedan, whose *The Feminine Mystique* effectively launched the second wave of feminism. Friedan argued that middle-class women were suffering due to the hegemony of what she called the "mystique of feminine fulfillment," which narrowly prescribed for women the role of housewife-mother (1963, 14). Drawing on the humanistic psychology of Rogers and Maslow, she maintained that what made the feminine mystique so insidious was that it prevented the modern woman from "realizing her true nature" (303). Friedan wrote, "our culture does not permit women to accept or gratify their basic need to grow and fulfill their potentialities as human beings" (69). For feminists like Friedan, then, the moral traditionalism that was rampant in the suburbs of 1950s America was a political problem because it was stifling the self-realization of half the population. Theirs was a "politics of authenticity" (Berman 1970), which resonated deeply with the romanticism of New Agers.

Notably, the feminist attraction to the religion of the heart has longstanding roots, as nineteenth-century movements such as Spiritualism, Devotionalism, Christian Science, and New Thought allowed women "greater participation and recognition than was available in mainline Protestant denominations" (Gross 1996, 35; Tumber 2002). Yet it wasn't until the 1960s that the alliance between the religion of the heart and feminism reached its apex. What made this possible were the wider social and institutional changes that occurred during this period. Between 1964 and 1972 the Civil Rights Act, the Equal Rights Amendment, and the Equal Employment Opportunity Act were passed in the US, each of which

---

[8] Indeed, this is also true of the civil rights movement, the New Age movement, the environmental movement, the gay liberation movement, and nearly all of the other social movements that emerged around this period. While they certainly contained elements that were hostile to liberalism, even in its romantic form, liberal democracies found ways to accommodate them. In short, these movements successfully *reformed* the liberal political order, they did not revolutionize it.

served to advance the struggle for equal rights for women and other disenfranchised identity groups. Of course, these amendments were not passed without a struggle, but as Peter Clecak (1983, 183) notes, what matters is that they were "ratified in the court of public opinion." These legal changes led to a drastic increase in the number of women enrolling in higher education, holding positions of authority in society, and running for public office, not to mention increased public attention devoted to "women's issues" such as unequal employment opportunities, earnings discrimination, and inequitable divisions of household responsibility. Moreover, as the legal order was remade to reflect a romantic liberal social imaginary, feminine ideals were similarly recrafted (Brown 2009, 176). And while young women increasingly rejected the traditionalist conceptions of piety championed in the churches, they simultaneously searched elsewhere for a viable religious alternative. In time, "the spirituality of the New Age emerged in the late twentieth century...as a new site of ideal femininity" (415).

The Sexual Revolution and Romantic Expressivism

One of the most significant legacies of the 1960s is the sexual revolution it set off. This was supported by a range of technological innovations and social changes—contraception, the automobile, television, women entering the workforce en masse (Illouz 1997, 57)—but the dramatic shift in sexual norms couldn't have occurred without a widespread acceptance of romantic expressivism. Indeed, the sexual revolution was fundamentally about challenging the status of deviance so long attributed to those who diverged from traditional biblical sexual morality. It had many facets, but a core component was the movement for gay liberation, which challenged the norms of heterosexual propriety that had been taken for granted only years before. Although some gay liberationists framed their struggle in Marxist terms, most celebrated Mill's romantic liberal notion of "experiments in living." They channelled the romantic attack on "straight" society, decisively rejecting both the "[b]iblical threats of hell-fire" as well as the claim that homosexuality is an illness. For these activists, "a person should not struggle against desires and inclinations, she should not squash patterns of behavior which represent the core of her being, her actual self that demands fulfillment" (Friedman 1990, 156). Indeed, McLeod remarks that gay liberationists "wanted to talk openly and without inhibitions about sex, and to affirm not only the joys of sex, but the advantages of multiple partners" (2007, 184). Gay activists challenged traditionalist assumptions about the meaning of marriage, championing instead romantic notions of self-fulfilment and free love, ultimately leading to the legalization of same-sex marriage in a host of Western nations (Macedo 2015).

Of course, the sexual revolution was not merely about the fight for gay rights and freedoms. At its most basic, it targeted the boundary between private and public, thereby extending the legacy of the Women's liberation movement. Brown (2011, 191) explains, "It challenged the acceptance in the late 1950s that the state had the right to supervise, if not regulate, sexual behaviour." In this way, the sexual revolution was similarly predicated upon a politics of authenticity, demanding "radically liberal social reforms" in order to enable "individuals to express their authentic personalities" (Berman 1970, 221). That is, the sexual revolution was fundamentally romantic liberal in nature, concerned as much with individual self-expression as political empowerment.

Multiculturalism and the (Expressivist) Politics of Recognition

What political theorists call the "politics of recognition" partakes of romantic expressivism as well. Feminists and gay activists sought (and continue to seek) public recognition of their identities, aspiring not only to a legal system but also a public culture, that offers their true selves equal respect and concern. This is a fundamental tenet of our romantic liberal imaginary, and it helps to illuminate another political development that is a by-product of the romantic liberal uprising: multiculturalism.

Drawing on Hegel, Charles Taylor (1992) argues multiculturalism emerges from the human need to receive recognition of one's identity by others. In a similar vein, Francis Fukuyama (1992, 135) argues it is ultimately the struggle for recognition that serves as "the primary motor of human history." Whether or not Fukuyama is right about this, it is difficult to make sense of the dramatic changes in public policy regarding national identity, citizenship, and immigration across Western nations since the 1960s without reference to the demand for equal recognition by previously disenfranchised identity groups.

Writing of the ethnic revivals of the twentieth century, which spurred the spread of multicultural policies across the globe, beginning with Canada's adoption of an official policy of multiculturalism in 1971, Kymlicka (1995, 67, 19) argues "the ethnic revival is essentially a matter of self-identity and self-expression" and "accommodating ethnic and national differences is only part of a larger struggle to make a more tolerant and inclusive democracy." In other words, according to Kymlicka (2007, 20), "multiculturalism should be seen as an intrinsic part of a larger process of liberalization and democratization." These processes were propelled, he argues, by the human rights revolution—of which the civil rights, women's and gay liberation movements are exemplars—that challenged the ethnic, gender, and sexual hierarchies entrenched, since their inception, in the primary institutions of Western liberal democracies (88).

One might argue that the delegitimation of these various social hierarchies belongs to a distinct social process—what we might call an *equality revolution*—altogether separate from the spread of a romantic liberal imaginary. While it might be true that increasing social and political equality and the widespread acceptance of romantic expressivism need not, and indeed have not, always coincided, I would argue these processes were deeply interdependent in the West during the 1960s.

Prior to the 1950s, liberal democracies granted far more freedom to some (able-bodied white Christian males) than others (non-Christians, women, blacks, indigenous peoples, the disabled, and other minority groups). Thus, we might say liberal democracies of this period betrayed their own ideals, as they failed to treat their citizens equally. What allowed this, among other things, was the moral traditionalism and authoritative ethic regnant in these societies; not only did this ethic demand deference to authority but it also stringently enforced ascriptive statuses and social roles, which privileged WASP culture and its presumptive representatives. Accordingly, the moral traditionalism and associated social norms of the 1950s coded those identity groups that conformed to the narrow cultural ideals of the period as more "civil" than others and therefore more worthy of public recognition and political power (Alexander 2006). This helps to explain why the rise of a romantic liberal imaginary helped to propel the equality revolution.

First, by attacking the authoritative ethic and the institutions that supported it, the counter-culture both loosened the grip of WASP culture on people's consciousness, as well as multiplied the number of respectable, as opposed to feckless, cultural options. As Clecak (1983, 218) observes, "the concept of normality was widened to encompass difference—racial and physical differences, differences in gender, mental and emotional differences, and differences in preferred ways of living." Second, as a result of the widespread acceptance of a romantic expressivist conception of freedom, individuals became less defined by ascriptive social roles than by their inner lives. Thus, a shift in conceptions of freedom entailed a transformation in prevailing ideas of personhood and citizenship, which enabled a radical expansion in conceptions of *who is owed freedom*. Once again, Clecak captures the process aptly: "Instead of being ignored or going unnoticed, discrimination on grounds of membership in every arbitrary or cultural category was called to public attention. It was scrutinized, protested, and actively lobbied against in the political, bureaucratic, and judicial arenas" (186). Clecak therefore concludes, "when taken together, the various categories of dissenting minorities add up to a clear majority of Americans who worked to widen and deepen the rights of persons in these decades" (187). In turn, while we might be able to distinguish the equality revolution from the spread of a romantic expressivist conception of freedom, in actuality, the two processes were deeply interconnected.

The 1960s and Its Aftermath

Just as New Agers challenged traditional assumptions regarding how one ought to worship or connect with the sacred, so too did environmentalists challenge traditional conceptions of the natural world, feminists challenge traditional conceptions of what it means to be a woman, and gay activists challenge traditional conceptions of acceptable sexuality. Of course, speaking in these terms belies my primary point: that these were not entirely separate or distinct movements, but rather *different aspects of the same romantic liberal revolt.* Indeed, what too few have acknowledged (and thus what I have emphasized) is that many of the moral, social, and political developments birthed in the 1960s were animated by a distinctly romantic liberal social imaginary, which presupposes a romantic expressivist conception of the human condition, and thereby interprets liberal principles and institutions through a romantic lens.

Of course, that countless people today fail to acknowledge this should not surprise us. Many who came of age during this period did not conceive of themselves as invoking and championing a common social imaginary. Given their romantic predilections, they tended to understand themselves as standing alone, challenging the pervading traditions, institutions, and norms, on the basis of pure heart-felt conviction—free of precedents and political debts. In their own eyes, they were not spokespeople for a new tradition, so much as celebrants of a post-tradition era. But as we have seen, this self-understanding denies social reality.

*   *   *

What of today? Are these historical developments still relevant to us, fifty years on? No doubt it would be mistaken to reduce the personality of twenty-first-century liberal democracies to the transformations wrought during the 1960s. Much has occurred in the last half-century that hasn't been accounted for. And yet I believe it is difficult to overstate the degree to which we in twenty-first-century liberal democracies are living in a world produced by the 1960s and its aftermath. We can find support for this by examining our primary and secondary institutions, as I do in Chapter 6. Or we can simply survey the generation that came of age in its wake. In carrying out the latter we find that millennials are, to a striking extent, carrying forward the cultural legacy of their parents—the counter-cultural baby boomers. Ideals and norms that were once considered radical or fringe in the heyday of the counter-culture are largely taken for granted by today's young adults. This explains why, for instance, millennials are the most "socially progressive" (or romantic liberal) than any generation in history (Greenberg and Weber 2008; Winograd and Hais 2011). And it also illuminates why "spirituality" is more popular among the young (Houtman and Mascini 2002, 464; Heelas and Woodhead 2005, 110; Alper 2015). In turn, whether one likes it or not, the romantic liberal social imaginary birthed in the 1960s lives on, in both tangible and intangible respects—it permeates our institutional spheres, our social structures, our political aspirations, and, as we have seen, our religious landscape. This is why I call the social order we in post-1960s liberal democracies inhabit *romantic liberal modernity.*

Conclusion

My genealogy in this chapter has largely remained at the level of philosophical ideas. I have said little of the institutional dynamics that precipitated this mass romantic liberal revolt. We might therefore ask: what enabled an entire generation to adopt the romantic critique of society? And how did their proposed solution—to reconcile romanticism with liberal institutions—create the social conditions conducive to the flourishing of the religion of the heart? In the following chapter I offer a thoroughly institutionalist analysis of the 1960s, which re-narrates the historical account outlined above from a macro-sociological perspective. In so doing, I illuminate what occurred during this period at an institutional level, and how the developments set off in the 1960s produced the institutional conditions many of us in the early twenty-first century largely take for granted.

5
The Making of Romantic Liberal Modernity

In the last chapter I offered a genealogy of the rise of romantic liberalism. I argued that many of the major moral, social, and political upheavals of the 1960s were animated by, and served to crystallize, the romantic liberal social imaginary which legitimates the social order of twenty-first-century liberal democracies. This imaginary, however, did not emerge out of thin air, nor was it universally supported. As Mary Douglas (1986, 8) reminds us, "thinking depends on institutions." Indeed, while meaning systems require individuals for their propagation and reproduction, they ultimately depend on, and find their origins in, social institutions.

But what is an institution? In *The Good Society* Bellah and his co-authors (1991, 40) define institutions as "patterns of social activity that give shape to collective and individual experience." Thus, institutions are both constraining and enabling—they "form individuals by making possible or impossible certain ways of behaving and relating to others." Moreover, institutions come in many different shapes and sizes—from a handshake, to a marriage contract, to a market exchange. Yet, even the most idiosyncratic social institutions tend to belong to one or another wider *institutional sphere*—collections of institutions which share a set of what Bellah et al. call "normative patterns" (1991, 288). Indeed, it is for this reason that sociologists speak of modern liberal society as an "interinstitutional system," comprised of multiple institutional spheres whose varying moral and symbolic logics order our everyday experience and social interactions—often without our even being aware of their doing so (Friedland and Alford 1991, 232).

I believe if we are to make sociological sense of the making of romantic liberal modernity, we first need to understand how the counter-culture and its associated movements—conceived as a collection of secondary institutions that were underwritten by an expressive ethic and the moral tradition of expressive individualism—challenged and reformed the central institutional spheres of Western liberal democracies. So, in this chapter I retell the story I narrated in the preceding chapter, but from a perspective which is attuned to the fact that modern societies are institutionally—and thereby morally—differentiated. This approach not only affords a more sociologically sensitive understanding of what happened during and in the wake of the 1960s, but also sheds light on why the religion of the heart is so well adapted to romantic liberal modernity.

The Spiritual Turn: The Religion of the Heart and the Making of Romantic Liberal Modernity. Galen Watts, Oxford University Press. © Galen Watts 2022. DOI: 10.1093/oso/9780192859839.003.0006

Institutional Differentiation and Moral Diversity

Recall from Chapter 1 that the core thesis of the secularization paradigm is one of *institutional differentiation*. According to Durkheim ([1893] 2014), it is precisely this process—the result of the division of labour—that demarcates modernity as a distinctive period. Moreover, as sociologist Steven Tipton (2002, 31) notes, Durkheim considered it an essential sociological task to determine "how the division of labor in modern society carries over into the division of moral understanding in modern culture." Following this line of inquiry, cultural sociologists hold that with differentiation, modern individuals inhabit multiple institutional spheres wherein a specific moral tradition, ethical style, and organizational structure reigns supreme.[1]

For instance, in the marketplace, individuals are generally conceived as rational consumers and producers engaged in free exchanges; in a court of law, they are generally conceived as agents imbued with certain inalienable rights, and expected to abide by the rules of rational deliberation; and in the family, they are generally conceived as unique individuals holding special relationships of affection to one another, whose mutual obligations stem primarily from fellow feeling.

Importantly, there exists a relatively symbiotic relationship between particular moral traditions and the organizational structures in which they are embedded. That is, each moral tradition "relies on a given social institution's structural arrangements, practices, and relationships to frame the moral activity and character it articulates" (Tipton 2002, 21). Indeed, it is this mutualistic relationship that makes it such that our experience of a particular institutional context tends to reaffirm the plausibility of the moral tradition and ethical style inscribed therein.

This is not to say that individuals are wholly determined by institutions; individuals can and often do resist institutional imperatives. So, the examples I offered above shouldn't be viewed as set in stone. Indeed, while a specific moral tradition, ethical style, and organizational template might reign supreme in a given institutional sphere, they are never uncontested. Why is this? For one, the logic of institutions is, by their very nature, "imperial" (Tipton 2002, 33). That is, the nature of institutional differentiation is such that, as Tipton puts it, "the individual attempts to take the ethical outlook predominant in one sector of social life (whichever he is involved in and identified with) and to generalize it to the whole" (Tipton 1982, 279). Thus, *inter*-institutional conflict is constant and inevitable. For another, in resisting one institution's moral logics, one is, wittingly or not, drawing on another—as it is institutions that ultimately provide us with "a sense of self" (Friedland and Alford 1991, 243). Moreover, *within* institutional spheres there are always those who seek to replace the reigning moral tradition

---

[1] My discussion of moral differentiation owes much to Steven Tipton (see especially Tipton 1982, 2002).

why Moral?

with those of a competing institutional context, thereby making *intra*-institutional conflict equally endemic to modern social life.

We can therefore conclude that institutional change is ultimately the result of moral clashes both *between* and *within* institutional spheres. These conflicts sometimes lead to the wholesale replacement of one moral tradition with another, and at other times produce "moral hybrids"—whereby seemingly contradictory meaning systems, ethical styles, and organizational structures are combined (Tipton 2002, 33). Roger Friedland and Robert Alford (1991, 254) explain, "Individuals, groups, and organizations struggle to change social relations both within and between institutions. As they do so, they produce new truths, new models by which to understand themselves and their societies, as well as new forms of behavior and material practices." This insight remains critical for making sense of what occurred during, and in the wake of, the 1960s.

The Counter-Culture as Expressive Institution

It is a sociological axiom that life in modern society is scattered across institutional fields. But differentiation produced by the division of labour has led many to speak of modern life as fragmented and alienating. This criticism has had diverse spokespeople. Weber echoed it when he famously described modernity as an "iron cage."[2] And Marx similarly decried the forms of alienation experienced in capitalist modernity. But ever since Rousseau this has been especially the cry of those who espouse a romantic expressivist conception of the human condition. These individuals have sensed in modernity a lack of wholeness, an inability to express their spontaneous impulses, and an inner fragmentation which mirrors that which exists in the structures of society. They have also sensed inside of themselves a false self, derived from society, and a true self, derived from God or Nature. Of course, as we saw in the last chapter, this self-understanding is precisely what spurred the 1960s counter-culture. The youthful romantics of the era lamented the disenchantment of the world—that is, the loss of mystery, the fragmentation of everyday life, and a nagging sense of meaninglessness—and they sought, in imperialist fashion, to remake the world in their image.

An institutionalist perspective urges that the power of this cultural criticism was, in fact, dependent upon a whole array of secondary institutions which emerged in and around this era: the demonstrations, sit-ins, rallies, protests, and marches, the music festivals (the birth of Rock 'n' Roll and the icons it supplied),

---

[2] A more accurate translation of Weber would be "steel shell" (see Baehr 2001).

the new academic disciplines, consumer culture, and more. With these, new vernacular ("groovy," "free love," "far out") emerged, new modes of interacting, everyday rituals, and communal forms were cemented, and new identities made possible. Additionally, books and artwork produced by the Beat poets, New Age authors, and "tenured radicals" revived the romantic critique of modernity, adapting it to fit the cultural sensibilities of a new generation. While media outlets like *Rolling Stone*, *Ramparts*, and *The Village Voice* "played important roles in defining the counter-culture and propagating its spirit and its ideas" (Kimball 2000, 227)—for instance, by giving a global platform to the counter-culture's charismatic leaders (e.g., the Beatles, Janice Joplin, Jimi Hendrix, etc.).

Each of these expressive secondary institutions served to inscribe and naturalize the moral tradition of *expressive individualism*, and an attendant *expressivist ethic*. According to Tipton, expressive institutions privilege "intuitive, affective knowledge" (2002, 29). "[T]he expressive style of ethical evaluation is mainly oriented toward the agent's feelings, the feelings of others around him, and to the particular situation in which they find themselves, as discerned by intuition. An act is right because 'it feels right,' most simply, or because it expresses the inner integrity of the agent and is most appropriate to the situation" (Tipton 1982, 16). Moreover, an expressivist ethic presupposes as its ideal organizational structure couples in love, or circles of brethren joined in intimacy, engaging in transparent communication about their emotions and inner states. It should be evident, then—however much it conflicts with the anti-institutional self-conception of the counter-culturalists themselves—that the moral uproar born in this period was only made possible by the formation of these myriad expressive institutions. That is, they offered a social base from which the counter-culture could contest the moral traditions, ethics, and organizational structures that reigned in competing institutional spheres.

Moral Conflict across Institutional Spheres

Below, I examine the way, during the 1960s, counter-culturalists mobilized an expressivist attack upon the moral traditions regnant in rival institutional spheres, consolidating the crystallization of a romantic liberal imaginary, and reconstituting the religious sphere of liberal democracies in the process. Conceiving of institutions as normative patterns of social activity, which become embedded in specific material contexts, serves to shed light on how the counter-culturalists challenged, with varying degrees of success, the moral vocabularies and ethical styles inscribed in the economic sphere, the legal-political sphere, and the private sphere of 1950s society. Indeed, while the counter-culture ultimately failed to remake society in its image, it nonetheless significantly transformed the institutional structures of liberal democracies.

The Expressivist Challenge to the Economic
Sphere's Utilitarian Ethic

One of the central institutional spheres in modernity is the capitalist market, or the economic sphere. Within this institutional field a moral tradition of *utilitarian individualism* is normalized. This is not to be confused with the philosophical tradition, utilitarianism. Rather, utilitarian individualism dates back to the writings of Hobbes and Locke, who regard the individual as "the sole proprietor of his own person and his capacities or skills." On this view, human actions "are essentially understood as utilities or means toward the satisficing of egoistic ends" (Cortois 2019, 23). Moreover, within the economic sphere a *utilitarian ethic* and attendant organizational structure—which presuppose a market economy and link "free, equal, and self-interested individuals through exchange and contract, whether as buyers and sellers or investors and entrepreneurs" (Tipton 2002, 26)—are naturalized. That is, within the economic sphere individuals are conceived (and lauded) as *homo economicus*, or what C. B. Macpherson (1962) famously called "possessive individualists"—bent on maximizing their utility as efficiently as possible.

In the 1960s, romantic youth railed against the utilitarian ethic endemic to the market, which they argued encouraged a life of shallow selfishness, and neglected the deeper dimensions of human life. This was evident, for instance, in the counter-cultural celebration of bohemian and alternative lifestyles, living off the land, and Timothy Leary's famous motto, "turn on, tune in, drop out." As Tipton (1982, 19) puts it, "the counterculture challenged utilitarian culture at the most fundamental level. It asked what in life possessed intrinsic value, and to what ends ought we act. Do ever more money and power add up to life's meaning, or do they obscure it?" Indeed, counter-culturalists sought to pollute the life of rational calculation, tarring it with terms such as "straight," "bourgeois," and "the Man." In romantic fashion, they mounted a direct challenge to the materialism and egoism they saw as inherent to the worlds of business, industry, and work.

Yet despite this attack upon the utilitarian ethic of the marketplace, history evinces that the expressive individualism of the counter-culture ultimately failed to overthrow it. For utilitarian individualism remains firmly anchored within the economic sphere of society, and has arguably expanded its influence since the 1960s as a result of the neoliberal economic policies enacted around the globe in the 1980s. Nevertheless, this is not to say the counter-cultural attack had no impact. Indeed, in the aftermath of the 1960s, the economic sphere—on both the production and consumption sides—has institutionalized something of a *moral hybrid*. As I explain in the next chapter, the counter-culture's confrontation with the utilitarian ethic of the market ultimately produced what scholars call "new" or "soft" capitalism (see Boltanski and Chiapello 2005; De Keere 2014), which combines, unevenly, the vocabularies of expressive and utilitarian individualism. In the wake of the 1960s, the economic sphere was permanently transformed.

The Expressivist Challenge to the Legal-Political Sphere's Rationalist and Authoritative Ethics

Another central institutional sphere in modern liberal democratic societies is that of the state, or what I call the legal-political sphere. Within this sphere, *moral individualism* is the reigning moral tradition—the language of rational liberalism *par excellence*. Moral individualism emphasizes the moral equality of all persons, and the obligation to never treat others as mere means. It stresses our capacities for free will, rational deliberation, and moral regulation. And as sociologist Liza Cortois (2019, 28) points out, "Since the Declaration of Independence (1776) and the Declaration of the Rights of Man and Citizens (1789), moral individualism has acquired . . . a direct juridical translation."

Prior to the 1960s, the moral individualism naturalized in the legal-political sphere of liberal democracies primarily privileged a *rationalist ethic* (although not comprehensively, as I discuss below). This ethic privileges "reason-giving debate and rational virtue" and "requires schooling in systematic knowledge" (Tipton 2002, 24). Moreover, a rationalist ethic presumes "the organizational structures of assemblies for disciplinary discussion and hierarchies of expertise" as well as "application of reasoned conclusions in policy and practice" (24). In short, moral individualism demands rule-following, self-discipline, and institutionalizes impersonality, impartiality and predictability.

Not surprisingly, the expressive individualism of the counter-culture and its sibling movements like those for women's and gay liberation led its proponents to target the overly rationalized impersonality they alleged pervaded public and civic life in the 1950s; that is, they attacked the rationalist ethic that sponsored most modern legal and political institutions. Counter-culturalists and 1960s activists argued that abstract rules and regulations, insensitive to personalities, relationships, and circumstances, stifle individuality and alienate the "head" from the "heart." They also challenged the universalism presupposed by moral individualism, which emphasizes our rational faculties as opposed to our need for authentic self-expression. In short, they channelled the romantic critique of rational liberalism, charging modern bureaucratic life with repressing the subjective and the emotional.

With hindsight, we can see the hardcore romantics of the 1960s failed in their task of overthrowing the moral individualism underlying the liberal political order. As Cortois observes, moral individualism, in its rationalist mode, continues to pervade in a variety of institutional fields including higher education (especially science departments), law (especially in legislative and judicial functions), and governance (state bureaucracy). In fact, moral individualism has emerged in the twenty-first century as something of a "globalized culture" that finds institutional supports and protections in international organizations such as the UN, European Union, and the International Committee of the Red Cross. And as cultural sociologist Jeffrey Alexander (2006a) demonstrates, the tradition of moral individualism remains firmly entrenched in what he calls the "Civil Sphere" of democratic societies (albeit discursively framed differently across national contexts).

But the moral individualism inscribed in the legal-political sphere of the 1950s was not limited to a rationalist mode. On the contrary, numerous laws were interpreted through the lens of an *authoritative ethic*, which, as we saw in the previous chapter, endorses the virtue of obedience, as well as presupposes "organizations structured by chains of command, in which those above issue orders and those below obey them" (Tipton 2002, 21). And recall, this ethic classifies individuals according to "ascriptive statuses and highly role-specific commands" that "separate and rank persons by age, sex, and seniority" (22, 23). For this reason, while liberal democratic states in the 1950s naturalized the tradition of moral individualism in their constitutions and charters they nevertheless assumed it right and just to deny certain classes of persons the full scope of liberal freedoms, while enforcing moral behaviour. Thus one cannot make sense of the panoply of legal reforms which occurred during and in the wake of the 1960s—regarding both the public life issues of political and social inclusion of previously disenfranchised groups, and the private life issues of public obscenity, homosexuality, divorce, abortion, gambling, drinking, blasphemy, and more—without reference to the institutional transformations engendered by the legal-political sphere's encounter with the expressive institutions of the counter-culture. In other words, from an institutionalist perspective, the romantic liberal legal revolution was ultimately the result of a clash between the counter-culture's expressivism and the authoritative ethic privileged in various corners of the 1950s legal-political sphere.

As we learned in the last chapter, this clash ultimately led to "a variety of legislative measures, executive orders, and legal decisions" which "enhanced the rights of persons to due process, to access to decisions affecting them, and to personal privacy" (Clecak 1983, 187). Moreover, this revolution was principally fuelled by a *reformulation of the value of individual liberty*; that is, justifications offered for liberal legal and political institutions and principles were, in many instances, recast to reflect a romantic expressivist understanding. Thus, writing in the 90s, Lawrence Friedman (1990, 36) remarked, "The central concepts of modern legal culture are choice, consent, freedom, and individual rights. These are old terms, but what they mean in the 1980s is startlingly different from what they meant to Jefferson or Locke." Indeed, it is just as likely today for rights discourses and legal principles to be framed and interpreted by judges and jurists within an expressivist register, which stresses the obstacles to authentic self-expression, as that of a rationalist one, which focuses on the intrinsic and equal worth of all human beings (Gustavsson 2014).

Furthermore, as liberal democratic governments embraced a more romantic expressivist conception of freedom in their interpretation of moral individualism, they have become more sensitive to, and affirmative of, the politics of recognition and authenticity. Increasingly, Western states have publicly acknowledged the historical plight of minority groups, offering various forms of accommodation, recognition, and representation in order to ensure their individual members receive equal recognition and respect in the public sphere, and equal opportunities to realize their true selves in the private sphere. That is, in the wake of the romantic liberal revolt, liberal governments have frequently admitted the need for, in addition to the standard civil and political rights for individuals, group-specific rights and public policies, as a means of securing the expressive freedom of individual members of both historically disenfranchised and disadvantaged identity groups and national minorities (Kymlicka 2007). Indeed, this is a defining feature of romantic liberal modernity.

The Expressivist Challenge to the Private Sphere's Authoritative Ethic

The private/public distinction is central to the liberal tradition. It is also, not coincidentally, central to the fact of institutional differentiation. By "private sphere" I refer to the institutional sphere that is imperfectly captured by the concept of civil society—symbolically independent of the economic and legal-political spheres, at least in principle.[3] It includes the realms of the family, voluntary associations, and religious organizations. Importantly, this does not mean the private sphere is asocial or free of a shared symbolic order or moral tradition. By no means. As Mark Cladis (2003, 18) explains, "The private...does not occur outside of social conventions, but occupies a set of conventions that constitute a somewhat distinctive realm."

I argued in the last chapter that the private sphere in the 1950s was governed by a pervasive and entrenched moral traditionalism. Although the institutional fields of the family, popular culture, and religion institutionalized distinct discourses, and while there certainly existed deviant social institutions, an authoritative ethic largely reigned supreme in private life. This meant that, within the private sphere, social roles were strictly ascribed and enforced across and within institutional contexts, and there existed comparatively little room for personal choice or self-

---

[3] Although I recognize the economic sphere is often referred to colloquially as the "private sector," my conception of the private sphere largely excludes the world of the market.

expression, as the symbolic order privileged the good of the community, not the individual. Friedman (1990, 27) sums things up aptly: "It was a God-fearing, hard-working, disciplined, traditional self, as far as private life was concerned."

While counter-culturalists may have railed against the egoism of the market-place, and the overly rationalized nature of civic and public life, their chief goal was to challenge the authoritative ethic and attendant moral traditionalism that informed the private sphere prior to the 1960s. They did this by spotlighting and scrutinizing the myriad ways in which private life in the 1950s was repressive, alienating, conformist, backwards, patriarchal, unjust, and ultimately unfree. Of course, the changes did not take place overnight. But, in time, the romantic expressivist assault successfully, and profoundly, transformed the private sphere, replacing an authoritative ethic with an expressivist one. Moreover, this was a change that occurred "from below," thereby spurring changes "from above"—the reforms that occurred in the legal-political sphere, associated with the romantic liberal legal revolution, were ultimately responses to the moral transformations taking place in the private sphere (Friedman 1990, 35).

This naturally held massive implications for the religious sphere. Sociologist Rhys Williams (2007, 48) informs us, "Religious language and meanings become entwined with culturally approved ways of thinking, acting, and being. Religion helps legitimate cultural forms and, in turn, becomes a legitimate mode of expression within a culture." Indeed, the close associations and affinities in the 1950s between the moral tradition of biblical religion and the authoritative ethic that governed private life meant religious organizations were placed under intense scrutiny by counter-culturalists. As a result, many 1960s romantics considered "religion" utterly antithetical to their commitment to expressive individualism. Interestingly, it did not matter whether some religious denominations and spokes-people allied themselves with the counter-culture, engaging in both critical self-reflection and political activism. There was sufficient religious opposition to the upheavals of the period that "religion" became a polluted term in expressive social contexts. This is why we cannot make sense of the religious sphere of romantic liberal modernity without accounting for the wider romantic liberal revolt.

Secularization theorists contend that the 1960s exacerbated the decline of religion. But armed with a broader conception of religion this story becomes suspect. Rather, what took place was a _reconstitution_ of the religious sphere itself. Prior to the sixties the religious sphere was comprised primarily of those groups that explicitly labelled themselves "religious" (e.g., churches, synagogues, temples, etc.) But in the wake of the 1960s, as expressive individualism rose to become the primary moral tradition of the private sphere, this no longer held true.

Alongside the various expressive institutions associated with the broader counter-culture, the New Age and Human Potential movements—its religious wings—produced their own social institutions: conferences, communes, retreats, research centres, not to mention best-selling books and magazines. These served to contest the tradition of biblical religion and its privileged authoritative ethic, granting increased authority and legitimacy to the expressivist religion of the heart. And in the process, these movements served not only to *reconfigure* the religious sphere of liberal democracies but to *expand* it as well, bringing into its jurisdiction social institutions, organizations, and groups that did not themselves explicitly identify as "religious."

This was made possible by the distinctive character of the religion of the heart, which enables its adherents to locate God or the superempirical potentially anywhere—in both "religious" and "secular" settings—and which affords religious bricolage of dizzying proportions. No doubt, the Charismatic Christian revivals of this period breathed new life into the congregational domain, creatively combining the language of biblical religion with an expressivist ethic. But the fact is much of the religious activity subsequent to the 1960s has taken place *outside* of the churches. Thus, what occurred in the wake of the 1960s was a *contraction* of the old religious sphere (as church religion declined), and its *expansion* into novel territory (as the religion of the heart spread)—and this was ultimately the result of the counter-culture's successful transformation of the private sphere.

The Religion of the Heart in Romantic Liberal Modernity

As a result of the counter-culture's romantic expressivist challenge to the economic, legal-political, and most importantly, the private sphere, the institutional dynamics of liberal democracies were fundamentally altered. Moreover, what began in the 1960s has only intensified and expanded.

In what follows I sum up the key ways these institutional changes have gradually produced an array of conditions conducive to the spread of the religion of the heart. These fall into four categories: moral, political, epistemological, and economic. My argument is that the religion of the heart, since the 1960s, has served as a dominant framework of religious meaning for romantic liberals, and that this is because the very institutional reforms that brought about the decline of Christendom simultaneously created conditions conducive to the flourishing of the religion of the heart.

Moral (Expressive Individualism and the Rights Revolution)

One way of summing up the period of time elapsed since the 1960s is, as Francis Fukuyama (1999, 39) has put it, the "Worldwide Liberal Revolution." In the wake of the Cold War, Fukuyama triumphantly declared "the end of history," prophesying that liberal democracy had emerged victorious in the war of political ideologies (47). Though highly controversial, and in hindsight premature,

Fukuyama was describing a real phenomenon. In the wake of the 1960s, what occurred was no less than a liberal democratic revolution, which took a distinctive shape in the West—which I have characterized as the rise of romantic liberalism. As we have seen, the replacement of an authoritative ethic with an expressivist one in the private sphere threw into doubt the interpretation of biblical religion which, in many instances, served to legitimate the former. This was primarily a moral shift, but one that was crucial for eroding the authority of "religion" for many sixties youth (Hout and Fischer 2014, 433).

But more than this, the rise of romantic liberalism expanded the legal-political sphere to incorporate a wide range of previously disenfranchised identities, and transformed the boundaries of the private and public in order to enable these individuals more expressive freedom and self-determination. This rights revolution, Michael Ignatieff writes, "took off in the 1960s in all industrialized countries, and it is still running its course. Just think for a minute about how much rights talk there is out there: women's rights, rights of gays and lesbians, aboriginal rights, children's rights, language rights, and constitutional rights" (2007, 1). And noting the degree to which the rights revolution was propelled by a romantic liberal social imaginary, Clecak (1983, 185) remarks, "During these years prevailing ideas of personhood changed, largely as a consequence of political and cultural dissent launched in the sixties. A neo-Romantic concept of the essential equality of persons spread through many regions of society." Similarly, Rosenblum (1987) notes, "Many of liberalism's elements remain—individualism, liberty, tolerance— but they are apprehended in a fresh way, and valued for new reasons. They no longer rest on a defense of rational liberty, but on satisfying romantic longings" (123–4). As a result of this shift, we can speak confidently of the degree to which a romantic liberal "rights-consciousness" has become "embedded in our cultures in the Atlantic world" (Taylor 2007, 486).

The rights revolution made it such that the religion of the heart—which is, in effect, a religious expressive individualism—would be considered a viable religious alternative, especially among romantic liberals. For one, the religion of the heart, in romantic liberal fashion, sacralizes individual liberty, and authorizes a self-ethic. As a result, it places a premium on the values of tolerance, self-expression, and self-realization. This makes it especially well adapted to the hyper-diverse character of liberal democracies—especially in urban areas. Political scientist Ronald Inglehart (1977) has spoken of a value shift in Western societies from "materialism" to "postmaterialism," which he traces back to the 1960s. Of course, this shift is not universal, but rather has a distinct class character. Expressive individualism—and therefore the religion of the heart—is predominant among the middle classes, and, as I discuss in the next chapter, finds support in some institutional fields more than others. However, given that the middle class reflects the "part of society that dominates its culture and defines the moral aspirations of the rest" (Madsen 2002, 109), the popularity of expressive individualism among this cohort is not insignificant. Thus, remarking on the success of the religion of the heart in the twenty-first-century West, Anneke van Otterloo et al. (2012, 247) write, "It is this new cultural climate—in which individual liberty had become more and conformity to external authority less important—that damaged the meaning-providing potential of Christianity and made people susceptible to... 'inner spirituality'." Furthermore, an expressivist ethic is central to what Paul Heelas and Linda Woodhead (2005, 81) call "subjective wellbeing culture," the "most widespread cultural expression" in the liberal democratic West. In a word, the religion of the heart flourishes in romantic liberal modernity because "there are many features of our civilization that foster it" (Campbell 1978, 152).

Political (Romantic Liberalization and Privatization)

The secularization paradigm holds that with institutional differentiation and the shift to modernity, the religious sphere becomes one "sub-system of society" among others (Dobbelaere 1984). Following this line of thought, I have argued the religious sphere in modernity belongs primarily (although not entirely) to the private sphere, or the realm of civil society. Thus, I agree with secularization theorists that religion no longer serves to legitimate the entire social order since, as we have seen, distinct moral traditions and ethical styles govern different institutional spheres. Of course, this isn't to suggest that religion can no longer serve important social functions. But it does mean that the scope of religious authority in modernity is reduced (Fenn 1972; Chaves 1994).

Here we are once again presented with the close relationship between the liberal distinction between private and public and the fact of institutional differentiation. Religion belongs to the private sphere—is "privatized"—insofar as it does not receive explicit legitimation in the primary institutional spheres of society (e.g., the economic or legal-political spheres). Of course, not all religious groups accept this privatized status. José Casanova (1994) has charted the emergence of various religious movements that seek to contest the structural boundaries separating institutional spheres in modernity, as well as the liberal tradition that legitimates them. Indeed, it is useful to keep this in mind when considering the elective affinity between romantic liberalism and the religion of the heart.

Romantic liberalism offers romantic justifications for liberal principles and institutions. That is, romantic liberals seek to protect individuals from the potential despotism of custom and convention, allowing them to engage in their own religious quests, or to find and express their true selves. They do so primarily by reformulating the value of individual liberty, and recasting the private/public settlement. Because romantic liberals acknowledge the romantic yearnings of citizens to express their true selves, however they understand this, they conceive of the private sphere (and therefore the religious sphere) as a site of romantic expressivist self-discovery. On this view, the private sphere is the personal sphere, referring to the space within which one ought to have the freedom to examine and express oneself in whatever way one chooses, so long as one does not infringe on another's right to do so. At the same time, for romantic liberals, religious convictions must remain confined to the private sphere, so as to prevent unresolvable conflicts within the public sphere. This division is predicated on a desire for institutional/moral equilibrium: romantic liberals view the private sphere as a necessary antidote to the disciplinary character of civic or public life, and the egoistic character of life in the market. While modern individuals may find their public lives stifled by formal legalism, bureaucracy, and the demand for disciplined impartiality, or their economic lives filled with egoistic competition and instrumental rationality, both of which impede their creative impulses, they are afforded a private space within which to realize their true selves. Or, put in more institutionalist terms: romantic liberals believe the moral individualism naturalized in the legal-political sphere, and the utilitarian individualism naturalized in the economic sphere, needs to be counterbalanced by an expressive individualism in private life.

Casanova (1994, 58) distinguishes between "public civil religions" and "private domestic cults." The religion of the heart is the latter—an essentially *private religion*. By this I mean that adherents of the religion of the heart do not seek to contest its privatized nature: they accept the romantic liberal private/public settlement, and agree that religion ought to be "consigned to the private sphere—the sphere of the voluntary group, the family, or the individual" (Cladis 2003, xxxi). Linda Woodhead (2013, 47–8) makes this clear when she suggests that "spirituality" "has a particularly strong tie to personal life," understood as the "sphere of intimate relationships," and that its "thrust lies in its emotional, moral and motivational aspects rather than in its orientation to a set of concrete political goals." Indeed, the religion of the heart does not orient its adherents, as public civil religions do, to politically mobilize against rival religious or secular movements, nor to institutionalize a political party. Rather, the religion of the heart aims to enchant private life, to emancipate the spirit from the arid legalism and secular rationality of modern life, and liberate the individual from whatever its adherents perceive to be an impediment to realizing their true selves—be it oppressive moral traditions, social expectations, or civic duties.

The elective affinities between romantic liberalism and the religion of the heart should now be apparent: romantic liberalism offers philosophical justification for what is central to the religion of the heart—self-realization and the enchantment of private (or personal) life. Additionally, romantic liberals propose a private/public settlement that harmonizes well with the effectively private character and ambitions of the religion of the heart. And finally, romantic liberal modernity, understood as a social order, provides the religion of the heart with vital legal protections and substantial institutional support (as I demonstrate in the following chapter).

Epistemological (Pluralism and Subjectivization)

The shift to romantic liberal modernity produced not only religious pluralism but pluralism of manifold kinds. For instance, immigration policies enacted in the 1970s began to dramatically increase the number of foreign-born residents and citizens in liberal democracies (Williams 2007, 44). As a result, most Western nations are today multicultural and ethnically pluralistic to historically unprecedented degrees (Kymlicka 2007). These demographic changes dovetailed with the counter-cultural demand for recognition, thereby animating official multicultural policies that endorsed forms of integration more sensitive to immigrants' cultural identities, as opposed to a strict accommodationism. It is therefore largely due to the shift from rational to romantic liberalism that, as sociologist Peter Beyer (2013, 5) puts it, "Concepts like diversity, pluralism, multiculturalism, accommodation, integration, tolerance, and inclusion have ... become constants in Canadian public debates and official policy." Of course, this also remains true of most other liberal democracies (Franck 1999). Furthermore, increased cultural and ethnic pluralism has, in tandem with a widespread acceptance of the romantic liberal ideals of tolerance and self-expression, led to more inter-faith and mixed-race marriages, making cultural hybridity more and more the norm rather than the exception (Livingston and Brown 2017). In short, the 1960s kicked off dual processes of romantic liberalization and mass migration that have given new meaning to the fact of pluralism.

I've already noted how the high value placed on tolerance by the religion of the heart makes it well adapted to life in post-1960s liberal democracies. As Colin Campbell (1978, 154) puts it, "The increasingly pluralistic character of modern society, with its many and diverse ethnic and cultural groups has made the acceptance of toleration a necessary feature of social and political life." But the fact of pluralism becomes especially relevant in light of the claim, advanced by secularization theorists, that pluralism leads to religious decline. Recall from Chapter 1 that Peter Berger once argued modernity pluralizes institutions and plausibility structures, forcing religious worldviews to compete with one another, thereby engendering religious decline. Similarly, Taylor (2007, 718) speaks of how the late modern world "fragilizes" belief systems inasmuch as it relativizes them. However, these perspectives presuppose a religion with a rationalist or doctrinal epistemology. By contrast, there are good sociological reasons to think that experiential epistemology, central to the religion of the heart, is well suited to the extreme pluralism of romantic liberal modernity.

Ironically, Berger provides us with the theoretical framework to make sense of this, for he observed that in pluralizing institutions and plausibility structures modernity simultaneously forces individuals to look *within* for epistemic authority: "modernization and subjectivization are cognate processes" (Berger 1979, 20). Moreover, due to its experiential epistemology, the religion of the heart is less susceptible to rational or sceptical critique than those religious forms that espouse rationalist or doctrinal epistemologies. In fact, Campbell (1978, 152) has even suggested that this religious tradition rides on the back of humanist and secular criticisms of established religion, turning such attacks "to its own advantage." In agreement, cultural sociologists Dick Houtman and Stef Aupers (2010, 11) argue that widespread attraction to "spirituality" reflects a "psychological adaptation to a massively rationalized world."

This helps to explain why the religion of the heart is most popular among the highly educated, or those most familiar with the rationalist ethic and empiricist cultures that pervade in academic institutional contexts. That is, the pluralism and rationalism characteristic of romantic liberal modernity may well be conducive to the experiential epistemology at the core of the religion of the heart, which locates the grounds of truth within personal experience.

Economic (Neoliberalization)

Of course, none of the above was possible without the policies of global economic liberalization established over the past half-century; and in speaking of these changes, we need not restrict our focus to the liberal democratic West. As Fukuyama has observed, while political liberalism may not have found much traction (in the sense of being enshrined in legal and political institutions) beyond the West, economic liberalism—in the form of market institutions, or capitalism—certainly has. When he wrote of the "larger pattern that is emerging in world history," Fukuyama had in mind the spread of capitalist institutions across the globe (1999, 45). Moreover, it is reasonable to think that the moral, social, and political changes outlined above would not have occurred without these sweeping economic reforms. For instance, Ignatieff (2007, 92) observes that the rights revolution was "the product of the most sustained period of affluence in the history of the developed world." Similarly, it was this rise in affluence that fuelled increased migration (McLeod 2007, 119). And all of this occurred only because technological innovations made possible by industry produced new modes of telecommunication, transportation, and commercial exchange that set in motion what we today call globalization. Indeed, more than anything else, it is capitalism that has "connected" the nations of the world, creating the sense (certainly not felt by everyone) that we live in a "global village." Furthermore, these processes were profoundly amplified with the move towards increased economic liberalization and privatization in the 1980s, spearheaded by Thatcher in the UK and Reagan in the US—which many today refer to as neoliberalism.

From an institutionalist perspective, neoliberalism reflects the *imperialism of the moral tradition and ethical style of the economic sphere*—utilitarian individu-alism is adopted and applied by neoliberal actors without regard for institutional boundaries or competing moral traditions. In other words, neoliberal policies seek to remake the world in the image of the market: they dissolve barriers to trade between nations, and give unprecedented freedom to corporations, while at the same time rolling back the social and economic protections—rooted in the tradition of moral individualism—afforded by the welfare state. It should therefore come as no surprise that neoliberal policies, truly global in their scale and impact, have produced a twenty-first century that is characterized by fundamental polarities and asymmetries. For instance, while the world economy has grown exponentially since the 1980s, the distributions of wealth both across and within nations are radically uneven (Picketty 2017). Neoliberalism has produced a few big economic winners and a lot of big economic losers (Stiglitz 2015). Lastly, in giving new meaning to Joseph Schumpeter's ([1942] 2008) phrase, "creative destruction," neoliberal policies have sped up the rate of social change and technological innovation, leading to severe disruption of individuals' lives both in the developed and developing worlds. As a result, re-skilling, part-time contract work, and economic precarity have become the norm for a growing portion of the world's population.

A critical question is to what degree the religion of the heart can be understood as an ally of neoliberalism. I leave it until Part III to answer this question. But what cannot be denied is that, since the 1980s, they have been historically linked to one another.

Conclusion

In light of its affinities with the moral tradition of expressive individualism and an expressivist ethic (aligned with both the counter-culture and the rights revolutions), its privatized nature (prescribed by romantic liberalism), its experiential epistemology (adaptable to pluralism), and the way it invests private life with cosmic meaning, I call the religion of the heart *the spirit of romantic liberal modernity*. And if my argument is correct, while the religion of the heart may not legitimate the *entire* social order, it nevertheless serves a critical social function. For unlike radical romanticism, today's religion of the heart does not seek to disrupt or alter the basic structures of the romantic liberal order, nor does it incite revolutionary impulses. Rather, by enabling the romantic liberal to locate herself within a horizon of ultimate meaning, whilst circumscribing her expressivist ambitions to the private sphere, the religion of the heart ensures the stability and survival of romantic liberal modernity.

Still, it remains to be explained how and where the religion of the heart finds institutional support in the twenty-first century. I argued above that as the counter-cultural attack successfully transformed the private sphere in the 1960s, so too was the religious sphere reconstituted. The changes have taken time, but half a century later the outcome is clear. What originated as relatively marginal expressive institutions in time blossomed into extensive institutional fields and networks, whose impacts have been seismic and sweeping. Indeed, in the twenty-first century the term "counter-culture" is a misnomer, as the moral tradition of expressive individualism has risen to become the *lingua franca* of not only the private sphere but also a number of primary institutions. As a result, there exists an extensive institutional order in post-1960s liberal democracies that lends support, in both direct and indirect ways, to the religion of the heart. I call this the *romantic liberal institutional order*, and I argue that it constitutes the religious sphere of romantic liberal modernity. Much like the New Age, Human Potential, and Charismatic movements did in the 1960s, these various institutional fields serve as plausibility structures for today's religion of the heart. That is, they make possible the re-enchantment of the world, not by removing the fragmentary and alienating dimensions of modern life, but by offering those with romantic needs an outlet for them.

6

Mapping the Romantic Liberal
Institutional Order

> [W]hat we think of as spiritual is actively produced within medical,
> religious, and arts institutions, among others. It is not unorganized or
> disorganized, but rather organized in different ways, within and
> adjacent to a variety of religious and secular institutional fields that
> inflect and shape various spiritual practices.
>
> (Bender 2010, 23)

The 1960s set off a series of moral, social, and political upheavals which fundamentally altered the social order of liberal democracies. As a result, the religious
sphere of today is not what it once was. No longer is religion isolated to the
congregational domain—that is, the panoply of organizations and groups
(Christian and otherwise) which self-identify as "religious." With the naturalization of expressive individualism and an expressivist ethic into an array of secondary and primary institutions, the religion of the heart today receives direct and
indirect institutional support in both "religious" and "secular" institutional fields.

In this chapter I shift my focus from the recent past to the present. I draw from
the existing literature on "spirituality," as well as my own empirical research, in
order to map the romantic liberal institutional order—that is, the seven institutional fields that collectively constitute the religious sphere of romantic liberal
modernity. These comprise: (1) the holistic milieu, (2) the Charismatic wing of the
congregational domain, (3) popular culture and entertainment media institutions,
(4) arts institutions, (5) healthcare institutions, (6) educational institutions, and
(7) certain dimensions of the economic sphere. Collectively, these secondary and
primary institutions give life to the religion of the heart, serving as plausibility
structures as well as sites of socialization.[1]

After charting the nature of this institutional order, I then outline the social
pathways by which individuals in romantic liberal modernity become socialized to

---

[1] I am not suggesting these institutional fields are inherently religious. I recognize that there are
many who actively participate in these institutional contexts yet do not subscribe to the religion of the
heart (or any other religion, for that matter). My point is simply that, given the expressivist ethic
inscribed in each of these fields, they are *capable* of functioning as plausibility structures for the religion
of the heart. In turn, my analysis in this chapter is best thought of as concerned with the supply side of
today's religious sphere.

The Spiritual Turn: The Religion of the Heart and the Making of Romantic Liberal Modernity. Galen Watts,
Oxford University Press. © Galen Watts 2022. DOI: 10.1093/oso/9780192859839.003.0007

espouse the religion of the heart. I have argued that the religion of the heart can be thought of as the religion of preference among romantic liberals. Yet it goes without saying that not all romantic liberals are "spiritual"—that is, not all endorse or subscribe to this cultural structure in one form or another. Why, then, do romantic liberals embrace the religion of the heart when, in fact, they do? And what do these social pathways look like? I believe the answers to these questions illuminate much about the nature of life in romantic liberal modernity.

The Holistic Milieu

While some commentators contend the religious ferment of the 1960s fizzled out by the 1980s, the reality is rather different. Although it took decades to come to fruition, the counter-culture and its religious wings eventually gave birth to a vast associational territory, which comprises a range of services and activities where the language of expressive individualism and an expressivist ethic is naturalized, and where "spiritual" discourses are pervasive. In *The Spiritual Revolution* Paul Heelas and Linda Woodhead (2005, 13) call this network of secondary institutions the "holistic milieu," and it includes: yoga studios, meditation groups, silent retreats, Twelve Step meetings, aromatherapy and acupuncture clinics, wellness workshops, and life-coaching seminars, among other spaces where subjective life is catered to explicitly. It also comprises the "mind, body, spirit" sections in bookstores, along with the countless newspaper articles, magazines, online blogs, and social media pages that discuss "spirituality." Historian Matthew Hedstrom (2012) contends that book culture has been pivotal to the spread of "spirituality" since the nineteenth century. This trend has far from abated. Indeed, nearly all of my SBNR informants had participated in the holistic milieu—either by means of engaging in one or more of these activities, or reading relevant literatures (or both).

Organizationally, the holistic milieu holds clear resemblances to what Colin Campbell ([1972] 2002, 15) once called the "cultic milieu," which he argued in the 1970s was becoming ever more important for understanding the character of religion in the West. Campbell described the cultic milieu as the "cultural under-ground of society," which is kept alive "by the magazines, periodicals, books, pamphlets, lectures, demonstrations and informal meetings through which its beliefs and practices are discussed and disseminated." He also contended that because of its inclusive and open nature, "individuals who 'enter' the cultic milieu at any one point frequently travel rapidly through a wide variety of movements and beliefs and by so doing constitute yet another unifying force." Campbell was well aware of the implications the romantic liberal revolt would have for the religious sphere of modern societies, and so presciently predicted that it would eventually come to resemble ever more the cultic milieu. A wealth of recent scholarship on "spirituality" makes clear that he was right (see Partridge 2004; Heelas and Woodhead 2005; Houtman and Aupers 2010; Watts 2018).

The Charismatic Wing of the Congregational Domain

While the SBNR moniker might be most prevalent in the holistic milieu, it would be mistaken to think the religion of the heart is confined to this institutional site. This cultural structure is, in fact, institutionalized across an array of institutional fields. Now, each of these fields sponsors a distinct discursive iteration, not to mention embeds it within its own set of norms, practices, and rituals. But this should not distract us from noting the cultural similarities across these various institutional contexts, allowing them to serve as plausibility structures for "spirituality."

For instance, we find the religion of the heart in a Charismatic Christian form in the congregational domain, the holistic milieu's competing associational territory. Of course, secularization theorists measure religious trends according to the degree to which the congregational domain diminishes in membership and moral authority, and for this reason diagnose modernity as corrosive of religion. Yet, while the congregational domain has certainly suffered setbacks in recent years, certain pockets of it are booming. These are those religious denominations which belong to, or share affinities with, the Charismatic movement: notably, Pentecostalism, neo-Pentecostalism, and prosperity theology. In fact, Matthew Lee et al. (2013, 34) found that one out of every four (27 percent) Americans identifies as Pentecostal or Charismatic Christians, leading them to conclude that we've seen nothing less than the "pentecostalization of Christianity" in recent years. So, while much of the congregational domain remains hostile to the religion of the heart, this religious form has nevertheless found traction among Christians like Amy Kim via the Charismatic movement. Indeed, since the 1960s, as expressive individualism has risen to become the primary moral tradition of private life, Charismatic Christianity has flourished. In fact, I believe the holistic milieu and the Charismatic wings of the congregational domain are the *primary sites of socialization* as regards the religion of the heart.

Popular Culture and Entertainment Media Institutions

Lynn Schofield Clark (2007, 9) remarks, "popular culture expresses the zeitgeist of an era, speaking to deep-seated beliefs that are consistent with what we believe are the best qualities of our collective society." Similarly, Gordon Lynch (2012, 89) argues, "In late modern societies, public media are the primary institutional structure through which forms of the sacred are experienced, reproduced, and contested." Only recently have scholars begun to pay attention to the ways popular culture and entertainment media institutions serve as sites of religious socialization. This is most odd given the seminal role music and popular culture played in giving voice to the expressive individualism of the 1960s counter-culture—not to mention the way New Age discourse was embraced by celebrities of the time. Picking up on these insights, Anneke van Otterloo et al. (2012, 254) ask, "Could it be ... that precisely the powerful modern institutions of market and media now play major roles in socializing young people into this type of spirituality, or at least priming them for it?" Indeed, it can. The religion of the heart in its various forms is often disseminated today via popular films, television, video games, and music. For instance, many Disney films naturalize expressive individualism, depicting traditionalism as backward, and valorizing the nonconformist misfit (Watts 2018). Moreover, as a number of scholars have shown, "spiritual" themes can be found in a wide variety of popular films, television shows, and video games (Shimazono 1999; Partridge 2004; Houtman and Aupers 2010; Erb 2014; Kaler 2018). And talk of "spirituality," "personal growth," and "self-development" has become a staple of therapeutic daytime talk shows, like those of Dr. Phil or Oprah Winfrey (Travis 2007, Lofton 2011). Finally, romantic expressivism remains central to popular music today (Watts 2018). Thus, Giles Beck and Gordon Lynch (2009, 352) conclude, "the most fruitful places to look for the cultural transmission of alternative spiritual identities and ideologies among younger adults is popular culture."

Arts Institutions

Romantics have always considered the arts to be one of the primary channels by which one connects with the divine or the superempirical. Thus, in the sixties it was commonplace for New Agers to champion the religious significance of art. This explains why, according to a large portion of my informants, the arts are the most "spiritual" of professions. Based on her research with SBNR "metaphysicals" in the US, Courtney Bender (2010, 38) observes, "almost all took for granted the self-evident link between spirituality, inspiration, and artistic, creative experience." For these heirs to the romantics, art is the means by which one both discovers one's true self and expresses it. Through creating music, literature, or fine art, one gives external form to the uniqueness that lies within.

In *Creative Spirituality: The Way of the Artist* Wuthnow notes, "Artistic expressions of spirituality correspond especially well with this current interest in the experiential aspects of spirituality" (2001, 22). Likewise, Altglas (2014) writes in *From Yoga to Kabbalah*, "the artistic milieu represents an ideal of creativity, a personal quest of self, and the transcendence of economic and institutional constraints" (296). Of course, whether or not artists actually transcend these constraints is an open question; but either way, it remains the case that the arts retain a kind of moral purity from a romantic perspective—which is why a substantial portion of my informants were either engaged in artistic practices or aspired to be. The religion of the heart, in all its discursive forms, valorizes the artistic ideal of the creative genius who, in mining their inner depths, creates beautiful works of art, and thereby enchants the world.

Of course, it would be wrong to suggest that all arts institutions are "spiritual" in the sense that they legitimate the religion of the heart equally. Some artistic milieus are more amenable to "spirituality" than others. However, as Bender (2010, 41) observes, "distinctions between spiritual and nonspiritual artists are not always distinct, as 'secular' arts organizations...also include and support artists who evoke spiritual rationales and discourses to explain their endeavors." Thus, as with popular culture, it is very difficult to definitively measure the extent to which a specific arts institution functions as a site of socialization for the religion of the heart because while some artists may conceive of their practice in terms antithetical to its cultural structure, others might be unable to make sense of their practice without it.

Healthcare Institutions

"Healing is, I think, a very very important part of spirituality." This statement, made by one of my SBNR interviewees, lends credence to Taylor's (2007, 507) claim that "the search for spiritual wholeness is often closely related to the search for health." Indeed, across the board my informants affirmed that "spirituality" is inextricably linked to both mental and physical health. As Amanda Porterfield (2001, 195) aptly puts it, "wellness itself has taken on spiritual dimensions."

Prior to the 1960s, the institutional sphere of medicine and healthcare largely presupposed a mind-body dualism (Lynch 1985; McGuire 2008). Counter-culturalists vehemently attacked this paradigm. Instead, they endorsed the holistic assumptions of Complementary and Alternative Medicine (CAM) in one or other of its many forms: homeopathy, hydrotherapy, naturopathy, aromatherapy, osteopathy, biofeedback, and reflexology. While these alternative approaches—each of which bears cultural affinities to the religion of the heart—remained relatively marginal in the 1980s, by the turn of the century a prominent religious studies scholar could confidently declare: "we are now seeing a large-scale reemergence of holistic ideas about health and illness" (Bowman 1999, 183). In fact, the label "alternative medicine" is quite misleading. For, in recent years, CAM has moved from the institutional margins into the primary healthcare institutions (Heelas and Woodhead 2005, 72; Campbell 2007, 97; Heelas 2008, 67). What's more, there is a burgeoning academic literature devoted to incorporating "spirituality" into healthcare contexts. And most intriguing is that CAM is not merely popular among counter-culturalists and their progeny, but finds increasing traction among evangelical Christians (Brown 2014, 61; Yi and Silver 2015, 598).

Of course, not all sectors of healthcare are equally welcoming of "spirituality" (see Grant et al. 2004). In highly rationalized or bureaucratized spaces, with little to no opportunity for human contact or self-expression, the religion of the heart will likely find little institutional support. But with the post-1960s shift to "person-centred" and "caring-focused" medicine has come mounting opportunities for "spirituality" to find traction in healthcare institutions (see Baldacchino 2017). Thus, Heelas and Woodhead (2005) found those involved in the holistic milieu populated healthcare institutions in large numbers: as psychiatric nurses, social workers, nurses, and care workers.

However, the healthcare profession that was said to have the most "spiritual" significance, according to my informants, was psychotherapy. Indeed, nearly all of them saw talk therapy as "spiritual" in nature. Why might this be? Psychotherapy's emphasis on private life and its methodological individualism harmonize well with the religion of the heart, for both presuppose a conception of psychological health that is deeply informed by expressive individualism. Of psychotherapy, Jeffrey Alexander (2013) writes:

> In all these different manifestations, the philosophy is much the same. The instruction is to turn away from external things and authorities and to move inward toward the self, to recognize and take on board the irrational and regressive impulses and beliefs that threaten to engulf the self. It is about providing an experience of private life, of protecting it from the intrusions of the public sphere, of nurturing the self so it can experience fuller and more balanced emotions and become healthy enough, not only to participate in modern disciplines, but to sustain love and friendship. None of this can be done by the community or the state, by money or social movement. Social subjectivity must be nurtured in private spaces that allow individuals to experience themselves and others in an emotional relationship of confrontation, dialogue, and respect.   (145)

As one SBNR interviewee asserted, "I think it is to know yourself. That is the deepest spiritual question."

Educational Institutions

In the 1960s, counter-culturalists took critical aim at the institutional sphere of education—what they disdainfully deemed the "knowledge industry." They argued educational institutions had been colonized by instrumental rationality and a sterile positivism that left no room for emotion, spontaneity, intuition, or mystery, producing docile, unfeeling, and rationalistic subjects. This critique was given systematic treatment by critical theorist Herbert Marcuse in *One-Dimensional Man*—a book that gave voice to the New Left and helped to inspire some of the counter-culture's more radical wings.

Despite this attack, however, the romantic counter-culture was ultimately unsuccessful in fundamentally revolutionizing the educational sphere. As noted in the previous chapter, it remains—especially in the sub-sector of higher education—governed primarily by a rationalist ethic, the very same kind that sponsors the legal-political spheres of modern society. Thus, analytic reasoning, reliance on the natural and social sciences in their positivist modes, and objectivity as an aspirational ideal are given pride of place, as are bureaucratic decision-making procedures that valorize universal rules and regulations. In short, the disciplines of civilized life live on in the sphere of education.

Nevertheless, expressive individualism has made inroads since the sixties, reforming certain sub-sectors of the educational sphere in quite dramatic ways. We can see this, for instance, in the post-1960s shift towards "child-centred learning," which encourages treating every child as a unique individual with special needs, as well as the increase in student autonomy in classrooms (Friedman 1990, 135). We can also see it in the stress placed today on experiential activities within the mainstream educational system (Heelas 2007), as well as in the turn to subjectivity in much postmodern theorizing (see Alexander 1995). Finally, there has been a marked interest in integrating "spirituality" into educational contexts in recent years (e.g., Miller 2000). Hence why Heelas and Woodhead (2005, 93) found that many participants in the holistic milieu had education-related occupations: primary school teacher, college lecturer, art teacher, special needs teacher, adult education, educational therapist, and religious education advisor.

The Economic Sphere: New Forms of Consumption and Changing Conceptions of Work

In the previous chapter I argued that the counter-culturists' moral attack on the economic sphere in the 1960s produced a moral hybrid—an uneven synthesis of utilitarian and expressive moral vocabularies, ethical styles, and organizational structures. This is, of course, one of the great ironies of this period: the romantic critique of capitalism was ultimately subsumed into the very capitalist world it once sought to overcome (Boltanski and Chiapello 2005). We find this moral hybrid most evidently at two sites within the economic sphere.

First, in modes of marketing and consumption. As the 1960s romantics ridiculed the conformity of mass society, marketers adapted their strategies. Dick Houtman et al. (2011, 19) explain, "Marketing gradually gave way to branding, associating products with young, hip, cool, adventurous and non-conformist images and lifestyles. Corporations started challenging consumers to assert their self-dependence and personal authenticity by setting themselves apart from the dull grey masses." They conclude, "Contemporary consumer culture has come to breathe the rebelliousness and non-conformism of the 1960s counter culture." Indeed, in the wake of the sixties, marketing has been increasingly oriented by the romantic values of personal authenticity and self-expression, as opposed to those of efficiency or utility. In fact, the growth of the holistic milieu is itself evidence of this transformation in the economic sphere.

The second site is in changing conceptions of work. With the rise of "soft capitalism" many sectors of business have embraced a vocabulary of expressive individualism that champions "bringing life back to work," "personal growth through work," and "unlocking human potential" (Heelas 2008, 69). This has dovetailed with the emergence of new managerial strategies and techniques, not to mention a whole array of corporate trainings, weekend courses, online lectures, and seminars, which emphasize "empowerment," "creativity," and "leadership" in order to maximize productivity and increase profits (Nadesan 1999, 12). At the same time, there is now a growing business literature—some explicitly "spiritual," some not—which endorses an iteration of the religion of the heart that combines utilitarian and expressivist language (see Bouckaert and Zsolnai 2012; Bregman 2014).

Of course, economics played a key role in spurring this. With the shift to a post-industrial society—dependent upon a service economy, novel information technologies, and entrepreneurship—new skills have become economically valuable. Social theorists Luc Boltanski and Ève Chiapello (2005, 97) list the qualities valorized by what they call the "new spirit of capitalism": "autonomy, spontaneity . . . conviviality, openness to others and novelty, availability, creativity, visionary intuition, sensitivity to differences, listening to lived experience and receptiveness to a whole range of experiences." Not surprisingly, these are precisely the qualities championed by the romantics of the 1960s. As a result of these developments, it has become much harder to distinguish between the economic and private institutional spheres, as the expressivist ethic inscribed in private life has now found an esteemed, if not central, place in professional life.

Yet it would be wrong to think the differences have been erased. While an expressivist ethic has found its way into certain workplaces—chiefly, those in the information technology, creative, and communication industries—much of industry remains firmly committed to opposing ethics—be they rationalist or authoritative. So, just as the religion of the heart finds support in particular sub-sectors of the healthcare and educational institutions and not others, the same applies here. Those sectors of the economic sphere that naturalize a vocabulary of expressive individualism are far more amenable to the religion of the heart than those that do not. As Nancy Ammerman (2014, 180) reminds us, "some jobs are simply more plausible as spiritual narratives than others."

* * *

It should be apparent by now that the religion of the heart is far from lacking institutionalization, as it finds support across a wide array of secondary and primary institutions which collectively constitute the religious sphere of twenty-first-century liberal democracies—what I call the romantic liberal institutional order. Moreover, as expressive individualism—and the religion of the heart, with it—have risen to become the dominant moral and religious traditions institutionalized in romantic liberal modernity, so too has the self-understanding they naturalize. This explains why the polarization of "institutional religion" and "subjective spirituality" has achieved the status of common sense: both expressive individualism and the religion of the heart encourage their adherents to view their true selves as *pre-social* and *independent of society and its traditions*, thereby denying their status *as* traditions.

The great irony, of course, is that this self-understanding is only plausible in a society where these traditions, and the social institutions that support them, are taken for granted—or have become, as Laurence Cooper (2016) puts it, "the air we breathe." Indeed, this would simply not be possible in a social order where the moral tradition of expressive individualism and its attendant expressivist ethic were unknown or received little social support.

Of course, this self-understanding is not exclusive to adherents of the religion of the heart, but is in fact shared by romantic liberals, more generally. Hence why so many today remain adamant that their innermost convictions stem from deep within them, as opposed to flowing out of the shared tradition to which they belong. In turn, we might say just as the 1960s counter-culturalists failed to acknowledge the extent to which the counter-culture itself relied upon a whole collection of social institutions in order to mount an attack upon competing institutional spheres, so too has it become commonplace for both adherents of the religion of the heart and romantic liberals more generally, to deny their social and institutional debts.

What Leads to an Interest in "Spirituality"?

Still, given that not all individuals in romantic liberal modernity take an interest in "spirituality," it warrants asking what distinguishes those who do from those who do not. Though we cannot deduce universal maxims, examining the life histories and interview accounts of my informants reveals clear cultural sociological patterns. That is, exposure to, engagement with, and embrace of "spirituality" follow established social pathways.

In what follows I draw from my interviews with SBNRs and Charismatic Christians in order to outline the nature of these pathways. I argued above that the holistic milieu and the Charismatic wings of the congregational domain serve as the chief sites of socialization as regards the religion of the heart. What this means is that while the five complementary institutional fields remain capable of transmitting the religion of the heart, they nevertheless *depend upon these key associational territories to do so.* That is, their naturalization of expressive individualism, along with an expressivist ethic, enables them to serve as plausibility structures for "spirituality," but due to their marked internal diversity, this function is only made possible by the fact that legitimation is secured elsewhere. It follows that the holistic milieu and the Charismatic wings of the congregational domain constitute the core of the religious sphere in romantic liberal modernity— disseminating and legitimating discourses of "spirituality." Indeed, it is for precisely this reason that among my informants an interest in "spirituality" could always be traced back to an engagement with one or other (or both) of these associational territories.

Social Pathways into the Holistic Milieu

There is no single path into the holistic milieu, but recurrent themes among my SBNR interviewees are what we might call *personal crises* and *problems of meaning.* What I mean is that for almost every one of my SBNR informants, an interest in "spirituality" begins with a story of dissatisfaction or suffering that resulted in them asking one or all of the following questions: "Why is this happening?" "Is this all there is?" and/or "Who am I?"

Of course, almost everyone asks one or more of these questions at some point or another. But in the case of my informants, the poignancy of these questions ultimately led to a kind of crisis. Recall Leslie Parker. Although she was introduced to "spirituality" at a young age as a result of her parents' participation in the holistic milieu, it wasn't until she suffered from a serious addiction—what prompted a tidal wave of existential questioning—that her interest level grew. Similarly, Michael Wallace never thought twice about "spirituality" until he suffered an identity crisis upon entrance into university. In both cases, a personal crisis catalysed a hunger for "spirituality."

For clarity's sake I have classified the types of personal crises—to be understood as ideal types—according to the following two criteria. First, the specific *content* of the crisis (what the crisis is primarily *about*). And second, the *origins* of the crisis (the *conditions* that precipitated it). They are as follows: (1) the need to find meaning in suffering; (2) disenchantment with utilitarian individualism; and (3) struggles with self-identity. I argue (1) is a historical universal, bound up with the human condition, while (2) and (3) are modernity-induced.[2]

---

[2] I thank Dick Houtman for suggesting this typology.

The Need to Find Meaning in Suffering (Historical Universal)

In *On Purpose: How We Create the Meaning of Life*, Paul Froese (2016, 45) writes, "It is modernity that enhances meaninglessness." Indeed, the rationalized, pluralistic, and fragmenting nature of modernity has led many to feel haunted by the spectre of nihilism (see Berger and Luckmann 1995). But it would be wrong to reduce the problem of meaning to the shift to modernity. As Taylor (2007, 680) wisely reminds us, "When we break down the hunger for meaning into more concrete needs, one is for an answer to the problem of suffering and evil." Like Taylor, I believe such a need is a historical universal, not one that only arises in modern conditions. Of course, the need to find meaning in suffering may be more acute in liberal modernity, but it would be wrong to suppose that the need itself can be eradicated by a change in social organization.

Accordingly, the first social pathway by which my SBNR informants found their way into the holistic milieu begins with a personal crisis catalysed by the universal need to find meaning in suffering. For example, in our interview Charlene, 32, described an adolescence plagued by depression. She was in and out of therapist offices, struggling tremendously with the question, "Why me?" She was desperate to know what ultimate purpose her pain served. In high school, a counsellor introduced her to mindfulness meditation and "spirituality." They would sit in his office, meditate, and "talk about life, and what really matters." This was her first introduction to the holistic milieu. Gradually, she got increasingly involved, to the point where she eventually started a business as a reiki practitioner and yoga instructor. As she tells it, the most important lesson she's learned is that her past struggles were not for naught. Rather, they've been instrumental to helping her realize that she is a "healer," whose life's purpose is to "spread compassion and love."

Another illustrative case is offered by Philippa, 24, who when we spoke had recently graduated from law school. Philippa recounted that her interest in "spirituality" sparked when her mother was diagnosed with breast cancer. Although she'd practised yoga since the age of twelve, it was only once her mother fell ill that she began to consider the "spiritual side of it." She movingly described the moral disorientation she experienced once her mother passed—she was angry at the world, but felt immobilized by grief. In response, Philippa continued to practise yoga, and started psychotherapy, where she learned to be "more present, more self-aware, and mindful of my thoughts, feelings, and sensations." In session, she learned to allow herself to be "vulnerable," or "to feel [her] feelings." When asked how "spirituality" entered into this process Philippa responded, "spirituality says to look within yourself to find that there's more."

Lastly, in our interview, Liam, 30, described a traumatic childhood. His parents went through a messy divorce, which caused him to develop a rare and crippling anxiety disorder. As a teenager he struggled with suicidal ideation and engaged in self-harm. Liam was first introduced to "spirituality" in a World's Religions class in high school. He liked Buddhism because it taught, "All life is suffering." "I related to that more than anything else." Still, he didn't pursue it. Liam struggled with substance abuse in his teens. At nineteen, he found himself in a long-term treatment facility, where he got clean and sober. It was there that his interest in "spirituality" was reawakened. Upon his release from rehab Liam joined NLF. When asked to explain his decades-long commitment to "AA spirituality" he replied: "I see a picture bigger than my own pain, or bigger than my own life. 'Cause that's where I get stuck in, that's chronically where I get stuck."

Disenchantment with Utilitarian Individualism (Modernity-Induced)

The second social pathway into the holistic milieu begins with a personal crisis spurred by disenchantment, in one form or another, with utilitarian individualism. In fact, the accounts of my informants echo in a striking manner the romantic charges brought against "straight society" in the sixties.

Consider Charles, 21, an engineering student who was drawn to the holistic milieu after suffering from depression in his third year of university. Charles admitted that, before this, he'd never had an interest in "spirituality." He was too focused on achieving top grades. However, his preoccupation with "being the best at everything" led him to suffer a "mental breakdown." The breakdown compelled Charles to re-evaluate his life, read a number of "spiritual" books, and take up a host of holistic activities (yoga, meditation, psychotherapy). He shared that since his breakdown his outlook on life has changed quite a bit. "People today define 'success' in terms of how many material things they own, how many things they have. The bottom line for most is money and material things. And that's the true problem. They don't have a deeper meaning to their life than that."

Another illustrative case is provided by Samara, 33, an aspiring artist who, upon turning thirty, suffered "a bit of a crisis." She explained that this was spurred by a mounting feeling of burnout, coupled with the realization that, owing to an obsession with advancing her career, she'd failed to attend to her "inner needs." This revelation came to her during an intimate conversation with one of her best friends—herself a yoga instructor. Samara shared that since having this conversation she's reduced her workload, and instead sought to "connect with that inner voice and get in touch with myself." She's done this in order to "really understand what's worth my energy and time." "Because I've given too much attention to my brain—I'm a very cerebral person—I feel I've neglected my heart. And now I feel like I need to listen to that."

Charles and Samara each channel the romantic critique of utilitarian individualism, which holds that life is simply about the dogged "pursuit of one's own material interest" (Bellah et al. 1985, 33). Although their reasons might differ, each became dissatisfied, indeed disenchanted, with utilitarian individualism. And in seeking an alternative, expressive individualism did not suffice—they sought, in addition, a *religious* language through which to articulate their romantic frustrations, and an institutional field wherein they could seek a resolution. They found these, respectively, in the religion of the heart and the holistic milieu.

Struggles with Self-Identity (Modernity-Induced)

The third social pathway begins with a personal crisis that finds its origins in the range of identity troubles caused by late-modern social conditions. One of the consequences of the romantic liberal revolt of the 1960s has been a proliferation of the range of identity options available to individuals, in tandem with a weakening of the structures that once secured stability in people's identities. Neo-modernization scholars speak of this as "the great dis-embedding," which has been endemic to modernity but has rapidly intensified over the last half-century (Beck and Beck-Gernsheim 2002). In fact, Anthony Giddens (1991, 28) goes so far as to suggest, "To live in the 'world' produced by high modernity has the feeling of riding a juggernaut." With increasingly complex institutional differentiation, life in the twenty-first century remains segmented, compartmentalized, and highly diversified. Giddens notes that this can engender moral confusion and existential disorientation (83). These troubles show up especially in the realm of self-identity—leading Berger et al. (1973, 74) to aver, "it should not be a surprise that modern man is afflicted with a *permanent identity crisis.*"

Of course, many in romantic liberal modernity don't experience this. However, there are those for whom this sense of inner fragmentation is severe. In romantic fashion, these individuals sense acutely a conflict or division within themselves. Houtman and Aupers (2007, 309) write, "Robbed of the protective cloak of 'pregiven' or 'self-evident' meaning and identity, the late-modern condition conjures up nagging questions that haunt the late-modern self: 'What is it that I really want?' 'Is this really the sort of life I want to live?' 'What sort of person am I, really?'" We see this play out in the accounts of my informants.

Zamir, 21, said he only became interested in "spirituality" after his girlfriend left him. The break-up seriously shook his sense of self. As Zamir sees it, throughout the relationship he worked tirelessly to change himself in order to meet his partner's expectations. But this shapeshifting ultimately failed—leaving him hurt, confused, and doubtful about whether anyone would like him "for who I really am." In the face of uncertainty and self-doubt, Zamir read a swath of "self-help books with a spiritual side to them." He took from them the following lesson: "If someone doesn't like me for who I am then that's their problem. This is who I am."

Amanda, 26, offers another example. For most of university, Amanda thought little of "spirituality." Instead, her priorities were to "party, socialize, and study." However, in her fourth year she developed severe anxiety. From an early age, she'd assumed she would go to law school. But when the time came to apply, it struck her that she'd never really considered why. This realization set off an anxiety attack—she doubted who she really was, and what she should be doing with her life. To help her cope, her boyfriend gave her a book by New Age author Wayne Dyer. "So basically, when I read that book, I was like, 'This is insane!' But also, 'This doesn't *not* make sense to me.' It made sense. 100 percent." Amanda continued to read "spiritual" literature, as well as seek out conversation partners who shared her budding interests. After consulting a tarot card reader, she eventually decided to ditch her plan to go to law school. Instead, she enrolled in a music production program. When asked why she replied, "If you're going to be an artist you are connecting with the deepest parts of yourself, and expressing them. And self-expression is of the highest order to me right now."

Identity issues are endemic to modern social life, so it should come as no surprise that individuals are drawn to discourses that enable them to construct a stable sense of self. And in imbuing one's inner states with cosmological significance, the religion of the heart offers individuals a degree of certitude otherwise unavailable to them.

Social Pathways into the Charismatic Wing of the Congregational Domain

There exist two ideal-typical social pathways into the Charismatic wing of the congregational domain. The first path follows roughly the same sociological lines as entrance into the holistic milieu—that is, it begins with a *personal crisis* caused by the need to find meaning in suffering, disenchantment with utilitarian individualism, and/or struggles with self-identity. However, the second path—distinctive to the congregational domain—is what I call the *move from traditionalist Christianity to seeker-sensitive evangelicalism*, which I believe reflects the conservative evangelical's accommodation to romantic liberal modernity.

From Traditionalist Christianity to Seeker-Sensitive Evangelicalism

What distinguishes this path into the Charismatic wing of the congregational domain is its starting place: individuals who follow it were raised in a home where there was *strict familial religious socialization*.[3] Recent scholarship suggests that one of the key drivers of the increase in "nonreligion" is family socialization (Thiessen and Wilkins-Laflamme 2017, 2020). Individuals are far more likely to identify as "nonreligious" if they grew up in a home where either there was no religious socialization or they were given the choice to be religiously committed. By contrast, children raised in homes where religious socialization is "strict"— where parents don't give them a choice about their level of religious involvement—are far more likely to identify as "religious." Summing up this research sociologist Joel Thiessen (2016, 10) writes, "family as primary socialization agent significantly impacts religious and secular socialization tactics."[4]

Accordingly, individuals who follow this path are almost always raised in homes where familial religious socialization is strict.[5] More often than not, parents subscribe to a socially and theologically conservative ideology, which children are expected to conform to. Yet, having been raised in romantic liberal modernity, these young people experience a significant tension between the authoritative ethic they encounter at home and the expressivist ethic they encounter in other corners of the private sphere. What subsequently occurs is what anthropologist James Bielo (2011, 31) calls a process of "deconversion," where the young person begins to question or doubt their parents' religious worldview. However, this is followed by a "reconversion" to the religion of the heart in its Charismatic Christian form. As Bielo notes, this deconversion-reconversion narrative is framed by insiders as a desire for "something more real, more genuine, more meaningful, more relevant, more honest, more biblical—something more." Indeed, Amy Kim provides a clear illustration of this: "I was looking for a place that would help me in my spiritual journey in a way that grows me, and where knowing Jesus is central." Yet, in my view, reconversion to Charismatic Christian discourse is not insignificantly motivated by an attempt to reconcile the moral traditionalism young people like Amy were raised in with their commitment to romantic expressivism. In other words, it enables evangelicals who have been raised in comparatively traditionalist homes to reconcile the theological conservatism of their childhood with the expressivist ethic naturalized across the romantic liberal institutional order.

---

[3] "Religious socialization" here means socialization into a tradition that understands itself as "religious" and willingly embraces this label.

[4] This would explain why the vast majority of my SBNR informants grew up in homes with either no, or comparatively less strict, religious socialization.

[5] For the classic statement on "strictness" see Dean Kelley's *Why Conservative Churches Are Growing*. For a revised statement which persuasively suggests "strictness" must be defined relative to culture see Neuhouser 2017.

Conclusion

Over the last three chapters I've sought to make clear that the popularity of the religion of the heart is ultimately the result of a decades-long transformation that I have called the making of romantic liberal modernity. Beginning in the 1960s, cultural and religious transformations helped produce moral, social, and political reforms that, at least in Western liberal democracies, enabled historically excluded identities and ways of being to be recognized as worthy of equal concern and respect to unprecedented degrees. These reforms were animated by, while also serving to consolidate, a romantic liberal social imaginary that treats individual liberty, understood as authentic self-expression, as a sacred value, and which offers romantic justifications for liberal legal and political institutions. However, this same social imaginary tends to blind its most loyal adherents to their social and institutional debts. Thus was born a new social order—romantic liberal modernity—which sustains and generates conditions ripe for the flowering of the religion of the heart—and which, paradoxically, produces subjects who fail to see, let alone appreciate, their commonality.

7

Romantic Liberal Modernity and Its Critics

> A society is not constituted simply by the mass of individuals who comprise it, the ground they occupy, the things they use, or the movements they make, but above all by the idea it has of itself. And there is no doubt that society sometimes hesitates over the manner in which it must conceive itself. It feels pulled in all directions.
>
> (Durkheim [1912] 1995, 425)

Equipped with an understanding of the nature of the religion of the heart, its historical development, and the basis and nature of its institutionalization in romantic liberal modernity, a defining feature of recent public and academic debates about "spirituality" now becomes clear: *socio-moral assessments of the religion of the heart largely hinge on evaluations of the current social order*. In other words, what one thinks of "spirituality" depends predominantly on how one assesses romantic liberal modernity and its discontents. This may seem implausible. But the fact is that many critics charge the spiritual turn with epitomizing or exacerbating what they perceive as central failings of post-1960s liberal democracies. In my accounting, we can identify at least five general concerns: According to critics, the shift from "religion" to "spirituality" signals: (1) the ascent of subjectivism and irrationality; (2) the decline of community and the weakening of moral commitment; (3) a crisis in civic membership and political solidarity; (4) the triumph of neoliberalism; and (5) a novel form of social control and source of collective unfreedom. While debates about "spirituality" may be quite young, these concerns reflect longstanding anxieties about the character and constitution of liberal modernity. Indeed, critics have been ringing these alarm bells for some time.

Are these concerns legitimate? The simplicity of this question betrays the truth: it cannot be answered in a straightforward manner. It depends as much on theoretical and normative presuppositions as it does on empirical facts. Or put another way, what one thinks of the religion of the heart depends on what one thinks of romantic liberal modernity, which in turn depends upon the assumptions about our social condition, values, and vision of the good society that one holds. Indeed, *we all assess romantic liberal modernity according to our own lights*.

Let me therefore make clear my allegiances. I believe strongly that the moral impulses behind romantic liberal modernity are worth defending—even if romantic liberal societies have often failed to live up to their animating ideals. Thus, if

The Spiritual Turn: The Religion of the Heart and the Making of Romantic Liberal Modernity. Galen Watts, Oxford University Press. © Galen Watts 2022. DOI: 10.1093/oso/9780192859839.003.0008

Bellah and his co-authors (1985, 303) are correct that *we all stand, consciously or not, within a tradition*, then I cannot deny that my feet find themselves planted firmly within that of romantic liberalism.

And yet, I recognize that should critics' concerns be valid then there exist compelling reasons not only to be highly suspicious of the religion of the heart but also to condemn the social order in which it finds a sympathetic and protective home. For, as we shall see, critics contend that, owing to a range of philosophical, moral, and sociological reasons, romantic liberal societies will not, indeed cannot, realize their own ideals—and what's more, that the religion of the heart serves only to conceal and strengthen these internal contradictions.

In this chapter I make the case that critics who raise these concerns, in important respects, either misunderstand or fail to appreciate the distinctive character of romantic liberal modernity. I begin by sketching these five broad concerns and the presuppositions informing them, identifying their representative thinkers, and making clear how their respective assessments of the religion of the heart hinge, in crucial respects, on their respective assessments of romantic liberal modernity.[1] Following each sketch, I draw from the Durkheimian tradition, and the secondary literature it has spawned, in order to, in some cases refute, while in others merely recast, critics' concerns. The aims of this undertaking are threefold: first, to advance a Durkheimian interpretation of the romantic liberal tradition that pays due attention to the social and institutional preconditions necessary to realize its animating ideals. Second, to raise doubt about the legitimacy of these sweeping critiques—or at least certain aspects of them. And third, to use the Durkheimian tradition in order to flag, as well as reframe, the specific concerns of critics that call out for more careful empirical investigation. In short, I draw from the Durkheimian tradition in order to provide a more realistic picture of how the contemporary social order actually operates—as well as, in ideal terms, how it ought to.

Common Criticisms of "Spirituality" and Romantic Liberal Modernity

The Ascent of Subjectivism and Irrationality

Recall that, since its inception, the liberal tradition has been championed by those heirs of the Enlightenment who stress, above all else, the ideals of disinterestedness, reason, impartiality, and self-restraint, while encouraging distrust of the emotions and anything that resembles irrationalism. Among committed

---

[1] For a systematic outline of the social-cum-political theoretical traditions that inform the dominant critiques of "spirituality" see Watts 2020.

rationalists, the stability and survival of liberal democratic institutions requires respect for expertise and rational deliberation—along with the institutions that support them. In light of the allegedly growing penchant for privileging feelings over facts, emotion over reason, and the heart over the head this camp has received renewed support in recent years: many today fear that romantic liberal modernity is overrun by irrationality and subjectivism, often in the form of conspiracy theories, which threaten the authority of science and reason, while undermining civil discourse. This explains why expressive individualism and the religion of the heart have received considerable criticism in recent years. Critics of this kind remain antagonistic to "spirituality" insofar as it places epistemic authority in subjective feelings and personal experience—a position exemplified by the work of the so-called New Atheists.

For instance, as host of the BBC special "Enemies of Reason," Richard Dawkins (2015) warns his audience, "There are two ways of looking at the world: through faith and superstition, or through the rigours of logic, observation and evidence, through reason. Yet today, reason has a battle on its hands." According to Dawkins, "We live in dangerous times when superstition is gaining ground and rational science is under attack," and the severity of this danger is no more evidenced than by the rising popularity of "spirituality"—a trend that unquestionably signals the triumph of the "irrational mind."

Of course, Dawkins is not alone in thinking this. In a polemical essay titled "Religion Poisons Everything," Christopher Hitchens (2007) proudly asserts that he "distrust[s] anything that contradicts science or outrages reason," and therefore fervently dismisses what he perceives as the intellectual immaturity of those who embrace the religion of the heart. Sam Harris (2014, 6) similarly writes, "to walk the aisles of any 'spiritual' bookstore is to confront the yearning and credulity of our species by the yard." While Daniel Dennett (2007) is adamant that those who take an interest in "spirituality" "are deluding themselves" (306). And more recently, cognitive scientist Steven Pinker (2018) dismisses what he calls "New Age flimflam," concluding in *Enlightenment Now*, "A 'spirituality' that sees cosmic meaning in the whims of fortune is not wise but foolish" (427, 434).

According to these critics, the spiritual turn is a symptom of the tide of irrationality and subjectivism which has come to characterize romantic liberal modernity. They contend that "by accepting multiple, simultaneously valid truths" the religion of the heart "makes us into idiots" (Webster 2012, 32, 42). But they also have more political concerns. According to Dawkins, to indulge in "irrationality" of this kind, even in the private sphere, is not harmless, but rather "profoundly undermines civilization." He therefore warns, "Reason has built the modern world. It is a precious but also a fragile thing which can be corroded by apparently harmless irrationality." On this view, the rise of the religion of the heart is extremely dangerous, threatening to undermine intersubjective agreement and the universal standards of reason.

A Durkheimian Reformulation: Balancing Rationalist and Expressive Institutions

In championing liberalism, Durkheim identified the liberal tradition with the moral individualism inscribed in the legal-political sphere—which he saw embodied in France's 1789 Declaration of the Rights of Man and of the Citizen. He did this because he believed an autonomous and robust legal-political sphere is required to counterbalance the utilitarian individualism inscribed in the economic sphere, as well as serve as a basis for political solidarity in liberal democratic societies. In turn, Durkheim would have had great sympathy for the critiques proffered by those who see in the spiritual turn a potential threat to the liberal democratic project. Indeed, he believed that a just society requires an enduring and resilient rationalist ethic within the public sphere in order to ensure the healthy functioning of democratic institutions (e.g., public deliberation grounded in the rule of reasons, public trust in the empirical sciences, and an impartial rule of law).

However, there is reason to think that Durkheim's rational liberalism requires supplementing. Indeed, Durkheim himself gave surprisingly short shrift to the *need for private enchantment*—the "continuing need that human beings have to make their worlds meaningful" (Alexander 1995, 2). This seems to me a serious omission. Romantic needs are in fact *needs*, which cannot be rationalized away, nor wholly fulfilled by means of participation in a moral community. Moreover, given the necessity of bureaucracy and rational-legal authority in differentiated and pluralistic societies it seems unavoidable that the public sphere will remain somewhat alienating and fragmenting in nature.

Accordingly, on this issue I believe we must supplement the Durkheimian tradition with the insights of Rousseau, as interpreted by Mark Cladis (2003, 221): "In Rousseau, we find two kinds of religious vocabularies—the religion of the heart, which addresses the inwardness of the private life, and civil religion—which addresses the public life of the citizen." This vision, it seems to me, sums up the best of romantic liberalism: aware of the fact that a comprehensively rationalist society would be a "science-fiction nightmare" (Berger et al. 1973, 204), romantic liberals advocate for a clear separation of private and public spheres—with romantic needs for enchantment, aestheticism, and self-realization confined to the former. Thus, I agree with the early Romantics that modernity is disenchanting, and therefore accept that the private sphere must remain the site of enchantment—where individuals seek meaning, intimacy, and refuge. And for this reason, I see no problem *ceteris paribus* with the religion of the heart serving to imbue private life with cosmic meaning in romantic liberal modernity. In fact, this seems to me a vital social function.

Yet these critics' concerns are not wholly misplaced. In light of Durkheim's recognition that liberal democracies require an autonomous rationalist legal-political sphere it is appropriate and warranted to fear the colonization of the public by the private, as pure privatism and subjectivism cannot uphold just institutions. Moreover, with the recent burgeoning of conspiracy theories and growing lack of public trust in scientific institutions, it is not by any means hyperbolic to fear that science may be under siege (see Houtman et al. 2021). Thus, a Durkheimian reformulation of romantic liberalism would reframe the concern as follows: *to what degree does the religion of the heart and the expressive individualism it naturalizes function in romantic liberal modernity to colonize those institutional spheres that require a rationalist ethic, such as the legal-political sphere?*

The Decline of Community and the Weakening of Moral Commitment

Liberal modernity has long been criticized for naturalizing a supposedly atomistic individualism. For instance, in *Democracy's Discontent* political theorist Michael Sandel (1996, 13) argues that liberalism dissolves community as a result of the conception of the self it endorses—which he characterizes as "free and independent, unencumbered by aims and attachments." While philosopher Alasdair MacIntyre ([1983] 2007) contends in *After Virtue* that liberal theory makes moral consensus impossible because it rejects the authority of tradition. Importantly, these critiques are not merely philosophical in nature, as these critics contend that this self-understanding remains widespread in romantic liberal modernity—leading Sandel to proclaim that "the moral fabric of community is unravelling around us" (Sandel 1996, 3). Moreover, sweeping pronouncements such as this are a staple of what might be called "communitarian" social science. For instance, in *The Fall of Public Man* Richard Sennett (1976, 340) charges the rise of romantic expressivism and its attendant ideal of personal authenticity with eroding public life, concluding that our "absorption in intimate affairs is the mark of an uncivilized society." While James Davison Hunter (2000, 157, 217) singles out "therapeutic individualism"—which he traces to "Romantic modernism"—to blame it for the "death of character."

One version of this concern focuses on the *moral limitations perceived to be intrinsic to expressive individualism*. The best known is found in *Habits*. Bellah and his co-authors (1985, 246, 235) argue that "spirituality" lacks "any effective social discipline" and fails to "provide practical guidance." They also warn of its "inner volatility and incoherence" and its "difficulty with social loyalty and commitment," charging the religion of the heart with enabling the individual to run wild, without any moral accountability (236). For instance, some have criticized "spirituality" on the grounds that it discounts the importance of community, and gives too much authority to personal experience (Casanova 1992;

Bruce 2006, 2017).[2] In fact, Steve Bruce (1998, 23) has even called the methodo-logical individualism at the core of the religion of the heart "bad sociology" insofar as it discounts the role of social structures in shaping social life—thereby exacerbating the threat of anomie in romantic liberal modernity. According to these critics, then, "spirituality" lacks a centralized institution that can ensure generational transmission and socialization, and for this reason is considered incapable of mustering the moral resources necessary to produce a vital and robust communal life, or "challenge the dominance of utilitarian values" (Bellah et al. 1985, 224).

A second version of this concern is more radical, rejecting outright the romantic liberal settlement. Proponents of this view—generally conservative in spirit—conceive of romantic liberal modernity as morally bankrupt, and antithetical to the type of community they desire. For instance, MacIntyre ([1983] 2007, xv) writes, "what liberalism promotes is a kind of institutional order that is inimical to the construction and sustaining of the types of communal relationship required for the best kind of human life." While social critic Christopher Lasch ([1979] 1991, 25) likewise laments that "self-absorption defines the moral climate of contemporary society." And more recently, philosopher Patrick Deneen (2018, 18) has called romantic liberalism an "anti-culture," contending that it "has ruthlessly drawn down a reservoir of both material and moral resources that it cannot replenish." While Robert George (2013, 167) has pilloried "the expressive individualism and social liberalism" which he contends reigns in romantic liberal modernity.

These conservative commentators are especially concerned about the decline of authoritative biblical religion in romantic liberal modernity, and therefore endorse what we might call *public enchantment*. It should not surprise us then that they have heaped copious derision and scorn on the religion of the heart and those who embrace it. For example, Martin Marty (2005, 47) describes religionless spirituality as "banal" and "solipsistic." Likewise, in his discussion of "New Age spirituality," Lasch ([1979] 1991, 245) suggests that it "is rooted in primary narcissism." While David Koyzis (2015) similarly writes, "mere spirituality leaves the ego in charge."[3] Put briefly, these critics view in the religion of the heart everything they despise about romantic liberal modernity—namely, its individualism, expressivism, and pluralism.

A Durkheimian Reformulation: Anomie and Egoism in Romantic Liberal Modernity

Philosophical critiques of liberal political theory like those of Sandel and MacIntyre are, as I see it, basically correct. Liberal theorists have too often

---

[2] For an overview of these debates see Oh and Sarkisian 2011; Berghuijs et al. 2013.
[3] Similar critiques include Douthat 2008; Brooks 2019b.

espoused sociologically naïve conceptions of the self, and claimed a degree of neutrality that does not, in fact, exist. Nevertheless, liberalism need not be understood so narrowly. Durkheim, by contrast, took a sociological, or communitarian, view of liberalism—conceiving of it as a tradition of moral individualism, deeply collective in nature (see Cladis 1992). This is significant because it makes apparent that when critics claim that liberalism is an "anti-culture" or that it lacks "any appeal to common good" (Deneen 2018, 20, 29), they are *confusing empirical description with normative judgement.*

Indeed, as Bernard Yack (1988, 157) points out, while liberal theory might presuppose an unencumbered self, "The unencumbered self's real-world analogues are as much socially constituted—fully encumbered—individuals as all others." In agreement, philosopher Stephen Macedo (1990, 18) writes, "in becoming more permissive a society may not be disintegrating at all, nor its members drifting apart. It may simply be changing and acquiring a new, more liberal morality." Durkheim would agree. As we've seen, romantic liberal modernity is not without shared cultural traditions, social practices, or moral norms. On the contrary, within each institutional sphere a distinctly liberal moral tradition reigns supreme.

It follows that conservative portrayals of romantic liberal modernity are profoundly misleading because they tend to conflate romantic liberal theory and romantic liberal practice.[4] And this criticism also applies to their portrayals of "spirituality." In fact, these critics make the same mistake as secularization theorists, insofar as they theorize the spiritual turn as consisting of a shift from an institutionalized form of religiosity to one that is free-floating, bereft of institutional support, and lacking any internal consistency. It also follows that in rejecting romantic liberal modernity, conservative critics "are actually rejecting one form of community for another, rather than recommending community per se over dissociated individualism" (Yack 1988, 159). And if this is true, then it warrants asking whether the normative vision preferred by conservatives merits *dis*embedding denizens of romantic liberal modernity from their already existing social forms.

From a Durkheimian perspective the problem with the conservative vision of the good society is that it is utterly incompatible with the pluralistic and differentiated character of twenty-first-century liberal democracies. Or, to invoke the terms of Benjamin Constant, conservatives fail to realize that most of us in modernity have a deep need for a liberty suited to modern times, not one suited to antiquity (see Constant [1820] 1988). Indeed, there is often a deep sense of "nostalgia for the pre-modern moral community" running through the writings of these critics (Macedo 1990, 15). Of course, this is not in itself condemnable, but

---

[4] For an excellent philosophical study that advances this very argument see Stout 1988.

I believe conservative rhetoric about community largely masks a quite parochial conception of the good society, which cannot account for, or cope with, as Macedo puts it, "the ideological complexity of modern states" (24). Consequently, it is hard to imagine how a comprehensive conservative ideal could be instated in the twenty-first century without a significant reduction in modern freedom (and simultaneous increase in human misery).

Still, Durkheim would concede that conservatives flag important areas of concern. For instance, they're not wrong to suggest that romantic liberal modernity encourages "loose connections" (Deneen 2018, 34). This is, in part, a by-product of institutional differentiation, but it also derives from the degree to which expressive individualism and the religion of the heart sacralize individual liberty, self-expression, and self-realization. No doubt, for this reason romantic liberal modernity will never satisfy those who long for a state of *Gemeinshaft*. But this does not mean romantic liberals have nothing to fear.

As W. Watts Miller (2003, 110) remarks, Durkheim's *Suicide* is an "exploration of the pathologies of the modern world," that is, the pathological forms of individualism that are central to liberal democratic societies. In this study Durkheim identifies four distinct types of suicide, each of which he argues represents a different social pathology: anomie, egoism, fatalism, and altruism. However, the two most common pathologies in modernity are *anomie* and *egoism*, which he suggests "spring from society's insufficient presence in individuals" (Durkheim [1897] 1951, 220). Durkheim's use of these terms can sometimes confuse,[5] so for the sake of simplicity we can think of *anomie* as referring to a *lack of social integration*, while *egoism* refers to a *lack of moral regulation*. According to Durkheim, these pathologies derive from different social origins. Anomie stems from a lack of communal belonging and is specific to modernity; its symptoms include feelings of social isolation, loneliness, and a pervasive sense of meaninglessness. Egoism, on the other hand, is deeply human, but is naturalized and amplified by the utilitarian individualism inscribed in the economic sphere, and amounts to a kind of excessive selfishness, or myopic preoccupation with advancing one's own self-interest. Moreover, Durkheim maintained that egoism tends to engender an irrational desire for more—which he called a "malady of infiniteness" (Durkheim

---

[5] For Durkheim ([1897] 1951, 219), egoistic suicide results "from man's no longer finding a basis for existence in life" whereas anomic suicide results "from man's lacking regulation." Thus "egoism," as it is understood in *Suicide*, is to be distinguished from the kind of "egoism" which Durkheim writes about in other contexts. As W. Watts Miller (2003, 4) makes clear, when Durkheim speaks of egoism in other contexts he is referring to "the unfettered, morally unconstrained pursuit of self-interest," however, in *Suicide* it is the pathology referred to as "anomie" that implies this meaning. Anomic suicide, then, results from insatiable desires that ultimately lead to misery. Like Philip Smith (2020, 33–4) I find Durkheim's use of these terms in *Suicide* counterintuitive, if not confused. Moreover, it seems to me that popular uses of "egoism" and "anomie" are quite at odds with Durkheim's technical use of these terms in *Suicide*. For this reason, I employ these terms, not in their strict Durkheimian senses, but rather in their more popular formulations.

[1961] 2002, 43)—such that if our selfish desires are not curbed, they become insatiable and thereby tortuous (Durkheim [1897] 1951, 208).

Durkheim consistently argued that anomie and egoism were the key threats to liberal democratic societies, holding the potential to exacerbate injustice and engender untold human suffering. Yet, in diagnosing these social pathologies he also proffered a potential solution. While he championed moral individualism as the basis for political solidarity, as we saw above, Durkheim was well aware that the state was too distant from individuals to combat these pathologies. Consequently, he looked to civil society, arguing that it is the role of associational or voluntary groups to socially integrate and morally regulate individuals in liberal democracies (Durkheim [1957] 2003). Within such groups, Durkheim maintained, individuals will derive a sense of identity, meaning, and purpose—thereby staving off anomie—while also having their egoism curbed. For by internalizing the group's norms, their selfish desires would be tempered and the malady of infiniteness would be avoided (Marske 1987, 9).

A useful way of understanding the conservative critique of romantic liberal modernity, then, is through the Durkheimian lenses of anomie and egoism. Conservatives fear that, given the expressive individualism inscribed in the private sphere, romantic liberal societies cannot provide the moral or religious resources necessary to stave off the threats of meaninglessness and moral disintegration, and that what is required instead is that biblical religion function as a comprehensive sacred canopy. Less radical critics, such as Bellah and his co-authors, share this fear, but propose a less drastic solution: rather than reject the tradition of expressive individualism, they simply seek to limit its scope (see Tipton 1986, 171). In this, we see the significant debts *Habits* owes to Durkheim. However, while Bellah and his co-authors may accept that expressive individualism is naturalized in the private sphere of romantic liberal modernity, they also lament this fact in a way that romantic liberals do not. This is chiefly because they believe this moral tradition remains incapable of staving off the threats of anomie and egoism. Indeed, it is for this reason that they criticize "Sheilaism"—which they correctly conceive as a religious expressive individualism—and instead champion the tradition of biblical religion. But in making this claim, I would argue, the authors of *Habits* fail to fully heed the Durkheimian tradition.

Recall from chapter 1 that, according to Durkheim, religion always consists of two elements: collective representations and *ritual*. While I've refrained from discussing it until now, it is difficult to overstate the importance of ritual in Durkheim's thought (Marshall 2002; Weiss 2012). Indeed, in *The Elementary Forms of Religious Life*, Durkheim challenges the cognitivist (Protestant) conception of religion, which holds that religious belief precedes ritual. He argues, by contrast, that religious (as well as moral) conviction is a *by-product* of ritual participation. Accordingly, from a Durkheimian perspective, discourses— religious or otherwise—require rituals in order to become intellectually plausible and morally persuasive. Furthermore, recent cultural sociological thinking has extended this Durkheimian inheritance, arguing that cultural structures and the discourses they inform "are polysemous," in that they "sustain a range of interpretations" (Eliasoph and Lichterman 2003, 736, 757). Now, this does not mean cultural structures allow infinite interpretations. They do not. But empirical studies nevertheless demonstrate that "the same symbol or collective representation can take on different meanings in different contexts" (736). It follows that *the same discourse can encode different meanings and values by means of different collective rituals and social practices.*

So, from a Durkheimian perspective a crucial limitation of the analysis of both expressive individualism and "spirituality" offered in *Habits* is its narrow focus on discourse or language, without regard for how these are encoded through ritual and everyday practice (Lichterman 1996; Wilkinson 2010). And the import of this limitation becomes apparent when we consider the reason why Bellah and his co-authors prefer biblical religion to the religion of the heart: taking at face value the self-understanding typical of romantic liberals they presume that the religion of the heart, or "radical religious individualism," as they call it, "delivers not the autonomy it promises but loneliness and vulnerability instead" (1985, 247). Thus, like conservatives, the authors of *Habits* conflate theory (or in this case, discourse) and practice, presuming the latter mirrors the former. But given the Durkheimian insights outlined above, there is good reason to doubt this.

Accordingly, the question becomes: to what degree is Bellah and his co-authors' characterization of "spirituality" empirically accurate? In other words, *are they correct in asserting that the religion of the heart fails to mitigate the pathologies of anomie and egoism? Or might their inattention to ritual and practice distort social reality?*

The Crisis in Civic Membership and Political Solidarity

Another camp, closely related to those who perceive in the religion of the heart and romantic liberal modernity the dissolution of community, fear the civic consequences of the spiritual turn. These critics seek to ensure that the legal-political sphere retains sufficient autonomy and vitality to uphold democratic institutions. And in taking their cue from Tocqueville, they tend to view expressive individualism in terms of its deleterious consequences for civic life.

In *Democracy and America* Alexis de Tocqueville ([1835] 1998, 206) famously asserts that individualism encourages the following self-conception: "They owe nothing to any man, they expect nothing from any man; they acquire the habit of always considering themselves as standing alone, and they are apt to imagine that their whole destiny is in their hands." Tocqueville feared that were this self-understanding to become widespread it could lead to a new kind of despotism, one where "each nation is reduced to nothing better than a flock of timid and industrious animals, of which the government is the shepherd" (359).

These insights have been systematized in the work of political scientist Robert Putnam (2000), who has charted a consistent decline in "social capital"—the social ties that bind us together—over the twentieth century. According to Putnam, "it is in the voluntary organizations of civil society—churches, families, unions, ethnic associations, cooperatives, environmental groups, neighbourhood associations, support groups, charities—that we learn the virtues of mutual obligation" (Kymlicka 2002, 305). Consequently, Putnam and others like him fear that "the individualism promoted so strongly in recent years militates against maintaining faith in standards that may be necessary for fostering public life" (Ricci 2004, 187).

Of course, *Habits* shares this concern. For like Putnam, Bellah and his co-authors take as authoritative Tocqueville's ([1835] 1998, 120) conviction that, "Religion in America...must be regarded as the first of their political institutions." In turn, these critics contend that religion ought to be concerned not just with private enchantment, but with public life as well. Thus Bellah et al. (1985, 237, 238) champion the ideal of a "public church," which they associate with the "mainline churches" or "religious center." Indeed, part of the reason why they advocate for biblical religion is because they see this tradition as "concerned with the whole of life—with social, economic, and political matters as well as with private and personal ones" (220).

This sheds light on why this group of critics have tended to be wary of "spirituality." Much like Bellah and his co-authors, they fear a "crisis in civic membership" as a result of the eclipse of biblical religion by the religion of the heart (Bellah et al. 1985, xvii). And they worry, with Putnam (2000, 74), that "privatized religion...embodies less social capital." According to these thinkers, religion ought to encourage active participation in democratic life, sufficient at the very least to shore up the autonomy of the legal-political sphere. These concerns are articulated forcefully in the work of sociologist Bryan Turner (2011, 267), who argues, "The evolution of weak or passive citizenship is parallel, in my interpretation of modern society, to the evolution of passive religiosity or spirituality." Turner further laments, "Privatized forms of religious activity do not contribute significantly to the vitality of civil society, but simply provide psychological maintenance to the individual" (225).

In sum, according to this camp, the dominance of expressive individualism in the private sphere prohibits the cultivation of political solidarity and stifles civic engagement. Accordingly, "spirituality" is considered dangerous because it encourages a turning inward, away from civic duties—or leads to the subsuming of the public under the private. In fact, these critics fear that to the extent that the religion of the heart erodes the authority of biblical religion and the congregational domain, liberal democratic institutions shall deteriorate from neglect.

A Durkheimian Reformulation: Religion as a Source of Private Enchantment, not Civic Virtue or Political Solidarity

While Durkheim might have maintained that the tradition of moral individualism should serve as a kind of civil religion for liberal democracies, he did not believe it should reign supreme across institutional spheres (Watts Miller 2003, 88). This is for the following reasons. First, much like Benjamin Constant, he recognized that it is a rare few in liberal democracies who hold the view that the good life is one of active political participation. But more importantly, in his view what is most commendable about liberal societies is the degree to which they allow for moral pluralism, or what Nancy Rosenblum (1998, 17) calls "the possibility of shifting involvements." In fact, Irving Horowitz (1982, 371) contends that central to Durkheim's political thought is the belief that "democratic institutions will be strong to the degree that society is pluralist in nature." So, while he certainly believed a liberal community requires a common "faith"—in the form of a shared commitment to moral individualism—Durkheim did not champion a totalizing civil religion. Instead, he sought only to protect the autonomy of the legal-political sphere, for that way citizens in liberal democracies would have a shared basis for solidarity (Cladis 2005).

In this way, the Durkheimian tradition holds much in common with neo-Tocquevillian critics who accept the romantic liberal settlement. Yet it would be wrong to view their theories of liberal democracy as identical. As M. J. Hawkins (1994, 476) notes, unlike Durkheim, "Tocqueville's theory of intermediary bodies laid considerable stress on their participatory and educational aspects," and in fact Tocqueville generally saw the proliferation of voluntary groups as an "intrinsically healthy process." By contrast, Durkheim held a less sanguine view of the potential of associational groups to produce the kind of solidarity that would enhance national unity. This is because he recognized that voluntary associations within civil society are just as likely to foster the kinds of qualities and forms of commitment that impede democratic and civil deliberation in a pluralistic society, or that they will have no civic impact at all. Indeed, in Durkheim's view, any honest look at civil society reveals that "[a]nomie and aggressive self-interest coexist alongside powerful solidaristic social groups, whose members do not have the psychological latitude to look outside and identify as citizens" (Rosenblum 1994, 546). He would have therefore suggested that critics like Putnam demand too much of voluntary associations "in expecting them to be the main school for, or a small-scale replica of, democratic citizenship" (Kymlicka 2002, 306).

Additionally, while Tocqueville may have considered religion the first political institution in America, Durkheim would argue this is no longer appropriate. Neo-Tocquevillians tend to evaluate all religious forms with reference to an ideal of voluntaristic Protestantism, which is expected to serve as a social glue, moral framework, sacred canopy, and source of civic virtue simultaneously. The problem with this model, from a Durkheimian perspective, is that in the increasingly differentiated, pluralistic, and porous nature of romantic liberal modernity, where a wide range of public institutions that did not exist in Tocqueville's time serve various civic and social functions (for instance, the welfare state), it may well be "rather out of date" (Alexander 2006, 99).

Here, again, we see where a more thoroughly Durkheimian perspective departs from the neo-Tocquevillianism of *Habits*. Unlike Bellah and his co-authors, Durkheim wouldn't look to religious groups in order to provide civic virtue or stoke political solidarity in romantic liberal modernity. And while he would agree with them that religious associations continue to play a crucial function in romantic liberal modernity, he would frame their role differently. Rather than viewing such associations as the seedbeds of democratic life, Durkheim would conceive of these associations as what Berger (1976) calls "mediating structures," which serve to stave off anomie and temper egoism in individuals—in other words, as *key sites of social integration and moral regulation*.

And yet, I do not wish to downplay the apparent need for political solidarity and civic-mindedness. But, once again, a Durkheimian reformulation of romantic liberalism would hold that the majority of voluntary associations in civil society—including religious groups—should not be expected to supply this. Instead, we must look to the legal-political sphere, and rest our hopes in *a robust conception of national citizenship*, which reflects the tradition of moral individualism. In other words, Durkheim was well aware of the degree to which "the spread of liberal individualist values goes hand in hand with the strengthening of an identification with national community" (Yack 1988, 161), and therefore maintained that political solidarity ought to find its roots at the national level.[6]

Still, it remains the case that Durkheim said relatively little about how this is meant to occur. For this reason, cultural sociologist Jeffrey Alexander has recently extended and refined this Durkheimian line of thought in the formation of what he calls Civil Sphere Theory. Alexander fundamentally rejects the tenets of Putnam's civil society theory, which holds that all voluntary associations should serve as schools of civic virtue. Instead, Civil Sphere Theory recognizes that many voluntary associations, including religious groups, "play no effective role in society's civil sphere" (Alexander 2006, 2013). However, Alexander makes sure to add, "they may perform important functions in their respective noncivil spheres" (103). According to Alexander, the "Civil Sphere" (what I have been calling the legal-political sphere) comprises a range of regulative institutions (law, voting, parties, office) and communicative institutions (public opinion, mass media, polls, civil associations, and social movements), which collectively serve

[6] Thus, Durkheim pre-empts the more recent scholarship on "liberal nationalism" (see Tamir 1993; Miller 1995; Kymlicka and Banting 2017).

to create and sustain a "solidary sphere, in which a certain kind of universalizing community comes to be culturally defined and to some degree institutionally enforced" (31). In other words, it is within the Civil Sphere where the tradition of moral individualism finds an institutional home.

Importantly, the institutional order that comprises the Civil Sphere is quite distinct from what I call the romantic liberal institutional order—the collection of secondary and primary institutions that naturalize an expressivist ethic and constitute the religious sphere in romantic liberal modernity. While the former institutional order belongs to (and is largely commensurable with) the legal-political sphere, the latter is primarily oriented towards the private sphere. Thus, a Durkheimian romantic liberalism would postulate the following as an ideal: *while the Civil Sphere serves the need for political solidarity and civic-mindedness, the romantic liberal institutional order serves the need for private enchantment.*

Of course, whether or not this ideal is reflected in reality is unclear, and indeed the issue cries out for empirical investigation. But the point I wish to stress is that a Durkheimian reformulation of romantic liberalism would take seriously critics' concern about the state of civic membership, but reframe it differently. And once we reframe it in light of Durkheimian insights we see that it takes a quite similar form as those who fear the ascent of irrationality or subjectivism, albeit with a slightly different emphasis: *to what extent do discourses of "spirituality" colonize or invade the legal-political sphere (or Alexander's Civil Sphere), thereby impeding the cultivation of civic virtue and political solidarity?* It would seem, then, that we need a better understanding of when and where the religion of the heart erodes the influence and authority of this competing institutional sphere.

The Triumph of Neoliberalism

A fourth camp tends to interpret romantic liberal modernity as shot through with class conflict, where moral debates and avowed religious convictions conceal or mystify the material interests which structure and shape them. Thus, whereas romantic liberals might view "spirituality" as laudably enchanting the private sphere, these scholars—significantly influenced by Karl Marx—tend to see it as operating to legitimate capitalist relations of production by turning us into the kind of subjects that capitalism requires. Indeed, there has been a concerted effort by some critics to present "spirituality"—in one or other of its discursive iterations—as intimately tied to neoliberalism.[7]

---

[7] See, for example, Lau 2000; Possamai 2003; Carrette and King 2005; Wood 2007; McGee 2005; Comaroff 2009; Rindfleish 2005; Kim 2012; Redden 2012; Maddox 2012; Martin 2014; Altglas 2014; Crockford 2017; Jain 2020.

For instance, in *Selling Spirituality: The Silent Takeover of Religion* Jeremy Carrette and Richard King warn of "a silent takeover of 'the religious' by contemporary capitalist ideologies by means of the increasingly popular discourse of 'spirituality'" (2005, 2). They condemn what they call "capitalist spirituality" for doing little to challenge the status quo in romantic liberal modernity—which they interpret as "a lifestyle of self-interest and ubiquitous consumption" (57, 5). Indeed, according to Carrette and King, neoliberalism "has removed the social dimension of religion and created a spirituality of the self—of the *consuming* self" (68). They further contend that what goes by "spirituality" almost always operates as a "psychological sedative for a culture that is in the process of rejecting the values of community and social justice" (83), concluding, "Privatized spirituality emerges here as the new *cultural prozac* bringing transitory feelings of ecstatic happiness and thoughts of self-affirmation, but never addressing sufficiently the underlying problem of social isolation and injustice" (77).

Another illustrative example is found in Craig Martin's conspicuously titled *Capitalizing Religion: Ideology and the Opiate of the Bourgeoisie.* Martin (2014, 12) confesses at the outset that he's "interested in rhetorics and discourses that naturalize or legitimate a capitalist system." And, as we might expect, talk of being "spiritual but not religious," according to Martin, is one such discourse. "Capitalism does not sustain itself, but requires ideology for its maintenance. The self-help and spirituality publishing industry is, arguably, one of the ideological state apparatuses of late capitalism" (89). Martin argues that the holistic milieu and associated institutions serve to interpellate subjects, thereby leading them to "produce, consume, and accommodate themselves to the regnant mode of production" (35). It follows, he says, that SBNR discourse is a "domesticated ideology of the status quo" (52). Martin also gives critical attention to the methodological individualism at the core of the religion of the heart. He remarks, "this ideology simultaneously obscures the constitutive role of social structures in the creation of individuals and their desires, as well as the structural causes of individual suffering" (157). Thus, according to Martin, "spirituality" serves a number of ideological functions in romantic liberal modernity: it deflects critical attention away from social structures, thereby quelling social criticism, and it acclimates middle-class workers "to our prison" (70, 126)—hence why he deems "spirituality" the "opiate of the bourgeoisie."

These studies usefully illuminate what are central and recurring claims advanced from within this camp. These are as follows: first, discourses of "spirituality" are considered an ideological channel for the utilitarian individualism inscribed in the economic sphere, and therefore charged with bolstering neoliberalism. And second, the religion of the heart is criticized for emphasizing "individual responsibility over structural dismantalization" (Jain 2020, 164). In other words, by naturalizing methodological individualism, the religion of the heart is singled out for deflecting criticism of, if not legitimating, unjust social or economic conditions.

A Durkheimian Reformulation: Religion
as Counterforce to Egoism

Durkheim did not agree with Marx that capitalist relations of production are inherently alienating or exploitative. In fact, he believed that the institution of private property was a necessary, and indeed moral, feature of modern life, seeing in it an extension of the sacralization of the individual. Yet, as Paul Vogt notes, "While Durkheim believed in the sacredness of the right of property, this belief by no means led him to a laissez-faire individualism of the sort advocated by classical economists and political conservatives of his day." On the contrary, "he was clearly an advocate of what was called at the time 'the new liberalism'—a kind of liberalism that was perfectly willing to accept state intervention in social and economic life in order to strengthen individual rights and liberties" (83). In fact, a century before the term "liberal egalitarian" was coined, Durkheim was articulating this philosophical doctrine's basic tenets. As Will Kymlicka (2006, 14) notes, liberal egalitarians such as John Rawls and Ronald Dworkin view inequalities that are morally arbitrary— that is, the result of brute luck—as unjust and therefore in need of rectification. In a strikingly similar spirit, Durkheim argued economic arrangements should be structured so that individuals are rewarded for what they merit (Filloux 1993, 208).

And yet Durkheim would have disagreed with the means by which contemporary liberal egalitarians derive their conclusions (Herzog 2018, 116). In Durkheim's view, when contemplating what justice requires, we should not reason abstractly, but rather begin by reflecting upon the moral traditions we have inherited (Durkheim [1887] 1993, 69–70). In other words, for Durkheim, "Justice is relative to social meanings," not universal principles (Walzer 1983, 312). Thus, he came to endorse left-liberal (or what we might call social democratic) economic arrangements because he believed that they were necessary in order to realize the normative ideals of individual liberty and moral equality inherent to the tradition of moral individualism (Vogt 1993, 85).

Despite their differences, then, the Durkheimian and Marxist traditions entail quite similar commitments to moral equality and social justice. However, Durkheim, unlike Marx, refused to reduce the good society to particular economic arrangements. Indeed, as a result of his conception of social life, Marx tended to see all modes of domination and oppression as the result of class conflict, and therefore assumed that once capitalism was transcended, there would be no need for a state (Lukes 2015). But Durkheim disagreed. In his view, state institutions such as the rule of law and rights regimes will always be necessary in a differentiated and pluralistic society in order to resolve disputes among individuals and ensure relative peace. Durkheim was therefore adamant that just economic arrangements were necessary but far from sufficient to realize a good society, arguing in *Socialism and Saint-Simon*: "the social question . . . is not a question of money or force; it is a question of moral agents" (Durkheim [1928] 1959, 129).

It follows that the Durkheimian tradition does not presuppose that social life in romantic liberal modernity is fundamentally and inalterably conflictual. While Durkheim would certainly concede that egoism fuels a significant part of social life, he would nevertheless contest critics' claim that all action is instrumental and self-interested—or, as Martin (2014, 402) puts it, that "the way people talk and think about the social world is rooted in material interests and social domination." For by universalizing the utilitarian individualism of the economic sphere in their theories, Durkheim would argue that these critics fail to account for the fact of institutional differentiation, and the existence of plural moral traditions in romantic liberal modernity. As Alexander (2006, 33) fittingly phrases it, "We are no more a capitalist society than we are a bureaucratic, secular, rational one, or indeed a civil one."

And yet, Durkheim was not naïve to the pitfalls of capitalism. In fact, we find a trenchant critique of capitalism embedded in his conception of human nature. According to Durkheim, *humans have two opposing natures* or *selves*—one "natural," the other "social" (Durkheim [1960] 1965). Our "natural self," he argues, is fundamentally *egoistic*, while our "social self" *derives from society, is the source of morality*, and reflects "the best part of us" (Durkheim [1951] 1953, 27). While it's unclear whether Durkheim, in discussing our "natural self," actually meant natural (in the sense of asocial),[8] the important point is that *he identified it with the tradition of utilitarian individualism*. In other words, according to Durkheim, the moral logic of the economic sphere, if left unchecked, exacerbates the pathology of egoism, thereby engendering within individuals an irrational and insatiable desire for more—and undermining their flourishing. Therefore, Durkheim evidently recognized the dangers of capitalism. In fact, he spent much of his life railing against those who sought to expand its scope (see Durkheim [1897] 1951, 218). Yet, as we've seen, he did not agree with Marx that capitalist relations of production are inherently alienating, nor that they should be abolished. Instead, he advocated that utilitarian individualism be tightly circumscribed within the economic sphere, and that it be counterbalanced by competing institutions and moral traditions (Cladis 1992, 146).

Accordingly, while Durkheim would share with critics a fear that discourses of "spirituality" are "fundamentally shaped by an economic ideology" (Carrette and King 2005, 17), he would also argue that such a claim should not be accepted without empirical evidence, given the fact of institutional differentiation and the existence of plural moral logics. Thus, a Durkheimian romantic liberalism would hold only that *there is cause for concern to the extent that the religion of the heart serves to naturalize the utilitarian individualism of the economic sphere, and thereby exacerbates egoism in romantic liberal modernity*. Additionally,

---

[8] For more on this issue see Fish 2013; Bowring 2016.

Durkheim would share critics' concern about the degree to which discourses of "spirituality" impede the quest for social justice by means of deflecting criticism of unjust social conditions or social structures. But he would frame this concern differently: rather than viewing methodologically individualistic discourses as *inherently* problematic, *he would focus on the degree to which they are totalizing in individuals' lives—that is, the extent to which they impede the adoption, when called for, of competing discourses.* This is because Durkheim believed that different social situations and dilemmas demand different moral logics for their resolution. Indeed, this is another reason why he championed pluralism and shifting involvements—for Durkheim, the good society can only be realized if citizens have access to multiple social perspectives and moral traditions, and are able to summon these when necessary.

A New Form of Social Control and Source of Collective Unfreedom

A final concern focuses on the disciplinary nature of the religion of the heart—and with it, romantic liberal modernity—and the degree to which, under the guise of "self-realization," they covertly produce unfree political subjects. To give some context to this critique, it's necessary to say a few things about its key theoretical influence: Michel Foucault.

While Foucault says little in his scholarship about his own normative commitments, it is not difficult to discern that he is radically sceptical of, if not outright hostile to, liberal modernity. Indeed, *contra* the claims of liberals—rational and romantic—he argues that the emergence of liberalism did not mark moral progress, but rather a shift in disciplinary regimes—from one of "exceptional discipline" to "one of a generalized surveillance" (Foucault 1984, 115). In short, in Foucault's rendering, romantic liberal modernity is interpreted as a social order of unrelenting discipline and normalization, where the rhetorics of freedom and individuality conceal myriad and insidious relations of power that dominate us as much from within as from above.

In recent years, the work of Foucault has become incredibly popular for analysing romantic liberal modernity—and with it, the religion of the heart. For instance, in *Governing the Soul: The Shaping of the Private Self* social theorist Nikolas Rose applies a Foucaultian schematic to conduct a genealogy of romantic liberal subjectivity. He writes, "Liberal democratic polities place limits upon direct coercive interventions into individual lives by the power of the state" (Rose 1989, 10). Consequently, they covertly maintain control by means of "governmental technologies of the self" (249). One such technology, Rose suggests, is discourses of self-help and "spirituality," whose "power lies in their capacity to offer means by which the regulation of selves—by others and by ourselves—can be made consonant with contemporary political principles, moral ideals, and constitutional exigencies" (261). Rose concludes, "the language of autonomy, identity, self-realization and the search for fulfillment acts as a grid of regulatory ideals," which serve to produce romantic liberal subjects (quoted in Redden 2011, 655).

This is not an uncommon critique. In fact, many others have presented discourses of "spirituality" as carriers of romantic liberal regimes of power and discipline.[9] While these studies might differ in their specifics, the following two claims recur almost across the board. First, that discourses of "spirituality," in naturalizing a self-ethic and endorsing an ideal of self-realization, function as a disciplinary mechanism in romantic liberal modernity. In other words, these critics endorse a view of the religion of the heart as deeply normalizing, or as legitimating "prescriptions and rules" and "promot[ing] certain attitudes while discouraging others" (Altglas 2018, 81). And their concern is that the freedom heralded by "spirituality" is not what it seems: rather than enabling freedom from social constraints, "becoming one's true self," in fact, entails conformity to collective values and moral ideals.

The second claim is that "spiritual" discourses serve to discipline individuals, through processes of subjectification, into becoming what Andrea Jain (2020) calls "neoliberal spiritual subjects"—subjects who are harmoniously adapted to neoliberal economic and political structures. Ronald Pursuer (2018, 2) contends that "spirituality" emphasizes "the sovereignty of autonomous individuals who can navigate the vicissitudes of late capitalist society by becoming self-regulating and self-compassionate, governing themselves, and by freely choosing their own welfare, well-being, and security." While Sam Binkley (2014, 4) argues that humanistic psychology functions as "one of the chief instruments of neoliberal government, the very leitmotif of neoliberal life itself." Accordingly, these critics share with those who view in romantic liberal modernity the triumph of neoliberalism the conviction that the religion of the heart serves to naturalize the utilitarian individualism inscribed in the economic sphere, thereby extending the moral logic of the market into ever new spheres of social life.

A Durkheimian Reformulation: Balancing the Need for Moral Community with the Need for Shifting Involvements

It is impossible to make sense of this critique without first coming to grips with Foucault's scholarship and interpretive framework. Philosopher Ronald Beiner (1995, 350) observes: "What is interesting about Foucault's unique rhetoric is that he steadfastly resists pronouncing explicit moral-political judgments, yet of course

---

[9] See, for example, Nadesan 1999; Rimke 2000; Bell and Taylor 2003; Philip 2009; Erjavec and Volčič 2009; Williams 2014; Trifan 2016; Godrej 2017; Altglas 2014, 2018; Pursuer 2018; Jain 2020.

he is judging all the time." Beiner suggests this is because, given Foucault's social schema—which holds that social life is shot through with relations of power and domination—"one must avoid at all costs spelling out a normative vision, since it would ineluctably become the ground for a repressive regime of 'normalization'." If Beiner is right, then the question becomes: why does Foucault reject processes of normalization—whereby external ideals serve to regulate the actions of individuals through their willing consent—so vehemently? I maintain, following Seyla Benhabib (1992, 16), that the reason is that Foucault is ultimately committed to something like "super-liberalism," which values, along with *radical individual freedom*, diversity, heterogeneity, eccentricity and otherness.[10] That is, Foucault champions an ideal of "pure untrammeled freedom," which implies that all social norms are constraining, coercive, and ultimately oppressive (Taylor 1989, 489). Indeed, it seems to me that only by espousing such a conception of freedom can Foucault fail to see the difference between medieval forms of discipline and those of liberal democratic societies (Walzer 1988, 200).

In turn, it is enlightening to contrast Foucault's conception of freedom with Durkheim's. According to Durkheim, to act *freely* is to act morally, and to act morally is to heed one's "social self." Our "social self," as we have seen, has its origins in the moral communities we belong to (Durkheim [1951] 1953, 17). Yet while our "social self" may derive from society, it exists *within* us, and ultimately constitutes *who we truly are*. Indeed, for Durkheim our identities are comprehensively shaped by the moral traditions we imbibe, and the strength of our moral convictions depends in large part upon our participation in the collective rituals associated with those traditions.

Moreover, the reason Durkheim argues that our "social self" reflects "the best part of us" is because it counters the egoism of our "natural self." He writes, "Everything which is a source of solidarity is moral, everything which forces man to take account of other men is moral, everything which forces him to regulate his conduct through something other than the striving of his ego is moral" (Durkheim quoted in Bellah 1973, 136). This is why Durkheim opposed the libertarian presumption that freedom amounts to a mere lack of external constraints. Given his conception of human nature, Durkheim argued that individuals wholly governed by their "natural self"—their selfish desires—are, in important respects, unfree. In his view, it is only by submitting to our "social self" that we become truly free: "The individual submits to society and this submission is the condition of his liberation" (Durkheim [1951] 1953, 37).

And lest we fear that Durkheim's positive conception of freedom could legitimate an authoritarian regime that "forces individuals to be free" it is important to keep in mind two claims. First, that moral motivation, for Durkheim, must not

---

[10] Similar critiques of Foucault include: Taylor 1985; Beiner 1995; Seigel 1999; Berkowitz 1999.

stem from external coercion but rather from attachment to the collective through periodic ritual. And second, Durkheim was a liberal. In other words, while he may have advanced a positive conception of freedom, politically, he defended human rights—especially the right to negative liberty. Thus, unlike Foucault, Durkheim recognized the very real differences between self-discipline, whereby one *legislates oneself*, and the kind of discipline that is *imposed by others* through force—and on this basis advocated for the liberal protection of individual rights against state authoritarianism.

What fundamentally distinguishes Durkheim from Foucault, therefore, is that Durkheim recognizes the crucial difference between *power* and *authority* (Seligman 2000, 25). As Massimo Rosati (2009, 35–6) observes, authority can be understood as *legitimate power*, such that, "If power works through coercing our will, moral authority works through the voluntary subjugation of our will." Foucault's unwillingness to make this distinction leads him to suppose that individuals who voluntarily submit to a regime of normalization are merely coerced by other means. But from a Durkheimian perspective this is deeply misleading. For, in actual fact, "community and authority are two sides of the same coin, two aspects of the same phenomenon" such that one presupposes the other (40). Indeed, for Durkheim, there is a world of difference between being forced to conform to a community's standards because there are no other options (power), and deciding to conform because one identifies with the community (authority). What's more, if one is to have solidarity one must have an authority that individuals submit to. Those following in the footsteps of Foucault can only deny the latter by rejecting the former.

By contrast, Durkheim does not conceive of the moral traditions indigenous to a society as oppressive regimes of normalization, which impede individual free-dom, but rather as *enabling* true freedom, or autonomy, through moral action. For, in his view, *all that we are we owe to society*, thus it makes no sense to seek escape. And yet, crucially, Durkheim did not embrace social determinism. Rather, he rejected both social determinism as well as the radical freedom championed by Foucault, instead promoting a conception of "freedom as voluntary responses to one's own socially constituted beliefs and loves" (Cladis 1992, 30). Cladis usefully sums up this view: "autonomy, for Durkheim, no longer refers to being free from influences. It refers, rather, to the freedom to understand how one has been influenced, and then to go on to influence others, often in novel and critical ways" (40). Indeed, Durkheim's conception of real freedom paradoxically entails both submission to society (in the form of heeding one's "social self") while simultaneously developing a critical attitude towards it—which he referred to as "enlightened allegiance" (Durkheim [1961] 2002, 116).

The differences between Foucault-inspired critics of romantic liberal modernity and those of a Durkheimian ilk should now be apparent. For the former, the moral tradition of expressive individualism and the religion of the heart insidiously serve as disciplinary mechanisms, by means of processes of subjectification and nor-malization. In this vein, Altglas (2018, 101) laments that "'spirituality' makes the self the locus of discipline and conformity to collective values and incentives." However, from a Durkheimian perspective, this fact does not necessarily warrant criticism. In fact, given the importance of shared norms and moral traditions to the good society this should be expected and potentially encouraged.

Romantic liberalism at its best seeks to balance the value of expressive freedom with the need for solidarity. The problem with critics who view in the spiritual turn a new form of social control and source of unfreedom, from a Durkheimian perspective, is that *they give ultimate weight to the former and none to the latter*—the exact *opposite* error conservatives make. Durkheim would contend that the radical individualism implicit in these critics' thought is premised upon nothing short of a vision of the good society comprising wholly unencumbered and atomistic individualists—where a society does not in any meaningful sense exist. A world without overarching moral traditions may, for Foucault, embody absolute freedom, but from a Durkheimian perspective it is more likely to mean chronic anxiety, moral disorientation, and anomie.

Having said this, while Durkheim advocated that citizens in liberal democracies be members of smaller, more local, moral communities within civil society, he also feared that too much social integration and moral regulation into a *single* group could stifle individuality and erode individual liberty. Indeed, he recognized that voluntary groups are just as likely to become what sociologist Lewis Coser (1974, 4) refers to as "greedy institutions"—that is, social institutions that "seek exclusive and undivided loyalty" while attempting to "reduce the claims of competing roles and status positions" on their members. While greedy institutions integrate individuals into a moral community that can be incredibly personally fulfilling, they simultaneously serve to undermine the possibility for shifting involvements.

Accordingly, while Durkheim would not share with critics the view that moral traditions and social norms are inherently oppressive, he would share with them *a concern about the degree to which specific moral traditions and social norms are totalizing in individuals' lives, thereby stifling their ability to shift involvements and experience moral pluralism.* Furthermore, he would share with these critics a concern about the degree to which the religion of the heart functions to produce "neoliberal subjects"—that is, "social selves" comprehensively constituted by the utilitarian individualism naturalized in the economic sphere. But here too the concern would be recast: rather than viewing processes of normalization and moral regulation as inherently problematic, Durkheim would *scrutinize the sub-stance of the specific moral traditions used to constitute subjects, as well as the degree to which subjects are capable of shifting involvements.*

In this chapter I have drawn from the Durkheimian tradition in order to problematize, and in some cases dispute, many of the claims critics make about the current social order, along with the social functions they allege the religion of the heart fulfils (or fails to fulfil) within it. But I've also identified a number of unresolved concerns, which a Durkheimian interpretation of romantic liberalism cannot afford to ignore or dismiss. And to the extent that these concerns are legitimate, accurately capturing social reality, romantic liberals like myself have good reason to worry. So, it's important that these concerns be made as clear as possible.

I think we can boil down the core challenges to the religion of the heart, and its place in romantic liberal modernity, to the following two concerns:

(1) *To what extent does the religion of the heart mitigate or exacerbate the pathologies of romantic liberal modernity—anomie and egoism?*
(2) *Does the religion of the heart lead to a colonization of competing social spheres, thereby impeding shifting involvements and the adoption of rival social perspectives and moral traditions?*

Consider: critics who perceive in the spiritual turn the ascent of irrationality and subjectivism fear a distinct version of (2): the colonization of the rationalist public sphere by the expressivist private sphere. Those who lament the decline of community and moral commitment are chiefly concerned with (1), as they tend to give primacy to the threats of anomie and egoism, understood as a lack of social integration and moral regulation, charging the religion of the heart with dissolving communal ties in romantic liberal modernity. The Tocquevillian concern regarding civic membership and political solidarity, when reframed by the Durkheimian tradition, ultimately amounts to (2): though we should not expect the religion of the heart (or any religion, for that matter) to serve as a source of civic virtue and political solidarity in romantic liberal modernity, it is imperative that it not impede citizens from retaining a commitment to the moral individualism inscribed in the legal-political sphere (or Alexander's Civil Sphere). Furthermore, critics who argue that "spirituality" serves to produce "neoliberal subjects" raise both concerns. In submitting that the religion of the heart conceals a utilitarian individualism behind expressivist language they highlight (1)—specifically, the dangers of unfettered egoism. While their fear that the religion of the heart undermines the possibility for deflecting criticism of unjust social structures points to (2), for it implies that this methodologically individualistic religious discourse is so totalizing—or "greedy"—in individuals' lives that they remain incapable of adopting competing social perspectives or moral traditions and engaging in shifting involvements. And finally, once we translate the concern about social control and unfreedom into a Durkheimian register we see that it amounts to a distinct version of (2)—that is, a fear that specific social norms are so "greedy" that they prohibit identification with alternative norms and moral traditions, as well as impede both social critique and shifting involvements.

These two unresolved concerns cry out for empirical investigation. But, as should be clear by now, not just any methodological approach will do. For if we are to take seriously the insights contained in my Durkheimian defence of romantic liberalism then we must heed the following guidelines.

First, in accepting the facts of institutional differentiation and moral diversity, we should resist the tendency to paint romantic liberal modernity with too broad a brush. As sociologist Gary Alan Fine (1979, 744) puts it, "Culture, like all aspects of social life, is situationally grounded and, thus, sociologists should bracket grand theorizing about culture in favor of examining it in situ." Indeed, we ought not assume that we know, prior to our investigation, what moral traditions or collective values are dominant.

Second, given the pivotal role ritual plays in Durkheimian thought, attending to discourse without ritual or practice will not suffice. For cultural structures and the discourses they inform are powerless without concomitant rituals to encode them with distinctive meaning and sacred value. Moreover, it is through participating in collective ritual that our "social self" is constituted. As Durkheim ([1961] 2002) puts it, "our individuality is not an empty form. It consists of elements that come to us from outside" (215). This insight is particularly salient given the distinctive character of the religion of the heart, which champions a teleology of self-realization, while positing an absolute distinction between the true inner self and the outer world of social norms and institutions. According to Durkheim, however much we phenomenologically experience our true self as emerging from deep within us, it is incontrovertibly *social* in nature—intimately and profoundly shaped by the institutional contexts we traverse and the social practices we engage in. Accordingly, he would argue that any responsible empirical investigation of the religion of the heart should focus on the sites and spaces within which particular conceptions of the "true self" are socially constructed and meaningfully encoded through collective ritual and shared practice.

It should be clear, in turn, why such an enquiry requires participant observation. It is only by means of prolonged study using ethnographic methods that we can discern the social contextualization of the religion of the heart. Thus, the following three chapters consist of Durkheimian cultural sociological investigations, each of which is guided by critics' unresolved concerns regarding the pathologies of anomie and egoism, and the issue of shifting involvements.

Of course, it would be wrong to suppose that these case studies can resolve critics' concerns decisively. All the same, I believe they can still garner lessons and insights that will ultimately prove illuminating.

An Overview of the Case Studies

The case studies that comprise Part III each look at a particular voluntary association within the romantic liberal institutional order where, through collective ritual, the religion of the heart is discursively encoded, enfleshed, and imbued with moral authority. Chapter 8 examines the meeting of Alcoholics Anonymous, New Life Fellowship (NLF), where I met Leslie Parker. Chapter 9 centres on the neo-Pentecostal church, C3 Toronto (C3T), where I encountered Amy Lee. And Chapter 10 covers Tomorrow's Leaders (TL), the Toastmasters public speaking club where I was introduced to Michael Wallace.

One could be forgiven for wondering why I chose such seemingly disparate comparative case studies. Yet it is precisely this superficial diversity that interests me. In fact, one of the reasons I chose these field sites is because they powerfully illustrate how the religion of the heart circulates across both "religious" and "secular" contexts. In other words, they help me to drive home the argument that I advanced in the preceding chapter: that the religious sphere of romantic liberal modernity is not what it used to be.

As a means of grappling with critics' unresolved concerns I analyse each of these sites as independent moral communities, which not only institutionalize a particular version of the religion of the heart but also instantiate a distinctive collective identity on the basis of a shared conception of the "true self." Each chapter begins with a brief historical description of the specific field site, which is then followed by a mapping of how the ten tenets of the religion of the heart take discursive form at each of them. Next, I break down the nature, and individual components, of the collective rituals institutionalized at each group. In this task I rely significantly on previous academic studies of these three organizations. Importantly, my aim is not to offer wholly novel (and therefore potentially controversial) sociological interpretations of these field sites. Rather, I'm interested in marshalling existing scholarship in order to bring certain aspects of these groups into view—aspects that our self-understanding has led us to miss—which bolster my normative arguments regarding the character and constitution of both the religion of the heart and romantic liberal modernity more generally. Then, after making clear how these three groups can be conceived as *institutionalizing specific collective rituals which encode and enflesh a specific conception of the true self*, I revisit critics' unresolved concerns—identifying both where and when their criticisms are warranted, as well as where and when they are not. I conclude each chapter with a discussion of those aspects of my empirical findings which suggest that even when critics are correct, their renderings of the religion of the heart—and by proxy, romantic liberal modernity—often obscure or overlook significant issues, thereby oversimplifying what is, in reality, far more complex.

PART III
THE ROMANTIC LIBERAL SUBJECT

8

Moral Reform and Shifting Involvements at a Twelve Step Group

Outside of the church stand a motley group of young people forming a semi-circle, as each smokes a cigarette. Holding my breath, I walk past the group and enter the building. Inside I'm bombarded with activity; people of all stripes crisscrossing the lobby, moving in and out of rooms. I make my way down to the basement, where New Life Fellowship (NLF) meets once a week. The rec room the group rents, though not large, fits up to a hundred attendees some nights. I find a seat near the back.

The majority who attend NLF regularly are under thirty-five, though as usual I spot a number of men (and a few women) who look older. They generally sit alone, wearing faces of sorrow and shame, staring at the ground. Surrounding these scattered nomads are various small groups of individuals, whose demeanours reflect a quite different emotional state: they converse in a matter-of-fact way about the day's events, what they had for supper, the weather. This all seems routine to them.

With only a few minutes until the hour the room is near capacity. Greeters remain at the door, dutifully shaking hands with stragglers, who then look in desperation for free seats. The room is now full of chatter, though many sit in silence. The range of emotions alive in the room is dizzying—it's not uncommon to find deep-throated laughter emanating from one corner, while a person cries softly in another. Suddenly, one of the members, a young woman who can't be more than twenty, calls the meeting to order. She asks for a moment of silence. Within seconds, the room transforms from a chaotic mix of babble and shuffling to one of absolute and focused silence. Most close their eyes. The silence holds for a few moments. Then the whole room begins to recite in unison, "God, grant me the serenity to accept the things I cannot change, the courage to change the things I can, and the wisdom to know the difference." The meeting has begun.

A Brief History of Alcoholics Anonymous

AA began in the 1930s as a branch of the Oxford Group, an American evangelical and ecumenical movement founded in the early twentieth century. Theologically,

The Spiritual Turn: The Religion of the Heart and the Making of Romantic Liberal Modernity. Galen Watts,
Oxford University Press. © Galen Watts 2022. DOI: 10.1093/oso/9780192859839.003.0009

the Oxford Group owed much to Pietism, with its emphasis on experiencing the Holy Spirit as a prerequisite for salvation. However, in his history of the movement, Bill Pittman (1988, 122) argues that the group's closest historical precedent can be found "in the sweeping enthusiasm of the Methodist movement."

In 1935, Bill Wilson joined the Oxford Group. A failed stockbroker from Akron, Ohio, Wilson had struggled for years with his drinking. In the hopes the group could help him stay sober, Wilson threw himself into it, eventually starting what in Akron became known as "the alcoholic squadron of the Oxford Group" (Jensen 2000, 30). According to AA lore, the fellowship of Alcoholics Anonymous began when Wilson met a man named Robert Holbrook Smith (known to AA members as "Dr. Bob"). In developing the basic teachings of the program—which were eventually distilled into the fellowship's basic text, *Alcoholics Anonymous*—Wilson and Smith adopted many of the principles of the Oxford Group. But they also drew from a number of other sources for inspiration.

After reading the work of Carl Jung, Bill came to believe alcoholism was a disease that could only be cured by means of a "spiritual experience" (Kurtz 1979, 33). In fact, it was arguably AA that began the trend of drawing a sharp symbolic boundary between "spirituality" and "religion," thereby popularizing the moniker "spiritual but not religious" (Fuller 2001, 112). A seeker by nature, Wilson was also significantly inspired by William James. While detoxing in a hospital Wilson read James's *Varieties of Religious Experience*, which proved, for him, revelatory.

AA's organizational structure is essentially democratic. When there are issues that affect the fellowship globally, decisions are made at the group level and gradually communicated upwards to what's called the AA General Services Office, located in New York. Moreover, individual AA groups have significant autonomy regarding how they operate. As Ernst Kurtz and William White (2015, 60) observe, "there really is no single entity as 'Alcoholics Anonymous'—only AA members and local AA groups that reflect a broad and ever-increasing variety of AA experience." This is all the more striking in light of the fact that today AA boasts over 2 million active members and 120,000 groups in approximately 175 countries (A.A. General Service Office 2020).

How do these myriad groups, structured in such a decentralized manner, retain anything in common? First, no matter where it exists AA remains explicitly apolitical. In other words, in meetings, members "do not talk politics" (Jensen 2000, 63). Thus, we might say AA both assumes the romantic liberal separation of private and public spheres, while identifying itself expressly with the former. Second, all AA groups consider *Alcoholics Anonymous*, or the "Big Book" as it's known to members, canonical (Antze [1987] 2003)—that is, AA discourse remains authoritative at all AA groups, thereby ensuring a degree of unity across the global fellowship.

New Life Fellowship (NLF)

In many respects, NLF's weekly meeting differs little from other AA meetings. It takes place in the basement of a local church. In meetings, members sit in rows on old metal chairs, facing a table where the chairperson and speaker sit. One hears many of the same readings read aloud, along with a collective recitation of the Serenity Prayer, at both the beginning and close of the meeting. And like many other Twelve Step groups, NLF presents itself as officially "spiritual but not religious" (McClure and Wilkinson 2020). All of this is run of the mill in AA wherever you go.

Yet local differences do exist. Despite the uniformity of AA discourse, embodied in its written and oral traditions, we nevertheless find "different cultural expressions of core AA elements" (Westermeyer 2014, 159). In this way, AA groups exhibit their own *idioculture*, which Fine (1979, 734) characterizes as "a system of knowledge, beliefs, behaviors, and customs shared by members of an interacting group." Now, in order to map NLF's idioculture we need to examine the dramatic changes in demography that transformed it into the group it is today.

Roughly five years ago, a large number of young queer- and trans-identifying people joined the meeting. As Pat recalled, because it was a young persons' meeting, NLF attracted many of the queer youth who suffered from addiction in Toronto. Another early member, Robin, shared that as Pat and Hal—the first two explicitly trans-identifying NLF members—began showing up regularly to the meeting, it became known as a safe space for the trans community in the city. Queer and trans alcoholics and addicts found in NLF an AA meeting where they could share about their experiences being trans, and where they didn't need to hide their gender or sexual identities. NLF soon developed a reputation for welcoming those who belonged to the LGBTQ+ community with open arms.

AA groups tend to reflect their surrounding environments (see Cahn 2005; Christensen 2010). So, as Toronto transformed in the wake of the 1960s from being a "bastion of Britishness and Protestantism" (Levine 2014, 88) to "the world's most diverse city—and one of the trans-/queer-friendliest" (Raj 2017, 154), Toronto AA groups have changed with it. Indeed, there is an undeniable sense in which the city is far more "Toronto the Queer" than the "Toronto the Good" of yesteryear. So, for many young queer and trans people, the city serves as a kind of sanctuary, an escape from what they've experienced as an unaccepting and hostile world.

Over time, queer and trans members like Pat and Hal were conferred the moral authority that comes with sobriety and seniority in AA (Hoffman 2006, 676). And they gradually remade the group in order to cater in both explicit and implicit ways to the queer and trans community. This shows up, for instance, in the group's decision to change all male pronouns (He, Him) contained in the "Big

Book" to genderless ones (They, Them) when read aloud. They also changed the wording of the "AA Preamble," so that rather than reading in meetings, "Alcoholics Anonymous is a fellowship of men and women..." they instead read, "Alcoholics Anonymous is a fellowship of people..." Additionally, the group included in the chairperson's weekly statement the following disclaimer: "There are members of the LGBTQ community here tonight."

However, NLF's idioculture is most evident, not in the explicit inclusion of statements, or changes in recited literature, but rather in what might be called the *performative force* contained in the core members' public statements and self-presentations. To give some examples: Leslie Parker, whom we met earlier, regularly refers to her higher power as "She" during her shares, while another member, Fran, confidently refers to theirs as "Goddess." Indeed, it's not uncommon to hear members share things to the effect of, "You can call your higher power whatever you want," "The basic text of AA is so patriarchal," and "We are a bunch of weirdos and freaks at this group," with resolute sincerity and good-humour.

What's more, there is a distinctive *normative aesthetic* at NLF: among core members, body piercings and tattoos in abundance, peculiar hairstyles, and eccentric fashion styles are the norm. Indeed, nearly all the core members of the group don clothing, wear their hair, and decorate their bodies in ways that defy the norms of professional society. Moreover, these aesthetic displays make the individual in question's gender identity difficult to discern. The force of this kind of self-presentation is crucial to understanding NLF's idioculture—its *queer subcultural identity*.

Because the group's members share a common identification with the LGBTQ+ community, loaded with its own political commitments and discursive understandings, they exert a considerable degree of influence over NLF's idioculture—and thereby give formative shape to what Durkheim would call its *collective conscience*, referring to the totality of sacred beliefs and sentiments common to a moral community (see Durkheim [1893] 2014, 63).[1] In other words, because these queer- and trans-identifying members are, by all outward indications, the unspoken leaders of the meeting, they set the group's tone and authorize its moral norms. Indeed, they wield significant influence within the meeting—modelling what "good sobriety" looks like, and exhibiting, by their examples, how one ought to "work the program."

And yet, despite NLF's idiosyncrasies, members remain steadfastly committed to the AA program. In fact, their distinctive collective conscience is only made

---

[1] "Collective conscience" is not a perfect translation of the French original, *conscience collective*. But as Smith (2020, 15) makes clear, it is customary to accept this translation "while noting that a residuum of 'awareness' or 'self-awareness' or even 'reflexivity' rests somewhere deep inside the term."

possible because of the group's abiding commitment to AA discourse—a particular iteration of the religion of the heart.

The Religion of the Heart at New Life Fellowship: AA Discourse

Experiential Epistemology

"At the very heart of all the experience of Alcoholics Anonymous," writes historian Ernest Kurtz (1979, 191), "lay experience." This is true in multiple respects. First, it is an unspoken rule that one must always speak from experience, and restrict one's shares in meetings to "I statements." Members commonly preface their shares with, "*I* am not an expert and *I* only have my experience, but this is what works for *me*." Second, it's generally accepted within the fellowship that reason, or science, are not useful when it comes to recovering from alcoholism. As Liam put it, "the biggest fallacy is that I can think my way out of my problems." Working the Twelve Steps allows AA members to *experience* what they need to stay sober, and meetings are where they "*feel* God's presence." And third, the truth of the program ultimately derives from its efficacy in helping the alcoholic to stay sober. As Kurtz explains, "most members of Alcoholics Anonymous come to an understanding of their God through His felt rather than believed effect in their lives" (175).

Immanence of God or the Superempirical

The third step of the Twelve Steps reads, "Made a decision to turn our will and our lives over to the care of God as we understood Him." While the wording of this step clearly reflects AA's evangelical roots, NLF members take seriously the qualification, "*as we understood Him*." During their shares in meetings, members speak of "God" variably in terms of a "higher power," "Spirit of the Universe," "Force," "Divine Energy," "Creator," "Goddess," "God-X," "She," "Invisible Sky Friend," and even "Whatever word you're comfortable with." How NLF members label God or the superempirical seems less important than the fact that it's considered a power *greater and other than egoistic*, and that it's something that can be *experienced directly* (Rudy and Greil 1989, 45). As anthropologist Maria Gabrielle Swora (2004, 188) puts it, "The Twelve Steps move the alcoholic toward an understanding of the world as sacred, or in AA's terms, as spiritual." Indeed, NLF members assume they can access mystical or divine guidance by *going within* and listening for "God-thoughts" or intuitions. In this way, AA discourse posits access to an immanent divinity.

Benevolent God/Universe

It is perhaps not surprising that AA members—many of whom have suffered from experiences of childhood abuse, trauma, or mental illness—yearn for a loving and benevolent "higher power" in their lives. In fact, it is common to hear at NLF that members struggled with the "God-thing" upon entering AA because of the negative associations they held towards "religion," but that once they learned their higher power did not have to be judgmental or vengeful they embraced it. As one trans member of NLF, Lars, put it: "my God loves me for exactly who I am." While Farouk described his higher power as "the most loving and forgiving thing I can think of." Thus, members of NLF carry forward the Jamesian legacy of a religion of healthy-mindedness. However, rather than aim for the "wonderful inner paths to a supernatural kind of happiness," as James tantalizingly put it, NLF members simply seek a higher power that doesn't wish for them to suffer or struggle in vain.

Redemptive Self as Theodicy

AA discourse teaches that every event in life is meaningful. As Leslie Parker averred, "I had to go through what I went through in order to get to this place." And another NLF member explained, "I am able to accept what happened to me because I can now see the lessons in them." AA members learn to narrate their lives in a way that imbues all of their past experiences with "spiritual" significance. In fact, there is a clear narrative structure or script that informs AA stories. In early childhood the feeling of being "different" plagues the alcoholic. Alcohol becomes a means of quelling or coping with this feeling. However, as a result of their alcoholism the individual experiences a series of increasingly dire negative consequences. This self-destructive cycle ends only when the alcoholic "hits bottom" and "surrenders," upon which they have a "spiritual experience" and commence to rebuild their lives under the guidance of their "higher power" (see Rudy and Greil 1983, 9).

Needless to say, this is a deeply redemptive life narrative—and every committed AA member learns to adapt it to their past and present circumstances. Furthermore, AA discourse teaches members that their negative experiences were *necessary* in order to help those who continue to suffer from alcoholism. This is because only those with experiences of alcoholism are said to be able to reach the alcoholic. As anthropologist Paul Antze ([1987] 2003, 173) observes, veteran AA members see their experiences with alcoholism "as having 'elected' them to a unique therapeutic mission." Lastly, in adopting this narrative as their own, AA members learn to look out for signs of their higher power's presence in their lives. Swora (2004, 203) explains, "For many AA members, nothing in the world happens arbitrarily or by mistake; there are no coincidences in God's world."

Self-Realization as Teleology

AA discourse postulates self-realization as the end suffering serves, and the ultimate purpose of the alcoholic's life. Members commonly say things like, "In pain and suffering you find growth," and "My worst moments taught me the most valuable lessons." Yet realizing one's true self is given a distinct framing at NLF. Members often distinguish between who they were *when they were in active addiction*—what they refer to variously as their "alcoholic self," "ego," or "when I was sick"—and who they are *now that they are clean and sober*—what they refer to as their "true" or "recovering" self (Pollner and Stein 2001, 47). Amara shared that, upon getting sober, she asked her AA sponsor whether she needed to seek forgiveness from her higher power for what she'd done while drinking. Her sponsor replied that she didn't need to because her higher power knew that she wasn't really her true self when she was drinking—that who she is *truly* is *who she is when sober*. Thus, "getting sober" for members of NLF amounts to far more than remaining abstinent; it entails a life-long quest to become who they were meant to be, or who they truly are. Indeed, NLF institutionalizes an expressivist ethic whereby members are expected to seek out their true self and live accordingly.

Self-Ethic (Voice from Within)

Among NLF members, the false alcoholic self is conceived as a *by-product of an oppressive society and culture*. They learn to interpret their lives prior to getting sober as a fall from grace as a result of corrupt socialization—the result of heteronormativity, homophobia, materialism, and other societal sources—which they must undo in order to realize their true recovering selves. Typical of the religion of the heart, then, NLF members conceive of their true self as *pre-social*, or free of social or cultural influences, while construing society as the source of corruption and iniquity.

Of course, AA discourse does not merely presuppose a pre-social self, but also that members can become inwardly connected to an immanent divinity: it is generally accepted at NLF that one is "being true to oneself" or "living one's truth" when one is attuned to, or following the will of, one's higher power. As a result, members spend considerable time trying to distinguish their false "alcoholic self" from their true "recovering self."

Virtue Is Natural

It is a staple of the redemptive self that although individuals may have struggled and committed wrongful acts, at the beginning, "goodness was there" (McAdams 2006, 235). In realizing one's "recovering self" the alcoholic is assumed to simultaneously reconnect with, and embody, that inner pre-social core. This follows from NLF members' conception of the "ego" of the alcoholic as the by-product of a corrupt society. However, members also accept the AA precept that alcoholism is essentially a *disease of egoism*—or as one member put it, a "disease of more."

Here we can see how NLF members challenge and revise the evangelical underpinnings of AA. Rather than viewing the alcoholic as innately selfish (which would resemble something like original sin), these young people tend to view their egoism as a by-product of the culture and society they were raised in. Yet while acknowledging its social origins, they nevertheless accept that they, as individuals, acted selfishly and must therefore take responsibility. In turn, to undertake the AA program of recovery is not merely to remain abstinent, but also to cultivate the virtues of honesty, humility, tolerance or open-mindedness, and selflessness. Indeed, members encourage one another to cultivate these virtues in both subtle and overt ways. And yet, despite the moral dimensions of "getting sober," most members of NLF shy away from invoking explicitly moral language. Instead, they prefer framing their personal transformations in medical terms—as a process of "healing," "recovering," or "becoming whole."

Sacralization of Individual Liberty

The value of individual liberty is foundational at NLF. Members are adamant that individuals must freely choose to join the fellowship, that no member has the authority to offer anything more than "suggestions" to another, and that the fellowship itself must operate according to the principle of "attraction rather than promotion." AA discourse therefore takes seriously the value of negative freedom: NLF members rail against the external authorities they perceive to be trying to constrain their true selves. For these young adults a life not lived from the inside is no life at all.

At the same time, AA discourse also encodes a conception of positive freedom, which emerges directly out of members' experiences with addiction. In interviews members shared, "My experience with the Twelve Steps is that I have freedom from debilitating fear and anxiety today," "I'm more free in sobriety than when I was drinking," and "I finally have the freedom to choose how to live my life." For AA members, a life of complete self-determination was experienced as a nightmare. Under the influence of their addictions, they experienced a radical unfreedom, despite a relative lack of external constraints. Thus, AA discourse holds that real freedom, or autonomy, comes from dependence upon one's higher power, for only in this way can the alcoholic avoid the clutches of their alcoholic self (Kurtz 1979, 216).

Mind-Body-Spirit Connection

As I noted in Chapter 3, the mind-body-spirit connection tenet is ambiguous, in that it allows for rich interpretive variety. And yet it remains central to AA discourse: "Alcoholism" as understood by founder Wilson is a "disease" which affects mind, body, and spirit (Kurtz 1979, 164). Indeed, *Alcoholics Anonymous* outlines in systematic fashion how each of these dimensions are interconnected: the alcoholic's mind is said to be plagued by an obsession with alcohol, leading to a compulsion to drink. Meanwhile, the alcoholic's body is believed to have an allergy to alcohol such that when alcohol is consumed they immediately crave more, thereby leading to a vicious cycle. And finally, the alcoholic is said to suffer from a "spiritual malady," which only a "spiritual experience" can cure. Thus, "AA teaches that the physical, mental, and spiritual components of each alcoholic's individual life are mutually connected" (Kurtz 1979, 204).

Methodological Individualism

As with all other versions of the religion of the heart, AA discourse focuses on personal transformation rather than structural change (Mercadante 2015). Though NLF members might view their alcoholic self as a by-product of corrupt and oppressive societal norms, they nevertheless believe they must take personal responsibility for their recoveries from alcoholism. What this means is that members learn to accept that if they are to "recover," they must refrain from focusing on society's ills, and, as they say in the program, "sweep their own side of the street." AA discourse therefore presupposes an ideal of self-responsibility and a methodological individualism; recovery from addiction is an individual process, which can only be achieved by means of personal, not societal, reform.

AA Meetings as Collective Rituals

I have argued that AA discourse—a discursive variant of the religion of the heart—is morally authoritative at NLF. But as I stressed in Chapter 7, a Durkheimian perspective holds that discourses are powerless without concomitant collective rituals. It is worth emphasizing that this doesn't mean that rituals merely play one key role among many in socializing individuals to accept specific symbolic systems and moral traditions. Rather, it means that, for Durkheim, processes of meaning construction, socialization, identity acquisition, and moral formation have their foundations in ritual—that is, the *entirety of social life is only made possible because of ritual.*

It will be useful, then, to examine Durkheim's theory of ritual in more detail. For Durkheim, all rituals begin with *human assembly*. The reason for this is that when individuals gather together their collective presences produce a kind of social energy or "electricity," which Durkheim refers to as *collective effervescence* (Durkheim [1912] 1995, 217). Sociologist Randall Collins (2004, 35) usefully defines this as a "condition of heightened intersubjectivity." Of course, mere assembly is not sufficient to produce this state—shared action and awareness, as well as shared emotion, are also required: collective attention strengthens shared emotion, which in turn increases individual emotional energy, thereby intensifying the shared experience. So, we might say *rituals are patterned and coordinated forms of human behaviour which, by channelling and orienting collective attention and emotion, enable the construction, and reaffirmation, of a distinct collective conscience.* As we shall see, different rituals accomplish this differently. But from a Durkheimian perspective, what all rituals share is a propensity to produce collective effervescence, which in turn makes possible the following ritual effects.

First, the collective representations or discourses that structure the ritual are *sacralized* as a result of their association with the emotional arousal and heightened intersubjectivity experienced by participants. At the same time, the ritual encodes these shared symbols with meaning, such that they come to define reality for the group—giving life to its collective conscience.

Second, through ritual the "social self" is (re)constructed and strengthened. This is because the experience of collective effervescence transforms members "through a emotional structuring of their sensory and sensual being," in light of that which the group holds sacred (Shilling and Mellor 1998, 196).

Third, rituals reify and affirm the group's moral standards. This takes place because ritual participants *feel moral* when they are "acting with the emotional energy derived from the heightened experience of the group" (Collins 2004, 39). Thus, a by-product of ritual is that the collective representations held sacred by a moral community are reaffirmed and strengthened in the minds of the participants, bolstering their attachment to the group itself.

Furthermore, according to Durkheim, without regular and repeated ritual participation, commitment to the group and its moral ideals—and with them, the "social self"—eventually dissipates. Indeed, sacred symbols are only respected to the extent that they are "charged up with sentiments by participation in rituals" (Collins 2004, 37). Resultantly, "When the practices stop, the beliefs lose their emotional import, becoming mere memories, forms without substance, eventually dead and meaningless" (37).

It should be clear, then, why I place ritual centre stage in my analysis. The religion of the heart, as a cultural structure, will hold little private or public significance unless *repeatedly revivified through collective ritual*. So, in this section, I analyse NFL's weekly meeting as a specific type of collective ritual, identifying and delimiting its key components. I focus on weekly meetings because it is at these where NLF members assemble, thereby reaching a heightened condition of intersubjectivity. At the same time, I recognize that this ritual is not the sole source of moral (re)formation for NLF members. Indeed, as we will see, weekly meetings are often supplemented by personal rituals, which enable members to bolster their commitment to the group's collective conscience (Durkheim [1912] 1995, 214).

Erection of Symbolic Boundaries

All rituals draw boundaries between insiders and outsiders (Giesen 2006, 343). NLF does this in a number of ways. First, AA discourse makes a categorical distinction between "alcoholics" or "addicts" and "normal people" or "social drinkers." And this symbolic boundary is constantly reinforced as members are expected to introduce themselves as "alcoholics" whenever they speak in meetings. AA discourse, in demarcating and reifying a distinct collective identity, serves to enable a deep bond among members that is kin-like (Swora 2001, 5). Crucial, then, is the symbolic role "alcoholism" plays in the construction of moral community in AA. Not only does this heuristic serve to distinguish insiders from outsiders, but it also *presupposes an entire moral order*: the alcoholic is believed to suffer from excessive egoism or selfishness, which can only be diminished by means of working the Twelve Steps. This is why acceptance and internalization of AA discourse is so critical to the formation of community at NLF—until members view themselves as suffering from a "spiritual malady" that only AA can cure, they will likely feel no need to commit to the group.

Demarcation of a Distinct Social Environment

How is acceptance of this discourse achieved? The answer lies in the social environment AA groups like NLF create. It is noteworthy that meetings take place in an enclosed and private setting, where individuals remain anonymous. Both this physical separation and the requirement of anonymity serve to enable the creation of a distinct social environment, where the speech norms and codes of behaviour differ markedly from those that pervade elsewhere in romantic liberal modernity.

Newcomers at AA meetings are almost always plagued by shame; the struggling addict is used to feeling as though they have to hide aspects of who they are and what they've done. Indeed, it is not uncommon for alcoholics to feel stigmatized in their societies (Jensen 2000, 105). In turn, it is significant that, in the rooms of AA, members are not merely allowed, but in fact expected, to divulge these hidden aspects of their lives. This, of course, reflects an expressivist ethic, but it takes a distinct form in AA. That is, within the rooms, "members invert public reality by making stigma the norm" (Young 2011, 713). Time and again I've heard at NLF how relieved and inspired newcomers were to listen to others share about things they've said, thought, or done while in "active addiction"—things that might be considered taboo or even immoral outside the rooms of AA. Events that would likely be met with horror in public life are listened to without condemnation in meetings.

Of course, this also occurs in talk therapy. But what distinguishes the AA meeting is its *publicness* (O'Reilly 1997, 166). Jensen (2000, 108) explains, "As alcoholics confess their most hidden secrets to their higher power and other alcoholics, the secrets begin to lose their power." Second, the meetings consist of a series of monologues, so "cross-talk"—commenting on another person's share— is prohibited. This serves not only to prevent potential conflicts but also to reinforce the value of individual liberty—members must not be preached at, as assent must come from within. Finally, laughing at one's past misdeeds serves to distance one's present self from the "alcoholic self" who committed them, thereby facilitating moral reform (Pollner and Stein 2001, 48).

Again, NLF institutionalizes a distinctly AA version of an expressivist ethic, which contrasts sharply with much of public life in romantic liberal modernity. For members, AA meetings are experienced as a kind of haven, where masks can be set aside and authentic selves can engage in intimate emotional exchanges. For individuals who are suffering from shame and self-loathing the degree of emotional honesty found at NLF is experienced as exhilarating and energizing. This is critical to the production of collective effervescence in AA, as this emotional energy is harnessed in order to strengthen members' commitment to both AA discourse and the group itself. In turn, by creating a social environment where members can identify with one another, and where the public confession of one's "bad behaviour" is made normative, each meeting serves to galvanize NLF members, reinforcing their commitment to the program and reconstituting their selves in light of AA discourse.

The Performative Uses of Storytelling

Storytelling is endemic to human life. As Taylor (2016, 317) observes, we are language animals, so "through my story, I define my identity." Narrative psychologists have extended this insight, arguing that "we ultimately make meaning out of our lives through stories" (McAdams 2006, 289). The religion of the heart, as a cultural structure, only gains plausibility and force when encoded in the narratives individuals tell about themselves and their lives. Indeed, this is why groups like NLF are so crucial to study, for they serve as the sites of collective storytelling, where shared narratives are internalized by individuals in order to make sense of their pasts, presents, and futures. As Wuthnow (1994, 301) observes, "People in groups do not simply tell stories—they become their stories."

Carole Cain contends that AA stories "are part of the process of cultural transmission," and serve a number of functions. First, they reframe AA discourse into a narrative form, naturalizing the religion of the heart. Second, they encode what it means to be an alcoholic, enabling individuals to identify themselves as alcoholics and also label others. And third, the "AA story is a cognitive tool" or "a mediating device for self-understanding," meaning the AA member "learns to tell and to understand his own life as an AA life, and himself as an alcoholic" (Cain 1991, 215). What Cain is pointing to is the way storytelling, when performed in the distinct social environment offered by AA meetings, functions to reconstitute members' sense of self in light of AA discourse.

How does this work? Stories are not merely told, but *lived*. Or, put another way, in narrating their lives according to AA discourse, NLF members literally *reinterpret* (and therefore *reconstitute*) their selves. "Every telling of one's story involves a number of acts of identity," writes Jensen (2000, 115). "The speaker reaffirms an identity with his or her former self (I am the person who did these things, the person who takes responsibility for these things) even as he or she creates (with each retelling) an increased sense of distance from that self."

So, we might say, "Speakers come to know themselves and others as they speak" (113). Or, a bit more provocatively, storytelling at NLF serves to "make up" people (Weegman and Piwowoz-Hjort 2009, 273). Each time a member shares publicly they construct and reinforce the pure and pristine "true recovered self" they now identify with, as well as the contaminated or "polluted alcoholic self" they reject (Pollner and Stein 2001, 47). And as members share their stories in meetings they learn to model forms of behaviour that embody the latter—they literally *perform their recovering self*.

Additionally, telling one's story is not merely descriptive, but also *prescriptive*. For each telling is an act of self-constitution in light of the moral ideals and collective values encoded at NLF. As Jensen (2000, 113) observes, "as [AA members] speak, sharing the stories of their lives, constructing heroes, they do so by taking on the values of the community." He adds, "Each time they speak, they reinforce those values. So, they construct heroes that are like the heroes of the community." At NLF the heroes are those veteran members such as Pat and Hal who have achieved long-term sobriety, belong to the queer and trans community, and embody the AA virtues. These members come closest to embodying the group's collective conscience, which comprises a combination of liberal Christian ideals—humility, selflessness, honesty, and tolerance—and a queer subcultural identity.

Of course, stories are not merely *told*, but in a very real sense *enfleshed*. What I mean by this is that the act of telling stories does not merely reconstitute the speaker's sense of self, but quite literally *how they experience the world*. Again, Durkheim's notion of collective effervescence is critical in this regard. By stoking emotional energy within individuals and orienting and affixing this energy to those sacred forms that are central to the collective identity of the group, rituals serve to reconfigure individuals on a physiological level (Shilling 2005, 215).

This illuminates how, despite epistemically privileging personal experience, AA discourse avoids leading to solipsism or anarchy. The key thing to bear in mind is that *all experience requires interpretation*: AA discourse provides a particular narrative script, or heuristic, with which newcomers learn to *interpret their experiences*. Indeed, it is not an exaggeration to suggest that unity in AA is predicated upon a *shared interpretation of the alcoholic identity and experience*. By reading AA literature and listening to experienced members share, newcomers learn that as "alcoholics" their experiences were the result of a "spiritual malady." They are socialized into AA discourse by *identifying* with the experiences described (and indeed prescribed) by veteran members (those who have internalized the AA discourse). And this process is such that *once the newcomer begins to interpret their experiences through AA discourse, they begin to actually have new experiences which lend credence to its plausibility*.

Leslie Parker described listening intently at her first visit to NLF to veteran members sharing their experiences with alcoholism. The narratives they recounted—what they'd done, how they felt, what they aspired to—all "resonated" with her in such a way that she identified with them, and as a result, began to accept as true the AA stories they used to interpret their experiences. In other words, Leslie's *experience of identification* granted plausibility and thereby authority to AA discourse. As the weeks went by, Leslie continued to listen to NLF members share about having "God-thoughts" and "spiritual experiences"—and soon enough she too began to experience these. And in time, she learned that, as an "alcoholic," she experiences life in a way that "non-alcoholics" do not.

Leslie's case enables us to see that while an experiential epistemology is institutionalized at NLF, AA discourse serves as a means of framing experiences in such a way that it feeds and supports a particular conception of her "true self." And this sheds light on how the ideal of self-realization can serve well-defined collective ends. Though certainly amenable to individual interpretation, as Durkheim would expect, the *true self at NLF is very much socially constituted*— fundamentally reflective of the group's collective conscience. Thus, as members begin to internalize AA discourse as encoded at NLF they quite literally come to experience the world in a way that reaffirms its plausibility. "God-thoughts," which members like Leslie interpret as emanating from a source beyond the group, in fact, reflect the *distinct moral ideals of the group itself*, and the lessons individual members learn to distil out of the day's events are similarly shaped by its collective values. In turn, active engagement in NLF meetings serves to produce commitment to the group by means of identity (re)constitution.

Practices of Self-Cultivation

NLF's weekly meeting stands out as the primary locus of socialization, where members' "social selves" are born and reaffirmed. Yet, upon introduction to the AA program, members quickly learn that merely going to meetings is not sufficient to achieve "emotional sobriety." On the contrary, according to veteran members "working the program" requires engaging in various practices of self-cultivation in order to stay in "fit spiritual condition" and realize one's true self.

The first of these is remaining abstinent from alcohol and mind- or mood-altering drugs. Ironically, while some medical professionals view this as an extreme measure, from a sociological perspective, the requirement of abstinence is crucial to securing both solidarity and commitment, as it serves to bolster the "alcoholic" identity and strengthen the bond between alcoholics. Second is the practice of psychological identification. Jensen (2000, 98) explains, "As they identify with others in the program, newcomers take on a new persona" (98). As a result, "listeners, also alcoholics, commune with speakers and are transformed by their stories" (24). Indeed, identification is critical to the process of identity reconstitution in AA. Moreover, this is very much a learned skill; newcomers are encouraged by their sponsors and veteran members to "ignore the differences" and "focus on the similarities," which amounts to disregarding those aspects of their biography that clash with AA discourse, and highlighting those aspects of their life (especially the emotional states) that can be related to the narrative told by the speaker. Again, this is central to community formation, for it is only through members collectively identifying as "alcoholics"—as "being in the same boat"—that solidarity is made possible (Trevino 1992).

Accordingly, the most important practices of self-cultivation found in NLF are *abstinence, storytelling,* and *psychological identification.* Yet there are others. These include practices of "recalling the last drink," "helping the newcomer" (often called "Twelfth Stepping"), prayer and meditation in order to connect with one's higher power, and monitoring one's thoughts and feelings for traces of the alcoholic self. Members learn to look out for polluted thoughts and feelings of resentment, fear, and self-centeredness, as they are taught that "the alcoholic who is not drinking but taken over by these dangerous emotions is not truly sober but is merely 'dry', on an 'emotional binge'" (Swora 2001, 13). Members also regularly consult with each other in order to discern whether or not a particular desire they might have is selfish or reflective of their true recovering self. In all of this, NLF members regularly engage in forms of self-cultivation in order to revivify and reaffirm their commitment to one another, and to the group's collective conscience.

The Pathologies of Romantic Liberal Modernity
at New Life Fellowship

Having systematically outlined how NLF functions as a site of collective ritual, we can now take up the first concern regarding the religion of the heart: *whether or not it can offer a corrective to the pathologies of romantic liberal modernity—anomie and egoism.*

Recall that one group of critics charge "spirituality" with producing anomic and/or egoistic individuals. They argue that by sacralizing individual liberty, "religious individualism" gives too much authority to the individual, producing social atomism. For instance, Bellah et al. (1985, 232) criticize what they call "communities of personal support" where "community and attachment come not from the demands of a tradition, but from the empathetic sharing of feelings among therapeutically attuned selves." And they further criticize "spirituality" on the grounds that it allegedly "lacks any effective social discipline" (246). Similarly, Carrette and King (2005, 58) view Twelve Step programs like AA as "not a cure for our sense of social isolation and disconnectedness but ... in fact, part of the problem." They further argue groups like NLF have "played into the hands of a neoliberal ideology of religion" (68). Translating these terms into a Durkheimian register, we can say these critics fear that with the rise of neoliberalism, and the accompanying spread of utilitarian individualism, AA members like those at NLF are solely being socialized by the moral logic of the economic sphere.

It is useful to distinguish between two distinct criticisms contained in the above accounts. First, critics argue groups like NLF, which naturalize "spirituality"—and thereby expressive individualism—cannot produce robust moral community and therefore cannot stave off anomie. Second, critics argue that AA groups like NLF, even when they can create moral community, do so not by naturalizing expressive individualism, but rather by naturalizing the utilitarian individualism of the economic sphere, thereby exacerbating egoism. Let's take these up in turn.

Regarding the problem of anomie, it is not difficult to see what would give critics this impression. At NLF the value of individual liberty is firmly entrenched—members take their own personal experiences as authoritative, there exist minimal overt social norms or regulations, moral language is eschewed, and members join the group on the basis of self-interest (e.g., to stay sober). Moreover, the lack of explicit authorities and the extensive negative freedom members have to decide for themselves what their recoveries require would seem a recipe for weak attachment and commitment. It is therefore not by any means obvious how a place like this could serve as a site of social integration and belonging.

And yet, as I have demonstrated, it does. This process begins once the newcomer commences identifying as an "alcoholic," which entails internalizing AA discourse. By actively participating in meetings, NLF members reconstitute their selves in consonance with the collective values and virtues encoded in the narratives shared. In this, we can see Durkheim's conception of human nature at work. As members internalize the values of the group, they begin to *identify with them* (what they call their "recovering self") such that they eventually *desire to abide by them*. As a result, doing "what feels right" or listening to "one's inner self"— ostensibly self-interested and void of communal obligation—in reality, reflects the collective conscience of the group at work *within* the individual—their "social self." Thus, the normative tasks of healing, becoming whole, and self-realization—all of which smack to communitarians and conservatives of rugged individualism—are, contrary to critics' claims, deeply moral and collective in nature.

One of the primary reasons why these critics have tended to miss this, I believe, is due to their assumptions about the relationship between the individual and community—which sociologist Paul Lichterman (1996, 11) calls the "seesaw model." On this view, it's assumed that the good of the individual is necessarily at odds with the good of the community, such that the advancement of one implies erosion of the other. So, when NLF members proclaim, "AA is a selfish program," or make statements like, "I go to meetings because it helps me stay sober," critics simply assume their rhetoric reflects a lack of commitment to the group. However, as Durkheim recognized, it is in fact when the individual *identifies* with the good of community, such that what he or she perceives as being in their self-interest is significantly shaped by the group's collective conscience, that commitment is strongest (Rosati 2009, 37). Therefore, at NLF, the practice of self-help ought not be understood as being at odds with an other-oriented way of being. As one NLF member affirmed, "the opposite of addiction isn't sobriety, it's connection."

This leads us to the other concern: is AA discourse, as encoded at NLF, a mere "capitalist spirituality"? Carrette and King (2005, 42) single out AA for contributing to "a new cultural malaise—the loneliness and isolation of contemporary individualism." Instead, they call for a revival of "the religious traditions," which encourage "identification with others" along with the moral ideals of "selfless love and compassion toward others" (83, 171).

I find this baffling in light of the fact that egoism is considered within AA discourse *a primary symptom of the disease of alcoholism*. In the *Twelve Steps and Twelve Traditions*—a text whose authority in AA is second only to *Alcoholics Anonymous*—the alcoholic is described thus: "we have demanded more than our share of security, prestige, and romance...Never was there enough of what we thought we wanted" (*Twelve Steps and Twelve Traditions* 1952, 71). "We had lacked the perspective to see that character-building and spiritual values had to come first, and that material satisfactions were not the purpose of living" (71). And finally, in sketching out a normative vision for the recovering alcoholic, the text reads: "Our desires for emotional security and wealth, for personal prestige and power, for romance, and for family satisfactions—all these have to be tempered and redirected. We have learned that the satisfactions of instincts cannot be the sole end and aim of our lives" (114). What's more, this normative vision persists in the testimonies of NLF members, and in the personal stories they narrated in meetings. For instance, as Hal shared in our interview, "our society doesn't have any meaning, and it tells us to value things that don't matter." They then added, "I was addicted to *more*. Nothing was ever enough. So, I was always miserable." Hal's representative example makes vivid that "getting sober" necessarily entails limiting one's insatiable desires, and becoming more selfless— precisely the *opposite* of egoism. Indeed, most NLF members describe their trajectories in recovery in terms of a shift away from an excessively egoistic life towards one that is guided by the moral ideals Carrette and King champion. Nor is this unique to NLF. As Kim Bloomfield (1994, 33) reports, "one of AA's main actions is its opposition to utilitarian individualism. The 'Big Book', the basic text of AA, is replete with references to the dangers of egotism and the pursuit of one's own interests without concern for others or one's higher power . . . The fellowship is a primary source in today's society voicing the need for limits against the limitlessness of utilitarianism." It would seem, then, that AA discourse challenges, much more than legitimates, the "lifestyle of self-interest and ubiquitous consumption" that Carrette and King allege reflects the status quo in romantic liberal modernity.

In sum, in accepting an alcoholic identity and learning to narrate one's life using AA discourse, NLF members are brought into a robust moral community that staves off the threat of anomie. Furthermore, rather than encouraging the egoism of the market, its members are taught that "working the program" requires challenging the utilitarian individualism they once accepted as authoritative (Trevino 1992, 194). Accordingly, active participation in meetings serves to morally regulate members, curbing their egoism.

Shifting Involvements at New Life Fellowship

We can now take up the second concern raised by critics: *does the religion of the heart at NLF lead to a colonization of competing social spheres, thereby impeding shifting involvements and the adoption of rival social perspectives and moral traditions?*

Talk of moral community and moral regulation has led some critics to fear that NLF traps its members in their identities as "alcoholics," stifling their ability to express or develop other potential selves. For instance, sociologist Micki McGee (2005, 187) argues that the "requirement of anonymity [in AA] cuts off the individual from any of his or her other identities." Critics like McGee fear that AA is a greedy institution whose members "must be so fully and totally committed to [it] that they become unavailable for alternative lines of action" (Coser 1974, 8).

At the same time, others worry that the symbolic boundaries legitimated at AA between "alcoholics" and "social drinkers" could fuel a kind alcoholic chauvinism—a concern raised by scholars who perceive in the AA fellowship a "sectarian" character (e.g., Jones 1970; Unterberger 1989).

At the base of these criticisms seems to rest anxiety about the degree of freedom members have to hold other commitments or to leave their groups. McGee (2005, 187) critically notes that the narrow emphasis placed on discussing one's alcoholic identity in meetings "separates his or her 'addict' identity from his or her other social roles." No doubt this is true. But it is important to point out that this also plays a central role in the cultivation of moral community. Indeed, this is the unavoidable *paradox of solidarity: exclusion is intrinsic to unity*. Durkheim would therefore argue that the strength of moral community at NLF would be far weaker without this emphasis, increasing the risk of anomie significantly. So, while McGee is correct that competing social identities are given far less priority in AA meetings, I would argue this shouldn't be lamented. Rather, *what should concern us is the degree to which the alcoholic identity is totalizing in members' lives*.

And based on my fieldwork I believe that while newcomers may seek in AA a comprehensive identity, the longer members stay in the program the more they are able and willing to invest in other social spheres. The reason for this is that in the early days of recovery from addiction, members are often searching for structure and order in their daily lives. As a result, they seek in AA discourse a totalizing identity. But the norm seems to be that this changes as time elapses. This was illustrated well by Pat who shared, "AA is not my whole life; I come to AA so that I can live a good life outside of these rooms." Accordingly, despite their constitutive nature, groups like NLF are not greedy institutions. Indeed, I've found that, typical of the religion of the heart more generally, for most NLF members *AA discourse is primarily circumscribed to private life*—thus being an alcoholic is far from totalizing in their lives.

Furthermore, although alcoholics might be taught to view themselves as having a kin-like relationship to one another, they are not taught to see their alcoholic identity as exclusive. In other words, being an alcoholic does not detract from, or conflict with, one's identity as, say, a sexual minority, a parent, or a citizen. And given its limited scope it is difficult to imagine AA discourse inspiring groups to separate themselves from society or fuelling social divisions. Indeed, the more reasonable concern is that groups like NLF incline members to accommodate themselves to the status quo (which I discuss below). So, it seems to me the fear of sectarianism is misplaced.

That said, AA discourse does constrain its members—at least as far as personal conduct is concerned. Indeed, it wouldn't serve as a successful site of social integration and moral regulation if it did not. This has led critics who see in the religion of the heart a new form of social control to contend the fellowship is inappropriate for women or gay men (among other minority groups), for whom "admitting powerlessness" may mean something quite different than it did for economically privileged white men who founded the fellowship (Sered and Norton-Hawk 2011). There is evident truth to this. The Big Book reflects its time and period. At the same time, the accounts of NLF members demonstrate just how malleable AA discourse is; they regularly reinterpret passages from *Alcoholics Anonymous* in order to accord with the group's queer subcultural identity. Moreover, this is not unusual. In her study of women's AA groups Jolene Sanders (2006, 4) found that "women in AA actively define the nature of their recovery experience in gender-specific and self-empowering ways." And Robert Kus (1987, 262) similarly found in his study of gay male AA members that "by conscientiously working the Twelve Steps, they begin to see being gay as a positive aspect of self rather than a negative one." These studies offer support to the argument that animates this chapter: groups adapt AA discourse to produce a distinct idioculture. Or, as Rachel Kornfield (2014, 417) puts it, "practice of AA across communities is not static or rigidly defined, illustrating instead how members interpret AA's principles to make them coherent within their broader cultural and social worlds."

Structural Critique and Generative Institutions

The question remains, however, whether or not AA discourse impedes the quest for social and economic justice by means of its methodological individualism. Critics who see in the spiritual turn the triumph of neoliberalism tend to zero in on the apolitical character of Twelve Step fellowships, as well as their anti-structuralism. For instance, in *The Globalization of Addiction* Bruce Alexander (2006, 299) lambasts groups like NLF because they "do not address the social causes of addiction." While McGee (2005, 182) contends that AA discourse "derails the opportunities for individuals to understand injuries or grievances as part of systematic social problems," further criticizing the program for endorsing "a worldview that is precisely the inverse of the 'sociological imagination'." These critics advance the claim that, as a result of their institutionalized methodological individualism, groups like NLF hamper their members from identifying and addressing the structural causes of romantic liberal modernity's social ills—and thereby legitimate social and economic injustice.

Of course, critics are right to contend that AA discourse is methodologically individualistic, and that it consequently foregrounds the actions of individuals in its heuristic. The religion of the heart is primarily concerned with private (or personal) life, and as a discursive expression of this cultural structure, AA discourse is no different. In meetings, NLF members are given a space within which they can realize their true selves, not engage in overt civic engagement or discuss public policy. And as Edmund O'Reilly (1997, 108) correctly notes, "the role of social pathologies in the genesis of individual alienation will never become a powerful theme in AA." This is ensured not only by AA discourse's anti-structuralism but also by the taboo placed on talk of politics in the rooms—a norm which serves as much to facilitate inclusive diversity as it does to quell social criticism.

Yet, as O'Reilly (1997, 108) points out, "This is not to suggest that AA members are incapable of, or enjoined from, social activism, only that platforms for it must be found outside of the boundaries of the program." In fact, "Nothing in AA precludes activism of any sort, provided it is not chemically buttressed." This is a crucial insight. Nearly every one of the members at NLF was engaged in some form of political activism outside the rooms of AA. For instance, Pat, one of the most longstanding members with twelve years of sobriety, talked at length about their experiences with community organizing, public protest, and political work in the queer and trans community. But more than this, Pat had no problem drawing on structuralist discourses when discussing these issues. And they were even willing to frame addiction as a result of an "oppressive" and "patriarchal" society—not altogether distinct from the critiques offered by Alexander, McGee, and Martin. When asked how they squared this structuralist framing with their commitment to AA, Pat responded that unless they accepted responsibility for their sobriety, they could not stay sober. In other words, when it came to their recovery, they wholeheartedly accepted the AA discourse of personal responsibility and self-realization. Yet, if asked to offer a structural critique, they had no trouble doing so.

Another illustrative example is offered by Neil who, like Pat, had been involved with a wide array of political organizing. Neil grew up queer in a small town, where he experienced extreme bullying. When we spoke, he was just finishing a doctorate in the humanities, and was a year sober. Neil told me he'd accrued two years of sobriety before, but then decided to "go out"—which he reflected on with regret. I asked him what he thought of the claim that his commitment to NLF might preclude him from engaging in structural critique or taking political action. He responded, "I can have all the most radical ideas about social justice, but unless I get sober I can't help anybody." Neil found that unless he internalized AA discourse, he was incapable of overcoming his addiction. I heard some version of this claim from nearly every other member of NLF I spoke to.

I think what Pat and Neil are spotlighting is *the utter uselessness of structuralist discourses in the face of acute and present suffering.* Faced with the pain of their addictions, outsourcing responsibility to "the system" simply didn't make sense. Thus, NLF members have learned to invoke *religious* (methodologically individualistic) discourses with respect to certain aspects of *their own lives* and *secular* (in this case, structuralist) discourses with respect to certain aspects of *those of others*. Put otherwise, when it comes to their *own* personal lives, AA discourse remains authoritative, but in thinking about the lives of *others*, they draw more readily on a structuralist perspective. This is, I would argue, a hallmark of romantic liberal modernity.[2]

Their examples also demonstrate the veracity of Wuthnow's (1998b, 28) observation that "self-help groups may provide some people with an opportunity to refashion their identity so that they can function more effectively as spouses and parents and citizens." Indeed, in his study of civic engagement in America Wuthnow reports, "across the nation many people who have participated in twelve-step groups have become involved in helping other people or working on civic projects." He therefore concludes, "Personal repair work is likely to go hand in hand with civic engagement, rather than conflicting with it" (217).

In agreement, I argue not only do groups like NLF not preclude shifting involvements and the experience of pluralism, but they often function as *generative institutions*.[3] We can best understand the nature of a generative institution by contrasting it with a greedy institution. If greedy institutions demand exclusive and undivided loyalty, generative institutions encourage shifting involvements and multiple social attachments. If greedy institutions serve to close the opportunities available to members to express other aspects of their selves or participate in competing institutional spheres, generative institutions encourage this, while at the same time serving as a source of psychic stability and communal belonging for their members. Finally, if greedy institutions risk obliterating "the private person as an autonomous actor" (Coser 1974 18), generative institutions bolster autonomy and independence, while also staving off the threat of anomie.

Critics who narrowly focus on the existence of apolitical and anti-structuralist discourse at Twelve Step meetings have paid little attention to the degree to which they serve to catalyse social and civic action far beyond the church basements they take place in. They have therefore dismissed their generative character. And while AA discourse may not highlight the structural sources of suffering, it does not preclude the adoption of social perspectives that do. Accordingly, one of the great advantages of taking a Durkheimian perspective is that it enables us to capture the wider complexity alive in romantic liberal modernity—and in so doing, we shall undoubtedly find that "one experience of associational life offsets others," and that "The lessons of one affiliation may provide countervailing force to the formative effects of another area of social life" (Rosenblum 1998, 49).

---

[2] This insight lies at the heart of Peter Berger's *The Many Altars of Modernity*. Berger came to the view that individuals in modernity variously invoke religious and secular discourses, pragmatically and contingently. I would argue this is equally true of individualistic and structuralist discourses.

[3] I thank Simon Coleman for this formulation.

Romantic Liberal Modernity and Communities of Redemption

Before I close this chapter, I want to highlight an aspect of social life that I believe critics of the religion of the heart from all camps tend, to their detriment, to either overlook or dismiss—the need for what I call *communities of redemption*.

Newcomers arrive at the proverbial doors of AA filled with shame and self-loathing. Whether the causes of these are partly (or even entirely) systemic does not detract from the fact that these feelings exist, and often plague individuals, stifling them from forming healthy relationships, engaging in projects, and enjoying life. As Wuthnow (1998b, 25) remarks, "Before they can be effective citizens, they have to relearn to be effective persons." This is easier said than done. Often newcomers at AA are so haunted by their pasts that they remain stuck in a cycle of addiction and self-destruction. McAdams (2006, 228) therefore argues, "for many addicts the only way to break the cycle is to create a new life story." However, the new story must be "more than just a few new words. It must instead integrate the addict in a caring and productive social environment." He further remarks that, in some cases, "a religious meaning may be the only kind of meaning that is powerful enough to exert the kind of redemptive force that the reform narrative seems to demand" (237).

In Chapter 6, I suggested that a central reason for the appeal of the religion of the heart in romantic liberal modernity is its ability to imbue suffering with meaning. The accounts of AA members exhibit this powerfully. We might say then that NLF functions as a site of private enchantment, where individuals' personal lives are imbued with cosmic meaning and purpose, and where they can achieve a sense of redemption. By internalizing AA discourse, members learn to reinterpret their pasts in order to make possible brighter futures. And in being redeemed, they learn to face the world outside the rooms with a sense of integrity and dignity. In turn, groups like NLF serve as communities of redemption, where feelings of shame and self-loathing can be confronted and overcome in the presence of supportive others. As Leslie Parker put it, "I came to AA and I felt like these broken pieces of me started getting fixed."

Is this only necessary for alcoholics and addicts, or for those, like them, who have tested the limits of their capacity for suffering? I doubt it. As human beings we can all feel guilty for wrongs we've committed or mistakes we've made. For most of us redemption is a felt need. Moreover, redemption is something that implies public recognition: it isn't real unless it is sanctioned by a community we hold to be authoritative. Thus, groups such as NLF serve a vital human need—one that I doubt even the most just society could eradicate.

Conclusion

In this chapter I've argued that groups like NLF, which institutionalize the religion of the heart, are considerably mischaracterized by critics. Contrary to popular criticisms, they do in fact serve as sites of social integration and moral regulation, staving off and tempering anomie and egoism. And they also serve as generative institutions—enabling their members to participate in shifting involvements and adopt rival social perspectives.

Of course, this is not to deny that members sometimes leave the group, quit the program, or fail to experience the necessary psychological identification for belonging. Because the alcoholic identity is not totalizing, and often restricted to private life, there is no guarantee that NLF members will not lose attachment to their group. No doubt, some critics will perceive this as evidence of romantic liberal modernity's communal deficiencies. And in some ways, they would be right. Anomie and egoism will always remain a potential threat in romantic liberal modernity, where the economic sphere institutionalizes utilitarian individualism and expressive individualism is institutionalized in the private sphere. But this is the price we must pay for the freedom to shift involvements and enjoy the benefits of pluralism.

And yet, having said this, it is a striking fact that while NLF members readily invoke structuralist discourses in order to diagnose and pinpoint society's ills, they remain unable, given their *self-understanding*, to acknowledge the extent to which their own convictions—and indeed their "recovering selves"—remain *dependent upon social sources*. In other words, the self-understanding naturalized by AA discourse leaves NLF members at risk of taking their AA group, along with the tradition of AA, for granted—and in so doing, makes them vulnerable to seeking the kind of radical freedom that only promises anomie. It follows that critics are on to something when they say that social and moral instability is intrinsic to the religion of the heart, given the self-understanding it engenders.

9

Prosperity and Positivity at a "Greedy Institution"

I can see the signs from a block away: ten feet tall with "C3 Church" plastered in bright green lettering, they stand out conspicuously on each street corner. As I walk up the entranceway stairs two C3T members eagerly greet me. "Welcome to church!" they cheer in unison. Once inside, I see a crowd of hip young people congregating around a makeshift coffee bar. The young Asian woman serving the coffee smiles at me. "Welcome to church!" she says enthusiastically.

In the auditorium, where the worship service takes place, the overhead lights are dimmed and music blares. I can barely make out the face of the member who hands me a "Newcomer" pamphlet and "I Gave Online" card. Onstage a seven-piece band is playing. With arms extended high in the air, the worship team jumps and swings to the sonorous tune. The song lyrics flash across two massive monitors that hang at the back of the stage. Most in the audience sing along, and many have their eyes closed with their arms stretched towards the ceiling. Meanwhile, worship music fills my ears, so loud I can hear nothing else. Around me strangers engage in ecstatic displays of affect, amidst a colourful lightshow.

All of a sudden, one of the singers onstage, a young blonde woman, speaks into the microphone, "Do you feel that? That is God! He's here with us!" The woman next to me, who until now was standing motionless, raises her hands, closes her eyes, and begins to sway. The emotional intensity in the room is palpable.

As the worship team ends its third song, pastor Sam—white, physically fit, with short blonde hair and a collection of arm tattoos—walks onstage. Dressed in black skinny jeans, sleek leather boots, and a tightly fitted t-shirt, he has a commanding presence—far more than his thirty-two years would suggest. In a thick Australian accent he shouts, "Let's give a hand for God! Praise God! Come on! Praise God!" The room erupts in cheers and applause.

A Brief History of C3 Church

C3T belongs to the larger neo-Pentecostal or Charismatic Christian church movement, C3 Church, founded by Phil and Chris Pringle in 1980 in Sydney, Australia. As of early 2019, C3 Church boasts over five hundred churches in sixty-

The Spiritual Turn: The Religion of the Heart and the Making of Romantic Liberal Modernity. Galen Watts, Oxford University Press. © Galen Watts 2022. DOI: 10.1093/oso/9780192859839.003.0010

four countries, with more than 112,000 members worldwide.[1] Scholars distinguish between classical Pentecostalism and the wider Charismatic movement. Although C3 churches share much with classical Pentecostalism, their theological and cultural debts partake of a wider set of influences, as they belong to a particular wing of the Charismatic revival, known as the "prosperity gospel" (Coleman 2000, 27). So, not only can we find traces of Methodism, Pietism, the Holiness movement, and Schleiermacher's inductive theology at work at C3, but we also find substantive linkages to the American metaphysical religious traditions, Christian Science and New Thought (Bowler 2013). That said, the 1960s counter-culture played a crucial role in neo-Pentecostalism's development, for it gave rise to what anthropologist Simon Coleman (2000, 24), borrowing from James Davison Hunter, calls "the 'Californication' of conservative Protestantism," whereby conservatives "accommodated to the anti-institutional, therapeutic, cultural preferences of the baby boomers." According to Hunter (1982, 43, 44), it was during this era that conservative evangelicals embraced a "psychological Christo-centrism," which stresses "the potentiality of the human individual who is 'under the lordship of Jesus Christ'." In agreement, historian Kate Bowler (2013, 7) contends that the prosperity gospel reached maturity "in the ripe individualism of post-1960s America." Thus, it was only in the latter half of the twentieth century when the Pentecostal "emphasis on spirituality rather than religious institutions" (Poloma 2003, 15) combined with an American obsession with prosperity.

Although Pentecostalism in Australia didn't originate directly from the US, C3 Church borrows much from the American gospel of prosperity. For instance, we find in C3 theology both traces of what Bowler (2013) refers to as a "soft" prosperity gospel, which stresses the physical and psychological benefits of channelling or harmonizing with the Holy Spirit, as well as "hard" prosperity rhetoric, which promises material blessings through the faithful enactment of biblical principles. But perhaps the most manifest theological inheritance is the C3 conviction that church growth is proof of divine blessing (Shanahan 2019, 5). Hence why Marion Maddox (2012) refers to churches like C3 as "growth churches."

C3 Toronto (C3T)

Pastor Sam has said in interviews with media that he aspires to "make Jesus famous." So it should come as no surprise that C3T's approach to evangelization, like that of other growth churches, involves utilizing the most innovative and up-to-date methods in digital marketing. Of course, it helps that many of the church's members work in the creative industries—marketing, photography, public relations, and the arts. In fact, the congregation is almost entirely made up of

---

[1] See https://c3churchglobal.com/home.

university or college-educated (aspiring) middle-class millennials. The church's army of creative class volunteers comprises entrepreneurs, models, marketers, publicists, hospitality workers, and filmmakers—all of whom donate their expertise, time, and money to grow C3T's "brand." And grow the church has. In five years, C3T has morphed from a prayer service attended by eleven people to a membership of over fifteen hundred, with three "campuses" across the city.[2]

The demographics of C3T members are ethnically and racially varied. One finds whites, blacks, and Asians scattered across the auditorium on any given Sunday. Attracting a significant number of first- and second-generation immigrants, C3T in many ways reflects the "hyper-diverse environment" of Toronto itself (Reimer et al. 2016, 498). And the vast majority of members were, like Amy Lee, raised in conservative Christian households where they experienced strict familial religious socialization.

C3T's social hierarchies resemble those of the larger C3 movement, making it a microcosm of the church's global structure. All decisions are ultimately made by pastor Sam and his wife, Jess, who seem to endorse what Coleman (2000, 95) calls the "One Shepherd principle"—the notion that the "congregation 'is' its pastor" and therefore the senior pastor "does not have to answer to higher ecclesiastical structures or a body of elders." Indeed, all decision-making power resides with Sam and Jess, and the closer one is to them the more power and moral authority one has—what veteran members referred to as belonging to the "inner circle."

Pastor Sam regularly claims that C3T is not about "religion" but rather about "faith." By this he means that, as church pastor, his sole obligation is to "connect people with God," such that they can develop a relationship with Jesus Christ. Sam therefore eschews making political statements or taking a stand on controversial issues—both from the pulpit and in public interviews. Indeed, it is for this reason that C3T members like Amy Kim tend to speak of the type of Christianity found at C3T as "relational"—which they contrast with "rule Christianity." The idea is that members are ostensibly allowed to figure out for themselves, in relationship with Christ, how they ought to live their faith. In this way, C3T members espouse a distinct version of the religion of the heart, which I call *Charismatic Christian (CC) discourse*.

The Religion of the Heart at C3 Toronto: Charismatic Christian Discourse

Experiential Epistemology

In sermons and interviews with C3T members it is consistently emphasized that *divine truth is revealed solely in personal experience*. These Charismatics are

---

[2] See https://c3toronto.com.

adamant that we should not simply seek to *know about God*, but should chiefly seek to *know God* by means of ecstatic and overwhelming experience (Poloma and Pendleton 1989). As Phil Pringle puts it in *Faith: Moving the Heart and the Hand of God*, "Faith and feelings go hand in hand" (2005, 31). On this view, Jesus or the Holy Spirit is not a distant figure, ever out of reach, but rather one made wholly accessible to the ordinary believer. Moreover, although C3T members accept that the Bible is inerrant, they conceive of it "not as a text to be memorized but as a personal document, written uniquely for each" (Luhrmann 2004, 523). Or, as Jesse Davie-Kessler (2016, 7) aptly summarizes: "Without inspiration from God channeled by the Holy Spirit into the born-again reader...the Bible [is] meaninglessness."

Immanence of God or the Superempirical

Of neo-Pentecostalism Philip Richter (1997, 100) writes, "The God of the Charismatics is above all an immanent God who acts in the world." "One of the attractions of Charismatic churches has been their offer of a direct, unmediated and unpredictable encounter with a God who is anything but dead" (108). The following testimony by C3T member, Alison, is illustrative:

> I put my headphones on and threw on a track, an album that I'd listened to maybe a thousand times. It's a punk band. Anyway, I start walking and the lyrics are literally like talking to me about my situation right now in a way where I was like, 'What? Oh my Gosh! God is talking to me through this song!' I mean, I've sang this song a million times and all of a sudden it sounds like God is talking to me about where I'm at, and where I need to be looking.

Alison explained: "I do truly believe that He talks to people in their own way. So, for me, it was that." For this young Charismatic, God chose to intervene in her life in the form of a song she'd heard many times over. In Alison's interpretation, this was God's loving way of helping her identify an area of her life she had until then failed to adequately attend to—which gives credence to the widespread observation that Charismatics "view divine experiences or events as sources of vitality that mediate God with human lives" (Young So 2009, 250).

Benevolent God/Universe

Talk of "relational Christianity" at C3T signals a move away from the judgemental and condemning God Amy Kim recalls growing up with, to one that wants her to be happy and actualize her full potential. As theologian Harvey Cox (1995, 201, 259) puts it, according to Charismatics, "God is more lover than judge," and it is widely believed that Christians "have a powerful cosmic ally and a secure standing in God's eyes." Pastor Jess offered an instructive example when she preached, "He is not a bad God. He wants you to find life. He wants you to find fulfilment," adding, "I don't think we are ourselves when we are in fear, when we are angry, or anxious. Those are not God's desires for you." This testimony vindicates Hunter's (1982, 42) observation that, within evangelicalism, "if one is spiritual, one is by and large, happy and contended." In actual fact, CC discourse goes further: *faithful Christians are promised not just emotional well-being, but also prosperity.*

Redemptive Self as Theodicy

One regularly hears pastor Sam preach, "God created you for a purpose, for a reason," "If you step out in Faith, you will see a God story in your life," and "Those who endure trials will become the most effective." On this view, all pain and suffering serve a redemptive purpose, thereby imbuing negative experiences with cosmic meaning. C3T members are taught that if they are struggling it is because God has a lesson for them to learn, or because they need this in order to realize their potential. Phil Pringle writes, "Our faith grows through trial. As God passes faith through a test, it is purified, strengthened, and enlarged" (2003, 173). Yet, in CC discourse the redemptive self is always narrated in the form of a conversion narrative, which follows a particular script. In unpacking this script Coleman (2000, 119) writes, "The convert learns that their previous life was one of 'darkness' as opposed to present enlightenment and revelation. 'Something lacking' has been replaced by plenitude, as identity is discovered through the 'full Gospel' and 'in Christ'. God, indeed, 'has a plan' for every believer's life." And as Alison's example illustrates, once the believer has internalized this canonical narrative, they eventually learn to look for (and find) evidence of God's intervention in their lives.

Self-Realization as Teleology

One hears over and over again at C3T slogans like: "Don't try to be someone else," "We should never feel bad about wanting growth," "God has a bold and courageous, alive and active, version of you on the other side," and "God has created you for a unique purpose." And in *Faith* Pringle writes, "People are on a desperate search to find out who they are. It's in Christ that we find ourselves" (2005, 148). In their study of Hillsong Church, another Australia-based growth church, Matthew Wade and Maria Hynes (2013, 176) report that members were drawn to it because of its "potential for a superior kind of self-actualization through the subsumption of the self within a cause greater than themselves." Indeed, while growth churches may be theologically conservative, they nevertheless embrace the language of expressive individualism (Stromberg 1986). The underlying belief is that Christian piety leads to self-realization—or what Gerardo Martí (2012, 140) refers to as becoming one's true *prosperous self.*

Self-Ethic (Voice from Within)

How do C3T members conceive of the true prosperous self? Characteristic of the religion of the heart, the true self is conceived as *pre-social* in origin, derived from a divine source. Accordingly, members constantly seek to distinguish between the authentic voice within—equated with the "Holy Spirit"—and that of the false self—equated with "the enemy" or "the Devil." This is because the voice of the Holy Spirit not only is believed to reflect one's true identity, but also is perceived as a source of limitless power. Thus, campus pastor George preached one Sunday, "Get more of God in you. More of God in you means more power. And more power means more of you." The logic here is that the more one aligns one's words and actions with the Holy Spirit within, the more one becomes both *like God* as well as *true to oneself.* As George put it, "More God, more power, more you."

Virtue Is Natural

Phil Pringle preached at C3 Canada conference, "Jesus promises freedom from anxiety, depression and mental illness." The prosperity gospel, Bowler (2013, 14) observes, is characterized by "an optimistic theology of human capacity." In this way, CC discourse reformulates the doctrine of original sin to mean "failing to realize one's true self." And in realizing one's true self through cultivating faith one is promised a number of godly gifts—health, virtue, and even wealth. For, as Bowler remarks, according to the prosperity gospel, "people share in God's healing power by activating their faith and tapping into God's spiritual laws" (142). Furthermore, C3T members tend to channel their Romantic forerunners by offering critiques of the wider culture, which they view as a source of disorder and despair. In his sermons Sam frames C3T as an antidote to the social isolation and nihilism that he believes pervades the secular city. So, while orthodox Christians may view humanity as eternally plagued by original sin, CC discourse, as encoded at C3T, posits a corrupt society replete with demonic powers, which serves as the primary obstacle preventing Christians from realizing their true prosperous selves.

Sacralization of Individual Liberty

One of the most striking aspects of CC discourse is the degree to which it sacralizes individual liberty while remaining theologically conservative. As we've seen, relational Christianity presupposes a God who respects the autonomy of all believers. As one of the campus pastors explained, "I feel like there's a door in our heart, and the handle is on the inside. God is a gentleman, so will never barge in. He will keep knocking, but we have to be the ones to let Him in." At C3T, individual commitment must rest upon the believer making a conscious and autonomous choice to continually "accept Jesus." And yet, at the same time, just as with NLF members, the ideals of self-sufficiency and independence are perceived by C3T members as misplaced insofar as they lock individuals into a state of dependence on their temporary whims and ungodly desires. Accordingly, for these Charismatics, real freedom comes only from aligning oneself with God's will—that is, the authentic voice within.

Mind-Body-Spirit Connection

Pastor Sam regularly preaches, "You will reproduce what you repeat," "If you want to see blessing in your world, you need to speak blessing into your world," and "You need to be speaking about the good things that God is doing in your world." Coleman argues that the prosperity gospel emerges from "distinctive theological tenets and linguistic ideologies" (2006, 27–8). He uses the term "positive confession" to capture the Charismatic Christian belief that "words spoken 'in faith' are objectifications of reality" (28). On this view, "affirmative repetition, visualization, imagination, mood redirection, and voice scripture" are conceived as "prayerful habits" that can "achieve results" (Bowler 2013, 60). Accordingly, among Charismatics the relationship between mind, body, and matter is rendered holistic and interdependent (Hollenweger 1986, 6)—for, according to CC discourse, bodily healing can occur through the faithful recitation of scripture, while mental illness may simply signal a lack of faith.

Methodological Individualism

In his study of American evangelicals sociologist Christian Smith characterizes their approach to social change as what he calls the "personal influence strategy": "working through personal relationships to allow God to transform human hearts from the inside-out, so that all ensuing social change will be thorough and long-lasting" (quoted in Lichterman 2005, 143). Similarly, Bowler (2013, 255) argues that proponents of the prosperity gospel hold that all social, cultural, and institu-tional barriers to change can only be overcome by means of personal transform-ation. We see this view reflected in Phil Pringle's proclamation one Sunday, "Circumstances don't need to change, we need to change." Characteristic of the religion of the heart, then, CC discourse endorses a methodological individualism that views the individual (Christian) as the primary (and sole) unit of social change. The prescription for social ills is simple: *more faith*. Of course, discourses of charity are common at C3T, as members are expected to give back by means of tithing and volunteering their time for the church. But one rarely, if ever, hears a sermon that ventures beyond discussions of charity and personal development. In this sense, CC discourse never strays beyond the personal, even when it's forced to confront the political.

C3 Worship Services as Collective Ritual

"Charismatics and Pentecostals tend to call themselves 'anti-ritualistic'," notes Ronald Schouten (2003, 29). Yet the reality belies this self-image. Schouten argues that what distinguishes Charismatic Christian rituals from those of mainline Christianity "is the primacy of experience" (32). Durkheim would surely agree. In this section I consider how Sunday worship services function as experience-based collective rituals which legitimate and reinforce CC discourse as it is encoded and enfleshed at C3T. I focus on the role of worship services because I agree with Margaret Poloma and Brian Pendleton (1989, 417) that religious experiences play a central role in establishing and revitalizing neo-Pentecostal religious institutions. In fact, I would argue that worship services serve as the principal plausibility structures for CC discourse at C3T, such that members' initial and sustained commitment depends significantly upon the ability of the church to enable members to "encounter the Holy Spirit." Put otherwise, by provoking certain kinds of sensations, and providing an authoritative discourse (CC discourse) with which to interpret them, C3T creates the basis for what Stephen Hunt et al. (1997, 6) call "an experience-led fundamentalism."

Worship, Atmosphere, and Aesthetics

There is nothing more central to guaranteeing ritual success at churches like C3T than the roles worship, atmosphere, and aesthetics play in provoking particular kinds of sensations in their members.[3] Yet this tailoring of experience begins long

---

[3] On this see Cox 1995; Jennings 2008; Meyer 2010; Brahinsky 2012; Inbody 2015.

before one enters the church, and is the product of meticulous forethought on the part of the pastoral team.

As visitors near the church on Sunday mornings, members of the "First Impressions Team"—each of whom have been selected because they embody the "C3 personality," which pastors Phil and Chris describe in a C3 promotional video as "fun, playful, bright, colourful, energetic, youthful, hospitable, attractive, beautiful, authentic, creative, generous, and compelling"—bombard them with boundless smiles and cheerful greetings. The aim of these fixtures is both to impress and to make visitors feel desired each step of the way into the church. And they work. Nadia recounted her first experience at C3T: "Everyone was so nice! They genuinely seemed interested in me—they wanted to know my name, and why I was there. They lavished me with attention. It felt so good."

While pastor Sam has ambitions to purchase property for the church, C3T's main campus operates out of a secondary school. As a result, throngs of church members spend hours on Sunday mornings transforming the staid school hallways into vibrant scenes of leisure and comfort. As Miranda Klaver (2015b, 431) observes, the aim is to signal to visitors that "church is a place different from the busy and stressful everyday lives of visitors." Thus, upon entering the foyer of the school one encounters a coffee bar, colourful C3 displays, a stylized literature table, an ATM machine, and an array of fashionable young adults dressed in hipster garb. James Wellman et al. (2014, 654) argue that this atmosphere and aesthetic functions to decrease "cultural membership capital barriers that prevent outsiders from participating." In other words, by borrowing "sensate strategies from pop culture," C3T reduces the potential for alienation, especially among those who have no religious memory (Brahinsky 2012, 225). Indeed, it is no coincidence that C3T's foyer resembles other common sites of leisure in romantic liberal modernity such as the shopping mall, the sports arena, or the movie theatre, all of which are designed to provide a "feeling of worry-free comfort" (Maddox 2012, 153).

Yet I would argue these aesthetic trimmings serve chiefly to *prime individuals to be receptive to experiencing the Holy Spirit*—which periods of worship are strategically and indeed powerfully designed to elicit. Thus, the real power of the Sunday service as public ritual lies in periods of worship, where state-of-the-art technologies, professionally produced music, and emotional regimes work together to produce feelings of ecstasy and awe, while simultaneously enforcing a particular discursive framework (CC discourse) with which to interpret them.

Consider, first, the role of lighting and stage design. As one enters the auditorium, where the service takes place, the lights on the audience are dimmed, while the stage is illuminated by a colourful lightshow, and it's not uncommon for a fog machine to run in the background. This allows the congregation to rest in relative anonymity during worship, thereby facilitating what Ibrahim Abraham (2018, 15) calls "self-forgetfulness." Meanwhile, onstage one finds a six- to eight-person band that not only produces the worship music that resounds throughout the room, but simultaneously "model the correct way to experience the presence of God" (Jennings 2008, 163).

Much like NLF, then, C3T creates a distinct *social environment*. However, it does so less by normalizing distinct speech norms (as at NLF) than by normalizing distinct *behavioural norms*. As Bobby Alexander (1989, 117) observes, "the defiant behavior of ecstatic display is a rejection of behavioral standards to which mainstream society subscribes, for example, poise, dignity, and composure." Indeed, C3T worship services are sites of what we might call *embodied enchantment*— where individuals are both allowed and expected to act on their spontaneous bodily impulses, and "reach beyond their individual selves" (Shilling and Mellor 2011, 23).

Also critical to producing collective effervescence is the role of worship music. Mark Jennings (2008, 171) contends, "music is the most important technology for creating a space in which an experience understood as a divine-human encounter can take place" (see also Goh 2008). But what distinguishes contemporary worship music from the hymnals of old is that it taps into widespread cultural tastes, while endorsing what Joel Inbody (2015, 351) calls a "specialized vocabulary" (CC discourse) through which individuals learn to interpret their bodily sensations. This is a powerful combination, for it promises ritual participants not merely the emotional energy derived from listening to the type of music they already enjoy, but also "allow[s] [them] to feel as though they are channeling and experiencing the divine" (Wellman et al. 2014, 654). And insofar as the music is successful in this task it "effectively dislodges the ability to critique and question because it immerses worshippers in an enthralling entertainment experience" (Sanders 2016, 80).

The importance of embodied enchantment produced in worship cannot be overemphasized. Indeed, as Inbody (2015, 338) contends, it is in worship where Charismatics experience a "socially derived emotional energy... [which] makes the individual feel not only good, but exalted," leading them to interpret these experiences as a "spiritual phenomenon." He concludes, "It is the shared experience of [emotional energy], which increases solidarity, is attributed to religious symbols or entities, and entices individuals to return for subsequent interactions."

Language Ideology, Conversion Narratives and Symbolic Boundaries

In the last chapter, I discussed the performative nature of storytelling and its significance for identity-reconstruction at NLF. Much that I spoke of there can be applied here. However, what distinguishes C3T from NLF is its *language ideology*, by which I mean the set of "ideas about the nature of language, how it works, and how people should use it" that underlies CC discourse (Robbins 2012, 15). For as a result of this language ideology, which holds that *what one speaks becomes manifest in the material world*, speech of any kind takes on increased importance for remaking the self.

Coleman (2000, 118) identifies four different ways that language is applied to the self within Charismatic Christianity: The first, *narrative emplacement*, refers to the production of self-descriptions whereby believers locate themselves "in terms of a landscape of evangelical action, ideals and characters." For instance, one member described her conversion as follows: "I started noticing things that are unique to me because I'm reading creation. And I'm reading God's character in the Bible and I'm realizing He's actually always been in my life." The second, *dramatization*, implies acting out church sanctioned ideals—performing the "prosperous self." The third, *internalization*, refers to refashioning oneself through performative utterances. And the fourth, *externalization*, refers to the deployment of language as a means of altering the material world. CC discourse holds that prayer, when done with a "faithful heart," is sufficient to overcome any conceivable difficulty (Pringle 2005, 22). These various applications of language together serve to fuel "rituals of rupture," whereby C3T members make a complete break with their pasts, primarily by recounting over and over again their conversion narratives (Robbins 2012, 12). With each telling the false worldly self is identified and transcended in lieu of the true prosperous self.

Of course, we find such rituals of rupture at NLF. But because AA discourse is not informed by the same language ideology as that of CC discourse, storytelling holds different consequences at each moral community. For instance, while negative talk is considered the norm within the rooms of AA, at C3T it is vehemently avoided. And because there is no impulse to proselytize in Twelve Step fellowships, NLF members limit sharing their AA stories to their interactions with other AA members. So, a fundamental difference between NLF and C3T revolves around *when and where to share one's story*: NLF works on a principle of "attraction rather than promotion," meaning the sharing of one's story is generally confined to AA meetings. By contrast, C3T implicitly espouses a principle of "attraction and promotion," so members are encouraged to share their testimony at every available opportunity in order to enlarge the kingdom of God. This is why Manual Vásquez (2003, 162) identifies in Charismatic thought a "certain narrative compulsion"—they seem "compelled to share with others their testimonies of conversion." Unlike NLF, then, storytelling at CT3 is construed as a means of demonstrating faithfulness, as well as engaging in proselytization.

Yet conversion narratives do much more than reconstitute believers in light of CC discourse and aid them to evangelize. They also serve to erect and sustain symbolic boundaries that demarcate the church as a distinct community—both real and imagined—thereby shoring up its subcultural identity. CC discourse serves to separate "believers" from "nonbelievers" in a categorical sense, binding members to one another and solidifying a collective identity. Indeed, Brian Starks and Robert Robinson (2009) argue that evangelicals thrive in pluralistic societies primarily because they are adept at constructing a collective identity which perceives itself as both wholly Other and embattled. While the rhetoric found at C3T may not be as hostile to the secular world as that found among, say, orthodox or fundamentalist groups, we should not discount the role this symbolic boundary drawing plays in bolstering commitment and solidarity among members. C3T members are adamant that as "faithful servants of Christ" they are epistemically and morally different from those who are "not saved" or "have not met God." For instance, Nadia asserted, "There's so many people in this city that are broken. And I know because I was one. Unfortunately, the enemy, the devil, He knows how to lure you in. That's why people don't believe in God. Because they're so far away from the truth. But I can tell you that the only thing is the living God. Jesus Christ is the only way to get to God." Adopting CC discourse at C3T entails initiation into a moral community where membership is not only exclusive, but where the outside world is perceived as both wholly Other and in need of saving.

The Role of Pastors in Modelling the Prosperous Self

CC discourse enjoins members to make a radical break with their false self in order to realize their true prosperous self. Yet, as with NLF, what is considered authentic and how members learn to construe their true selves is considerably *socially constituted*, and significantly shaped by the group's collective conscience— regardless of the fact that this is not reflected in the self-understanding of members themselves. I argued in the last chapter that the recovered self at NLF was largely informed by a combination of expressivist-cum-liberal Christian values (humility, selflessness, emotional honesty, tolerance, acceptance of limitation) and a queer subcultural identity, which the veteran members of the group embodied. By contrast, the prosperous self at C3T is enfleshed and modelled by the senior pastors, Sam and Jess Picken, and reflects a synthesis of the following value-sets.

First, CC discourse as encoded at C3T sacralizes the values of today's *celebrity and fashion cultures*: physical attractiveness, charm, sex appeal, fame, novelty, and personal magnetism. Indeed, these qualities are reconceived within CC discourse as virtues that enable members to attract converts and grow the church. As Martí (2010, 53) notes, the pursuit of personal celebrity is not conceived as self-serving egoism, but rather "faithful fulfillment of a religious duty." Similarly, Maddox (2013, 111) contends that within growth churches "one's body, image and lifestyle are a walking evangelistic billboard." What's more, there exists a clear "performative style" that Charismatic pastors share. Klaver (2015a, 156) describes it thus: "church websites present the pastor and his wife together as the leading couple of the church. They always look happily married; have both a sparklingly white set of teeth; the pastor's wife is, usually good looking, thin, blond." Sam and Jess's ability to embody these performative standards works to legitimate their moral authority, as they are seen to "have the right look," as one member put it.

Second, CC discourse sacralizes the values of *growth* and *prosperity*—emotional and material. Emotional prosperity entails conformity to a specific emotional regime which I call *relentless positivity*.[4] Phil Pringle preached one Sunday, "Get out of dismay, defeat, discouragement and depression," making sure to remind the congregation, "God hates whining!" According to CC discourse, fear, dullness, and anxiety are the work of the devil and therefore are to be weeded out as soon as they crop up. This emotional regime is closely tied to the language ideology naturalized at C3T. Within C3 theology negative self-talk is believed to be the cause of depression and failure, thus even entertaining a negative thought is tantamount to conspiring with "the enemy." As Pringle (2005, 146) puts it in *Faith*, "When we believe the negatives, we diminish in size. When we diminish in size, we move backward. When we move backward, we move toward destruction."

Furthermore, among Charismatics, money is conceived as an index of faith, so it is expected that a prosperous self is one who enjoys material abundance (Coleman 2006, 178). But material prosperity entails more than simply getting rich. As Pringle (2003, 47) writes in *Keys to Financial Success*, "To prosper is to do well in every area of your life and achieve your goals." It is therefore insufficient to amass wealth—one must, in every facet of life, be a victor, not a victim (Sødal 2010). In our interview, Pastor Sam articulated the gist of this plainly: "I hate the option of moving backward. I have to continually keep moving forward. So, while I'm pushing people into their potential all the time, I'm also achieving too." Here Sam revealed a keen awareness of the degree to which his moral authority depends upon what Bowler (2013, 193) calls a "performance of victory." His ability to attract followers, to grow the church, to accrue wealth and status, and to "raise sensibilities that invoke the divine presence in such a way that is recognized and persuasive" (Klaver 2015a, 151) is what proves his worthiness. This is a necessary corollary of growth church theology: those who prosper are those who merit authority, while those who do not, merit none. Maddox (2012, 151) is therefore undoubtedly correct that for these Christians "becoming wealthier and more successful is not merely desirable, but a moral duty."

Lastly, CC discourse at C3T sacralizes *social conservatism*: many C3T members espouse socially conservative views on a wide array of social issues. Members are encouraged by leadership not to engage in sex before marriage, have abortions, or abuse drugs or alcohol. Traditional marriage and the nuclear family are valorized in church teachings, and within C3 churches one finds a gendered division of

---

[4] I borrow the idea of an "emotional regime" from Woodhead and Riis 2010.

labour, where women, even when in leadership, are expected to "submit" to their husbands (Miller 2016, 3009). And while C3T refrains from taking a public stance on homosexuality, the ethos is unapologetically heteronormative, if not homo-phobic. At the same time, C3T members believe individuals should have the freedom to choose for themselves how they wish to live. That is, according to these young Charismatics "relational Christianity" implies that individuals be allowed to work out their views in relationship with God, as opposed to being coerced by others (or the state) into conforming. In short, while socially conser-vative, C3T members nevertheless seem to tacitly endorse political liberalism.

It follows that the collective conscience of C3T reflects a combination of *celebrity culture, market values*, and a *strain of social conservatism*. That is, C3T members are expected to pursue fame, fortune, and victory, all while remaining sexually disciplined, hardworking, and self-responsible. And as I mentioned above, this collective conscience is powerfully enfleshed in the figures of Sam and Jess. In fact, I would argue that these senior pastors exert an influence upon the church far beyond the influence the veteran members at NLF exert upon their AA group. The reason for this largely has to do with the fact that CC discourse enjoins submission to leadership as a means to achieving faithfulness and positive freedom. As one member put it, "you must submit to leadership, because you're serving God, and you're doing God's work, when you serve your leader." While another shared that submission to one's senior pastors' "vision" demon-strates the virtues of "obedience and faithfulness." However, it also has to do with the role *charismatic authority* plays at C3T.

Many sociologists associate the concept of charismatic authority with Weber, for whom it refers to "a collective belief that a person [the leader of the group] is embodying the sacred, the extraordinary, the divine" (Giesen 2006, 352). However, a complementary notion can be found in the work of Durkheim, for whom charismatic authority refers to a "special relational structure between an individual who is able to 'put in play', so to speak, and to articulate the strong emotions, the aspirations, the pent-up feelings of the collectivity" (Tiryakian 1995, 273). In other words, charismatic authority, from a Durkheimian perspective, derives from *the production of collective effervescence*.

It should come as no surprise, then, that worship services play a critical role in securing the outsized moral authority of pastors Sam and Jess, as it's through the cultivation of embodied enchantment that they become "sacred persons" (Durkheim [1912] 1995, 412). Indeed, by virtue of their role as mediators of divine-human encounters, James Wellman et al. 2014, 664) remark, pastors "become sacred objects of congregations and serve as representations of the group." And, as a result, Sam and Jess significantly shape the "standards of right and wrong that are approved by the group, giving members a sense of purpose through service and a set of normative standards by which to guide their lives" (668).

Practices of Self-Cultivation

And yet, while worship services might play a central role in securing and sustaining the plausibility of CC discourse, they are not sufficient to reconstitute C3T members' selves. For a comprehensive conversion requires members to voluntarily engage in a wide array of practices of self-cultivation outside of the church.

The first of these is donating financially to the church, often (though not only) in the form of tithing (the biblical practice of donating one tenth of one's income to the church). According to Phil Pringle (2005, 164), "Tithing, in the truest sense, is not actually giving. The tithe belongs to God, not to us." Indeed, tithing is presented at C3 churches less as an option than a necessary condition for realizing one's true prosperous self. For, as Pringle warns in *Keys*, "We cannot expect a financial breakthrough in our lives if we are stealing from God or withholding from Him what He has requested from us" (Pringle 2003, 76).

In addition to tithing, members willingly engage in a host of practices outside of worship services in order to refashion their selves in conformity with the church's collective conscience. For instance, it is normal for members to read their Bibles daily, pray frequently, and habitually listen to both the church's podcast and worship music, as a means of reconnecting with the Holy Spirit. Many members I spoke to also consider it essential to attend and lead connect groups, serve on a team, and take part in one or more of the church's weekly prayer meetings. Additionally, the church regularly holds leadership retreats, conferences, socials, and community events which members are encouraged to partake in. And members are expected to engage in these activities in conformity with the emotional regime of relentless positivity, closely monitoring their thoughts and feelings for evidence of "the enemy" in the process. Accordingly, each of these practices of self-cultivation serves to reform the internal life of C3T members, eliciting certain affective-volitional states while repressing others. And it's for this reason that external sanctions are not necessary—C3T members willingly remake themselves in light of the church's collective conscience.

The Pathologies of Romantic Liberal Modernity and C3 Toronto

How does the religion of the heart institutionalized at C3T relate to the pathology of anomie? Interestingly, despite sharing the same cultural structure, CC discourse and "spiritual" discourses associated with the holistic milieu have provoked quite different responses from critics. While some have been quick to perceive the latter as symptomatic of atomistic individualism, most have generally reserved tamer criticism for the former (a fact that is itself curious). Yet there do exist those who fear that churches such as C3T cannot stave off feelings of anomie, owing to the value they place on individual freedom and the primacy they give to subjective experience.

For instance, of neo-Pentecostalism Bryan Turner (2011, 282) contends, "These religious orientations place few ethical demands on their followers." Stephen Hunt et al. (1997, 10) suggest the religiosity found at Charismatic churches "is not essentially rooted in any sense of community." And Marion Maddox (2013, 109) writes, "Rather than fostering the virtues of solidarity and community... Pentecostalism stresses the individual virtues of initiative, aspiration, self-belief and self-motivation."

Of course, it is wholly accurate to suggest CC discourse focuses on individuals, rather than community, given the value it places on personal experience. Yet, as we've seen, an emphasis on subjective experience—provided experiences are interpreted in line with the canonical discourse—can motivate intense commitment. That said, it is clearly the case that the form community takes at C3T is far from traditional. For within CC discourse self-advancement is reconceived as corporate advancement, and doggedly pursuing status, fame, and wealth is reframed as a form of spiritual vocation. But what critics fail to recognize is the degree to which the prosperous self "can only be rooted and supported within a face-to-face, voluntary community of believers who face an uncertain world together" (Martí 2012, 148). In other words, members come to depend upon their real church community as well the "imagined world community of Christians" to which they belong (Brison 2017, 660).

This dependence takes the following two forms. First, C3T members conceive of their church, and their attachment to it, as an irreplaceable source of moral and spiritual strength. As one member phrased it, "They speak life into you at C3." While another asserted, "I don't know where I'd be without the church. Everything I have I owe to C3 Toronto." Moreover, if members begin to struggle, either emotionally or financially, CC discourse holds that this is due to either a lack of faith or a weak service life. One ex-member even recounted being asked by a campus pastor, after breaking with church norms and disclosing that she was facing financial hardship, "How much are you giving? Are you still leading your connect group? How often are you praying?" Thus, because members learn to view their own well-being and prosperity as bound up with their commitment to the church, the fulfilment of communal obligations is considered a precondition for self-advancement. While it may be paradoxical, it would be wrong to see the virtues of self-belief and self-motivation as antithetical to those of commitment and community.

Second, because churches like C3T promise direct access to the Holy Spirit, members come to rely on them as sources of both cosmic meaning and unconditional love. For instance, Sage explained her longstanding commitment to C3T as follows: "So the biggest thing for me is God's love. Before C3 I never knew that was a thing in my life. I never knew it existed. And now it is my life source." Choral echoed this sentiment: "Every other church I'd ever gone to in my life,

I didn't feel like I belonged. I didn't feel there was God there. At C3 I felt the presence of God. I felt loved." Time and again members spoke of the importance of the "Holy Spirit encounter" as the reason why they remain C3T members. An ex-C3T member even described being terrified to leave the church out of fear that it was the only place where they could experience the Holy Spirit.

These testimonies make clear the degree to which community at C3T depends upon the church's success in providing access to an all-loving and powerful God. But they also highlight the central role religious experience plays in stimulating individual commitment and mitigating anomie. In agreement, Luhrmann (2004, 527) argues that the human-divine encounter normalized at C3T functions "to protect [members] against the isolation of modern social life." And Gerardo Martí (2010, 69) observes that growth churches command intense devotion in large part because they enable their members to believe that "when they go out into the world they are never truly alone."

In sum, despite the fact that CC discourse sacralizes values that many consider anathema to communal obligation, C3T manages to integrate its members into a cohesive and comprehensive moral community in the following ways. First, by convincing members that their own prosperity is contingent upon their faithfulness, members willingly submit to leadership, contribute to the church both financially and otherwise, and regularly engage in normalizing practices of self-cultivation. And second, by providing access to an all-powerful God, which members can viscerally experience, feelings of anomie are dissipated as the believer comes to inhabit a cosmically meaningful universe where every event, interaction, or experience is full of divine possibility.

Enchanting the Market Mentality

Does CC discourse as encoded at C3T mitigate the pathology of egoism? To answer this question, it will prove useful to re-examine what we mean by egoism. Recall from Chapter 7 that, according to Durkheim, egoism is naturalized by utilitarian individualism, the moral tradition inscribed in the economic sphere. In other words, the ideal-typical egoist is tantamount to *homo economicus*—he or she who lives according to what Robert Heilbroner (1992, 89, 26) calls "the market mentality," that is, "the drive to get ahead, to make money, to accumulate capital." Moreover, as we saw in Chapter 6, one of the perennial problems with utilitarian individualism is that it tends to disenchant; the drive to maximize one's utility for its own sake serves as a poor theodicy, hence why it has historically spurred interest in expressivism (e.g., the Romantic movement). I restate this because it clarifies a dimension of CC discourse that is as astounding as it is alarming: C3T seems to have succeeded in staving off the threat of anomie, not by challenging the market mentality but by *enchanting* it. What I mean by this is that CC discourse, rather than countering the utilitarian ethic of the economic sphere, *adopts it as its own* and *provides an expressivist theology to legitimate it.*

Recall that at C3T self-advancement is reconceived as a form of community advancement, such that "the pursuit of personal celebrity" is reinterpreted as "faithful fulfillment of a moral imperative" (Martí 2010, 60). The effect of this conceptual transformation cannot be underestimated. For by reframing egoistic behaviour as a form of divinely sanctioned altruism, CC discourse overcomes the inherent limitations of utilitarian individualism as a moral tradition. No longer is self-advancement the ultimate end of life; rather, the pursuit of individual prosperity is reconceived as the means by which members become "ambassador[s] of the kingdom of God" (Martí 2012, 137). Birgit Meyer (2007, 12) captures the implications of this succinctly when she writes that neo-Pentecostals "have not only embraced the logic of the market, but also form part of it." Indeed, what we find at C3T is a robust moral community that is founded upon a *sacralization of market values* and the *Christianization of homo economicus.*

Recall the role money plays as a symbol of faith at C3 Church. According to Phil Pringle, "Faith is the currency of heaven," and "when we give in the God economy, the return on investment is insane." Furthermore, money metaphors are everywhere in CC discourse, as is a preoccupation with measurement and numbers. One could even boil C3 Church's core message down to "the bigger the better." If churches are not gaining in size, if the number of souls saved is not increasing, or if the church's capital assets have not grown since the year prior, the assumption is that it is in a state of spiritual decay. It follows that churches such as C3T, rather than serving to mitigate egoism, in fact, *naturalize* and *exacerbate* it by offering a theology and theodicy that legitimates it.

Importantly, it does not follow that there is no moral regulation at these churches. On the contrary, there is intense regulation. The call to realize one's prosperous self is stringent and totalizing, demanding constant and vigilant self-discipline—which goes far beyond utilitarian individualism as ordinarily conceived. Indeed, the stress on material prosperity as a sign of faith arguably reshapes C3T members into Christian utility-maximizers, who fervently believe pursuing their own economic self-interest is aligned with God's will. It also follows that critics are right to draw attention to the intimate connections between the religion of the heart, in its Charismatic Christian form, and neoliberalism. Indeed, Mary Wrenn (2019, 426) sums things up well: "The Prosperity Gospel is...a spiritual articulation of neoliberalism."

C3 Toronto as "Greedy Institution"

I agree with critics who argue that CC discourse, like that institutionalized at C3T, rather than challenging the egoism of the market, amplifies it in an unprecedented way. But the question remains: *do churches such as C3T impede shifting involvements and the adoption of rival social perspectives or moral traditions?*

It might be useful to remind ourselves why a Durkheimian recasting of romantic liberalism couches the concern in this way. Although Durkheim would certainly fear that in naturalizing egoism, CC discourse is bound to produce a malady of infiniteness in its adherents, he also recognized that utilitarian individualism has a rightful place in the economic sphere of liberal democracies. It follows that we need to distinguish between the *personal* and *political* consequences of CC discourse.

Durkheim would contend that by encouraging egoism, C3T is bound to have deleterious personal consequences for its adherents, as their desires will always exceed that which they possess. But it does not necessarily follow that CC discourse entails accommodation to the status quo, nor precludes challenging social or economic injustices. Indeed, this follows logically from what I argued in Chapter 8. There I suggested that simply because NLF members, *qua* members of AA, take as authoritative anti-structuralist discourses which, by their very nature, encourage political quietism and accommodationism, this should not lead us to think they are incapable or unwilling to engage in social critique. Thus, it was perfectly acceptable in the eyes of NLF members to speak in a methodologically individualistic way when discussing their recoveries from addiction, while using a structuralist framework to discuss socio-political issues. This, I argued, is because being a member of NLF is not wholly constitutive of their selves, and therefore enables shifting involvements.

Of course, we can distinguish between the religion of the heart at NLF and that found at C3T by their varying relationships to egoism—while the former challenges it, the latter legitimates it. But my point is simply that we must distinguish analytically between the *problem of egoism* (personal) and *whether or not a particular discourse legitimates economic and social injustice* (political). And in order to determine the latter, we need to know the degree to which membership precludes other attachments and perspectives.

I now want to make the case that C3T is a "greedy institution" in the Coserian sense, which significantly reduces the likelihood of committed membership in other institutional spheres, or the adoption of rival social perspectives. We can best make sense of this by contrasting the "alcoholic" identity, as normalized at NLF, with the identity of "Christian" as normalized at C3T.

First, the former is restricted to the private sphere, whereas the latter is comprehensive, meaning C3T members are expected to live as faithful Christians in *all* areas of their lives, with their identities as Christians always holding primacy. As Paul Lichterman (2005, 35) explains:

> To be an evangelical is to carry a kind of identity, one that sustains strong boundaries between Christian truths and other religious or secular beliefs. To be evangelical is to make religious *certainty* a core part of one's identity—

certainty about what one's beliefs are, and that they are true. Evangelicals usually think of their Christian identity as their most basic, life-defining one—an identity that grows not from birth but from the moment when an individual explicitly states the intent to commit his life to Jesus Christ.

Indeed, the totalizing nature of the Christian identity at C3T encourages members to apply CC discourse across both "secular" and "religious" contexts, and conceive of every interaction as an opportunity to either evangelize or demonstrate their faithfulness. Thus, believers do not separate their identities, say, at work from those they adopt at church. On the contrary, work is conceived as a vocation, a means by which one uses one's spiritual gifts and talents for God's purposes (Martí 2010, 71).

Now, a sceptic might argue that C3T is merely "rhetorically greedy" and that in fact members do not close themselves off to competing commitments and perspectives. But this view is strongly challenged by the testimonies of ex-members— those who have, in their own words, "got out." For instance, when I asked one ex-member, Kwame, how much time and energy he saved for himself outside of church commitments while he was a church member he replied, "I didn't save any for myself." And evincing the fact that C3T, like other greedy institutions, encourages members to weaken their ties with rival institutions, as well as persons that might "make claims that conflict with their own demands" (Coser 1974, 6), another ex-member, Julia, shared that during her tenure at C3T she only spent time with other church members, and became emotionally estranged from her immediate non-Christian family because she feared they were threats to her faith.

Furthermore, it is a central feature of greedy institutions that they typically do not enforce conformity by means of external coercion, but rather "rely on voluntary compliance" (Coser 1974, 6). As I have shown, C3T members willingly submit themselves to the disciplines demanded of them, reconstituting their selves in light of the church's collective conscience. And as the interview accounts of Madge and Dan demonstrate, the ideal of submission allows little room for critical thought or questioning. "We've found that as you get more and more in, you can't think for yourself. And you're so clouded by a lot of the propaganda—I guess that would maybe be the word," Madge explained. Dan agreed: "I think when you're doing it, when you're in it, you don't question it. You can't." Both Madge and Dan expressed relief at "being one of the lucky ones to get out." They also described leaving C3T as a process of "deprogramming ourselves." And when asked what that means Dan replied, "I've been able to broaden the voices that I was listening to." So, while it's certainly true that not every single church member becomes a committed devotee, I would nevertheless contend that churches like C3T, generally speaking, function as greedy institutions.

In agreement, Matthew Wade (2016, 668, 665) draws attention to the way growth churches like C3T erect "psychological walls" in their adherents, thereby inspiring a "curious form of sectarianism." He further contends that they seek "to replace any void community groups, labour unions, more conventional faith-based collectives and the like [members] might otherwise have occupied" (668) Indeed, few of the C3T members I spoke to were involved in non-church activities that were not expressly concerned with professional development—itself conceived within CC discourse as spiritually salient. This is because there is intense pressure placed on newcomers to "go all in." In this way, C3T severely restricts the ability of members to embrace anything other than a theologized utilitarian individualism, which conceives of all structural or systemic solutions as misguided, since all problems are fundamentally "spiritual" in nature.

We can see, then, that many critics' concerns—at least when it comes to CC discourse—are legitimate. Those who fear the ascent of irrationality and subjectivism are correct that CC discourse may serve to impede the rationalist ethic within the public sphere, as C3T members are taught to trust "God's Word" over "the 'facts'" (Pringle 2005, 23). And those who fear a crisis in civic membership have every right to be alarmed that churches like C3T tend to endorse pure privatism, turning their members into passive citizens who, if they think of citizenship at all, do so in purely Christian-cum-economic terms. As a result of the moral hybrid naturalized at CC discourse all issues—be they political, social, or economic—are made sense of via a utilitarian ethic. Indeed, Jean Comaroff (2009, 28) captures the situation well when she asserts that Charismatic churches such as C3T "break down the separations between moral, economic, and political institutions" and "threaten the relative autonomy once enjoyed by each of these distinct spheres." Lastly, I agree with those who fear the religion of the heart may, in some instances, serve to legitimate unjust social and economic conditions by proscribing the adoption of counter discourses or alternative identities. For what we find at C3T is a Christianized market fundamentalism that can only perceive of social ills through the lens of Christian salvation, such that what the poor, the hungry, and the disenfranchised need is nothing more than a stronger faith.

Explaining the Rise of Charismatic Christianity

It would seem that CC discourse is ideologically allied to neoliberalism. However, we might still wonder: *is the rise of neoliberalism sufficient to explain the recent popularity of CC discourse?* Or put otherwise: can we reduce the C3T's success to the fact that it harmonizes well with the post-industrial service economies of the twenty-first century?

Admittedly, few critics have made this claim explicitly. For instance, Isabelle Barker (2007, 413) contends that CC discourse "reflects yet another response to neoliberal economic restructuring." Marion Maddox (2012, 153) draws attention to the way growth churches like C3T exhibit "a conscious and consistent effort to align the church's activities and message not with any national culture but with the culture of global capitalism." And William Connolly (2005, 874) suggests, "The right leg of the evangelical movement is joined at the hip to the left leg of the capitalist juggernaut." Rather than reducing CC discourse to neoliberalism these critiques instead highlight the legitimating role the religion of the heart in its Charismatic Christian form plays in romantic liberal modernity, pinpointing the elective affinities this discourse shares with neoliberalism's economic and political structures. Presumably, then, these critics would not rule out the possibility that there is more to the Charismatic Christian success story than its affinities with neoliberalism. Indeed, Barker (2007, 413) asserts as much: "I do not mean to interpret Pentecostalism's growth solely as a reaction to neoliberal globalization."

And yet, there has been relatively little effort to provide complementary non-economic explanations for the surge in attraction to CC discourse. I believe the reason for this stems from the nature of the interpretive frameworks so often used to study this phenomenon. While critics may not explicitly endorse a "reduction to neoliberalism" hypothesis, their analyses nevertheless theorize out of sight alternative, if supplementary, explanations. The problem with this is that the full picture is thereby obscured. Accordingly, below I outline three reasons for the popularity of CC discourse in romantic liberal modernity that extend beyond the economic.

The Need for Totalizing Communities of Enchantment

I have spoken at length about the many sources of disenchantment: the disciplines of civilized life can be experienced as stifling and alienating, the processes of rationalization and bureaucratization—necessary for the functioning of a modern liberal state—can produce crises of meaning (which are only exacerbated by pluralism), and in a differentiated society individuals remain ever vulnerable to anomie and identity crises. Picking up on this, Hunt et al. (1997, 7) have noted that churches like C3T provide a subculture in which people can "retreat from the impersonal modern world." Indeed, I described above how C3T brands itself as a haven in a heartless world, where individuals can finally feel like they belong. But the church does more than merely offer emotional support. It also serves as both a community of redemption,[5] and a *totalizing community of enchantment*.

By a totalizing community of enchantment, I mean the following: by institutionalizing the religion of the heart, C3T legitimates a theodicy, which enables its members to make sense of their suffering and gain a sense of cosmic purpose. Communities of enchantment re-enchant the world by assuring their members

[5] See Chapter 8.

that they live in a meaningful universe, that what they subjectively experience is not false, and that their lives matter. Of course, all communities that institution-alize the religion of the heart do this to some extent. But C3T stands out because of its "greediness." In short, *the greedier, the more totalizing, and the more totalizing, the more enchanting.*

At C3T, I encountered a degree of certainty about the meaningfulness of life among members that was unmatched at my other field sites. I therefore believe that one of the sources of its attraction is that, as a result of the efficacy of worship services in producing embodied enchantment, C3T enables its members to leave each Sunday with a high degree of confidence that the world is meaningful and that God loves them. And because of the comprehensive scope of the Christian identity at C3T, members do not need to cope with the epistemic and moral difficulties institutional differentiation throws up. In other words, totalizing com-munities of enchantment overcome the sense of inner fragmentation that is a staple of romantic liberal modernity—protecting their members from role con-flict, identity troubles, and the spectre of nihilism. And given the deeply human desire to inhabit a meaningful universe, attraction to totalistic groups may be an irrepressible instinct in some.

If I am correct about this, then we are confronted with what might be called the *paradox of enchantment*: in demanding a comprehensive scope in the lives and minds of members C3T successfully enchants the world. However, it does so only at the expense of wider solidarities across institutional spheres. Or, put in more general terms, *the more the threat of anomie is mitigated by a single community of enchantment, the less likely its members will be willing to question their closely held beliefs, and the less they will feel a sense of identification with those outside of their community.*

The Desire for Personal Empowerment

One of the central characteristics of CC discourse is the stress it places on personal empowerment. I've been amazed by the degree to which C3T members are convinced that "faith conquers everything" (Coleman 2006, 181). One reasonable explanation for this is the role self-efficacy—"the belief that one has mastery over the events of one's life and can meet challenges as they come up" (Goleman 1995, 89)—plays in a meritocratic society, be it neoliberal *or* social democratic. Simply put, those who believe in themselves are likely to perform better. So, it is not difficult to see how CC discourse might serve to bolster individuals' chances of economic success in romantic liberal modernity (even while obscuring the various ways in which equality of opportunity remains far from a social reality).

Yet there is more to the story. For a sense of self-efficacy is not merely useful in the economic realm. Consider Nel, who during our interview discussed the problems she once had with "desperately needing validation from men." For this young Charismatic, developing a relationship with God allowed her to realize she "didn't need the validation of men in order to feel loved." Another example is offered by Chinara, who reflected on her struggles with social anxiety for many years prior to joining C3T. "God completely healed me of that. I thought I would suffer with it for the rest of my life. And I feel so free now." These examples shed light on some of the ways CC discourse can grant people a sense of agency, the feeling that they are not simply at the mercy of brute circumstance. This is a powerful feeling, one that comes in handy when faced with hardship. Of course, the source of this hardship may lie in conditions of injustice or inequity that can only be remedied by systemic change. But it may also have more personal origins—trauma, relationship troubles, or illness—which cannot be overcome, when they can, without the kind of resilience and resolve that C3T impressively musters. Thus, we cannot ignore the fact that CC discourse often functions as a "tool of empowerment" (Chestnut 2012, 219), the applications of which are not only economic in character.

The Burdens of Negative Freedom

Of Pentecostalism in Latin America, Bernice Martin (1995, 117) writes, "the most important aspect of the inner-worldly asceticism of the Pentecostal ethic is its ban on alcohol, tobacco, drugs, gambling, violence and sexual promiscuity." "It deploys the moral core to re-establish personal integration, self-discipline and family stability for those ravaged by the excesses of bohemianism" (116). Martin's observations have been echoed by a number of other scholars of Latin American Pentecostalism (see Brusco 1995; Dawley 2018). Of course, it could be argued that in Latin America where, especially in poorer areas, "machismo" culture is pervasive, there is far more need for the kind of rigid social conservatism found in Pentecostal churches. Although this is probably true, I nevertheless believe that Martin's observations can apply to C3T.

While conversion narratives among C3T members follow a similar format, I found the life narratives of male and female members were markedly distinct. From the men, I often heard *a story of excess*, which included struggles with excessive drinking and drugs, compulsive consumption of pornography, failing to connect with other men, and other problems generally associated with "toxic masculinity." For these young men the world beyond the church was experienced as one of perpetual temptation and hostility, which enabled them to readily adopt the narrative of spiritual warfare they heard at C3T upon arrival. From the women, I often heard *a story of disappointment*, largely revolving around struggles with men, romance, and the perils of dating. Female members recounted stories of deception, insecurity, and abuse, such that the world outside the church was experienced as one of perpetual dissatisfaction.

If the stories of C3T members are any indication, it would seem that the impetus towards social conservatism found at C3T may be fuelled, at least in part, by negative experiences of living in romantic liberal modernity—or what conservatives call our "permissive society." These young people, men and women alike, seek in C3T a moral community where gender roles are clearly divided, where sexual and romantic expectations are explicit, and where future ideals are flexible yet prescribed. While this is not a return to the traditionalism of their parents, it is nevertheless hostile to the romanticism embodied in the liberation movements of the 1960s. I have little doubt that many romantic liberals will find these developments disturbing. While I sympathize with this view, I believe they call for more than mere denunciation. For it may be that the conditions of romantic liberal modernity (including increasing gender and sexual equality) stoke in certain individuals the desire for moral order, not so much because they are hostile to difference (although this may be the case), but rather due to the heavy burdens posed by negative freedom in an open society.

With the shift to romantic liberal modernity, social norms—especially within the private sphere—have become far more contested and far less clear. This can lead to confusion and anxiety. Moreover, young people can experience a lack of fetters on their private lives as both liberating and imprisoning depending on their social circumstances and levels of self-control. Finally, as individual liberty has become sacralized, both men and women have the freedom to choose their mates, producing a dating scene that resembles the neoliberal economy—characterized by a few big winners and manifold losers. Although this certainly doesn't apply universally, the appeal of C3T may have something to do with the way it institutionalizes a culture that challenges "toxic masculinity" by encouraging males to become respectful and dutiful young men who take care (economic and emotional) of their female partners. This doubtless serves to reinforce a conservative gender ideology and overall social conservatism, but the point is that such ideologies may derive some of their appeal simply as a result of the burdens and challenges thrown up by life in romantic liberal modernity.

Conclusion

In this chapter I have argued that while critics are wrong to think churches like C3T fail to stave off anomie, they are quite right to fear their political and economic consequences. C3T not only integrates its members into a moral community, but also enfolds them into a totalizing community of enchantment that naturalizes a moral hybrid, which hides a rugged utilitarian individualism behind expressivist language. I have also argued that critics are right to characterize CC discourse as an ally to neoliberalism, and as an impediment to progressive social change. Because C3T functions as a "greedy institution," demanding undivided loyalty and commitment from its members, members' willingness to shift involvements and adopt rival social perspectives is drastically reduced. Yet I've also sought to shed light on various non-economic reasons for the appeal of CC discourse, for I believe doing so helps us to better understand important, if complex, features of romantic liberal modernity that we have failed to adequately reckon with.

10

Public Performance and Political Ambivalences at a Public Speaking Club

The club meeting takes place in an inconspicuous office building in the downtown core. I take the main elevator up to the fifth floor. As the doors open, I can hear shuffling echoing through the hall. I follow the sound and find two people—an older white woman and younger black woman—in one of the boardrooms. The room is generic and sterile. Aside from two whiteboards there are no pictures on the walls. There is little colour. The long rectangular tables are set up to form a semi-circle, which faces a podium. And behind the podium a banner displaying "Tomorrow's Leaders" hangs precariously.

The older woman greets me. "Welcome. I'm Marie." I smile back and introduce myself. As I take a seat, Marie resumes setting up the meeting. I introduce myself to the younger woman, and ask if this is her first time attending a Toastmasters meeting. She nods, tells me her name is Savannah, and shares that she's here because she wants to start a business that will empower young women of colour to reach their "full potential." "Something like a motivational coach?" I ask. "Something like that," she replies.

With a few minutes until the meeting is scheduled to start, the room has filled in—there are now twenty of us. And as the hour strikes, Marie approaches the podium and calls the meeting to order. TL club meetings run like a well-oiled machine. We stick diligently to the agenda, allowing no room for delays or distractions. We hear three prepared speeches from members, a round of "table topics" (improvised speeches from the floor), and three speech evaluations. One member gives a speech about Barack Obama's autobiography. Another gives a speech on how to become a Distinguished Toastmaster. And the third gives a speech titled "How to avoid procrastination."

At the end of the meeting, the guests share what they thought of it. Savannah thanks the club for hosting her, and says she "learned a lot." After her, a young Sikh man who works in the tech sector shares that he enjoyed the meeting, but is terrified of public speaking. "I don't know what to say when I'm asked to speak. But I'll keep coming back."

I will later learn that most guests don't return, and even fewer join (I never saw Savannah again). In fact, membership at Tomorrow's Leaders fluctuates frequently, with members arriving as quickly as they leave. Midway through my

The Spiritual Turn: The Religion of the Heart and the Making of Romantic Liberal Modernity. Galen Watts, Oxford University Press. © Galen Watts 2022. DOI: 10.1093/oso/9780192859839.003.0011

fieldwork I asked Marie what she thought of this. She responded, "People have their own priorities. They have to do what's right for them."

A Brief History of Toastmasters International

Toastmasters began unofficially in 1905, when Ralph C. Smedley, the Director of Education at a YMCA in Bloomington, Illinois, came up with the idea of hosting a series of public speaking workshops tailored for young Christian men. Toastmasters International was formally established in 1924, when Smedley organized the first official club meeting at a YMCA in Santa Ana, California. Today, the organization oversees more than 16,000 clubs, with more than 358,000 members across 143 countries.[1]

While the initial focus of Toastmasters was public speaking, it now boasts far broader ambitions. Its website promises members they will "Enjoy unlimited personal growth," "Build self-confidence and self-awareness," and "Maximize [their] potential." In *Toastmaster*, the organization's flagship magazine, one of the feature articles was titled "On realizing one's potential and teaching others to do the same" (Glozek 2018, 26). And in promotional videos veteran members attest: "Toastmasters is really the best kept secret for self-development." Anthropologist Amir Hampel (2017, 445) observes, "public speaking courses are a lively sector in a broad self-help universe." Indeed, although Toastmasters may promote its own educational programs, it has long relied on the self-help publishing industry to both fuel demand for its services and provide the cultural texts that give it legitimacy.

In *Self Help, Inc.* Micki McGee (2005, 31) traces the history of self-help to the writings of Benjamin Franklin, "the quintessential self-made man" in American lore. Yet she also classifies Ralph Waldo Emerson as a forefather of the self-help tradition. In fact, McGee's history of self-help in North America overlaps uncannily with the history of the religion of the heart that I traced in Chapter 2, as she contends Transcendentalism, Christian Science, and New Thought have all played a pivotal role in shaping contemporary self-help discourse. Relatedly, McGee notes that a significant semantic shift took place during the mid-twentieth century: classic self-help literature, which previously spoke in traditional Christian terms (invoking concepts such as "mission," "individual calling," and "vocation"), was translated into the secular register of humanistic psychology (invoking concepts such as "self-actualization" and "self-realization") (40).

"One of the principal cultural reasons that psychology has so successfully reached wider audiences" argues Robert Fuller (2006, 224), "is its capacity to

---

[1] See https://www.toastmasters.org/about/all-about-toastmasters.

function as an unchurched source of American spirituality." In agreement, I would argue there has been no cultural tributary more influential in shaping self-help discourse than humanistic psychology. So, it is no accident that the historical development of Toastmasters International has followed an identical trajectory to that of the self-help tradition: one of *increasing psychologization*. While Toastmasters may have begun as a liberal Protestant organization— implicitly and explicitly endorsing the classical self-help tradition—at some point during the mid-twentieth century it secularized its brand, embracing the humanistic psychological language of "realizing your potential," "building self-awareness," and "achieving personal growth." The changes that have taken place at Toastmasters therefore parallel the wider developments that have swept across liberal democracies in the last half-century: a once publicly acceptable language of traditional biblical religion has gradually been replaced by that of romantic expressivist psychology.

Tomorrow's Leaders (TL)

TL meetings follow a standardized structure that is virtually the same at all Toastmasters clubs. Meetings consist of four parts: the business portion, formal prepared speeches, table topics, and speech evaluations. Roles are always assigned the week prior, with executive team members taking on the more demanding roles. And much like AA groups, Toastmasters clubs are organized democratically (Hampel 2017, 446). So, unlike C3T, there is no clear hierarchy of command.

TL meets every Monday for just over an hour and a half. Clubs range in their degrees of professionalism and overall strictness. Some require prospective members to audition before being accepted, while others are run simply for the purpose of entertainment. TL lies somewhere between these extremes. When I joined, membership sat at fifteen, and the average number of guests on any given week ranged from five to eight. But over the course of the year, membership numbers oscillated dramatically. At various points, the club had fewer than seven paid members, leading executive team members to worry they wouldn't be able to afford the boardroom rental fee.

TL tends to attract those under thirty-five. Most members are entrepreneurs, graduate students, or work in lower management, and thus are members of the educated middle class. It's worth noting, then, that, unlike NLF or C3T, membership at TL is not free. Guests are allowed to attend three meetings free of charge, but are then asked to either pay for membership or not return.[2] Another noteworthy aspect of TL is that it attracts a large number of first-generation

---

[2] TL membership cost 90 Canadian dollars per six months. However, membership costs vary from club to club.

immigrants hoping to hone their English skills in a public setting (these members predominantly come from China, India, and the Middle East).

Unquestionably, the appeal of Toastmasters clubs is related to the shift from an industrial to post-industrial economy. But economic advancement is not the sole reason members join. Rather, the motivations for becoming a member fall into two general categories: *professional advancement* and *personal growth* (though these reasons commonly overlap). I think it fair to say then that nearly all members join Toastmasters owing to a *pre-existing desire for personal change.* That is, they are hoping to "work on" some part of themselves, and they view membership at TL as a means to this end. Moreover, most arrive at TL with some *previous exposure and attraction to self-help discourse*—which is itself premised upon (as well as produces) a desire to improve oneself (Dunn 2016, 122).

TL presents itself in promotional materials as "nonreligious" or "secular" in nature. Yet, this is not to say members don't identify as "religious" or as "spiritual." In fact, a large number of the TL members I interviewed identified as such. Nevertheless, there exists a club mandate that members not talk about religion in club meetings. In this sense, TL meetings mirror in important respects the public sphere in romantic liberal modernity: members generally feel it appropriate and right to keep their religious identities and commitments private in order to avoid confrontation, and visitors seem instinctively to recognize this as proper custom. Yet, this should not lead us to think members' religious or moral commitments are left at the door. On the contrary, members *import their pre-existing ideals into meetings by adopting a shared language of self-help.* It's just that this tends to occur internally, so is not obvious. Here, again, we see an analogy to the romantic liberal public sphere: SH discourse at TL enables a kind of "overlapping consensus" (cf. Rawls 1993) across members' varying social identities and moral commitments.

The Religion of the Heart at Tomorrow's Leaders: Self-Help Discourse

I argued in Chapters 8 and 9 that institutionalized at both NLF and C3T are distinct discourses that encode their own versions of the religion of the heart. I think we find something quite similar at TL—what I call *Self-Help (SH) discourse.* However, there are two important differences between these sites.

First, TL can be distinguished from both NLF and C3T to the extent that *there exists little in the way of a canonical text or oral tradition* with which individual members can collectively identify and refer to. Recall that NLF members often reference *Alcoholics Anonymous* and the Twelve Steps, while C3T members appeal to the Bible and the moral authority of senior pastors. There exists no such text or external authority at TL. As a result, *the group allows for a greater degree of individual interpretation and negotiation regarding what ideals or values SH discourse ultimately naturalizes.*

Second, to the extent that SH discourse is indebted to humanistic psychology it remains, in a way that AA discourse and CC discourse arguably do not, amenable to both secular and religious interpretations. Fuller (2006, 229) writes, "cultural historians must pay attention not only to how psychological theories are constructed, but also to how they are consumed." He adds, "even many psychological concepts that are themselves devoid of deep metaphors invoking an ultimate horizon are nonetheless sometimes appropriated as technical instruments for achieving religiously significant goals." Fuller's emphasis on how psychological discourses are *consumed* is critical to understanding how and when the religion of the heart finds a home at TL. For I believe SH discourse—couched in the humanistic psychological register that it is—only signals or transmits the religion of the heart among TL members *who have been socialized in other corners of the romantic liberal institutional order* (for instance, the holistic milieu or the Charismatic wing of the congregational domain) to embrace this cultural structure. In short, *whether or not SH discourse is interpreted in a religiously meaningful way depends upon members' pre-existing attachments and associations.*

Experiential Epistemology

Given the variety of speeches one hears at TL it would be wrong to claim an experiential epistemology is axiomatic at the club. For instance, I've listened to speeches that invoked a staunch scientific materialism, as well as speeches that appealed solely to reason and our rational faculties. Yet the fact is these discourses are quite rare at TL, while SH discourse, which appeals to personal experience, intuition, and feeling, is commonplace. For instance, in one of his speeches, "How to Find Your True Self," Michael Wallace asserted, "To me, to learn about the universe you don't go out, you go in." And in her first speech at the club, Sandra, an accountant with a long history of engagement in the holistic milieu, shared that she's learned to always "listen to what my heart is telling me," because "it has never let me down." Of course, some in the room may have been sceptical of these claims, but upon conducting subsequent informal interviews it became clear these members' appeals to the epistemic authority of experience received wide affirmation. I think this can be explained by noting the way TL members, in order to be relatable and comprehensible to their peers, speak in the moral language of expressive individualism. And because of the secular nature of Toastmasters, they adopt SH discourse to do so.

Immanence of God or the Superempirical

Marie shared in a meeting, "I have done a lot of energy clearing to work on the blockages from my past. Through psychotherapy and other activities, I have tried to rid myself of those blockages." In a speech, Sandra spoke about her struggles trying to "attune to the source," and how she has the ability to "feel other people's energies." And in our interview Michael shared, "It feels to me sometimes that I tap into sources of knowledge that don't just come from this place and time, you know?" In *Religious Thought and the Modern Psychologies* Don Browning and Terry Cooper (2004, 75) argue the "horizon" of humanistic psychology is replete with "images of harmony" which are communicated by "monistic metaphysical metaphors." They contend that the metaphors of "flow," "energy," and "source" gesture toward, if not signify, a metaphysical system whereby "apparently independent parts are so interrelated, interdependent, and harmonious that they are all identified with one another and identical with the divine itself." Now, while I rarely heard the words "God," "super-natural," or "the divine" in TL club meetings, it became clear in interviews that metaphors like those above were often understood by the members who invoked them as reflective of a larger metaphysical picture whereby "God" (or some other equivalent term) was conceived as "an immanent spiritual power continuously available to those with proper metaphysical awareness" (Fuller 2001, 145).

Benevolent God/Universe

While overt references to the benevolence of "God" or the "Universe" are few and far between at TL, much that is said in meetings presupposes the notion that life is fundamentally good, and that the natural state of things is one of peace and personal wholeness. As Greg, a German-born entrepreneur, put it over coffee, "I feel like all you need to do is keep saying 'Yes' and life will pay off." And as Tenzin, the club's president, asserted in a speech, "Life is on our side, we just need to believe it." In this way, SH discourse endorses a rugged optimism, which holds that "If you follow the plan and stay true to the inner self, you can have, be, or do almost anything" (McAdams 2006, 126).

This orientation towards the positive dimensions of life is fundamental to SH discourse, and while it may not require the existence of a benevolent God or Universe, many TL members nevertheless presuppose one. Accordingly, Sandra explained in our interview, "I know that if it hurts it is not God's plan. Because if it is God's plan, it is always good." For Sandra, among other TL members, SH discourse presupposes a loving and caring God or Universe.[3]

---

[3] Of course, this isn't to say that for all TL members SH discourse entails metaphysical commit-ments. But, as I gleaned from interviews, for many this discourse was made *cosmically meaningful* as they interpreted it within the context of a benevolent God or Universe.

Redemptive Self as Theodicy

In the spring, TL hosted an inter-district speech competition. One of the contestants, Tim, gave a speech titled, "Be a Light." He began by sharing that his father was difficult to live with when he was growing up, that he was "not a nice guy," and that he'd held this against him for many years. He then disclosed that his father was recently diagnosed with Alzheimers. "And if this wasn't enough, I've had a bunch of huge personal challenges come my way." Tim went on to explain how these hardships taught him that he needed to forgive his father—which he analogized to "being a light in someone else's life." In essence, Tim's speech was a story of redemption, one where his suffering and negative experiences were redeemed in light of the lessons they eventually procured. This narrative structure is characteristic of many of the speeches at TL. I was even told by a veteran speaker of a rival club that unless your speech follows this format you have little chance of winning competitions: "People want to know how you overcame your personal trials. It's inspiring, they learn something, and it makes them feel good. So, it's what everybody wants to hear." Of course, as McAdams (2006, 20) reminds us, "The burgeoning popular literature on self-help offers a cornucopia of redemption tales." So, it shouldn't surprise us that TL members regularly share about how their personal hardships ultimately served redemptive purposes—making them stronger, wiser, or better off than they were before.

Self-Realization as Teleology

There is no concept more central to SH discourse than *personal growth*. As one article in *Toastmaster* puts it, "Toastmasters is a great place if you want to continue growing" (Dewey 2018, 6). And according to Tenzin, it is simply common sense that "we all come to Toastmasters in order to become the best version of ourselves." So, when a seasoned member visited from another club, she challenged TL members by asking: "What is one thing you can do to make sure you continue growing?"

Browning and Cooper (2004, 61) argue that the concept of personal growth reflects an "organic model of self-actualization," which was both secularized and systematized by humanistic psychologists like Maslow and Rogers. In agreement, Peter Morea (1997, 66) contends, "Secular humanistic psychology maintains that individuals can find values which give meaning to their lives by actualizing their true selfs [sic]" (70). Talk of personal growth, becoming one's true self, and realizing one's potential are ubiquitous at TL and central to SH discourse. In fact, the ideal of self-realization is one of the least contested of those regularly circulated at TL.

Self-Ethic (Voice from Within)

The cover of a Toastmasters International pamphlet reads: "Find Your Voice. Where Leaders Are Made." SH discourse, in holding self-realization as the ultimate end of life, presupposes the existence of a true self which, if attuned to, promises great power. Thus, in the first speech I ever heard him give, Tenzin declared, "Always be true to yourself and you will never be let down." Tenzin spoke in our interview about listening to the voice inside of him, which he felt was connected to "something bigger." And many other TL members celebrated in speeches the inner resources we all allegedly have within us to conquer the obstacles we face. Of course, SH discourse doesn't necessarily propose that we all have within us an inner divinity. But it does imply that within us lies "an infallible source of inspiration and guidance" (Fuller 2001, 128). Furthermore, the majority of TL speeches centred on the perils and pitfalls of social conformity—members' speeches regularly invoked the ideals of "challenging the system," "breaking the rules," and "finding one's own voice." Indeed, SH discourse implicitly endorses the self-understanding typical of romantic liberals: because the true self is conceived as *pre-social*, society and its institutions are seen as the cause of alienation and personal inauthenticity.

Virtue Is Natural

SH discourse is articulated through what Browning and Cooper refer to as "implicit metaphors of harmony," which are central to humanistic psychology and implicit in notions like "self-realization," "achieving your potential," and "finding one's purpose." These metaphors, they argue, "depict an image of the world where conflict can occur only if humans are somehow untrue to their own deepest selves" (Browning and Cooper 2004, 31). I have on occasion witnessed these ideas being contested both in and outside of club meetings, so they are not accepted as fact at TL. But it became clear upon conducting interviews that a large portion of members endorsed the high anthropology that undergirds this view. Thus, Sandra affirmed that to the extent that individuals realize their true selves, she sees no reason why they would harm, discriminate, or mistreat others. And similarly, according to Vivaan, if one attunes to what God or the Universe is telling them at any given moment, one could not fail to do the right thing. For these TL members, becoming virtuous and realizing one's true self are one and the same.

Sacralization of Individual Liberty

Browning and Cooper (2004, 59) write, "the cultural power and attractiveness of humanistic psychology are partially explained by its continuity with significant strands of individualism that have characterized American history." While McAdams (2006, 278) notes that self-help and humanistic psychological ideas flourish in "individualist cultures" which "prioritize personal autonomy." Indeed, if there is any single value that is considered sacred at TL and which goes wholly uncontested it is individual liberty. This is apparent not only in the statements often made by members (e.g., "I want to live my own life," "I am looking to become more independent," "I am searching for more freedom") but also in the rationales offered for joining (and leaving) the club, the egalitarianism inherent in the meeting structure, and the taboo surrounding giving unsolicited suggestions or commands to others. In short, we can say that *SH discourse naturalizes and normalizes the romantic liberal notion that our lives go better when lived from the inside.*

Mind-Body-Spirit Connection

Of all three sites I studied, the ambiguity inherent in this tenet was most stark at TL. For instance, according to Michael Wallace, "The moment you say, 'I can' something happens in your brain—your brain gets wired differently." Here Michael couches the mind-body-spirit connection in neurobiological terms, endorsing something like the idea that believing in oneself increases self-efficacy. Conversely, Sandra impressed upon me, "Mind is only a small piece. There needs to be a heart, soul, mind connection if we are to find peace. So, heart, soul and mind need to be in alignment." For Sandra, SH discourse holds that we need to "be in alignment" if we are to find health and happiness. Finally, Marie gave a speech titled "Thoughts Become Things," wherein she echoed New Thought teachings that resemble a secularized version of positive confession: "Are you interested in creating an awesome life? When we hold something in our mind, we can manifest it. If you think negative thoughts, guess what? You will have negative impacts in your life. See it in your mind, and you will have it!" So, while each of these TL members subscribes to some version of the mind-body-spirit connection, it's doubtful that they would agree on its specifics. This, I believe, makes evident another way in which SH discourse, owing to its ambiguity, affords wide interpretive variety.

Methodological Individualism

Over the course of a year, while I heard a handful of speeches and informal conversations which made reference to social structures as sources of constraints, as well as the need for collective solutions to societal problems, SH discourse— with its emphasis on individualistic solutions—was nevertheless dominant.

Exemplifying this trend, Tenzin declared in an impromptu speech, "If you want to change the world, become the change you want to see." Similarly, Shahed, a grad student in the natural sciences, asserted, "If you want a cleaner environment, don't litter. And if you want to change the world, start by making your bed." Finally, Zamir, an Iranian engineering student, offered his own spin on this theme in a speech: "You will change the world for the better by finding and pursuing your passion." This anti-structuralist bias should be expected, given that both the traditions of self-help and humanistic psychology have tended to view the individual as the sole unit of social change. In turn, SH discourse holds that social progress is possible only when individuals take responsibility and seek to realize their true selves.

Toastmasters as Collective Ritual

Paul Lichterman (1992, 443) argues that self-help books work to produce a "thin culture," by which he means that "readers read books believingly yet loosely, defining and redefining aspects of lived experience with a variety of partly discountable terms, and readers read in ongoing relation to a larger cultural arena—a repertoire of everyday reference points that orient one's sense of self." While Lichterman may speak narrowly of reading practices, I believe we can apply his insights to the experience of attending and participating in a TL meeting. For, in a sense, when members encounter SH discourse at TL meetings, through either speeches or informal conversations, much in the same way as Lichterman's readers, they interpret this discourse "in ongoing relation to other frameworks for situating personal selfhood in a social context" (422). In other words, *to the extent that SH discourse is made meaningful to members, it is only through their pre-existing social attachments and moral commitments.*

And yet, despite this discursive negotiation, it would be wrong to suggest SH discourse is not, to some extent, normative or structuring. As we learned in Chapter 7, a number of critics have argued that self-help and humanistic psychological discourses are carriers of romantic liberal regimes of power and discipline—that is, regimes of normalization and subjectification through which romantic liberal states "create individuals who do not need to be governed by others, but will govern themselves, master themselves, care for themselves" (Rose 1993, 291). Heidi Rimke (2000, 63, 73) writes, "these discourses and technologies contribute to the invention and scripting of selves," which are "remarkably congruous with the political programmes of liberal democratic society." Rebecca Hazleden (2014, 433) similarly contends, "Political selves are, therefore, *produced* by (inter alia) self-help." And Brigid Philip (2009, 161) argues that SH discourse "encourage[s] readers to judge their behaviour against distinctively liberal virtues." According to these scholars, working with a Foucaultian schematic, SH discourse serves as a "technology of the self" that privileges and produces, broadly speaking, *romantic liberal subjects*—that is, subjects who conceive of individual autonomy—understood as both freedom from external constraint, as well as freedom to express one's true self—as a necessary precondition of the good life.

While I disagree with its normative connotations, I think this critical account is empirically accurate. What's more, I think attendance at a Toastmasters meeting is far more normalizing than simply reading a self-help book, to the extent that it involves participation in collective ritual. Accordingly, I consider below how TL meetings function as collective rituals, identifying and analysing the various components that work together to (re)produce subjects who are well adapted to the basic structures of romantic liberal modernity.

Shared Social Norms

TL lacks many of the features of NLF and C3T that make them successful sites of socialization and identity reconstruction. The meeting takes place in a generic boardroom, and speech norms differ little from what one finds in "polite society." There is nothing clandestine about the weekly gatherings, and little is done to manufacture a sensory environment that will excite or overwhelm the senses. Moreover, there is no attempt by TL members to delineate or promote a distinct "Toastmasters" identity, so there are few, if any, symbolic boundaries demarcating insiders from outsiders. In fact, the social environment of TL meetings is aesthetically and atmospherically indistinguishable from other common spaces in romantic liberal modernity. Consequently, rather than serving to encode or enflesh a distinct collective identity, TL institutionalizes many of the same social norms that pervade the romantic liberal institutional order.

Having said this, owing to the pervasiveness and dominance of SH discourse, TL can be said to reify and intensify these norms, *making explicit what often remains only implicit in other expressive contexts.* For instance, in meetings, members and guests are always addressed *as* individuals (there are no collective speeches), rather than members of specific identity groups. Individuals are given the freedom to come and go as they please, with few expectations placed upon them. And they are repeatedly encouraged to make decisions according to, as Marie put it, "what's right for them." The implicit message communicated in club meetings, then, is that individuals are *independent* and *bounded entities*, thereby reifying and normalizing the romantic liberal "ideal of persons as self-determining and unpredictably self-transforming creatures" (Macedo 1990, 204). That is, members learn to think of their selves and others as separated (or in need of separation) by boundaries. Indeed, Hampel (2017, 433) maintains that Toastmasters clubs "promote a liberal ethos by setting up interpersonal boundaries within families, while advocating civil and equitable relations with strangers." In other words, they "dismantle logics of kinship" by helping members to "experience themselves as autonomous individuals" (459).

We see this illustrated powerfully in the case of Sandra. Born in Shanghai an only child, Sandra immigrated to Canada with her parents at the age of sixteen. In our interview Sandra recalled the difficulties she faced adjusting to Canadian culture: she felt out of place, confused, and ill-equipped to make friends. Soon after arriving she became anorexic, an eating disorder she struggled with for the next few years. Reflecting on these experiences, Sandra blamed her cultural upbringing—specifically her parents' emotionally closed and characteristically Chinese approach to child-rearing.

> My parents are not the best models of self-love, so I never learned that. I just learned how to please them. Basically, I sacrificed myself for my parents. I also think I internalized a lot of their trauma. I absorbed their emotions and fears. They don't have their own awareness. They are trapped in themselves. So they avoid pain. They fought all the time, and I found there was no space for me. And I think I developed the eating disorder because I wanted to disappear. You know, I didn't want to be here—physically, emotionally, psychologically. I unconsciously looked for ways to hide, looked for ways to not be here, looked for ways to cover myself up.

As a means of coping with her eating disorder, Sandra sought help from "spiritual" and self-help literature. She read books by popular authors like Deepak Chopra, Tony Robbins, and Don Miguel Ruiz. While working for a university degree in accounting at the behest of her parents, she continued her "spiritual" explorations. "Even though I was away from my parents there was so much struggle, all their voices in my head. I was trying to run away from it." Much of Sandra's interest in "spirituality" and SH discourse reflects an attempt to create psychic and cultural distance between her and her parents. "I realized at some point that I can't take on all of my parents' emotions, pains, and struggles. I have to kind of set a boundary between myself and them." Membership at TL has helped her to become more autonomous, loosening the constraining influences of her parents in her life.

Central to SH discourse is a message of personal agency: as Tenzin put it, "until you accept responsibility for your life, nothing is going to change." So, TL members learn to habitually think in terms of an ideal of self-responsibility. Needless to say, this emphasis on personal responsibility is a staple of liberal thought (Galston 1991, 230). Moreover, owing to the dominance of SH discourse, TL members speak often about the importance of becoming the "best version" of themselves. This suggests a normative ideal whereby the self must be regularly worked on. So, while TL may not privilege any specific practices of self-cultivation (members engage in everything from meditation, visualization, yoga, reading, watching documentaries, exercise, and more), a work ethic remains normative—members are encouraged, if not expected, to engage in self-work in order to realize their potential.

While a "thick" collective identity is not produced at TL, the club nevertheless engenders a "thin" culture, or collective conscience, on the basis of shared social norms. These norms derive from the nature of SH discourse—which naturalizes a *romantic liberal subjectivity*, along with what Macedo (1990, 4) refers to as "liberal virtues," or "those forms of excellence appropriate to citizens in liberal regimes and conducive to flourishing in the kind of society liberalism creates." These include: broad sympathies, a self-critical attitude, a willingness to experiment and try new things, tolerance, openness to difference, self-control, and active autonomous self-development (272). TL therefore resembles many sites across the romantic liberal institutional order—institutionalizing expressive individualism and naturalizing the romantic liberal ideals of individual freedom, self-expression, and self-realization.

Public Performances

Still, a Durkheimian perspective would hold that SH discourse, and the romantic liberal norms it legitimates, derive their moral force as a result of being rooted in shared experiences of collective effervescence. Of course, it is quite likely that, given the ubiquity of these norms in romantic liberal modernity, TL members arrive at the club having already been socialized to accept them, at least to some extent. But it's worth considering how club meetings might themselves serve to solidify or strengthen members' allegiances to SH discourse.

Aside from securing a discursive environment where SH discourse is naturalized, what distinguishes TL from other sites across the romantic liberal institutional order is its emphasis on *public performance*—that is, the giving of speeches. It is a central feature of TL meetings that every member in attendance will, at some point, have the proverbial spotlight directed on them, receiving the gaze of all. It's notable, then, that fear of public speaking is one of the most common phobias (Ebrhahimi et al. 2019). Most people are terrified of speaking before strangers in public, as it tends to conjure up threats of humiliation, psychic pain, and intense self-consciousness.

Recall that SH discourse holds that we have within us the inner resources (potentially divine in nature) to overcome the obstacles before us, and realize our true selves. The ritual of public performance serves to give credence to this conviction by creating conditions where individuals are, first, obliged to muster the courage to speak in front of the group (rely on their inner resources); second, to endure the experience of facing their fear of public speaking (which often entails intense bodily and emotional discomfort); and finally, where they are met with positive affirmation and applause (thereby being reassured that their fears of humiliation and embarrassment were misplaced). In short, by creating a controlled social environment where experiences of personal triumph are made highly likely, the ritual of public performance arouses in members considerable emotional energy, while vindicating a key tenet of SH discourse: that *we have more power within us than we know, and that should we rise to the occasion God/the Universe is on our side.*

Michael Wallace, who credited Toastmasters for helping him to overcome his "learned helplessness," offers an illustrative example. He described his first Toastmasters meeting in the following way: "I realized after giving that impromptu speech that I had control of my life, that if I wanted to do things I could do them. And after that, I just remember this feeling of freedom and liberation." Part of the power of the ritual of public performance at TL, then, derives from the fact that it invokes intense feelings of anxiety (in the lead up to giving a speech) followed by a great sense of relief and joy (after having completed one). So, with every speech members successfully give they learn that they have agency and a powerful inner resource (self-ethic), that fears and doubts are merely mental obstacles (mind-body-spirit connection), and that they are capable of personal change (self-realization).

Personal Narratives and Psychological Identification

In giving speeches, TL members inevitably end up sharing personal narratives. We've already seen in the previous two chapters just how important public storytelling is to reconstructing one's identity. At both NLF and C3T, members learn to narrate their life histories in light of the canonical discourses encoded at each moral community. I argued in Chapter 8 that the recovered self at NLF is informed by a combination of liberal Christian values and a queer subcultural identity. And in Chapter 9 I suggested that C3T's senior pastors, given their charismatic authority, model the prosperous self—which sacralizes the values of celebrity culture, growth and prosperity, and social conservatism.

What does the true self look like at TL? Because TL lacks a thick collective conscience, how talk of the "true self" is interpreted remains indeterminate. That is, while becoming one's true self may be widely considered a desirable normative ideal, what personal authenticity consists of remains open to individual interpretation. Thus, *rituals of pubic performance provide an opportunity for members to reaffirm their pre-existing social attachments and moral commitments, within the discursive ambit set by SH discourse.*

Consider Sandra. Upon graduating from university, following the instructions of her parents, Sandra found a job as an accountant in the corporate sector, which she described as "ego driven, cutthroat, and closed-minded." She soon moved into the not-for-profit sector, where she found welcome respite. Over the past few years, her familial and personal lives have followed quite different tracks. With her parents she is quiet, deferent, and soft-spoken, while in her private life she takes dance classes, reads palms, and blogs about the importance of living "spiritually." Accordingly, for members like Sandra, SH discourse in club meetings serves to reinforce her commitment to the religion of the heart in a New Age form. And when she gives speeches at TL, she affirms *her* true self—the roots of which lie, not in her familial context, but in her longstanding participation in the holistic milieu.

Angela, 32, offers a second, somewhat different, case. Of Polish descent, Angela studied sociology in undergrad, and then completed a Master's degree in sustainable international agriculture in Germany. While she was happy to identify as SBNR, Angela confessed to having little involvement in the holistic milieu, though she'd read and enjoyed various "spiritual" books. After completing her Master's, she found a communications job with the UN, which strengthened her commitment to green causes. A year later, Angela decided to move back to Canada in order to be closer to her parents. She joined TL in order to overcome her shyness and social anxiety: "I felt so uncomfortable in the spotlight and I didn't like that about myself." An environmentalist and vegan, she aspires to give talks about sustainability and agriculture. So, for those like Angela, who have minimal familiarity with the holistic milieu, SH discourse is interpreted in secular terms. And when she speaks of *her* true self in meetings, she summons her environmentalist commitments, rooted in her academic research and employment at the UN.

Of course, while TL members share their stories, structured as they often are by SH discourse, others may well come to *identify* with them. I argued in Chapter 8 that such practices of identification are strongly encouraged at NLF in order to ensure a stable and shared alcoholic identity. But this is not the case at TL. While members may identify with one another, they also may not. In fact, interviews with members suggest that failure to identify with others tends to be the norm. Yet there are occasions when one member, for whatever reason, identifies with another—and it is in these instances when identity (re)constitution takes place.

We see this in the example of Vivaan, 34, who emigrated from Pakistan to Canada a decade ago. Having completed a degree in computer engineering prior to arriving in Canada, Vivaan was fortunate enough to quickly find a job working for a telecom company in downtown Toronto. Two years later, his wife and three children left Pakistan to join him in Canada. In our interview, Vivaan referenced a specific speech Angela gave on the importance of setting goals if one's wishes to grow. This had a significant impact on him. "When I heard her give that speech, I said to myself, 'I don't have a goal. I just live day by day. So maybe I should do something?'" This realization led Vivaan to make a number of changes to his daily routine: he began waking up two hours earlier in order to have time to himself in the morning, and he also started going to the gym regularly—something he'd never done before. Vivaan was inspired by Angela, who invoked SH discourse to discuss how she engages in self-development, and in turn adopted it as his own.

These examples illuminate what distinguishes Toastmasters club meetings from other sites in romantic liberal modernity. First, SH discourse is both privileged and pervasive in a way that it is not at other sites. Second, Toastmasters clubs give their members a chance to narrate their lives publicly through the ritual of public performance. This is crucial because self-help discourse is, after all, *discourse* and therefore needs to be *spoken* and *heard*. As I emphasized in Chapter 8, the sites where individuals narrate their lives to an audience are key sites of identity—construction, because the act of telling stories reconstitutes a speaker's sense of self, and even how they experience the world. Thus, speeches provide TL members the opportunity to apply SH discourse in order to strengthen their commitments to the moral ideals they cherish. And by structuring their speeches according to SH discourse, and producing collective effervescence, members make it possible for others to adopt this discourse as their own—while adapting it to their own pre-existing moral commitments.

The Pathologies of Romantic Liberal Modernity at Tomorrow's Leaders

I have argued there exists little in the way of a "thick" collective conscience among TL members. None identify as "TL members" in a formative sense, and subscription to SH discourse, though common, does not require sustained or robust commitment to the club. Moreover, because members import their own conceptions of authenticity into meetings, while SH discourse may serve as a shared vernacular, its meaning is multiple, undercutting the cultivation of solidarity and mutual obligation among members. It follows that, despite the fact that TL serves to (re)produce romantic liberal subjects, it is not much of a *community*—largely failing to stave off anomie.

This would not surprise critics. Recall from Chapter 7 that Sandel (1996) argues that expressive individualism undermines community as a result of the conception of the self it endorses. Similarly, Deneen (2018, 74, 78) contends that romantic liberal modernity "makes humanity into mayflies," such that "Our default condition is homelessness." In response, I argued, following Bernard Yack, that critics like Sandel and Deneen mistakenly conflate romantic liberal theory (reflected in common self-understandings) and romantic liberal practice, and that those inhabiting romantic liberal modernity are indeed more socially constituted than their self-image lets on. Yet, as Yack (1988, 158) dutifully reminds us, while unencumbered selves may be a fiction of communitarian thought, "Socially constituted individuals with little sense of community are a distinct possibility."

In turn, given the degree to which TL fails to integrate individuals into a cohesive moral community, Sandel and Deneen are right to raise concerns about the degree to which SH discourse can exacerbate feelings of anomie. At the same time, the issues are more complex than their criticisms allow.

Recall that for early romantic liberals like Mill, freedom requires some distance and detachment from inherited and fixed customs and traditions. Offering a modern translation of this view, Macedo (1990, 207) writes, "one of the great attractions of liberal politics and its view of man is that they liberate persons from inherited roles, fixed hierarchies, and conventions that narrowly constrain individuality and scope of choice." Of course, critics argue this conception is bound to lead to an anomic and anti-social way of being in the world. But while this might be true in some cases, it is far from axiomatic.

Consider: we saw above how Sandra applies the religion of the heart in SH form—which holds that the true self is *pre-social* in nature—to become a self-directed autonomous individual, able to distinguish *her own self* from *that of her parents*. Now, while Sandra might adopt the *rhetoric* of being an "unencumbered" or pre-social self, the *social reality* is otherwise. The truth is that she has far from dispelled the influence of her parents in her person or life. At the age of thirty, she continues to live with and care for them, and allows them to exert considerable influence on her—both internally and externally. Moreover, she is firmly rooted in a circle of friends and work colleagues both in and outside of the holistic milieu—who, *whether she realizes it or not*, significantly constitute what she thinks of as *her* true self. Thus, Sandra's talk of shedding her false self—represented by the voice of her parents in her head—should not be construed as serving to ontologically unmoor her from *all* social ties. Rather, it simply allows her to become a more autonomous self-directed individual, whose parents' expectations are not *wholly constitutive* of her identity. Or, put otherwise, SH discourse aids Sandra not to rid herself of all constitutive attachments, but rather to question and revise those attachments that she did not herself consciously choose—a foundational principle of romantic liberalism. Of course, this fact may not be reflected in Sandra's own self-understanding, but it remains the reality regardless.

Recall also the case of Vivaan, who explained his motivation for joining TL as follows:

> Before I joined Toastmasters, I was not feeling whole. I had everything. I had a beautiful family. I had a job. I had a house. I had cars. Whatever I wanted I had it for a decent living. But I was not fulfilled. I kept thinking, 'If this is all that I wanted then, you know, I have it. So, what now?' I mean, more money is not going to make me happy. And my kids are here. I have everything, you know? I didn't seem to be missing anything in my life.

He continued,

But then I realized that I needed free time for myself. I did not have free time. Free time is when you have completely disconnected all the thoughts from your head, so your head is not compounded, you know? It's clear. You see, I was rushing. I was in a rush always: wake up, run for breakfast, run for train, run for job, run to come back, shopping, groceries, kids, playtime, volunteer time, prayer time. My parents live with me, so I have to take care of them. You know, doctor appointments, listen to my mum, so many things. But where am I? I was not there. I had no unique identity. So, I needed to find myself.

We saw above how Angela's speech had a significant impact on Vivaan, leading him to start waking up early and exercising regularly. Just like in the case of Sandra, Vivaan's quest to "find himself" did not entail shedding *all* of his constitutive attachments. On the contrary, Vivaan remains firmly rooted in his familial and religious communities—which give shape to *his* conception of the true self. Thus, his adoption of SH discourse served not to strip him of communal obligations, but rather to carve out enough space in his private life to allow him a semblance of authentic self-expression.

This is also true of Fatima, a Syrian refugee who joined TL in order to become, in her words, "more independent." In our interview, Fatima shared that she was raised to be a "rule follower," but now wishes to think for herself, and she sees membership at TL as instrumental to this process. She also disclosed that she recently divorced her husband, who abused her emotionally and physically. So, when Fatima spoke in our interview of "trying to focus on my own wants and needs, and not others" she was primarily referring to independence from an abusive ex-husband—reflective of a desire for autonomy and self-determination. Moreover, it was quite clear that she didn't aspire to shed *all* of her constitutive attachments, which included commitments to her cultural and familial communities, and inform what she considers *her* true self.

These examples make clear that it is wrong to presume, as critics have, that expressive individualism, the religion of the heart, and SH discourse entail an anomic and anti-social existence, liberating individuals from all of their constitutive attachments. In actual fact, *talk of shedding one's false self and realizing one's true self mostly entails shifting from one set of constitutive attachments to another.*

Still, there is a sense in which critics' fears remain legitimate. The fact that TL does not stave off anomie is not a problem in the cases of Sandra, Fatima, and Vivaan because they find social integration and formative attachments in other institutional contexts. Sandra has her family, friends, and place of work; Vivaan has his family and religious community; and Fatima has her family and cultural community. Thus, their true selves find their origins in their respective constitutive communities. But what of those who arrive at the doors of TL without such thick attachments and moral associations?

While Durkheim praised modernity for emancipating individuals from oppressive associations, affiliations, and hierarchies, he nevertheless contended that liberal citizens must balance the desire for individual emancipation with the need for social rootedness. As Kymlicka (1989b) notes, liberal theorists have tended to presume that human nature is such that citizens in liberal democratic societies will naturally seek formative attachments and communal affiliations. But critics may be right to think this naïve. And more recent liberal philosophers have expressed similar concerns. For instance, William Galston (1991, 225) identifies what he calls "a basic fact of liberal sociology: The greatest threat to children in modern liberal societies is not that they will believe in something too deeply, but that they will believe in nothing very deeply at all." Indeed, critics are right to see expressive individualism, the religion of the heart, and SH discourse as potentially encouraging individuals to shed *all* pre-existing social ties, thereby leaving them in a state of utter anomie, lacking any form of social integration. This is a worrying prospect.

What's more, while Sandra, Vivaan, and Fatima may have been protected from the threat of anomie, owing to being rooted in their respective communities, their self-understanding—naturalized by SH discourse—*obscures the social character of their true selves.* That is, none of them recognized that the contours and substance of the true selves they champion have their wellsprings in their respective formative communities—and thereby depend on their continued participation in these for their survival. Instead, each was convinced that the content and authority of their respective conceptions of personal authenticity derived not from the communities to which they belonged, but rather a *pre-social* source, which made itself known in personal experiences and private reflection. It is this social fact that leads critics to contend, "the loosening of social bonds in nearly every aspect of life—familial, neighborly, communal, religious, even national—reflects the advancing logic of liberalism and is the source of its deepest instability" (Deneen 2018, 38).

And yet, while true, it need not be so. Indeed, what's required is that these romantic liberals come to recognize that which they have refused to see: that *society and its institutions are not antithetical to the task of self-realization, but rather the foundation for its successful achievement.* In other words, the animating ideals of romantic liberalism need not be rejected, nor must the tradition of expressive individualism (and with it, the religion of the heart) be let go of. Rather, a more Durkheimian self-understanding is needed—for this would protect these romantic liberal subjects from seeking the kind of unattainable radical freedom that promises not autonomy, but anomie and disenchantment.

SH Discourse and the Romantic (Neo)Liberal Order

We have seen how SH discourse can exacerbate the pathology of anomie by inducing its adherents to shed their formative attachments, leaving them bereft of community and a sense of belonging. In these instances, the religion of the heart can be said to provide neither social integration nor moral regulation, proving critics correct. Of course, this is not a concern shared by critics for whom "spirituality" signals unrelenting and insidious moral regulation. For according to this camp, the real problem with SH discourse is not that it produces anomic selves but rather that it produces *comprehensively egoistic selves* (like those at C3T).

For instance, Andrada Tobias (2016, 142) contends that SH discourse serves "as a technology of neoliberal governmentality." Andrea LaMarre et al. (2016, 249) argue that it produces "neoliberal subjects" (249). Elena Trifan (2016, 50) writes, "personal development... is closely related to the neoliberal project." And Sam Binkley (2011, 94) maintains that SH discourse "summon[s] the individual to a highly autonomous task of psychological self-realization within a distinctly indi-vidualistic therapeutic regime. In short, this is a vision of psychological life as enterprise, one centered on the individual pursuit of well-being as one of calcu-lating self-interest, and a project of repudiation centered on the inherited depend-encies of social government."

These critics fear that groups like TL, which institutionalize SH discourse, serve to (re)produce *romantic neoliberal subjects* that are hostile to all government intervention, endorse personal over political solutions to injustice, and view achievement and inequality solely through the lens of personal responsibility. And in so doing, they echo wider social critiques that see in romantic liberal modernity nothing but a neoliberal order, where a rugged utilitarian individual-ism "governs as sophisticated common sense" (Brown 2015, 35).

Are these critics' concerns justified? To answer this question we must first note that TL, unlike C3T, does not preclude shifting involvements, and is about as far from a greedy institution as it gets. Members are not locked into their roles as Toastmasters members, TL demands minimal emotional, physical, or financial investment, and members remain active in other social spheres. Moreover, because talk of the "true self" is interpreted according to members' pre-existing commitments, which find their social origins elsewhere, it would seem that much depends on the nature of these pre-existing attachments and affiliations. How then does TL fare?

Critics are not wrong to be concerned. Consider, for instance, Marie, who shared in a speech that "her Bible" is a book titled *The Science of Getting Rich* by Wallace D. Wattles, a well-known nineteenth-century proponent of New Thought. We saw earlier that she endorsed a kind of secularized version of positive confession, whereby thoughts are presumed to produce the reality they describe. It is on this basis, Marie explained, that she rejects governmental interventions to cure poverty. As she sees it, poverty is best dealt with by teaching the poor to "think rich," enabling them to manifest the reality they desire. Tenzin, the club's president and a digital marketer by trade, offers a similar example. In one of his speeches, Tenzin invoked SH discourse to make the case that success is simply a matter of mindset: "You can be whatever you want to be, as long as you work hard enough." And in informal conversations he made clear his overriding allegiances to the market mentality: "I want to be rich, successful, all that. I want to wear nice clothes, have nice cars, you know. I mean, who doesn't?" Tenzin also voiced that his idols were figures like Jeff Bezos and Elon Musk—entrepreneurs who "took big risks" and so "deserve the money they make." And like Tenzin, Greg heaped praise on wealthy entrepreneurs, and stressed the overriding importance of willpower and ingenuity in becoming successful. This is why he'd spent thousands of dollars on self-development seminars and workshops: "I want to become invincible, even super-human." Greg also voiced his disdain for governmental taxation schemes and the welfare state more generally: "I feel like people should be able to keep what they earn. Otherwise, what's the point of working?"

In their own ways, Marie, Tenzin, and Greg approximate the "neoliberal subject" that progressive critics describe. Rather than suffering from anomie, these individuals have been formatively shaped by their occupations in the economic sphere, such that when they arrive at TL, they come with their true selves having been comprehensively constituted by the tradition of utilitarian individualism, albeit couched in expressivist rhetoric. And because of the degree to which the market mentality is all-encompassing in their lives, outside of club meetings there is a good chance they will remain closed to rival social perspectives and competing moral traditions. Thus, generally speaking, they are likely to approach questions of justice, equality, and citizenship through the moral logic of the market, viewing the purpose of government as enforcing the rule of law and facilitating ripe conditions for market competition and economic investment, while reconceiving civic engagement as "responsibilized entrepreneurialism and self-investment" (Brown 2015, 210). And because of the hegemony of methodological individualism in their lives, they are liable to overlook the myriad ways in which social structures impede the realization of genuine equality of opportunity—an ideal they endorse, at least in the abstract.

Yet, as we saw above, not all TL members have been comprehensively constituted by the economic sphere. For instance, when Sandra speaks of *her* true self in meetings, she invokes her participation in the holistic milieu and the post-materialist values she subscribes to. When Angela hears talk of realizing *her* true self, this signals her environmentalist commitments, rooted in her time at the UN. And Vivaan's true self derives its substance from the Muslim community he belongs to. For each of these members, SH discourse does not signal a full-throated egoism, but rather—much like AA discourse does for NLF members—a set of collective values that offer a counterforce to the utilitarian individualism inscribed in the economic sphere. It follows that the degree to which TL exacerbates or mitigates egoism is highly variable. For as a result of the diversity of members' pre-existing social attachments and moral commitments, SH discourse serves, in some instances, to encourage egoism, whereas in others it tempers it.

Self-Help and Shifting Involvements

And yet, while SH discourse might serve for members such as Sandra, Angela, and Vivaan as a source of moral regulation, its methodological individualism nevertheless obscures the structural sources of suffering, and thereby holds the potential to legitimate unjust social and economic conditions. So, critics may still be right that clubs like TL function to produce romantic *neo*liberal subjects, simply by virtue of "deflect[ing] attention away from structural inequalities" (Dunn 2016, 129), and leaving their members "caught in a cycle of seeking individual solutions to problems that are social, economic, and political in origin" (McGee 2005, 177).

But this is not what one finds. For much like AA discourse at NLF, while SH discourse may have been dominant in TL meetings, members such as Sandra, Angela, and Vivaan had no problem drawing on rival social perspectives, and indeed moral traditions, outside of club meetings. For instance, Vivaan asserted during our interview,

> The people before us paid taxes so that Canada would become a better country. I mean, imagine those years when Canada was being developed. They worked for countless hours, sacrificing for us and our families in order to make this country great. So, they didn't think selfishly. If those people would have thought, 'Oh, I don't want to pay my tax money to build these roads, or to make these cities, or to have healthcare for all,' none of this would be here. So, this is all about giving back. It is what has made this country so beautiful.

Vivaan went on to describe his vision of the good society as one where individuals are treated equally and with dignity, where their basic needs are met, and where diversity is celebrated. Moreover, he stressed that his recent passion for self-development, which led him to join TL, does not nullify his civic obligations, like voting and staying informed. Similarly, in our interview, Angela voiced her approval of a strong welfare state, high taxes on the wealthy, and the need for bold governmental action on climate change. And she spoke at length about the systemic problems that, in her view, have stifled achievement of these goals: "We won't see real change until new laws are passed, and governments are held to account." Finally, in our interview, Sandra criticized what she called "hyper capitalism," which she described as encouraging us "to consume more and more," instead of "looking within for happiness." In her view, the good society is one where individuals recognize their "interdependence" and where laws "work for the many, not the few." She concluded, "We're all in this together, right?"

While these TL members spoke in the language of SH discourse in TL meetings, they freely adopted other vocabularies outside of them. Indeed, just like NLF members, their commitment to SH discourse and its methodological individualism in their *private lives* did not preclude these TL members from adopting structuralist perspectives with regard to *public issues*, enabling them to discern the background social conditions that shape individual opportunities and advantages, as well as the systemic changes needed in order to realize a just society.

Critics might argue that members like Vivaan, Angela, and Sandra are far less representative than members like Marie, Tenzin, and Greg as adherents of SH discourse, and perhaps even the religion of the heart more generally. For instance, political theorist Wendy Brown (2015, 47) paints a picture of romantic liberal modernity wherein neoliberalism has become hegemonic. On this view, neo-liberalism has colonized popular consciousness in romantic liberal modernity, crowding out all rival visions of the good society.

But recent empirical studies suggest otherwise. For instance, sociologist Franz Höllinger (2004, 294) found that many individuals interested in "spirituality" support "ecological and left-liberal parties," as well as exhibit "an affinity to post-materialist values, environmentalism...and a certain tendency to civic engagement" (Höllinger 2017, 310). In his treatise on the "new spirituality" Gordon Lynch (2007, 19) observes "a fundamental sympathy to notions of democratic society, gender equality and a welcoming of diversity" as well as "a sympathy with, and often active engagement in, green and left-of-centre political concerns." And based on his empirical research in the UK, Paul Heelas (2008) has argued that "spirituality" can, and often does, serve "as a form of counter-culture to combat the sins of capitalism" (209). Thus, there are good reasons to think that, while neoliberalism may have dictated the policy agenda in liberal democracies since the 1980s, it is simply not the case that this shift has been equally totalizing at the level of individual consciousness.

Competing Visions of Romantic Liberal Modernity

The conflation of expressive individualism, the religion of the heart, and SH discourse with neoliberalism belies the fact that *the animating ideals of romantic liberalism have long inspired two competing visions of the good society*. TL members like Marie, Tenzin, and Greg carry forward a neoliberal vision of the good society whose roots can be roughly traced back to Benjamin Franklin, the original spokesperson for utilitarian individualism. In their accounts they champion the Franklin-indebted ideal of the "self-made" businessperson who gets rich by dint of their ingenuity and cunning, and endorse a vision of the good society as one where each vigorously pursues their own self-interest (a vision that finds its Christian counterpart at C3T). On this view, citizenship amounts to nothing more than contributing to the national economy—by means of either innovative production or hedonistic consumption.

Conversely, Vivaan, Angela, and Sandra carry forward the left-liberal vision first articulated by Ralph Waldo Emerson, the original spokesperson of expressive individualism, and a champion of what Leigh Eric Schmidt (2012, 286) refers to as the "spiritual left." Although regularly forgotten, left-liberalism has long been a force for progress in American life, with champions as diverse as John Dewey,[4] Jane Adams, and W. E. B. Dubois.[5] And like them, for these TL members, the good society is one where the principles of equal concern and respect are enshrined in legal-political *and* economic institutions, and where private life and public life exist in a healthy balance. That is, the vision espoused by romantic left-liberals seeks a middle-way between pure privatism and all-encompassing public duty, embracing, "both humanity and citizenship, morality and politics, individuality and social cooperation" (Cladis 2003, 196).

While I'm mindful of the fact that these are analytic categories that do not perfectly capture the content of individuals' subjectivities, I would argue that rather than reflecting *romantic neoliberal subjects*, members such as Vivaan, Angela, and Sandra more accurately reflect *romantic left-liberal subjects*—that is, subjects who fluently draw from the tradition of expressive individualism in the private sphere, while adopting the tradition of moral individualism when in the public sphere. Or, framed in Rousseauian terms: they adopt the religion of the heart with regard to their personal lives, and adopt the language of civil religion when speaking as citizens.

Conclusion

Critics are wrong to suppose that the religion of the heart in SH form necessarily signals a neoliberal subjectivity. The basic structures and animating ideals of romantic liberal modernity are compatible with both neoliberal and left-liberal visions of the good society—and we find both of these embodied and defended at TL. Of course, among critics hostile to the liberal tradition *in toto*, this distinction will mean little. But, in line with Durkheim, my own sympathies lie squarely with the latter.

And yet, as it stands, even the romantic left-liberal vision is too often hindered by the self-understanding it engenders. For while Vivaan, Angela, and Sandra were able to speak in eloquent terms about the social structural causes of poverty, inequality, and injustice, they failed to see the degree to which *their own left-liberal convictions drew their substance and authority from the moral individualism inscribed in the legal-political sphere of their society.* In other words, just as they failed to recognize the social character of their true selves in club meetings, so too did they fail to see the degree to which the shape and strength of their left-liberal commitments depend not merely on their individual willpower, but also on their

---

[4] On Dewey's debts to Emerson see Dewey 1903.
[5] For an incisive history of this tradition see Rossinow 2008.

continued participation in the legal-political institutions and attendant collective rituals that make them possible. As a result, while I celebrate the romantic left-liberal vision they champion, I also fear it remains dangerously precarious due to the self-understanding it too often legitimates. And thus, once again, I reiterate that while the animating ideals of romantic liberalism remain potent with promise, what is required is a shift in self-understanding. That is, I ask of my fellow romantic liberals that *we acknowledge and appreciate that which is already there, but which we largely take for granted.*

Conclusion

Seeing Ourselves Anew

> The ideal society is not outside the real one but is part of it.
> (Durkheim [1912] 1995, 425)

This book has traversed much territory. I began, following in the footsteps of contemporary cultural sociologists, by arguing that the shift from "religion" to "spirituality"—otherwise known as the spiritual turn—signals the ascent of an enduring cultural structure in Western modernity, which I call the religion of the heart. In Part I, I drew from a wide array of sociological, anthropological, and historical studies, supplementing these with my own empirical research, in order to offer a brief history of this religious tradition, and delineate its core contemporary tenets. And in Part II, I traced the rise of the religion of the heart to the 1960s. I argued it was during this period when a romantic liberal social imaginary crystallized in popular consciousness and swept across liberal democracies such as Canada, the US, and the UK, eventually reforming their institutional spheres and giving birth to a new social order—romantic liberal modernity. I contended that not only does the religion of the heart hold deep elective affinities with this romantic liberal social imaginary, but it also finds support and plausibility across the romantic liberal institutional order—a collection of primary and secondary institutions that constitute the religious sphere of post-1960s liberal democracies. I therefore concluded that the religion of the heart should be thought of as the spirit of romantic liberal modernity, or the preferred religious option among romantic liberals. With this established, I then brought clarity to the fault lines that divide critics of "spirituality," illuminating the striking degree to which debates about the religion of the heart track debates about romantic liberal modernity and its discontents.

Of course, in undertaking this explicative foray, my aims have not been merely to clarify for its own sake. Rather, I've sought to defend romantic liberal modernity against its detractors. And so, I drew from the Durkheimian tradition in order to challenge some of the core theoretical and normative presuppositions informing the dominant critiques of "spirituality" (and by proxy, romantic liberal modernity), spotlighting where critics either misconceive social reality or fail to appreciate what I argue are important normative values. In doing so, however, I identified two concerns raised by critics that I suggested warrant further empirical investigation—those regarding the pathologies of anomie and egoism, as well

The Spiritual Turn: The Religion of the Heart and the Making of Romantic Liberal Modernity. Galen Watts,
Oxford University Press. © Galen Watts 2022. DOI: 10.1093/oso/9780192859839.003.0012

as the question of shifting involvements. In light of the differentiated and plural-istic nature of romantic liberal modernity, as well as the stress Durkheim placed on ritual in his understanding of social life, I proposed that in order to properly assess the validity of these concerns, we must avoid impressionistic and abstract theorizing and instead examine the locales where this cultural structure is encoded and enfleshed through collective ritual. Accordingly, in Part III, I offered cultural sociological case studies of three sites where the religion of the heart is institu-tionalized in a specific discursive form.

In this closing chapter, I sum up the key lessons that these case studies impart—especially as they pertain to those who, like myself, seek to defend the animating ideals of romantic liberal modernity. Indeed, while I've spent considerable time and energy in this book contesting the often sharp censures of both "spirituality" and the social order in which it finds a welcome home, this work of retrieval has been doubly motivated by a quite different objective: *to engender within romantic liberals a shift in self-understanding, toward a heightened awareness of both the potential perils alive in romantic liberal modernity, as well as a deeper acknow-ledgement of our social and institutional debts.*

The Potential Perils of Romantic Liberal Modernity

I have argued that the spiritual turn is intimately bound up with the making of romantic liberal modernity—so intimately, in fact, that it is difficult, if not impossible, to separate the two. However, I have also acknowledged that not all of us who inhabit romantic liberal modernity are "spiritual"—that is, not all of us adhere to the religion of the heart. The reason I have not stressed the differences between romantic liberals who subscribe to the religion of the heart (the "spirit-ual") and those who show little interest in this religious meaning system (the "nonspiritual") is because I think *their similarities are far more substantial than their differences.* For to the extent that the latter identify with, and partake of, the moral tradition of expressive individualism, they share the same self-understanding as the former—only void of reference to the superempirical. That is, they understand their true selves as *pre-social,* uncontaminated by societal institutions or traditions. Indeed, this is why the case studies help us to better understand not just the nature of "spirituality," but also romantic liberal mod-ernity more generally. While expressive individualism may not entail the religion of the heart, *the religion of the heart always entails expressive individualism*—thus studying the former reveals much about the latter.

Of course, the case studies only offer a glimpse into life on the ground, as it were. Yet despite this limitation they still make evident that grand theorizing about post-1960s liberal democracies, while sometimes useful, often utterly fails to account for the rich complexity, ambiguity, and moral diversity of twenty-first-century life. In light of what we find at these voluntary associations I would argue that we, in romantic liberal modernity, inhabit a culture of narcissism and selfishness no more than one of sainthood and selflessness, find pockets of community and commitment no less than zones of apathy and alienation, and experience moral disorientation no more than moral certitude. In truth, we inhabit not a world of black and white, but rather an uneven mural of vibrant colour.

Of course, these three case studies have only scratched the surface, and for this reason much will be gained from future study of the many other sites across the romantic liberal institutional order where the religion of the heart (or "spirituality") is encoded and enfleshed—as well as where it is not. But despite their limitations, they nevertheless help us to identify some key tensions that arguably remain inherent in our social condition, and yet are neither well understood nor appreciated.

Modernity Is Disenchanting

The first of these centres around the nature of modernity itself. Differentiation and pluralism, in tandem with the bureaucratic, legalistic, and rationalist character of public life, make inevitable a certain degree of alienation, fragmentation, and disenchantment. Indeed, as discussed in Chapter 6, the disenchanting nature of romantic liberal modernity lies at the root of the religion of the heart's contemporary appeal. For romantic liberals who feel the pangs of disenchantment acutely—and, as a result, end up struggling with personal crises or problems of meaning—the religion of the heart is likely to retain an enduring plausibility, given its romantic expressivism, privatized nature, and sacralization of individual liberty. No doubt, not all will suffer from disenchantment sufficiently to motivate a turn to "spirituality." And there will always be those who stoically reject the desire for re-enchantment. However, given the character of romantic liberal modernity, there is good reason to think the threat of disenchantment will remain an inescapable reality for many.

Of course, conservatives would have little trouble agreeing. Nostalgic for a condition of *Gemeinschaft*, they have long railed against the shift from premodernity to modernity. But as I argued in Chapter 7, I think the implementation of a conservative vision would engender profound human suffering, and would produce far worse consequences than those it seeks to overcome. This is why I defend the romantic liberal ideal, which conceives of the private sphere as the appropriate site of enchantment. Still, I cannot deny that this solution reflects a compromise, or better yet, a "middle way," maintaining, as it does, "a commitment to both public and private spheres, even in light of conflict" (Cladis 2003, 189). Indeed, ensuring only a limited space of refuge from the disenchanting impacts of rationalization, the fragmenting nature of institutional differentiation, and the disorienting effects of pluralism may not suffice for some.

We saw in Chapter 9 how the burdens of negative freedom and a craving for existential and epistemic security led C3T members to seek solace in a totalizing community of enchantment, where they could be enfolded into a coherent and stable moral order, protected from the spectre of meaninglessness and the pain of identity crises. While this may be unfortunate, as it prohibits these individuals from shifting involvements and adopting rival social perspectives, it is also understandable. The desire to inhabit a meaningful order, free of doubt, is arguably deeply human—and it cannot be denied that romantic liberal modernity makes this difficult (though clearly not impossible) to achieve.

Yet given what we find at both NLF and TL, it would seem that the desire for a totalizing community of enchantment is not a necessity. Again, while differentiation and pluralism may create existential difficulties for some, many experience them as liberating, or at least not so disenchanting as to provoke crises of meaning. Perhaps, then, we must accept, given the paradox of enchantment, that there will always be a faction of individuals who find life in romantic liberal modernity hard to cope with, and will therefore seek solace where they can find it.

The Ever-Present Threat of Anomie

The second tension centres on the pathology of anomie. By sacralizing the values of individual freedom, self-expression, and self-realization, romantic liberal modernity affords unprecedented freedom from oppression, hierarchy, and tyranny, as well as the flowering of human diversity, while simultaneously disrupting entrenched patterns of social life, loosening communal attachments, and threatening its inhabitants with social isolation, loneliness, and purposelessness. Moreover, the experience of shifting involvements, while necessary in order to realize a just society and enable the blossoming of individuality, can also weaken formative attachments, and the ties that bind individuals to one another.

Importantly, this is not to suggest that the selves of romantic liberals are unencumbered. In Chapter 10, we saw that critics are correct that romantic liberal norms and values impinge themselves on us, relentlessly remaking us in their image. Rather, it is to acknowledge that while becoming a romantic liberal subject may entail normalization and subjectification, these processes do not ensure social integration or communal belonging. Indeed, it is for precisely this reason that Durkheim contended that individuals in modernity must be rooted in constitutive communities in civil society, actively and regularly partaking in the collective rituals of the social groups they belong to. Only in this way, he maintained, shall they be protected from the threat of anomie.

Aware of this Durkheimian insight, critics like Bellah and his co-authors in *Habits* caution us about the increasing dominance of expressive individualism, and the attendant shift from "religion" to "spirituality." As we saw in Chapter 7, they presume that a moral tradition for which self-realization is considered the telos of human life, and wherein the authentic self remains the source of ultimate meaning and moral guidance, cannot muster sufficient commitment to either integrate individuals into a cohesive moral community, or temper their selfishness. But as I made clear in Chapter 8, this is plainly wrong. Groups like NLF, which institutionalize the religion of the heart, do, in fact, serve to socially integrate and morally regulate their members. Moreover, they do so while encouraging their members to shift involvements and adopt contrasting social perspectives—functioning as what I called generative institutions. What this reveals is that, to the extent that the true self is shaped and informed by the collective ideals of the group itself, the religion of the heart, and expressive individualism, can indeed fulfil the function that critics claim they cannot.

Having said this, Bellah and his co-authors are right to be concerned. As we saw in Chapter 10, to the extent that the religion of the heart is not institutionalized in a specific moral community, it is likely to be impotent, and therefore unable to stave off anomie. Of course, by "moral community" I mean something far broader than a church, or even voluntary groups of the kind I have studied in this book. Indeed, it might well entail a more dispersed network of family, friends, or even colleagues, or indeed some other communal form. A moral community is not defined by its organizational structures, but rather the functions it fulfils—what matters is whether or not the group's collective conscience penetrates into its members, providing them with a framework of meaning and moral order with which to navigate the world with relative confidence.

I surmise that there are many in romantic liberal modernity who self-identify as "spiritual," but whose commitment to this cultural structure is not grounded in a community of this kind. And in such cases, not only is it unlikely that the religion of the heart will serve to stave off anomie, but it also remains unlikely to curb one's egoism. In fact, it remains a real possibility that, unbeknownst to the individual in question, their "spirituality" has become a vessel for utilitarian individualism (as we saw in Chapter 9). Of course, this equally applies to those who espouse the tradition of expressive individualism but care little for "spirituality." For unless one is firmly rooted in a constitutive community, anomie and egoism are never far away.

The Imperialism of the Market Mentality

This leads us to the third and final tension, which centres on the pathology of egoism. Critics who fear the triumph of neoliberalism are undoubtedly correct that the economic sphere inscribes an imperial moral logic of its own, and that if left unchecked, it will wreak havoc upon rival institutional spheres, undermining human flourishing in the process. One of the great dangers in a capitalist society is the imperialism of the market mentality—its overgeneralization into spheres where it does not properly belong.

Yet, as we saw in Chapter 6, utilitarian individualism tends to disenchant, as it produces within individuals a malady of infiniteness that leads individuals to not only take more than they need but also become miserable in the process. It follows that there seems to be, built into utilitarian individualism, a kind of safety valve, which makes it unlikely to succeed in colonizing all competing spheres. However, as we saw in Chapter 9, there are ways of circumventing this built-in limitation. Indeed, this is what makes C3T both unique and extremely disconcerting. While the desire to inhabit a totalizing community of enchantment is understandable, if lamentable, what is most striking about CC discourse is the way it enchants what should, by its very nature, disenchant. Moreover, by providing a theology to legitimate the market mentality, as well as functioning as a "greedy institution," C3T not only stifles shifting involvements, but also sacralizes and intensifies one of the most potent sources of economic inequality: an unrelenting and insatiable desire for more, without any regard for, or recognition of, reasonable limits.

This is why I share critics' concerns regarding the nature and impact of neo-liberalism. A society where utilitarian individualism has colonized all competing institutional spheres would be profoundly inhuman, as it would reduce all areas of social life—be they intimacy, romance, art, politics, or religion—to sites of market exchange and utility maximization. But, in Durkheimian fashion, I do not believe abolishing capitalist institutions is an effective or desirable solution. Rather, I contend, like left-liberals before me, that what is needed is that *the autonomy of spheres be protected and preserved*. In other words, the economic sphere must be prevented from colonizing either the private sphere or the legal-political sphere.

Of course, critics influenced by Marx might argue that, given the primacy of economic interests in determining social life, this is a false hope. But I would argue this cynical perspective obscures the complexity of our social condition. We are not merely *homo economicus*—or at least not yet. As we saw in Chapter 8, by sacralizing the qualities associated with selflessness and polluting those associated with selfishness, NLF works to temper the egoism of its members. And as we witnessed in Chapter 10, TL members such as Vivaan, Angela, and Sandra drew from the moral individualism inscribed in the legal-political sphere in order to champion a romantic left-liberal vision of the good society—a vision that is markedly different from that which falls under the banner of neoliberalism.

The Antinomy of the Romantic Liberal Self-Understanding

And yet, despite these encouraging facts, there still remains cause for concern. For while the collective rituals at NLF, in tandem with AA discourse, may have staved off the threats of anomie and egoism, this occurred *in spite* of the fact that NLF members largely failed to acknowledge their dependence upon the group itself. In other words, by conceiving of the recovering self as deriving its substance from a *pre-social* source, they devalued, if not dismissed, both its social character as well as the principal role collective ritual and practices of self-cultivation play in sustaining it.

Similarly, while TL members like Vivaan, Angela, and Sandra movingly drew from the moral individualism naturalized in the legal-political sphere in order to articulate a left-liberal vision of the good society, their self-understanding blinded them to the fact that, in so doing, they were invoking a *distinct tradition* to which they equally subscribed, and which exists only because of the norms, rituals, and institutions that give it life. In other words, they failed to grasp the extent of their commonality—and more pointedly, the *social preconditions of their shared convictions.*

This is, of course, one of the animating insights of *Habits.* Bellah and his co-authors (1985, 334) recognized that expressive individualism, along with its religious iterations, in construing the true self as antithetical to social institutions and norms, encourages their adherents to shed all of their constitutive attachments. And they correctly point out that if this "ontological individualism," as they call it, is pursued to its logical conclusion it will inevitably lead to anomie, and, in some cases, an intensified egoism. So, instead, they champion the tradition of biblical religion, which they argue holds that "society is as real as individuals."

The example of NLF members in Chapter 8, I believe, gives some indication of the ubiquity of the sociological imagination in romantic liberal modernity, and therefore the degree to which "ontological individualism" is not the only social perspective individuals readily adopt. Indeed, many today seem to have little trouble shifting from an individualistic perspective *in their personal lives* to a structuralist perspective when discussing either *the lives of others* or public issues more generally. It therefore seems to me mistaken to suppose that the language of individualism is so hegemonic that few recognize the larger social structures that determine the distribution of benefits and burdens in society. We might say, then, that it is not so much that romantic liberals deny the reality of society, as Bellah and his co-authors suppose, but rather that, for most of us, *society is construed only as a force of oppression.* That is, we have little problem identifying the social sources of racism, sexism, and other forms of discrimination and exclusion, but *see little that is social in the ideals we invoke to challenge these.*

Here we find the antinomy at the core of the romantic liberal self-understanding—in both its religious and secular forms. In construing the true self as pre-social, we gain the ability to identify those aspects of society that oppress and stifle our freedom, and which prevent us from realizing who we feel ourselves to be. But in the process, we lose sight of the fact that *what we celebrate as authentic to ourselves owes as much to society as that which we seek to overcome.* And, in overlooking our social and institutions debts, we—along with the things we value—are left increasingly vulnerable. For if our self-understanding is such that realizing our true self requires escape from society in all its forms, then the possibility that we shall willingly shed our constitutive attachments remains all too probable.

Reconceiving the True Self

We whose vision of the good society finds its roots in the romantic liberal tradition, whose ideals have been shaped by the legacies of the 1960s, and whose identities have been comprehensively constituted by romantic liberal modernity rest largely unaware of our social and institutional debts. As I have repeatedly shown, expressive individualism and the religion of the heart in its various guises encourage this self-understanding, engendering a kind of self-imposed amnesia that obscures from sight the origins of *who we are* and *where we come from*. As philosopher Jeffrey Stout (1988, 237) aptly puts it, "We have so little sense of common purpose in part because we have become so accustomed to a picture that hides the actual extent of our commonality from view."

It goes without saying that this study was only made possible owing to the excellent and extensive scholarship on "spirituality" that preceded it. I would have been lost without the cumulative efforts of the many who came before me. Additionally, in undertaking this cultural sociological analysis of contemporary religion, I thereby belong to, and partake in, a tradition of scholarship that has unquestionably shaped my moral ideals and, I am grateful to admit, instilled in me a deep sense of moral purpose—a benefit I've accrued as a result of active participation in the community of scholars (both real and imagined) to which I belong, and its unique collective rituals and practices of self-cultivation. Of course, this is only one of the many social, institutional, and indeed intellectual debts that I have amassed—each of which serves to give life and form to what I consider my true self.

Following Durkheim, I've come to see that the pursuit of authenticity does not—cannot—entail an escape from norms and institutions, for the *true self is not antithetical to society, but rather its creative expression*. Importantly, this is not to endorse sociological reductionism, whereby our true selves are considered merely the sum of social forces which operate over and above our conscious awareness. I am not suggesting we are cogs in a social machine, or that we lack any agency as individual actors. To make this claim would reflect a form of sociological imperialism no better than the imperialism of the market mentality that I have vehemently opposed. Rather, in endorsing a Durkheimian self-understanding, I seek only to open our eyes to the social conditions that make possible, and probable, the quest for self-realization. For were adherents of the religion of the heart to adopt this self-understanding, the risk of their shedding all of their constitutive attachments in the pursuit of self-realization would be significantly mitigated: they would recognize that becoming *who they truly are* does not require that they shed all of the layers of social and cultural conditioning that they have internalized, but rather *discernment of what is best within them and their society.*

Accordingly, NLF members would come to appreciate their dependence upon the tradition of AA, their homegroup and its collective rituals, and their fellow members in a way that would significantly reduce the chances of their taking these for granted. Moreover, they would see that their recoveries from addiction are equally the product of society as their addictions themselves—that *society liberates as much as it oppresses.* Among C3T members, this shift in self-understanding might awaken them to the deep affinities their theology shares with the moral logic of the economic sphere, as they would be more sensitive to the social character of their convictions. This may also spur the neoliberal subjects at TL to a similar realization. Of course, this is far from guaranteed, but such a shift in self-understanding would at least make this a possibility. And TL members like Vivaan, Angela, and Sandra would recognize the social character of the true selves they import into club meetings, thereby ensuring that they each remain firmly rooted in their formative communities. Moreover, this self-understanding, if extended beyond the private sphere, would awaken them both to their commonality, as well as the considerable extent to which their left-liberal vision of the good society relies on the existence of an autonomous legal-political sphere, the institutions that uphold and enshrine moral individualism, and their participation in the civic rites of their society.

Living up to Our Own Ideals

While I have sought to defend romantic liberal modernity against its many critics, challenging their often-exaggerated characterizations, along with the visions of the good society that inform them, the primary reason I wrote this book is to give romantic liberals a better sense of the tradition we belong to, and of the extent to which our convictions remain dependent upon both collective rituals and institutions. For while this self-understanding has, thankfully, not yet undermined the social conditions that give life to our shared romantic liberal social imaginary, I believe it has not only encouraged us to take these for granted but also prevented us from fully realizing its animating ideals.

The reasons for this are powerfully articulated in Durkheim's *The Elementary Forms of Religious Life,* wherein he makes the case that human beings are fundamentally *social,* and therefore rely on the existence of traditions, collective rituals, and institutions in order to realize the "best part of us." According to Durkheim ([1912] 1995, 425), "it is in the school of collective life that the individual has learned to form ideals." Moreover, not merely the shape, but also the strength, of our moral convictions depend on collective life: "The only hearth at which we can warm ourselves morally is the hearth made by the company of our fellow men; the only moral forces with which we can nourish our own and increase them are those we get from others" (427). As Durkheim makes clear, whether we realize it or not, the degree to which we feel motivated to live up to our own ideals depends considerably upon *our active and repeated participation in the collective rituals and institutions that give them life*. Unfortunately, the self-understanding common to most romantic liberals has obscured this, leading many of us to assume that the strength of our moral convictions depends wholly on factors internal to us. But this could not be more mistaken. Our true selves are also our "social selves," and these require regular renewal, through ritual, in the constitutive communities we belong to—be they our families, our voluntary associations, our professional occupations, and indeed our national societies. Consequently, if we have failed to live up to our own ideals, this may be, in part, because we misunderstand what makes this achievement possible.

In telling the story of the making of romantic liberal modernity, I have sought to catalyse a shift in self-understanding—to spur those who, like myself, remained blithely unaware of their social and institutional debts to reckon with their mutual dependencies. For by doing so, I submit, we shall come to know ourselves—and in knowing ourselves, we may be able to realize the "best part of us."

Research Methods

Method 1: Interviews

In early 2015, I began conducting qualitative research consisting of in-depth semi-structured interviews with Canadian millennials (born 1980–2000) who self-identify as "spiritual but not religious" in both Toronto and Kingston. I conducted and transcribed fifty interviews in total. Interviewees were recruited by multiple means: online recruitment notices, email list-servs, snowball sampling, posters placed in university campuses, coffee shops, and local community centres. Most of the interviews took place in person, with the specific location chosen by the interviewee, although some were conducted virtually. While the majority were university educated and middle class, my interviewees belonged to a diversity of ethnic, racial, and religious backgrounds. Many were brought up in a religious tradition, although not all were. I interviewed individuals raised in traditions as wide ranging as Protestant, Anglican, Catholic, Jewish, Buddhist, Ba'Hai, Hindu, and Muslim, as well as Atheist and Agnostic. I also interviewed men, women, and trans persons, heterosexual, homosexual, and polyamorous persons.

The interviews were loosely structured in three parts. The first part consisted of asking the interviewee about their life history; I asked them to recount formative experiences as they related to their "spirituality," enquired into their childhoods, family life, friendships, leisure activities, and private life. I did not pry but rather let the interviewees guide the conversation as they saw fit. This part of the interview encouraged narrative responses, where I listened to the interviewee reflect out loud without interruption. The second part of the interview, which usually began about forty-five minutes later, centred on exploring what "spirituality" meant to the interviewees. How they distinguished "religion" from "spirituality," and what "spirituality" was and was not, were among the questions asked during this time. The final part of the interview focused on discovering how "spirituality" manifest, or was experienced, in their everyday lives. I often asked interviewees to give specific examples of "spiritual" experiences, or to recount times when and how "spirituality" played a role in their decision-making, if ever.[1] I also asked what "spiritual practices" they engaged in, if any, as well as where and when "spirituality" was most salient for them, and why. While this was the pre-structured format that I began every interview with, on many occasions the interviews developed into something much more exploratory, heuristic, and improvised—as is expected from an in-depth approach.

Interview Methodology: Grounded Theory and Interpretivist Sociology

I approached and analysed my interview data using an inductive grounded theory method (see Strauss and Glaser 1967). Grounded theory is a particular style of qualitative analysis

---

[1] Heeding the advice of Beaman and Beyer (2013, 130) I paid careful attention to personal narratives about "spirituality" and meaningful life events.

that emphasizes the generation of theory grounded in primary data. Importantly, though most grounded theory begins without reference to existing theories in the field, this need not be the case. As pioneer of the method Anselm Strauss (1987, 306) makes clear, "there is no reason not to utilize extant theory from the outset—*providing* only that it too was carefully grounded in research—to direct the collection of new data in the service of discovering a new (and probably more encompassing) theory." Accordingly, I utilized contemporary cultural sociological accounts early on in the analysis process (notably Houtman and Aupers 2006, 2007; Campbell 2007), given their efficacy for making sense of my data.

My approach followed the following steps: I delimited my research scope to the study of "spirituality." Next, I collected primary data through interviews while simultaneously conducting an extensive literature review. I then transcribed all fifty interviews using Trint. This AI software transcribed my interviews, which I subsequently went through manually, making corrections and taking extensive notes. Next, I engaged in a process of open coding, followed by a stage of axial coding, which was then followed by more selective coding. These codes were generated with reference to, though not determined by, existing cultural sociological accounts, as well as my own discursive analysis of popular "spiritual" literature. Moreover, all coding was done manually, without software; I read over each transcript individually and marked codes by hand. Throughout the entire process I was constantly comparing my own observations with those in the existing literature.

In adopting a cultural sociological approach, I espouse an interpretivist conception of social research, which assumes that "the individual and society are inseparable; the relationship is a mutually interdependent one rather than a one-sided deterministic one" (O'Donoghue 2007, 16). In other words, such a theoretical framework allows for the acknowledgement of both individual agency and social structure in influencing human action by placing subjective meanings and their interpretations at the heart of social life. Moreover, interpretivist sociology is distinguishable from positivist and postmodern approaches insofar as it offers "as an alternative a human science that embraces, theorizes, and struggles with the humanity of both researchers and those they study" (Yanow and Schwartz-Shea 2006, 388).

Method 2: Participant Observation

In the Fall of 2017, I began conducting participant observation at three sites in downtown Toronto—a Twelve Step group, a non-denominational neo-Pentecostal church, and a Toastmasters International club meeting. My reasons for selecting these specific field sites are as follows.

First, after multiple site visits, I was confident that something like what, at the time, I was calling "self-spirituality" was present in both overt and covert forms (see Watts 2018). Of course, it took time to work out precisely how "spirituality" was institutionalized at each site, and how each group privileged a particular discursive expression of the same cultural structure. Yet, it became clear early on that these sites would make for credible comparative case studies.

Second, it was important to me that each site presented itself, and was generally located by members, at different points across what might be called the religious-secular spectrum. The Twelve Step group presented itself as "spiritual but not religious," the non-denominational church as "religious" (notwithstanding members' stress on "faith" rather than "religion"), and the Toastmasters club as "nonreligious" or "secular." This allowed me to make vivid the degree to which the religion of the heart operates without respect for the traditional religious/secular divide, as well as highlight the underlying cultural similarities these seemingly disparate groups and memberships shared.

Third, each of the groups I studied belongs to a larger organization that boasts many thousands of members across the globe. This meant not only that I could avail myself of the many excellent existing studies of these organizations, but also that in studying these established groups I might be able to discern more general lessons about romantic liberal modernity.

Though my first site visits took place in the Fall of 2017, I began officially conducting fieldwork in January 2018, and completed my last site visit on December 28, 2018. All three field sites are located in downtown Toronto.

New Life Fellowship, Twelve Step Group

New Life Fellowship (NLF) met once a week, in the evening, for an hour. Because AA is an anonymous program, and because of its vulnerable population, I do not disclose the day or time of the meeting. Moreover, due to the risks involved, I took extra precautions not to interfere with the group's activities while conducting fieldwork. For instance, I couldn't make my presence as a researcher known. In order to avoid engaging in deception I make sure not to quote anyone who did not give me their express consent to do so, nor do I include observations from meetings that could in any way be traced back to particular members. Most weeks I would quietly sit in the back of the room, listen intently, and wait until the meeting was finished to write down my observations. I never took notes in meetings in order to avoid making members uncomfortable. I conducted formal interviews with ten NLF members outside of meeting hours. And I attended two of the group's business meetings, where I was able to witness how members interacted with one another. Additionally, I read an array of AA approved literature, and listened to numerous AA speakers and podcasts. Owing to the sensitivity surrounding the principle of anonymity at AA, and the content often discussed in meetings, I have changed the name of the group, as well as provided pseudonyms for all of my informants.

C3 Toronto, Branch of C3 Church Global

Over the course of one year, I regularly attended C3 Toronto's weekly Sunday service, participated in their "Next Steps" program (their newcomer initiation program), attended one Thursday prayer service, and joined a "connect group," which ran for eight weeks in the summer. I also attended C3 Canada Conference, a three-day event held in downtown Toronto. I conducted formal interviews with seventeen members of C3 Toronto, including the senior pastor, Sam Picken, and conducted many other informal interviews. Unlike NLF and TL, C3 Toronto is not a pseudonym. The reason for this is that there is only one C3 church in Toronto, so it didn't make sense to provide one, as readers could easily identify the church, along with the senior pastors, through a quick online search. So, while all of the C3T members I quote directly have been given pseudonyms, this is not true of the senior pastors. In addition to interviews and field notes taken at C3 events, I treated as data C3 Toronto publicity (newsletters, emails, podcasts, Instagram posts, YouTube videos, and online marketing campaigns), as well as books authored by C3 Church founder and senior pastor, Phil Pringle.

Tomorrow's Leaders, Toastmasters International Club

In addition to attending TL's weekly meeting, I socialized with members outside of the group on a number of occasions. About once every fortnight I'd go for coffee either before or after club meetings with a single member or a small group of us. I was also an active participant in the club, eventually sitting on the executive committee as the club secretary (I was asked by executive team members to take on this role a few months into my fieldwork). As a result, I was privy to not only what took place during meetings but also how the executive team handled club business. I attended two Toastmasters International events outside of the club. The first was a training workshop for executive team members that had just acquired their roles, and the second was a regional conference held in North Toronto. I formally interviewed eight club members, and informally interviewed many more. I treated as data the field notes I took in club meetings, Toastmasters International publicity (both in print and online), *Toastmasters* magazine, and the official Toastmasters communication manuals.

Bibliography

A.A. General Service Office. 2020. "Estimated Worldwide A.A. Individual Group Membership." Last modified December 2020. Accessed July 25, 2021. https://www.aa.org/assets/en_US/smf-132_en.pdf.

Abraham, Ibrahim. 2018. "Sincere Performance in Pentecostal Megachurch Music." *Religions* 9 (192): 1–21.

Abrams, M. H. 1973. *Natural Supernaturalism: Tradition and Revolution in Romantic Literature*. New York: W. W. Norton & Company.

Ahlstrom, Sydney E. 1970. "The Radical Turn in Theology and Ethics: Why It Occurred in the 1960's." *The Annals of the American Academy of Political and Social Science* 387 (1): 1–13.

Ahlstrom, Sydney E. 1977. "The Romantic Religious Revolution and the Dilemmas of Religious History." *Church History* 46: 149–70.

Ahlstrom, Sydney E. 1980. "The Traumatic Years: American Religion and Culture in the '60s and '70s." *Theology Today* 36 (4): 504–22.

Albanese, Catherine L. 2007. *A Republic of Mind and Spirit: A Cultural History of American Metaphysical Religion*. New Haven: Yale University Press.

Alcoholics Anonymous. 1953. *Twelve Steps and Twelve Traditions*. New York: Alcoholics Anonymous World Services, Inc.

Alcoholics Anonymous. 2001. *Alcoholics Anonymous*. New York: Alcoholics Anonymous World Services, Inc.

Alexander, Bobby C. 1989. "Pentecostal Ritual Reconsidered: Anti-Structural Dimensions of Possession." *Journal of Ritual Studies* 3 (1): 109–28.

Alexander, Bruce K. 2006. *The Globalization of Addiction: A Study in the Poverty of the Spirit*. Oxford: Oxford University Press.

Alexander, Jeffrey C. 1995. *Fin de Siècle Social Theory: Relativism, Reduction, and the Problem of Reason*. New York: Verso.

Alexander, Jeffrey C. 2003. *The Meanings of Social Life: A Cultural Sociology*. Oxford: Oxford University Press.

Alexander, Jeffrey C. 2006. *The Civil Sphere*. Oxford: Oxford University Press.

Alexander, Jeffrey C. 2013. *The Dark Side of Modernity*. Cambridge: Polity Press.

Alexander, Jeffrey C., and Philip Smith. 2005. *The Cambridge Companion to Durkheim*. Cambridge: Cambridge University Press.

Alexander, Jeffrey C., and Philip Smith. 2010. "The Strong Program: Origins, Achievements, and Prospects." In *Handbook of Cultural Sociology*, edited by John R. Hall, Laura Grindstaff, and Ming-Cheng Lo, 13–24. London: Routledge.

Alper, Becky. 2015. "Millennials are Less Religious than Older Americans, but just as Spiritual." *Pew Research Center*, November 23, 2015. https://www.pewresearch.org/fact-tank/2015/11/23/millennials-are-less-religious-than-older-americans-but-just-as-spiritual/.

Altglas, Véronique. 2014. *From Yoga to Kabbalah: Religious Exoticism and the Logics of Bricolage*. Oxford: Oxford University Press.

Altglas, Véronique. 2018. "Spirituality and Discipline: Not a Contradiction in Terms." In *Bringing Back the Social into the Sociology of Religion: Critical Approaches*, edited by Véronique Altglas and Matthew Wood, 79–107. Boston: Brill.

Altglas, Véronique, and Matthew Wood. 2018. *Bringing Back the Social into the Sociology of Religion: Critical Approaches*. Boston: Brill.

Ammerman, Nancy T. 2014. *Sacred Stories, Spiritual Tribes: Finding Religion in Everyday Life*. Oxford: Oxford University Press.

Antze, Paul. [1987] 2003. "Symbolic Action in Alcoholics Anonymous." In *Constructive Drinking: Perspectives on Drink from Anthropology*, edited by Mary Douglas, 149–81. New York: Routledge.

Baehr, Peter. 2001. "The 'Iron Cage' and the 'Shell as Hard as Steel': Parsons, Weber, and the Stahlhartes Gehause Metaphor in the Protestant Ethic and the Spirit of Capitalism." *History and Theory* 40 (2): 153–69.

Baerveldt, Cor 1996. "New Age Religiosity as a Process of Individual Construction." In *The Fence, the Hare, and the Hounds in the New Age*, edited by Miranda Moerland, 33–48. Utrecht: Jan van Arkel.

Baldacchino, Donia. 2017. "Spirituality in the Healthcare Workplace: Conference Report." *Religions* 8 (12): 1–10.

Barker, Isabelle V. 2007. "Charismatic Economies: Pentecostalism, Economic Restructuring, and Social Reproduction." *New Political Science* 29 (4): 407–27.

Bartolini, Nadia, Robert Chris, Sara MacKian, and Steve Pile. 2017. "The Place of Spirit: Modernity and the Geographies of Spirituality." *Progess in Human Geography* 41 (3): 338–54.

Beaman, Lori G., and Peter Beyer. 2013. "Betwixt and Between: A Canadian Perspective on the Challenges of Researching the Spiritual but Not Religious." In *Social Identities Between the Sacred and the Secular*, edited by Abby Day, Giselle Vincett, and Christopher R. Cotter, 127–42. Burlington: Ashgate.

Beck, Giles, and Gordon Lynch. 2009. "'We Are All One, We Are All Gods': Negotiating Spirituality in the Conscious Partying Movement." *Journal of Contemporary Religion* 24 (3): 339–55.

Beck, Ulrich. 2010. *A God of One's Own: Religion's Capacity for Peace and Potential for Violence*. Cambridge: Polity.

Beck, Ulrich, and Elisabeth Beck-Gernsheim. 2002. *Individualization: Institutionalized Individualism and Its Social and Political Consequences*. London: Sage.

Beiner, Ronald. 1995. "Foucault's Hyper-Liberalism." *Critical Review* 3: 349–70.

Bell, Emma, and Scott Taylor. 2003. "The Elevation of Work: Pastoral Power and the New Age Work Ethic." *Organization* 10 (2): 329–49.

Bellah, Robert N. 1970. *Beyond Belief: Essays on Religion in a Post-Traditionalist World*. Berkeley: University of California Press.

Bellah, Robert N. 1973. *Emile Durkheim on Morality and Society*. Chicago: Chicago University Press.

Bellah, Robert N. 1976. "The New Consciousness and the Berkeley New Left." In *The New Religious Consciousness*, edited by Charles Y. Glock and Robert N. Bellah, 77–92. Berkeley: University of California Press.

Bellah, Robert N. 1990. "Finding the Church: Post-Traditional Discipleship." *The Christian Century* 107 (33): 1060–4.

Bellah, Robert N., Richard Madsen, William M. Sullivan, Ann Swidler, and Steven M. Tipton. 1985. *Habits Of the Heart: Individualism and Commitment in American Life*. Berkeley: University of California Press.

Bellah, Robert N., Richard Madsen, William M. Sullivan, Ann Swidler, and Steven M. Tipton. 1991. *The Good Society*. New York: Random House.

Bender, Courtney. 2007. "Religion and Spirituality: History, Discourse, Measurement." SSRC Working Papers. January 24, 2007. http://religion.ssrc.org/reforum/Bender.pdf.

Bender, Courtney. 2010. *The New Metaphysicals: Spirituality and the American Religious Imagination*. Chicago: University of Chicago Press.

Benhabib, Seyla. 1992. *Situating the Self: Gender, Community and Postmodernism in Contemporary Ethics*. Cambridge: Polity.

Berger, Peter L. 1967. *The Sacred Canopy: Elements of a Sociological Theory of Religion*. New York: Anchor Books.

Berger, Peter L. 1976. "In Praise of Particularity: The Concept of Mediating Structures." *The Review of Politics* 38 (3): 399–410.

Berger, Peter L. 1979. *The Heretical Imperative: Contemporary Possibilities of Religious Affirmation*. New York: Anchor Press.

Berger, Peter L. 2014. *The Many Altars of Modernity: Toward a Paradigm for Religion in a Pluralist Age*. Berlin: De Gruyter.

Berger, Peter L., Brigitte Berger, and Hansfried Kellner. 1973. *The Homeless Mind: Modernization and Consciousness*. Middlesex: Penguin Books.

Berger, Peter L., and Thomas Luckmann. 1966. *The Social Construction of Reality: A Treatise in the Sociology of Knowledge*. New York: Anchor Books.

Berger, Peter L., and Thomas Luckmann. 1995. *Modernity, Pluralism and the Crisis of Meaning: The Orientation of Modern Man*. New York: Bertelsmann Foundation.

Berghuijs, Joantine, Jos Pieper, and Cok Bakker. 2013. "New Spirituality and Social Engagement." *Journal for the Scientific Study of Religion* 52 (4): 775–92.

Berkowitz, Peter. 1999. *Virtue and the Making of Modern Liberalism*. Princeton: Princeton University Press.

Berlin, Isaiah. 1999. *The Roots of Romanticism*. Princeton: Princeton University Press.

Berlin, Isaiah. 2006. *Political Ideas in the Romantic Age: Their Rise and Influence on Modern Thought*. Princeton: Princeton University Press.

Berman, Marshall. 1970. *The Politics of Authenticity: Radical Individualism and the Emergence of Modern Society*. New York: Atheneum.

Besecke, Kelly. 2001. "Speaking of Meaning in Modernity: Reflexive Spirituality as a Cultural Resource." *Sociology of Religion* 62 (3): 365–81.

Beyer, Peter. 2013. *Growing up Canadian: Muslims, Hindus, Buddhists*. Montreal and Kingston: McGill-Queen's University Press.

Bibby, Reginald. 2017. *Resilient Gods: Being Pro-Religion, Low Religious, or No Religious in Canada*. Vancouver: UBC Press.

Bibby, Reginald. 2019. "So You Think You Are Religious, or Spiritual but Not Religious: So What?" In *Youth, Religion, and Identity in a Globalizing Context*, edited by Paul L. Gareau, Spencer Culham Bullivant, and Peter Beyer, 53–65. Boston: Brill.

Bielo, James S. 2011. *Emerging Evangelicals: Faith, Modernity, and the Desire for Authenticity*. New York: New York University Press.

Binkley, Sam. 2011. "Psychological Life as Enterprise: Social Practice and the Government of Neo-Liberal Interiority." *History of the Human Sciences* 24 (3): 83–102.

Binkley, Sam. 2014. *Happiness as Enterprise: An Essay on Neoliberal Life*. Albany, NY: State University of New York Press.

Bloomfield, Kim. 1994. "Beyond Sobriety: The Cultural Significance of Alcoholics Anonymous as a Social Movement." *Nonprofit and Voluntary Sector Quarterly* 23 (1): 21–40.

Boltanski, Luc, and Ève Chiapello. 2005. *The New Spirit of Capitalism*. London: Verso.

Bouchier, David. 1983. *The Feminist Challenge: The Movement for Women's Liberation in Britain and the United States*. London: MacMillan Press.

Bouckaert, Luk, and László Zsolnai. 2012. "Spirituality and Business: An Interdisciplinary Overview." *Society and Economy* 34 (3): 489–514.

Bowler, Kate. 2013. *Blessed: A History of the American Prosperity Gospel*. Oxford: Oxford University Press.

Bowman, Marion. 1999. "Healing in the Spiritual Marketplace: Consumers, Courses and Credentialism." *Social Compass* 46 (2): 181–9.

Bowring, Finn. 2016. "The Individual and Society in Durkheim: Unpicking the Contradictions." *European Journal of Social Theory* 19 (1): 21–38.

Brahinsky, Josh. 2012. "Pentecostal Body Logics: Cultivating a Modern Sensorium." *Cultural Anthropology* 27 (2): 215–38.

Braunstein, Ruth. 2021. "A Theory of Political Backlash: Assessing the Religious Right's Effectss on the Religious Field." *Sociology of Religion: A Quarterly Review*, Advance Online: 1–31.

Bregman, Lucy. 2014. *The Ecology of Spirituality: Meanings, Virtues, and Practices in a Post-Religious Age*. Waco: Baylor University Press.

Brison, Karen J. 2017. "The Power of Submission: Self and Community in Fijian Pentecostal Discourse." *American Ethnologist* 44 (4): 657–69.

Brooks, David. 2019a. "The Age of Aquarius, All over Again!" *The New York Times*, June 10. http://www.nytimes.com/2019/06/10/opinion/astrology-occult-millennials.html.

Brooks, David. 2019b. "The Morality of Selfism." *The New York Times*, December 20. https://www.nytimes.com/2019/01/03/opinion/self-care-individualism.html.

Brown, Callum G. 2007. "Secularization, the Growth of Militancy and the Spiritual Revolution: Religious Change and Gender Power in Britain, 1901–2001." *Historical Research* 80 (209): 393–418.

Brown, Callum G. 2009. *The Death of Christian Britain: Understanding Secularisation 1800–2000*. 2nd ed. London: Routledge.

Brown, Callum G. 2010. "What Was the Religious Crisis of the 1960s?" *Journal of Religious History* 34 (4): 468–79.

Brown, Callum G. 2011. "Sex, Religion, and the Single Woman c.1950–75: The Importance of a 'Short' Sexual Revolution to the English Religious Crisis of the Sixties." *Twentieth Century British History* 22 (2): 189–215.

Brown, Candy Gunther. 2014. "Feeling Is Believing: Pentecostal Prayer and Complementary and Alternative Medicine." *Spiritus: A Journal of Christian Spirituality* 14 (1): 60–7.

Brown, Wendy. 2015. *Undoing the Demos: Neoliberalism's Stealth Revolution*. Brooklyn, NY: Zone Books.

Browning, Don S., and Terry D. Cooper. 2004. *Religious Thought and the Modern Psychologies*. Minneapolis: Fortress Press.

Bruce, Steve. 1998. "Good Intentions and Bad Sociology: New Age Authenticity and Social Roles." *Journal of Contemporary Religion* 13 (1): 23–35.

Bruce, Steve. 2002. *God Is Dead*. Malden: Blackwell.

Bruce, Steve. 2006. "Secularization and the Impotence of Individualized Religion." *Hedgehog Review* 8 (2): 35–45.

Bruce, Steve. 2011. *Secularization: In Defence of an Unfashionable Theory*. Oxford: Oxford University Press.

Bruce, Steve. 2013. "Post-Secularity and Religion in Britain: An Empirical Assessment." *Journal of Contemporary Religion* 28 (3): 369–84.

Bruce, Steve. 2017. *The Secular Beats the Spiritual: The Westernization of the Easternization of the West.* Oxford: Oxford University Press.

Brusco, Elizabeth E. 1995. *The Reformation of Machismo: Evangelical Conversion in Gender in Colombia.* Austin: University of Texas Press.

Cahn, Peter S. 2005. "Saints with Glasses: Mexican Catholics in Alcoholics Anonymous." *Journal of Contemporary Religion* 20 (2): 217–29.

Cain, Carole. 1991. "Personal Stories: Identity Acquisition and Self-Understanding in Alcoholics Anonymous." *Ethos* 19 (2): 210–53.

Campbell, Colin. 1978. "The Secret Religion of the Educated Classes." *Sociological Analysis* 39: 146–56.

Campbell, Colin. 1987. *The Romantic Ethic and the Spirit of Modern Consumerism.* Cambridge: Basil Blackwell.

Campbell, Colin. [1972] 2002. "The Cult, the Cultic Milieu and Secularization." In *The Cultic Milieu: Oppositional Subcultures in an Age of Globalization*, edited by Jeffrey Kaplan and Helene Loow, 12–25. New York: AltaMira Press.

Campbell, Colin. 2007. *The Easternization of the West: A Thematic Account of Cultural Change in the Modern Era.* Boulder: Paradigm Publishers.

Campbell, Ted A. 1991. *The Religion of the Heart: A Study of European Religious Life in the Seventeenth and Eighteenth Centuries.* Eugene: Wipf and Stock Publishers.

Carrette, Jeremy, and Richard King. 2005. *Selling Spirituality: The Silent Takeover of Religion.* London: Routledge.

Carter, Ian. 2019. "Positive and Negative Liberty." Stanford Encyclopaedia of Philosophy. https://plato.stanford.edu/archives/win2019/entries/liberty-positive-negative/.

Casanova, José. 1992. "Private and Public Religions." *Social Research* 59 (1): 17–57.

Casanova, José. 1994. *Public Religions in the Modern World.* Chicago: The University of Chicago Press.

Casanova, José. 2006. "Rethinking Secularization: A Global Comparative Perspective." *Hedgehog Review* 8 (1–2): 7–22.

Castella, Tom de. 2013. "Spiritual, but Not Religious." *BBC News Magazine*, January 3. https://www.bbc.com/news/magazine-20888141.

Chaves, Mark. 1994. "Secularization as Declining Religious Authority." *Social Forces* 72 (3): 749–74.

Chestnut, R. Andrew. 2012. "Prosperous Prosperity: Why the Health and Wealth Gospel Is Booming across the Globe." In *Pentecostalism and Prosperity: The Socioeconomics of the Global Charismatic Movement*, edited by Katherine Attanasi and Amos Yong, 215–24. Basingstoke: Palgrave Macmillan.

Chopra, Deepak. 1994. *The Seven Spiritual Laws of Success: A Practical Guide to Fulfilling Your Dreams.* San Rafael, CA: Amber-Allen Publishing.

Christensen, Paul. 2010. "Struggles with Sobriety: Alcoholics Anonymous Membership in Japan." *Ethnography* 49 (1): 45–60.

Cladis, Mark S. 1992. *A Communitarian Defense of Liberalism: Emile Durkheim and Contemporary Social Theory.* Stanford: Stanford University Press.

Cladis, Mark S. 2003. *Public Vision: Private Lives: Rousseau, Religion, and 21st Century Democracy.* New York: Columbia University Press.

Cladis, Mark S. 2005. "Beyond Solidarity? Durkheim and Twenty-First Century Democracy in a Global Age." In *The Cambridge Companion to Durkheim*, edited by Philip Smith and Jeffrey C. Alexander, 383–409. Cambridge: Cambridge University Press.

Clark, Lynn Schofield. 2007. "Why Study Popular Culture? Or, How to Build a Case for Your Thesis in a Religious Studies or Theology Department." In *Between Sacred and*

Profane: Researching Religion and Popular Culture, edited by Gordon Lynch, 1–4. London: I. B. Tauris.

Clarke, Brian, and Stuart Macdonald. 2017. *Leaving Christianity: Changing Allegiances in Canada since 1945*. Montreal and Kingston: McGill-Queen's University Press.

Clecak, Peter. 1983. *America's Quest for the Ideal Self: Dissent and Fulfillment in the 60s and 70s*. Oxford: Oxford University Press.

Coffey, John. 2016. "Introduction: Sources and Trajectories of Evangelical Piety." In *Heart Religion: Evangelical Piety in England and Ireland, 1690–1850*, edited by John Coffey, 1–28. Oxford: Oxford University Press.

Coleman, Simon. 2000. *The Globalisation of Charismatic Christianity: Spreading the Gospel of Prosperity*. Cambridge: Cambridge University Press.

Coleman, Simon. 2002. "The Faith Movement: A Global Religious Culture?" *Culture and Religion* 3 (1): 3–19.

Coleman, Simon. 2006. "Materializing the Self: Words and Gifts in the Construction of Charismatic Protestant Identity." In *The Anthropology of Christianity*, edited by Fenella Cannell, 163–84. London: Duke University Press.

Coleridge, Samuel. [1912] 1951. *Selected Poetry and Prose of Coleridge*. Edited by Donald A. Stauffer. New York: Random House, Inc.

Collins, Randall. 2004. *Interaction Ritual Chains*. Princeton: Princeton University Press.

Comaroff, Jean. 2009. "The Politics of Conviction: Faith on the Neo-Liberal Frontier." *Social Analysis* 53 (1): 17–38.

Connell, John. 2005. "Hillsong: A Megachurch in the Sydney Suburbs." *Australian Geographer* 36 (3): 315–32.

Connolly, William E. 2005. "The Evangelical-Capitalist Resonance Machine." *Political Theory* 33 (6): 869–86.

Constant, Benjamin. [1820] 1988. *Constant: Political Writings*. Translated and Edited by Biancamaria Fontana. Cambridge: Cambridge University Press.

Cooper, Laurence D. 2016. "The New Spirituality, or The Democratization of Divinity and vice versa (Has the New Age Come of Age?)." *Perspectives on Political Science* 45 (4): 215–27.

Cortois, Liza. 2019. "Becoming an Individual: A Cultural-Sociological Study of Socialization into Individualistic Scripts." PhD Diss., KU Leuven.

Coser, Lewis A. 1974. *Greedy Institutions: Patterns of Undivided Commitment*. New York: The Free Press.

Cox, Harvey. 1995. *Fire from Heaven: The Rise of Pentecostal Spirituality and the Reshaping of Religion in the Twenty-First Century*. New York: Addison-Wesley Publishing Company.

Crockett, Alasdair, and David Voas. 2006. "Generations of Decline: Religious Change in 20th-Century Britain." *Journal for the Scientific Study of Religion* 45 (4): 567–84.

Crockford, Susannah. 2017. "After the American Dream: The Political Economy of Spirituality in Northern Arizona, USA." PhD Diss., London School of Economics.

Davie, Grace. 1994. *Religion in Britain since 1945: Believing without Belonging*. Oxford: Blackwell.

Davie-Kessler, Jesse. 2016. "'Discover Your Destiny': Sensation, Time, and Bible Reading among Nigerian Pentecostals." *Anthropologica* 58: 1–14.

Dawkins, Richard. 2015. "Richard Dawkins—Enemies of Reason (1/2)—Slaves to Superstition." September 18. YouTube video, 43:49, https://www.youtube.com/watch?v=AkYZKSmiaYY.

Dawley, William. 2018. "From Wrestling with Monsters to Wrestling with God: Masculinities, 'Spirituality,' and the Group-ization of Religious Life in Northern Costa Rica." *Anthropological Quarterly* 91 (1): 79–132.

De Keere, Kobe. 2014. "From a Self-Made to an Already-Made Man: A Historical Content Analysis of Professional Advice Literature." *Acta Sociologica* 57 (4): 311–24.

Deneen, Patrick. 2018. *Why Liberalism Failed*. New Haven: Yale University Press.

Dennett, Daniel. 2007. *Breaking the Spell: Religion as a Natural Phenomenon*. London: Penguin Books.

Devigne, Robert. 2006. *Reforming Liberalism: J. S. Mill's Use of Ancient, Religious, Liberal, and Romantic Moralities*. London: Yale University Press.

Dewey, John. 1903. "Emerson—The Philosopher of Democracy." *International Journal of Ethics* 13 (4): 405–13.

Dewey, Shannon. 2018. "Former Pastor Empowers Others to 'Rock Your Story'." *Toastmaster*, March.

Dobbelaere, Karel. 1984. "Secularization Theories and Sociological Paradigms: Convergences and Divergences." *Social Compass* 31 (2–3): 199–219.

Douglas, Mary. 1986. *How Institutions Think*. New York: Syracuse University Press.

Douthat, Ross. 2008. "The American Heresy." *The Atlantic*, December 20, 2019. https://www.theatlantic.com/personal/archive/2008/07/the-american-heresy/54277/.

Douthat, Ross. 2016. "The Crisis for Liberalism." *The New York Times*, November 19. https://www.nytimes.com/2016/11/20/opinion/sunday/the-crisis-for-liberalism.html/

Drescher, Elizabeth. 2016. *Choosing Our Religion: The Spiritual Lives of America's Nones*. Oxford: Oxford University Press.

Dunn, Cynthia Dickel. 2016. "Creating 'Bright, Positive' Selves: Discourses on Self and Emotion in a Japanese Public-Speaking Course." *Ethos* 44 (2): 118–32.

Durkheim, Émile. [1893] 2014. *The Division of Labor in Society*. Translated by W. D. Halls. New York: Free Press.

Durkheim, Émile. [1897] 1951. *Suicide: A Study in Sociology*. Translated by John A. Spaulding and George Simpson. London: Routledge.

Durkheim, Émile. [1951] 1953. *Sociology and Philosophy*. Translated by D. F. Pocock. New York: Routledge.

Durkheim, Émile. [1928] 1959. *Socialism and Saint-Simon*. Translated by Charlotte Sattler. London: Routledge & Kegan Paul Ltd.

Durkheim, Émile. [1960] 1965. *Montesquieu and Rousseau: Forerunners of Sociology*. Translated by Ralph Manheim. Toronto: Ambassador Books Ltd.

Durkheim, Émile. [1887] 1993. *Ethics and the Sociology of Morals*. Translated by Robert T. Hall. Buffalo: Prometheus Books.

Durkheim, Émile. [1912] 1995. *The Elementary Forms of Religious Life*. Translated by Karen E. Fields. New York: The Free Press.

Durkheim, Émile. [1961] 2002. *Moral Education*. Translated by Everrett K. Wilson and Herman Schnurer. New York: Dover Publications, Inc.

Durkheim, Émile. [1957] 2003. *Professional Ethics and Civic Morals*. Translated by Cornelia Brookfield. London: Routledge.

Dyer, Wayne. 1995. *Your Sacred Self: Making the Decision to be Free*. New York: HarperCollins Publishers.

Ebrhahimi, Omid V., Ståle Pallesen, Robin M. F. Kenter, and Tine Nordgreen. 2019. "Psychological Interventions for the Fear of Public Speaking: A Meta-Analysis." *Frontiers in Psychology* 10 (488): 1–27.

Eliasoph, Nina, and Paul Lichterman. 2003. "Culture in Interaction." *American Journal of Sociology* 108 (4): 735–94.

Emerson, Ralph Waldo. [1841] 2000. *The Essential Writings of Ralph Waldo Emerson.* Edited by Brooks Atkinson. New York: Random House.

Erb, Cynthia. 2014. "A Spiritual Blockbuster: *Avatar*, Environmentalism, and the New Religions." *Journal of Film and Video* 66 (3): 3–17.

Erjavec, Karmen, and Zala Volčič. 2009. "Management through Spiritual Self-Help Discourse in Post-Socialist Slovenia." *Discourse and Communication* 3 (2): 123–43.

Eskenazi, Elline Kay. 2010. The Roots of New Age Spirituality in United States Social History." PhD Diss., California Institute of Integral Studies.

Fawcett, Edmund. 2014. *Liberalism: The Life of an Idea.* Oxford: Oxford University Press.

Fenn, Richard K. 1972. "Toward a New Sociology of Religion." *Journal for the Scientific Study of Religion* 11 (1): 16–32.

Filloux, J. C. 1993. "Inequalities and Social Stratification in Durkheim's Sociology." In *Emile Durkheim: Sociologist and moralist*, edited by Stephen P. Turner, 205–22. London: Routledge.

Fine, Gary Alan. 1979. "Small Groups and Culture Creation: The Idioculture of Little League Baseball Teams." *American Sociological Review* 44 (5): 733–45.

Fish, Jonathan. 2013. "*Homo duplex* Revisited: A Defence of Émile Durkheim's Theory of the Moral Self." *Journal of Classical Sociology* 13 (3): 338–58.

Forman, Robert K. 2004. *Grassroots Spirituality.* New York: Imprint Academic.

Foucault, Michel. 1984. *The Foucault Reader.* New York: Pantheon Books.

Franck, Thomas M. 1999. *The Empowered Self: Law and Society in the Age of Individualism.* Oxford: Oxford University Press.

Friedan, Betty. 1963. *The Feminine Mystique.* New York: Dell Publishing.

Friedland, Roger, and Robert R. Alford. 1991. "Bringing Society Back in: Symbols, Practices, and Institutional Contradictions." In *The New Institutionalism in Organizational Analysis*, edited by Paul J. DiMaggio and Walter W. Powell, 204–31. Chicago: University of Chicago Press.

Friedman, Lawrence M. 1990. *The Republic of Choice: Law, Authority, and Culture.* Cambridge: Harvard University Press.

Froese, Paul. 2016. *On Purpose: How We Create the Meaning of Life.* Oxford: Oxford University Press.

Fukuyama, Francis. 1999. *The End of History and the Last Man.* New York: Penguin Group.

Fukuyama, Francis. 2018. *Identity: The Demand for Dignity and the Politics of Resentment.* New York: Farrar, Straus and Giroux.

Fuller, Robert C. 2001. *Spiritual but Not Religious: Understanding Unchurched America.* Oxford: Oxford University Press.

Fuller, Robert C. 2006. "American Psychology and the Religious Imagination." *Journal of the History of Behavioural Sciences* 42 (3): 221–35.

Galston, William. 1991. *Liberal Purposes: Goods, Virtues and Diversity in the Liberal State.* Cambridge: Cambridge University Press.

Garrett, William R. 1975. "Maligned Mysticism: The Maledicted Career of Troeltsch's Third Type." *Sociological Analysis* 36 (3): 205–23.

Gay, Peter. 1995. *The Naked Heart: The Bourgeois Experience: Victoria to Freud.* New York: W. W. Norton & Company.

George, Robert P. 2013. *Conscience and Its Enemies: Confronting the Dogmas of Liberal Secularism.* Wilmington: ISI Books.

Giddens, Anthony. 1991. *Modernity and Self-Identity: Self and Society in the Late Modern Age*. Cambridge: Polity.

Giddens, Anthony. 1992. *The Consequences of Modernity*. Cambridge: Polity Press.

Giesen, Bernhard. 2006. "Performing the Sacred: A Durkheimian Perspective on the Performative Turn in the Social Sciences." In *Social Performance: Symbolic Action, Cultural Pragmatics, and Ritual*, edited by Jeffrey C. Alexander, Bernhard Giesen, and Jason L. Mast, 325–67. Cambridge: Cambridge University Press.

Glendinning, Tony, and Steve Bruce. 2006. "New Ways of Believing or Belonging: Is Religion Giving Way to Spirituality?" *The British Journal of Sociology* 57 (3): 399–14.

Glock, Charles Y., and Robert N. Bellah. 1976. *The New Religious Consciousness*. Berkeley: University of California Press.

Glozek, John J. 2018. "Creating a Positive Impact." *Toastmaster*. February.

Godrej, Farah. 2017. "The Neoliberal Yogi and the Politics of Yoga." *Political Theory* 45 (6): 772–800.

Goh, Robbie B. H. 2008. "Hillsong and 'Megachurch' Practice: Semiotics, Spatial Logic and the Embodiment of Contemporary Evangelical Protestantism." *Material Religion* 4 (3): 284–305.

Goleman, Daniel. 1995. *Emotional Intelligence: Why It Can Matter More than IQ*. New York: Bantam.

Gradle, Sally. 2007. "A Spiritual Ecology: Finding the Heart of Art Education." *Journal of the Canadian Association for Curriculum Studies* 5 (1): 71–93.

Grant, Don, O'Neil, Kathleen, and Laura Stephens. 2004. "Spirituality in the Workplace: New Empirical Directions in the Study of the Sacred." *Sociology of Religion* 65 (3): 265–83.

Gray, John. 1995. *Liberalism*. 2nd ed. Minneapolis: University of Minnesota Press.

Greenberg, Eric H., and Karl Weber. 2008. *Generation We: How Millennial Youth Are Taking over America and Changing Our World Forever*. Emeryville: Pachatusan.

Grogan, Jessica. 2013. *Encountering America: Humanistic Psychology, Sixties Culture and the Shaping of the Modern Self*. New York: Harper Perennial.

Groothuis, Douglas R. 1986. *Unmasking the New Age: Is There a New Religious Movement Trying to Transform Society?* Downers Grove: InterVarsity Press.

Gross, Rita. 1996. *Feminism and Religion: An Introduction*. Boston: Beacon Press.

Gustavsson, Gina. 2014. "Romantic Liberalism: An Alternative Perspective on Liberal Disrespect in the Muhammad Cartoons Controversy." *Political Studies* 62: 53–69.

Hampel, Amir. 2017. "Equal Temperament: Autonomy and Identity in Chinese Public Speaking Clubs." *Ethos* 45 (4): 441–61.

Hanegraaff, Wouter J. 1996. *New Age Religion and Western Culture: Esotericism in the Mirror of Secular Thought*. New York: Brill.

Harris, Sam. 2014. *Waking Up: A Guide to Spirituality without Religion*. New York: Simon and Schuster.

Harvey, David. 2005. *A Brief History of Neoliberalism*. Oxford: Oxford University Press.

Hawkins, M. J. 1994. "Durkheim on Occupational Corporations: An Exegesis and Interpretation." *Journal of the History of Ideas* 55 (3): 461–81.

Hazleden, Rebecca. 2014. "Love Yourself: The Relationship of the Self with Itself in Popular Self-Help Texts." *Journal of Sociology* 39 (4): 413–28.

Hedstrom, Matthew S. 2012. *The Rise of Liberal Religion: Book Culture and American Spirituality in the Twentieth Century*. Oxford: Oxford University Press.

Heelas, Paul. 1993. "The New Age in Cultural Context: The Premodern, the Modern and the Postmodern." *Religion* 23: 103–16.

Heelas, Paul. 1996. *The New Age Movement: The Celebration of the Self and the Sacralization of Modernity*. Oxford: Blackwell.

Heelas, Paul. 2007. "The Holistic Milieu and Spirituality: Reflections on Voas and Bruce." In *A Sociology of Spirituality*, edited by Kieran Flanagan and Peter C. Jupp, 65–80. Burlington: Ashgate.

Heelas, Paul. 2008. *Spiritualities of Life: New Age Romanticism and Consumptive Capitalism*. Malden: Blackwell.

Heelas, Paul, and Dick Houtman. 2009. "Research Note: RAMP Findings and Making Sense of the 'God within Each Person, Rather than out There'." *Journal of Contemporary Religion* 24 (1): 83–98.

Heelas, Paul, and Linda Woodhead. 2005. *The Spiritual Revolution: Why Religion Is Giving Way to Spirituality*. Malden: Blackwell.

Heilbroner, Robert. 1992. *Twenty-First Century Capitalism*. Toronto: House of Anansi Press Inc.

Herrick, James A. 2003. *The Making of the New Spirituality: The Eclipse of the Western Tradition*. Downers Grove: InterVarsity Press.

Herzog, Lisa. 2018. "Durkheim on Social Justice: The Argument from 'Organic Solidarity'." *American Political Science Review* 112 (1): 112–24.

Hicks, Esther and Jerry Hicks. 2004. *Ask and It Is Given: Learning to Manifest Your Desires*. New York: Hay House, Inc.

Hitchens, Christopher. 2007. "Religion Poisons Everything." *Slate*, 25 April. https://slate.com/news-and-politics/2007/04/religion-poisons-everything.html.

Hoffman, Heath C. 2006. "Criticism as Deviance and Social Control in Alcoholics Anonymous." *Journal of Contemporary Ethnography* 35 (6): 669–95.

Hofstader, Richard. 1963. *Anti-Intellectualism in American Life*. New York: Alfred A. Knopf.

Hollenweger, Walter J. 1986. "After Twenty Years' Research on Pentecostalism." *International Review of Mission* 75 (297): 3–12.

Hollinger, David. 2011. "After Cloven Tongues of Fire: Ecumenical Protestantism and the Modern American Encounter with Diversity." *The Journal of American History* 98 (1): 21–48.

Höllinger, Franz. 2004. "Does the Counter-Cultural Character of New Age Persist? Investigating Social and Political Attitudes of New Age Followers." *Journal of Contemporary Religion* 19 (3): 289–309.

Höllinger, Franz. 2017. "Value Orientations and Social Attitudes in the Holistic Milieu." *The British Journal of Sociology* 68 (2): 293–313.

Horowitz, Irving Louis. 1982. "Socialization without Politicization: Emile Durkheim's Theory of the Modern State." *Political Theory* 10 (3): 353–77.

Hout, Michael, and Claude S. Fischer. 2014. "Explaining Why More Americans Have No Religious Preference: Political Backlash and Generational Succession, 1987–2012." *Sociological Science* 1: 423–47.

Houtman, Dick, and Stef Aupers. 2006. "Beyond the Spiritual Supermarket: The Social and Public Significance of New Age Spirituality." *Journal of Contemporary Religion* 21 (2): 201–22.

Houtman, Dick, and Stef Aupers. 2007. "The Spiritual Turn and the Decline of Tradition: The Spread of Post-Christian Spirituality in 14 Western Countries, 1981–2000." *Journal for the Scientific Study of Religion* 46 (3): 305–20.

Houtman, Dick, and Stef Aupers. 2010. "Religions of Modernity: Relocating the Sacred to the Self and the Digital." In *Religions of Modernity: Relocating the Sacred to the Self and the Digital*, edited by Dick Houtman and Stef Aupers, 1–30. Danvers: Brill.

Houtman, Dick, Stef Aupers and Willem de Koster. 2011. "The Myth of Individualization and the Dream of Individualism." In *Paradoxes of Individualism: Social Control and Social Conflict in Contemporary Modernity*, edited by Dick Houtman, Stef Aupers and Willem de Koster, 1–24. Burlington: Ashgate.

Houtman, Dick, Stef Aupers, and Rudi Laermans. 2021. *Science under Siege: Contesting the Secular Religion of Scientism.* New York: Palgrave Macmillan.

Houtman, Dick, and Peter Mascini. 2002. "Why Do Churches Become Empty, While New Age Grows? Secularization and Religious Change in the Netherlands." *Journal for the Scientific Study of Religion* 41 (3): 455–73.

Houtman, Dick and Paul Tromp. 2021. "The Post-Christian Spirituality Scale (PCSS): Misconceptions, Obstacles, Prospects." In *Assessing Spirituality and Religion in a Diversified World: Beyond the Mainstream Perspective*, edited by Amy L. Ai, Kevin A. Harris, and Paul Wink, 35–57. New York: Springer.

Humboldt, Wilhelm von. [1969] 1993. *The Limits of State Action.* Edited by J. W. Burrow. Indianapolis: Liberty Fund.

Hunt, Stephen. 1995. "The 'Toronto Blessing': A Rumour of Angels?" *Journal of Contemporary Religion* 10 (3): 257–71.

Hunt, Stephen, Malcolm Hamilton, and Tony Walter. 1997. "Introduction: Tongues, Toronto and the Millennium." In *Charismatic Christianity: Sociological Perspectives*, edited by Stephen Hunt, Malcolm Hamilton, and Tony Walter, 1–16. London: Macmillan Press.

Hunter, James Davison. 1982. "Subjectivization and the New Evangelical Theodicy." *Journal for the Scientific Study of Religion* 21 (1): 39–47.

Hunter, James Davison. 1991. *Culture Wars: The Struggle to Define America.* New York: Basic Books.

Hunter, James Davison. 2000. *The Death of Character: Moral Education in an Age without Good or Evil.* New York: Basic Books.

Huss, Boaz. 2007. "The New Age of Kabbalah." *Journal of Modern Jewish Studies* 6 (2): 107–25.

Huss. Boaz. 2014. "Spirituality: The Emergence of a New Cultural Category and Its Challenge to the Religious and the Secular." *Journal of Contemporary Religion* 29 (1): 47–60.

Ignatieff, Michael. 2007. *The Rights Revolution.* Toronto: House of Anansi Press.

Illouz, Eva. 1997. *Consuming the Romantic Utopia: Love and the Cultural Contradictions of Capitalism.* Berkeley: University of California Press.

Inbody, Joel. 2015. "Sensing God: Bodily Manifestations and Their Interpretation in Pentecostal Rituals and Everyday Life." *Sociology of Religion* 76 (3): 337–55.

Inglehart, Ronald. 1977. *The Silent Revolution: Changing Values and Political Styles among Western Publics.* Princeton: Princeton University Press.

Jain, Andrea R. 2020. *Peace Love Yoga: The Politics of Global Spirituality.* Oxford: Oxford University Press.

James, William. [1901] 1990. *The Varieties of Religious Experience.* New York: First Vintage.

Jay, Elisabeth. 1979. *The Religion of the Heart: Anglican Evangelicalism and the Nineteenth-Century Novel.* Oxford: Clarendon Press.

Jennings, Mark. 2008. "'Won't You Break Free?' An Ethnography of Music and the Divine-Human Encounter at an Australian Pentecostal Church." *Culture and Religion* 9 (2): 161–74.

Jensen, George H. 2000. *Storytelling in Alcoholics Anonymous: A Rhetorical Analysis.* Carbondale: Southern Illinois University Press.

Jones, Robert Kenneth. 1970. "Sectarian Characteristics of Alcoholics Anonymous." *Sociology* 4 (2): 181–95.

Josephson-Storm, Jason Ā. 2017. *The Myth of Disenchantment: Magic, Modernity, and the Birth of the Human Sciences.* Chicago: University of Chicago Press.

Jung, Carl. 1933. *Modern Man in Search of a Soul.* New York: Harcourt, Brace & World, Inc.

Kaler, Michael. 2018. "Neo-Gnosticism at the Movies." *Journal of Religion & Film* 22 (3): 1–17.

Kane, Anne. 1991. "Cultural Analysis in Historical Sociology: The Analytic and Concrete Forms of the Autonomy of Culture." *Sociological Theory* 9 (1): 53–69.

Kelley, Dean M. 1972. *Why Conservative Churches Are Growing: A Study in Sociology of Religion.* New York: Harper & Row.

Kim, Sung-Gun. 2012. "The Heavenly Touch Ministry in the Age of Millennial Capitalism: A Phenomenological Perspective." *Nova Religio: The Journal of Alternative and Emergent Religions* 15 (3): 51–64.

Kimball, Roger. 2000. *The Long March: How the Cultural Revolution of the 1960s Changed America.* San Francisco, CA: Encounter Books.

Kitchener, Caroline. 2018. "What It Means to Be Spiritual but Not Religious." *The Atlantic,* January 11. https://www.theatlantic.com/membership/archive/2018/01/what-it-means-to-be-spiritual-but-not-religious/550337/.

Klaver, Miranda. 2015a. "Pentecostal Pastorpreneurs and the Global Circulation of Authoritative Aesthetic Styles." *Culture and Religion* 16 (2): 146–59.

Klaver, Miranda. 2015b. "Media Technology Creating 'Sermonic Events': The Hillsong Megachurch Network." *Crosscurrents* 65 (4): 422–33.

Kornfield, Rachel. 2014. "(Re)Working the Program: Gender and Openness in Alcoholics Anonymous." *Ethos* 41 (4): 415–39.

Koyzis, David. 2015. "Liberalism and the Church." *First Things,* February 10, 2020. https://www.firstthings.com/blogs/firstthoughts/2015/06/liberalism-and-the-church.

Kurtz, Ernest. 1979. *Not-God: A History of Alcoholics Anonymous.* Center City: Hazelden Publishing.

Kurtz, Ernst, and William L. White. 2015. "Recovery Spirituality." *Religions* 6: 58–81.

Kus, Robert J. 1987. "Alcoholics Anonymous and Gay American Men." *Holistic Nursing Practice* 2 (4): 62–74.

Kymlicka, Will. 1989a. *Liberalism, Community and Culture.* Oxford: Oxford University Press.

Kymlicka, Will. 1989b. "Liberal Individualism and Liberal Neutrality." *Ethics* 99 (4): 883–905.

Kymlicka, Will. 1995. *Multicultural Citizenship: A Liberal Theory of Minority Rights.* Oxford: Oxford University Press.

Kymlicka, Will. 2002. *Contemporary Political Theory.* 2nd ed. Oxford: Oxford University Press.

Kymlicka, Will. 2006. "Left-Liberalism Revisited." In *The Egalitarian Conscience: Essays in Honour of G. A. Cohen,* edited by Christine Sypnowich, 9–35. Oxford: Oxford University Press.

Kymlicka, Will. 2007. *Multicultural Odysseys: Navigating the New International Politics of Diversity.* Oxford: Oxford University Press.

Kymlicka, Will, and Keith Banting, eds. 2017. *The Strains of Commitment: The Political Sources of Solidarity in Diverse Societies*. Oxford: Oxford University Press.

Laborde, Cécile. 2017. *Liberalism's Religion*. Cambridge, MA: Harvard University Press.

LaMarre, Andrea, Olga Smoliak, Carmen Cool, Hilary Kinavey, and Laura Hardt. 2019. "The Normal, Improving, and Productive Self: Unpacking Neoliberal Governmentality in Therapeutic Interactions." *Journal of Constructivist Psychology* 32 (2): 236–53.

Lasch, Christopher. [1979] 1991. *The Culture of Narcissism: American Life in an Age of Diminishing Expectations*. London: W. W. Norton & Company.

Lau, Kimberley J. 2000. *New Age Capitalism*. Philadelphia: University of Pennsylvania Press.

Lee, Matthew T., Margaret M. Poloma, and Stephen G. Post. 2013. *The Heart of Religion: Spiritual Empowerment, Benevolence, and the Experience of God's Love*. Oxford: Oxford University Press.

Levine, Allan. 2014. *Toronto: Biography of a City*. Madeira Park: Douglas and McIntyre.

Lichterman, Paul. 1992. "Self-Help Reading as a Thin Culture." *Media, Culture and Society* 14: 421–47.

Lichterman, Paul. 1996. *The Search for Political Community: American Activists Reinventing Commitment*. Cambridge: Cambridge University Press.

Lichterman, Paul. 2005. *Elusive Togetherness: Church Groups Trying to Bridge America's Divisions*. Princeton: Princeton University Press.

Lipka, Michael, and Claire Gecewicz. 2017. "More Americans Now Say They're Spiritual but Not Religious." *Pew Research Center*, September 6. https://www.pewresearch.org/fact-tank/2017/09/06/more-americans-now-say-theyre-spiritual-but-not-religious/.

Livingston, Gretchen, and Anna Brown. 2017. "Intermarriage in the U.S. 50 Years after Loving v. Virginia. *Pew Research Center*, May 18. https://www.pewsocialtrends.org/2017/05/18/intermarriage-in-the-u-s-50-years-after-loving-v-virginia/.

Lofton, Kathryn. 2011. *Oprah: The Gospel of an Icon*. Berkeley: University of California Press.

Luckmann, Thomas. 1967. *The Invisible Religion: The Problem of Religion in Modern Society*. New York: The Macmillan Company.

Luckmann, Thomas. 1999. "The Religious Situation in Europe: The Background to Contemporary Conversions." *Social Compass* 46 (3): 251–58.

Luhrmann, Tanya M. 2004. "Metakinesis: How God Becomes Intimate in Contemporary U.S. Christianity." *American Anthropologist* 106 (3): 518–28.

Lukes, Steven. 2015. "Marxism and Morals Today." *New Labour Forum* 24 (1): 54–61.

Lyon, David. 1993. "A Bit of a Circus: Notes on Postmodernity and New Age." *Religion* 23: 117–26.

Lynch, Gordon. 2007. *The New Spirituality: An Introduction to Progressive Belief in the Twenty-First Century*. London: I. B. Tauris.

Lynch, Gordon. 2012. *The Sacred in the Modern World: A Cultural Sociological Approach*. Oxford: Oxford University Press.

Lynch, James J. 1985. *The Language of the Heart: The Body's Response to Human Dialogue*. New York: Basic Books.

Macedo, Stephen. 1990. *Liberal Virtues: Citizenship, Virtue, and Community in Liberal Constitutionalism*. Oxford: Clarendon Press.

Macedo, Stephen. 2015. *Just Married: Same-Sex Couples, Monogamy and the Future of Marriage*. Princeton: Princeton University Press.

MacIntyre, Alasdair. [1983] 2007. *After Virtue: A Study in Moral Theory*. 3rd ed. London: Gerald Duckworth & Co.

Macpherson, C. B. 1962. *The Political Theory of Possessive Individualism: Hobbes to Locke.* Oxford: Oxford University Press.

Maddox, Marion. 2012. "'In the Goofy Parking Lot': Growth Churches as a Novel Religious Form of Late Capitalism." *Social Compass* 59 (2): 146–58.

Maddox, Marion. 2013. "'Rise up Warrior Princess Daughters': Is Evangelical Women's Submission a Mere Faire Tale?" *Journal of Feminist Studies in Religion* 29 (1): 9–26.

Madsen, Richard. 2002. "Comparative Cosmopolis: Discovering Different Paths to Moral Integration in the Modern Ecumene." In *Meaning and Modernity: Religion, Polity, and Self,* edited by Richard Madsen, William M. Sullivan, Ann Swidler, and Steven M. Tipton, 105–23. Berkeley: University of California Press.

Marler, Penny Long, and C. Kirk Hadaway. 2002. "'Being Religious' or 'Being Spiritual' in America: A Zero-Sum Proposition?" *Journal for the Scientific Study of Religion* 41 (1): 289–300.

Marshall, Douglas. 2002. "Behavior, Belonging, and Belief: A Theory of Ritual Practice." *Sociological Theory* 20 (3): 360–80.

Marshall, Joey, and Daniel V. A. Olson. 2018. "Is 'Spiritual but Not Religious' a Replacement for Religion or Just One Step on the Path between Religion and Non-Religion?" *Review of Religious Research* 60 (4): 503–18.

Marske, Charles E. 1987. "Durkheim's 'Cult of the Individual' and the Moral Reconstitution of Society." *Sociological Theory* 5 (1): 1–14.

Martí, Gerardo. 2010. "Ego-Affirming Evangelicalism: How a Hollywood Church Appropriates Religion for Workers in the Creative Class." *Sociology of Religion* 71 (1): 52–75.

Martí, Gerardo. 2012. "'I Determine My Harvest': Risky Careers and Spirit-Guided Prosperity in Los Angeles." In *Pentecostalism and Prosperity: The Socioeconomics of the Global Charismatic Movement,* edited by Katherine Attanasi and Amos Yong, 131–50. Basingstoke: Palgrave Macmillan.

Martin, Bernice. 1995. "New Mutations of the Protestant Ethic among Latin American Pentecostals." *Religion* 25: 101–17.

Martin, Craig. 2014. *Capitalizing Religion: Ideology and the Opiate of the Bourgeoisie.* London: Bloomsbury.

Martin, David. 2002. *Pentecostalism: The World Their Parish.* Oxford: Blackwell.

Marty, Martin. 2005. "Me, My Church and I." *Christian Century* 122 (2): 47.

Maslow, Abraham. 1970. *Religions, Values, and Peak Experiences.* New York: Viking Press.

McAdams, Dan P. 2006. *The Redemptive Self: Stories Americans Live By.* Oxford: Oxford University Press.

McClure, Paul K., and Lindsay R. Wilkinson. 2020. "Attending Substance Abuse Groups and Identifying as Spiritual but Not Religious." *Review of Religious Research.* Published online, March 13.

McGee, Micki. 2005. *Self-Help, Inc.: Makeover Culture in American Life.* Oxford: Oxford University Press.

McGraw, Phillip C. 1999. *Life Strategies: Doing What Works, Doing What Matters.* New York: Hyperion.

McGuire, Meredith. 2008. *Lived Religion: Faith and Practice in Everyday Life.* Oxford: Oxford University Press.

McLeod, Hugh. 2007. *The Religious Crisis of the 1960s.* Oxford: Oxford University Press.

Mercadante, Linda. 2015. "Sin and Addiction: Conceptual Enemies or Fellow Travelers?" *Religions* 6: 614–25.

Meyer, Birgit. 2007. "Pentecostalism and Neo-Liberal Capitalism: Faith, Prosperity and Vision in African Pentecostal-Charismatic Churches." *Journal for the Study of Religion* 20 (2): 5–28.

Meyer, Birgit. 2010. "Aesthetics of Persuasion: Global Christianity and Pentecostalism's Sensational Forms." *South Atlantic Quarterly* 109 (4): 741–63.

Meyer, Donald. [1965] 1980. *The Positive Thinkers: Religion as Pop Psychology from Mary Baker Eddy to Oral Roberts*. New York: Pantheon.

Meyer, Joyce. 1995. *The Battlefield of the Mind: Winning the Battle in Your Mind*. New York: Hachette Book Group.

Mill, John Stuart. [1859] 2016. *On Liberty, Utilitarianism, and Other Works*. Ware: Wordsworth Editions.

Miller, David. 1995. *On Nationality*. Oxford: Oxford University Press.

Miller, Elizabeth. 2016. "Hillsong: Australia's Megachurch." In *Handbook of Global Contemporary Christianity*, edited by Stephen J. Hunt, 297–316. Boston: Brill.

Morea, Peter. 1997. *In Search of Personality*. London: SCM Press.

Mounk, Yascha. 2018. *The People vs. Democracy: Why Our Freedom Is in Danger and How to Save It*. Cambridge, MA: Harvard University Press.

Murphy, Joseph. 1977. *Within You Is the Power: Unleash the Miracle Power inside You with Success Secrets from around the World!* New York: Penguin Random House.

Nadesan, Majia Holmer. 1999. "The Discourses of Corporate Spiritualism and Evangelical Capitalism." *Management Communication Quarterly* 13 (1): 3–42.

Næss, Arne. 1989. *Ecology, Community and Lifestyle*. Translated by David Rothenberg. Cambridge: Cambridge University Press.

Neuhouser, Kevin. 2017. "Strict but Not (Gender) Conservative: Refining the Strict Church Thesis in Light of Brazilian Pentecostalism." *Interdisciplinary Journal of Research on Religion* 13 (8): 1–28.

Nussbaum, Martha. 1997. "Women in the Sixties." In *Reassessing the Sixties: Debating the Political and Cultural Legacy*, edited by Stephen Macedo, 82–101. New York: W. W. Norton & Company.

O'Donoghue, Tom. 2007. *Planning Your Qualitative Research Project: An Introduction to Interpretivist Research in Education*. New York: Routledge.

Oh, Seil, and Natalia Sarkisian. 2011. "Spiritual Individualism or Engaged Spirituality? Social Implications of Holistic Spirituality among Mind-Body-Spirit Practitioners." *Sociology of Religion* 73 (3): 299–322.

Oppenheimer, Mark. 2014. "Examining the Growth of the 'Spiritual but Not Religious'." *New York Times*, July 18. http://www.nytimes.com/2014/07/19/us/examining-the-growth-of-the-spiritual-but-not-religious.html?_r=1.

O'Reilly, Edmund B. 1997. *Sobering Tales: Narratives of Alcoholism and Recovery*. Amherts: University of Massachusetts Press.

Osteen, Joel. 2004. *Your Best Life Now: 7 Steps to Living at Your Full Potential*. New York: Hachette Book Group.

Otterloo, Anneke van, Stef Aupers, and Dick Houtman. 2012. "Trajectories to the New Age: The Spiritual Turn of the First Generation of Dutch New Age Teachers." *Social Compass* 59 (2): 239–56.

Owen, J. Judd. 2015. *Making Religion Safe for Democracy: Transformation from Hobbes to Tocqueville*. Cambridge: Cambridge University Press.

Parsons, Talcott. [1974] 1984. "Religion in Postindustrial America: The Problem of Secularization." *Social Research* 51 (1): 493–525.

Parsons, Talcott. [1964] 1991. "Introduction." In *The Sociology of Religion* by Max Weber. Boston: Beacon Press.

Parsons, William B. 2010. "On Mapping the Psychology and Religion Movement: Psychology *as* Religion and Modern Spirituality." *Pastoral Psychology* 59: 15–25.

Partridge, Christopher. 2004. *The Re-Enchantment of the West*, Volume 1: *Alternative Spiritualities, Sacralization, Popular Culture, and Occulture*. London: T&T Clark International.

Peale, Norman Vincent. 1952. *The Power of Positive Thinking*. Westwood: Spire Books.

Peale, Norman Vincent. 1959. *The Amazing Results of Positive Thinking*. New York: Fawcett Crest Books.

Pew Research Center. 2018. "Being Christian in Western Europe." *Pew Research Center*. May 29. https://www.pewforum.org/2018/05/29/being-christian-in-western-europe/.

Philip, Brigid. 2009. "Analysing the Politics of Self-Help Books on Depression." *Journal of Sociology* 45 (2): 151–68.

Pickering, W. S. F. 1984. *Durkheim's Sociology of Religion: Themes and Theories*. Cambridge: James & Clarke Co.

Picketty, Thomas. 2017. *Capital in the Twenty-First Century*. Cambridge, MA: The Belknap Press of Harvard University Press.

Pinker, Steven. 2018. *Enlightenment Now: The Case for Reason, Science, Humanism and Progress*. New York: Penguin Books.

Pittman, Bill. 1988. *The Roots of Alcoholics Anonymous*. Center City: Hazelden Publishing.

Pollner, Melvin, and Jill Stein. 2001. "Doubled over in Laughter: Humor in the Construction of Selves in Alcoholics Anonymous." In *Institutional Selves: Troubled Identities in a Postmodern World*, edited by Jaber F. Gubrium and James A. Holstein, 46–63. Oxford: Oxford University Press.

Poloma, Margaret. 2003. *Main Street Mystics: The Toronto Blessing and Reviving Pentecostalism*. Walnut Creek, CA: AltaMira Press.

Poloma, Margaret M., and Brian F. Pendleton. 1989. "Religious Experiences, Evangelism, and Institutional Growth within the Assemblies of God." *Journal for the Scientific Study of Religion* 28 (4): 415–31.

Porterfield, Amanda. 2001. *The Transformation of American Religion: The Story of a Late-Twentieth-Century Awakening*. Oxford: Oxford University Press.

Possamai, Adam. 2003. "Alternative Spiritualities and the Cultural Logic of Late Capitalism." *Culture and Religion* 4 (1): 31–45.

Pringle, Phil. 2003. *Keys to Financial Excellence*. New Kensington: Whitaker House.

Pringle, Phil. 2005. *Faith: Moving the Heart and the Hand of God*. New Kensington: Whitaker House.

Pursuer, Ronald E. 2018. "Critical Perspectives on Corporate Mindfulness." *Journal of Management, Spirituality & Religion* 1–4.

Putnam, Robert D. 2000. *Bowling Alone: The Collapse and Revival of American Community*. New York: Touchstone.

Putnam, Robert D., and David E. Campbell. 2010. *American Grace: How Religion Divides and Unites Us*. New York: Simon & Schuster.

Raj, Rupert. 2017. "Worlds in Collision." In *Any Other Way: How Toronto Got Queer*, edited by Stephanie Chambers, Jane Farrow, Maureen Fitzgerald, Ed Jackson, John Lorinc, Tim McCaskell, Rebecka Sheffield, Tatum Taylor, and Rahim Thawer, 154–7. Toronto: Coach House Books.

Rambo, Eric, and Elaine Chan. 1990. "Text, Structure, and Action in Cultural Sociology." *Theory and Society* 19: 635–48.

Rawls, John. 1993. *Political Liberalism*. New York: Columbia University Press.

Rawls, John. [1971] 1999. *A Theory of Justice*. Revised ed. Cambridge, MA: Harvard University Press.

Redden, Guy. 2011. "Religion, Cultural Studies and New Age Sacralization of Everyday Life." *European Journal of Cultural Studies* 14 (6): 649–63.

Redden, Guy. 2012. "*The Secret*, Cultural Property and the Construction of the Spiritual Commodity." *Cultural Studies Review* 18 (2): 52–73.

Redfield, James. 1993. *The Celestine Prophecy: An Adventure*. New York: Warner Books.

Reimer, Sam, Mark Chapman, Rich Janzen, James Watson, and Michael Wilkinson. 2016. "Christian Churches and Immigrant Support in Canada: An Organizational Ecology Perspective." *Review of Religious Research* 58: 495–513.

Ricci, David M. 2004. *Good Citizenship in America*. Cambridge: Cambridge University Press.

Richter, Philip. 1997. "The Toronto Blessing: Charismatic Evangelical Global Warming." In *Charismatic Christianity: Sociological Perspectives*, edited by Stephen Hunt, Malcolm Hamilton, and Tony Walter, 97–119. London: Macmillan Press.

Rieff, Philip. 1966. *The Triumph of the Therapeutic*. Chicago: University of Chicago Press.

Rimke, Heidi Marie. 2000. "Governing Citizens through Self-Help Literature." *Cultural Studies* 14 (1): 61–78.

Rindfleish, Jennifer. 2005. "Consuming the Self: New Age Spirituality as 'Social Product' in Consumer Society." *Consumption, Markets and Culture* 8 (4): 343–60.

Robbins, Joel. 2012. "Transcendence and the Anthropology of Christianity: Language, Change, and Individualism." *Suomen Anthropologi: Journal of the Finnish Anthropological Society* 37 (2): 5–23.

Robbins, Tony. 1991. *Awaken the Giant Within*. New York: Simon & Schuster.

Rogers, Carl. 1961. *On Becoming a Person*. Boston: Houghton Mifflin Company.

Roof, Wade Clark. 1993. *A Generation of Seekers: The Spiritual Journeys of the Baby Boom Generation*. San Francisco, CA: Harper.

Roof, Wade Clark. 1999. *Spiritual Marketplace: Baby Boomers and the Remaking of American Religion*. Princeton: Princeton University Press.

Rorty, Richard. 1989. *Contingency, Irony, and Solidarity*. Cambridge: Cambridge University Press.

Rorty, Richard. 2003. "Religion in the Public Square: A Reconsideration." *Journal of Religious Ethics* 31 (1): 141–9.

Rosati, Massimo. 2009. *Ritual and the Sacred: A Neo-Durkheimian Analysis of Politics, Religion and the Self*. Burlington: Ashgate.

Rose, Nikolas S. 1989. *Governing the Soul: The Shaping of the Private Self*. New York: Free Association Books.

Rose, Nikolas S. 1993. "Government, authority and expertise in advanced liberalism." *Economy and Society* 22 (3): 283–99.

Rosenblum, Nancy L. 1987. *Another Liberalism: Romanticism and the Reconstruction of Liberal Thought*. Cambridge, MA: Harvard University Press.

Rosenblum, Nancy L. 1989. "Pluralism and Self-Defense." In *Liberalism and the Moral Life*, edited by Nancy L. Rosenblum, 207–26. Cambridge, MA: Harvard University Press.

Rosenblum, Nancy L. 1994. "Civil Societies: Liberalism and the Moral Uses of Pluralism." *Social Research* 61 (3): 539–62.

Rosenblum, Nancy L. 1998. *Membership and Morals: The Personal Uses of Pluralism in America*. Princeton: Princeton University Press.

Rossinow, Doug. 1998. *The Politics of Authenticity: Liberalism, Christianity, and the New Left in America*. New York: Columbia University Press.

Rossinow, Doug. 2008. *Visions of Progress: The Left-Liberal Tradition in America*. Philadelphia: University of Pennsylvania Press.

Roszak, Theodore. 1969. *The Making of a Counter Culture: Reflections on the Technocratic Society and Its Youthful Opposition*. Berkeley: University of California Press.

Rudy, David R., and Arthur L. Greil. 1983. "Conversion to the World View of Alcoholics Anonymous: A Refinement of Conversion Theory." *Qualitative Sociology* 6 (1): 5–28.

Rudy, David R., and Arthur L. Greil. 1989. "Is Alcoholics Anonymous a Religious Organization? Meditations on Marginality." *Sociological Analysis* 50 (1): 41–51.

Russell, Bertrand. 1946. *History of Western Philosophy*. New York: Routledge.

Saler, Michael. 2006. "Modernity and Enchantment: A Historiographic Review." *The American Historical Review* 111 (3): 692–716.

Sandel, Michael J. 1996. *Democracy's Discontent: America in Search of a Public Philosophy*. Cambridge, MA: The Belknap Press of Harvard University Press.

Sanders, George. 2016. "Religious Non-Places: Corporate Megachurches and Their Contributions to Consumer Capitalism." *Critical Sociology* 42 (1): 71–86.

Sanders, Jolene M. 2006. "Women and the Twelve Steps of Alcoholics Anonymous: A Gendered Narrative." *Alcoholism Treatment Quarterly* 24 (3): 3–29.

Schmidt, Leigh Eric. 2012. *Restless Souls: The Making of American Spirituality*. Berkeley: University of California Press.

Schouten, Ronald. 2003. "'Rituals of Renewal': The Toronto Blessing as a Ritual Change of Contemporary Christianity." *Journal of Ritual Studies* 17 (2): 25–34.

Schumpeter, Joseph A. [1942] 2008. *Capitalism, Socialism and Democracy*. 3rd ed. New York: Harper Perennial.

Seigel, Jerrold. 1999. "Problematizing the Self." In *Beyond the Cultural Turn: New Directions in the Study of Society and Culture*, edited by Victoria E. Bonnell and Lynn Hunt, 281–314. Berkeley: University of California Press.

Seligman, Adam B. 2000. *Modernity's Wager: Authority, the Self, and Transcendence*. Princeton: Princeton University Press.

Sennett, Richard. 1976. *The Fall of Public Man*. New York: Penguin.

Sered, Susan, and Maureen Norton-Hawk. 2011. "Whose Higher Power? Criminalized Women Confront the 'Twelve Steps'." *Feminist Criminology* 6 (4): 308–32.

Shanahan, Mairead. 2019. "'An Unstoppable Force for Good'? How Neoliberal Governance Facilitated the Growth of Australian Suburban-Based Pentecostal Megachurches." *Religions* 10: 1–16.

Sharma, Robin. 1997. *The Monk Who Sold His Ferrari: A Remarkable Story about Living Your Dreams*. Toronto: HarperCollins.

Sheldrake, Philip. 2013. *Spirituality: A Brief History*. West Sussex: Wiley-Blackwell.

Shibley, Mark A. 1998. "Contemporary Evangelicals: Born-Again and World Affirming." *The Annals of the American Academy of Political and Social Science* 558: 67–87.

Shilling, Chris. 2005. "Embodiment, Emotions, and the Foundations of Social Order: Durkheim's Enduring Contribution." In *The Cambridge Companion to Durkheim*, edited by Jeffrey C. Alexander and Philip Smith, 211–38. Cambridge: Cambridge University Press.

Shilling, Chris, and Philip A. Mellor. 1998. "Durkheim, Morality and Modernity: Collective Effervescence, Homo Duplex and the Sources of Moral Action." *The British Journal of Sociology* 49 (2): 193–209.

Shilling, Chris, and Philip A. Mellor. 2001. *The Sociological Ambition: Elementary Forms of Social and Moral Life*. London: Sage.

Shilling, Chris, and Philip A. Mellor. 2011. "Retheorising Emile Durkheim on Society and Religion: Embodiment, Intoxication and Collective Life." *The Sociological Review* 59 (1): 17–41.

Shimazono, Susumu. 1999. "'New Age Movement' or 'New Spirituality Movements and Culture'?" *Social Compass* 46 (2): 121–33.

Shklar, Judith N. 1989. "The Liberalism of Fear." In *Liberalism and the Moral Life*, edited by Nancy L. Rosenblum, 21–38. Cambridge, MA: Harvard University Press.

Siedentop, Larry. 2014. *Inventing the Individual: The Origins of Western Liberalism*. Cambridge, MA: The Belknap Press of Harvard University Press.

Simko, Christina, and Olick, Jeffrey K. 2021. What We Talk about When We Talk about Culture: A Multi-Facet Approach. *American Journal of Cultural Sociology* 9 (4): 431–59.

Smith, Christian. 2003. *Moral, Believing Animals: Human Personhood and Culture*. Oxford: Oxford University Press.

Smith, Christian, Brandon Vaidyanathan, Nancy Tatom Ammerman, José Casanova, Hilary Davidson, Elaine Howard Ecklund, John H. Evans, Philip S. Gorski, Mary Ellen Konieczny, Jason A. Springs, Jenny Trinitapoli and Meredith Whitnah. 2013. "Roundtable on the Sociology of Religion: Twenty-Three Theses on the Status of Religion in American Sociology—A Mellon Working-Group." *Journal of the American Academy of Religion* 81 (4): 903–38.

Smith, Philip. 2020. *Durkheim and After: The Durkheimian Tradition, 1893–2020*. Cambridge: Polity.

Sødal, Helje Kringlebotn. 2010. "'Victor, not Victim': Joel Osteen's Rhetoric of Hope." *Journal of Contemporary Religion* 25 (1): 37–50.

Sointu, Eeva, and Linda Woodhead. 2008. "Spirituality, Gender, and Expressive Selfhood." *Journal for the Scientific Study of Religion* 47 (2): 259–76.

Stark, Rodney. 1998. "Secularization: The Myth of Religious Decline." *Fides et Historia* 30 (2): 1–19.

Starks, Brian, and Robert V. Robinson. 2009. "Two Approaches to Religion and Politics: Moral Cosmology and Subcultural Identity." *Journal for the Scientific Study of Religion* 48 (4): 650–69.

Steensland, Brian, Lauren Chism Schmidt, and Xiaoyun Wang. 2018. "Spirituality: What Does It Mean and to Whom?" *Journal for the Scientific Study of Religion* 57 (3): 450–72.

Stiglitz, Joseph. 2015. *The Great Divide: Unequal Societies and What We Can Do about Them*. New York: Norton.

Stoll, Mark R. 2015. *Inherit the Holy Mountain: Religion and the Rise of American Environmentalism*. Oxford: Oxford University Press.

Stolzenberg, Nomi Maya. 2009. "Liberalism in a Romantic State." *Law, Culture and the Humanities* 5: 194–215.

Stout, Jeffrey. 1988. *Ethics after Babel: The Languages of Morals and Their Discontents*. Cambridge: James Clarke & Co Ltd.

Straus, Anselm L. 1987. *Qualitative Analysis for Social Scientists*. Cambridge: Cambridge University Press.

Strauss, Anselm L., and Barney Glaser. 1967. *The Discovery of Grounded Theory*. London: Aldine Transaction.

Streib, Heinz, and Constantin Klein. 2016. "Religion and Spirituality." In *The Oxford Handbook of the Study of Religion*, edited by Michael Stausberg and Steven Engler, 73–80. Oxford: Oxford University Press.

Stromberg, Peter G. 1986. *Symbols of Community: The Cultural System of a Swedish Church*. Tucson, AZ: University of Arizona Press.

Swora, Maria Gabrielle. 2001. "Personhood and Disease in Alcoholics Anonymous: A Perspective from the Anthropology of Religious Healing." *Mental Health, Religion & Culture* 4 (1): 1–21.

Swora, Maria Gabrielle. 2004. "The Rhetoric of Transformation in the Healing of Alcoholism: The Twelve Steps of Alcoholics Anonymous." *Mental Health, Religion & Culture* 7 (3): 197–209.

Tamir, Yael. 1993. *Liberal Nationalism*. Princeton: Princeton University Press.

Taylor, Charles. 1985. *Philosophy and the Human Sciences*. Cambridge: Cambridge University Press.

Taylor, Charles. 1989. *Sources of the Self: The Making of the Modern Identity*. Cambridge: Harvard University Press.

Taylor, Charles. 1991. *The Ethics of Authenticity*. Cambridge: Harvard University Press.

Taylor, Charles. 1992. *Multiculturalism and 'The Politics of Recognition'*. Princeton: Princeton University Press.

Taylor, Charles. 2004. *Modern Social Imaginaries*. Durham: Duke University Press.

Taylor, Charles. 2007. *A Secular Age*. Cambridge, MA: Belknap Press of Harvard University Press.

Taylor, Charles. 2016. *The Language Animal: The Full Shape of the Human Linguistic Capacity*. Cambridge, MA: Harvard University Press.

Thiessen, Joel. 2015. *The Meaning of Sunday: The Practice of Belief in a Secular Age*. London: McGill-Queen's University Press.

Thiessen, Joel. 2016. "A Sociological Description and Defence of Secularization in Canada." *Post-Christendom Studies* 1: 97–124.

Thiessen, Joel, and Sarah Wilkins-Laflamme. 2017. "Becoming a Religious None: Irreligious Socialization and Disaffiliation." *Journal for the Scientific Study of Religion* 56 (1): 64–82.

Thiessen, Joel, and Sarah Wilkins-Laflamme. 2020. *None of the Above: Nonreligious Identity in the US and Canada*. New York: New York University Press.

Tipton, Steven M. 1982. *Getting Saved from the Sixties: Moral Meaning in Conversion and Cultural Change*. Berkeley: University of California Press.

Tipton, Steven M. 1986. "A Response: Moral Languages and the Good Society." *Soundings: An Interdisciplinary Journal* 69 (1): 165–80.

Tipton, Steven M. 2002. "Social Differentiation and Moral Pluralism." In *Meaning and Modernity: Religion, Polity, and Self*, edited by Richard Madsen, William M. Sullivan, Ann Swidler, and Steven M. Tipton, 15–40. Berkeley: University of California Press.

Tiryakian, Edward A. 1995. "Collective Effervescence, Social Change and Charisma: Durkheim, Weber and 1989." *International Sociology* 10 (3): 269–81.

Tobias, Andrada. 2016. "Steps on Life Change and Spiritual Transformation: The Project of the Self." *Studia Ubb Sociologia* 61 (2): 125–44.

Tocqueville, Alexis de. [1835] 1998. *Democracy in America*. Translated by Henry Reeve and Francis Bowen. Ware: Wordsworth Editions.

Tolle, Eckhart. 2005. *A New Earth: Awakening to Your Life's Purpose*. New York: Plume.

Travis, Trysh. 2007. "'It Will Change the World if Everybody Reads This Book': New Thought Religion in Oprah's Book Club." *American Quarterly* 59 (3): 1017–41.

Trevino, A. Javier. 1992. "Alcoholics Anonymous as Durkheimian Religion." *Research in the Social Scientific Study of Religion* 4: 183–208.

Trifan, Elena. 2016. "I Am Worthy, I Want, and I Can: The Social Implications of Practicing Personal Development." *Studia Ubb Sociologia* 61 (2): 49–70.

Trilling, Lionel. 1971. *Sincerity and Authenticity*. Cambridge, MA: Harvard University Press.

Troeltsch, Ernst. [1912] 1992. *The Social Teachings of the Christian Churches*. 2 vols. Louisville: Westminster/John Knox Press.

Tschannen, Oliver. 1991. "The Secularization Paradigm: A Systematization." *Journal for the Scientific Study of Religion* 30 (4): 396–415.

Tumber, Catherine. 2002. *American Feminism and the Birth of New Age Spirituality: Searching for the Higher Self, 1875–1915*. Lanham: Rowman & Littlefield.

Turner, Bryan S. 2011. *Religion and Modern Society: Citizenship, Secularization and the State*. Cambridge: Cambridge University Press.

Turner, Bryan S. 2014. "Religion and Contemporary Sociological Theories." *Current Sociology Review* 62 (6): 771–88.

Unterberger, Gail. 1989. "Twelve Steps for Women Alcoholics." *The Christian Century* 106 (37): 1150–2.

Van der Veer, Peter. 2009. "Spirituality in Modern Society." *Social Research* 76 (4): 1097–120.

Vásquez, Manual A. 2003. "Review: Tracking Global Evangelical Christianity." *Journal of the American Academy of Religion* 71 (1): 157–73.

Versluis, Arthur. 2014. *American Gurus: From Transcendentalism to New Age Religion*. Oxford: Oxford University Press.

Voas, David. 2009. "The Rise and Fall of Fuzzy Fidelity in Europe." *European Sociological Review* 25 (2): 155–68.

Voas, David, and Mark Chaves. 2016. "Is the United States a Counterexample to the Secularization Thesis?" *American Journal of Sociology* 121 (5): 1517–56.

Voas, David, and Alasdair Crockett. 2005. "Religion in Britain: Neither Believing nor Belonging." *Sociology* 39 (1): 11–28.

Vogt, Paul W. 1993. "Durkheim's Sociology of Law: Morality and the Cult of the Individual." In *Emile Durkheim: Sociologist and Moralist*, edited by Stephen P. Turner, 69–92. London: Routledge.

Wade, Matthew. 2016. "Seeker-Friendly: The Hillsong Megachurch as an Enchanting Total Institution." *Journal of Sociology* 52 (4): 661–76.

Wade, Matthew, and Maria Hynes. 2013. "Worshipping Bodies: Affective Labour in the Hillsong Church." *Geographical Research* 51 (2): 173–9.

Walker, Andrew. 1997. "Thoroughly Modern: Sociological Reflections on the Charismatic Movement from the End of the Twentieth Century." In *Charismatic Christianity: Sociological Perspectives*, edited by Stephen Hunt, Malcolm Hamilton, and Tony Walter, 17–42. London: Macmillan Press.

Walsch, Neale Donald. 1995. *Conversations with God*, Volume 1. New York: G. P. Putnam's Sons.

Walzer, Michael. 1983. *Spheres of Justice: A Defense of Pluralism and Equality*. New York: Basic Books.

Walzer, Michael. 1988. *The Company of Critics: Social Criticism and Political Commitment in the Twentieth Century*. New York: Basic Books.

Watts, Galen. 2018. "On the Politics of Self-Spirituality: A Canadian Case Study." *Studies in Religion* 47 (3): 345–72.

Watts, Galen. 2020. "Making Sense of the Study of Spirituality: Late Modernity on Trial." *Religion* 50 (4): 590–614.

Watts, Galen. 2022. "The Religion of the Heart: 'Spirituality' in Late Modernity." *American Journal of Cultural Sociology* 10 (1): 1–33.

Watts Miller, W. 2003. *Durkheim, Morals and Modernity*. London: Routledge.

Weber, Max. [1922] 1946. "Science as a Vocation." In *From Max Weber: Essays in Sociology*, edited by H. H. Gerth and C. Wright Mills, 129–56. Oxford: Oxford University Press.

Weber, Max. [1922] 1991. *The Sociology of Religion*. Boston: Beacon Press.

Webster, David. 2012. *Dispirited: How Contemporary Spirituality Makes Us Stupid, Selfish and Unhappy*. Alresford: Zero.

Weegman, Martin, and Ewa Piwowoz-Hjort. 2009. "'Naught but a Story': Narratives of Successful AA Recovery." *Health Sociology Review* 18: 273–83.

Weiss, Raquel. 2012. "From Ideas to Ideals: Effervescence as the Key to Understanding Morality." *Durkheimian Studies* 18: 81–97.

Wellman, James K., Katie E. Corcoran, and Kate Stockly-Meyerdirk. 2014. "'God Is Like a Drug…': Explaining Interaction Ritual Chains in American Megachurches." *Sociological Forum* 29 (3): 650–72.

Westermeyer, Joseph. 2014. "Alcoholics Anonymous and Spiritual Recovery: A Cultural Perspective." *Alcoholism Treatment Quarterly* 32: 157–72.

Whitman, Walt. [1855] 2005. *Leaves of Grass*. New York: Penguin Books.

Wilkins-Laflamme, Sarah. 2021. "A Tale of Decline or Change? Working toward a Complementary Understanding of Secular Transition and Individual Spiritualization Theories." *Journal for the Scientific Study of Religion*. Advance Online, 1–24.

Wilkinson, Jennifer. 2010. "Personal Communities: Responsible Individualism or Another Fall for Public [Man]?" *Sociology* 44 (3): 453–70.

Williams, Rhys H. 2007. "The Languages of the Public Sphere: Religious Pluralism, Institutional Logics, and Civil Society." *Annals of the American Academy of Political & Social Science* 612: 42–60.

Williams, Ruth. 2014. "*Eat, Pray, Love*: Producing the Female Neoliberal Spiritual Subject." *The Journal of Popular Culture* 47 (3): 613–33.

Winograd, Morley, and Michael D. Hais. 2011. *Millennial Momentum: How a New Generation Is Remaking America*. New Brunswick: Rutgers University Press.

Wood, Matthew. 2007. *Possession, Power and the New Age: Ambiguities of Authority in Neoliberal Societies*. Burlington: Ashgate.

Woodhead, Linda. 1993. "Post-Christian Spiritualities." *Religion* 23: 167–81.

Woodhead, Linda. 1999. "Diana and the Religion of the Heart." In *Diana: The Making of a Media Saint*, edited by Jeffrey Richards, Scott Wilson, and Linda Woodhead, 119–39. London: I. B. Tauris.

Woodhead, Linda. 2010. "Real Religion and Fuzzy Spirituality? Taking Sides in the Sociology of Religion." In *Religions of Modernity: Relocating the Sacred to the Self and the Digital*, edited by Dick Houtman and Stef Aupers, 31–48. Danvers: Brill.

Woodhead, Linda. 2013. "New Forms of Public Religion: Spirituality in Global Civil Society." In *Religion beyond Its Private Role in Modern Society*, edited by Wim Hofstee and Arie van der Kooij, 29–54. Danvers: Brill.

Woodhead, Linda, and Ole Riis. 2010. *A Sociology of Religious Emotion*. Oxford: Oxford University Press.

Wordsworth, William. [1802] 1996. "My Heart Leaps up When I Behold." In *English Romantic Poetry: An Anthology*, edited by Stanley Appelbaum, 35. Mineola: Dover Publications.

Wray, Matt. 2013. *Cultural Sociology: An Introductory Reader.* New York: W. W. Norton.

Wrenn, Mary V. 2019. "Consecrating Capitalism: The United States Prosperity Gospel and Neoliberalism." *Journal of Economic Issues* 53 (2): 425–32.

Wuthnow, Robert. 1976. *The Consciousness Reformation.* Berkeley: University of California Press.

Wuthnow, Robert. 1994. *Sharing the Journey: Support Groups and America's New Quest for Community.* New York: The Free Press.

Wuthnow, Robert. 1998a. *After Heaven: Spirituality in America since the 1950s.* Berkeley: University of California Press.

Wuthnow, Robert. 1998b. *Loose Connections: Joining Together in America's Fragmented Communities.* Cambridge, MA: Harvard University Press.

Wuthnow, Robert. 2001. *Creative Spirituality: The Way of the Artist.* Berkeley: University of California Press.

Wuthnow, Robert. 2007. *After the Baby Boomers: How Twenty- and Thirty-Somethings Are Shaping the Future of American Religion.* Princeton: Princeton University Press.

Yack, Bernard. 1988. "Liberalism and Its Communitarian Critics: Does Liberal Practice 'Live Down' to Liberal Theory?" In *Community in America: The Challenge of Habits of the Heart,* edited by Charles H. Reynolds and Ralph V. Norman, 147–67. Berkeley: University of California Press.

Yanow, Dvora, and Peregrine Schwartz-Shea. 2006. *Interpretation and Method: Empirical Research Methods and the Interpretive Turn.* London: M. E. Sharpe.

Yi, Joseph, and Daniel Silver. 2015. "God, Yoga, and Karate." *Journal for the Scientific Study of Religion* 54 (3): 596–615.

Young, Lance Brendan. 2011. "Personal Construct Theory and the Transformation of Identity in Alcoholics Anonymous." *International Journal of Mental Health Addiction* 9: 709–22.

Young So, Tae. 2009. "Pentecostal Spirituality as Nurturing Vitality for Human Lives." *Journal of Pentecostal Theology* 18: 246–62.

Zinnbauer, Brian J., and Kenneth Pargament. 2005. "Religiousness and Spirituality." In *Handbook of the Psychology of Religion and Spirituality,* edited by Raymond F. Paloutzian and Crystal L. Park, 21–42. New York: Guilford Press.

Index

For the benefit of digital users, indexed terms that span two pages (e.g., 52–53) may, on occasion, appear on only one of those pages.